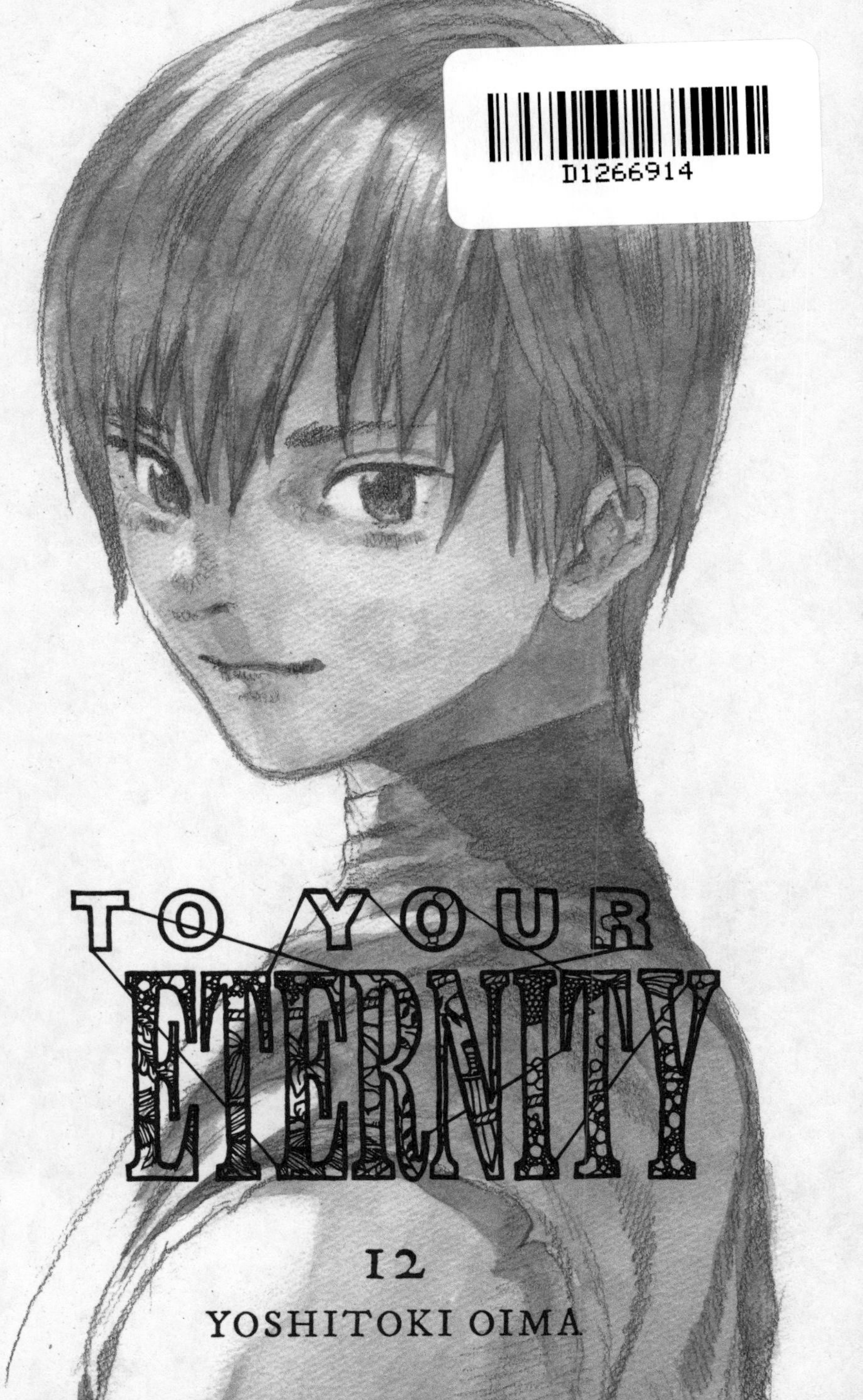

TO YOUR ETERNITY

12

YOSHITOKI OIMA

THE STORY SO FAR

After training in preparation for the Nokker attack,
Fushi obtains a wider field of perception.
On the battlefield in Renril await new comrades, discovered by Bon—
the three Immortals: Kai, Hairo, and Messar.

With the help of these Immortals and the cooperation from
Renril's townspeople, Fushi meets the Nokker attack with full force.
However, the hard-fought battle slowly chips away at not only his,
but also his allies' minds and bodies.

When Kahaku approaches the exhausted Fushi,
the Nokker living in his left hand goes berserk.
It attacks Fushi and steals his vessels, one after another.
The one who appears to save Fushi from this
predicament is none other than...

CHARACTERS

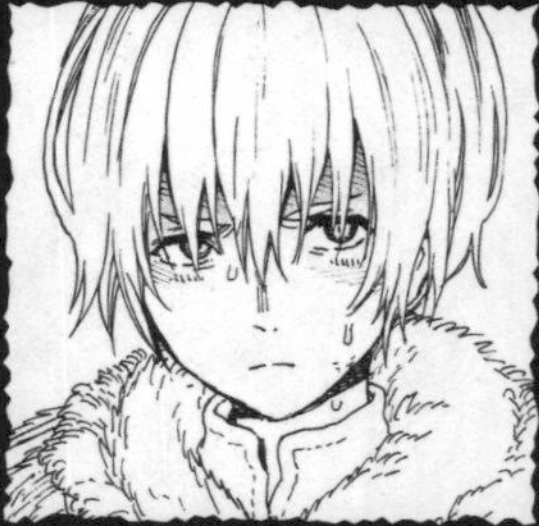

Fushi

An immortal being created to preserve this world by accumulating data. Over time, Fushi has acquired vessels and can transform into them. Through intense training, Fushi has gained a wider field of perception and the ability to create larger objects.

FRIENDS FUSHI HAS MET ALONG THE WAY

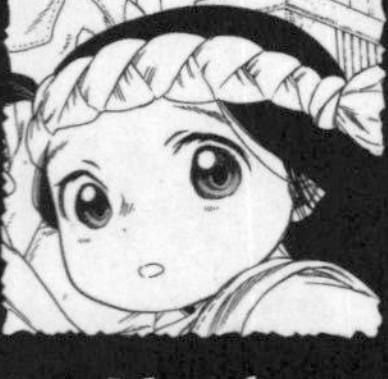

March

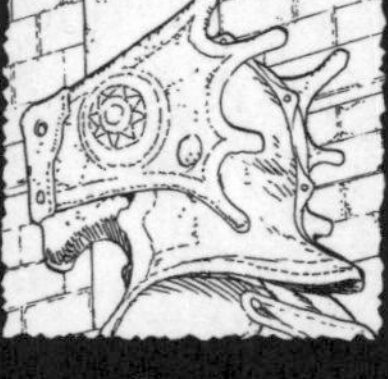

Gugu

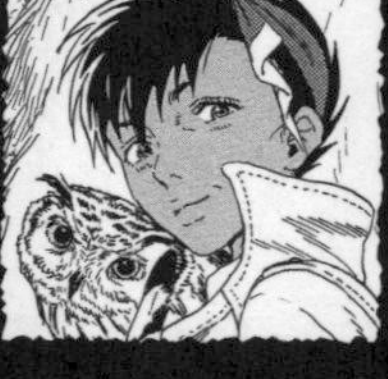

Tonari

Messar Robin Bastar

An old friend of Bon's. Possesses powerful firearms. Half-brother to the Princess of Renril, Alme.

Hairo Rich

Former head soldier of the Church of Bennett's main temple. Cannot feel pain.

Kai Renald Rawle

Soldier in the Uralis army. Has a strong physique, and is a proficient weapon make

Cam's Friends

Renril militia troops. They fight the Nokkers with Cam to protect their city.

Cam

A local militiaman from Renril who knows the truth about Fushi and his team. Cares for Yuiss.

Bonchien Nicoli la Tasty Peach Ura

Former Prince of Uralis. Ca see the dead. Searching for immortal allies for Fushi.

Horse

A white horse the Beholder created from Fushi's flesh. Sensitive to when Fushi is in danger.

Iddy

A girl of the Earthenware people. Has the ability to quickly detect changes around her.

Kahaku

Descendant of Hayase and the sixth successor to carry out her will. A Nokker live in his left arm.

Nokker

Their true forms, called "fye," are likened to souls. They slaughter in order to liberate humans from the pain that comes with living, and oppose Fushi and the Beholder for standing in their way.

The Beholder

Created Fushi in orde to preserve the world. Always watching Fush from nearby. Will one day be replaced by Fus and vanish.

CONTENTS

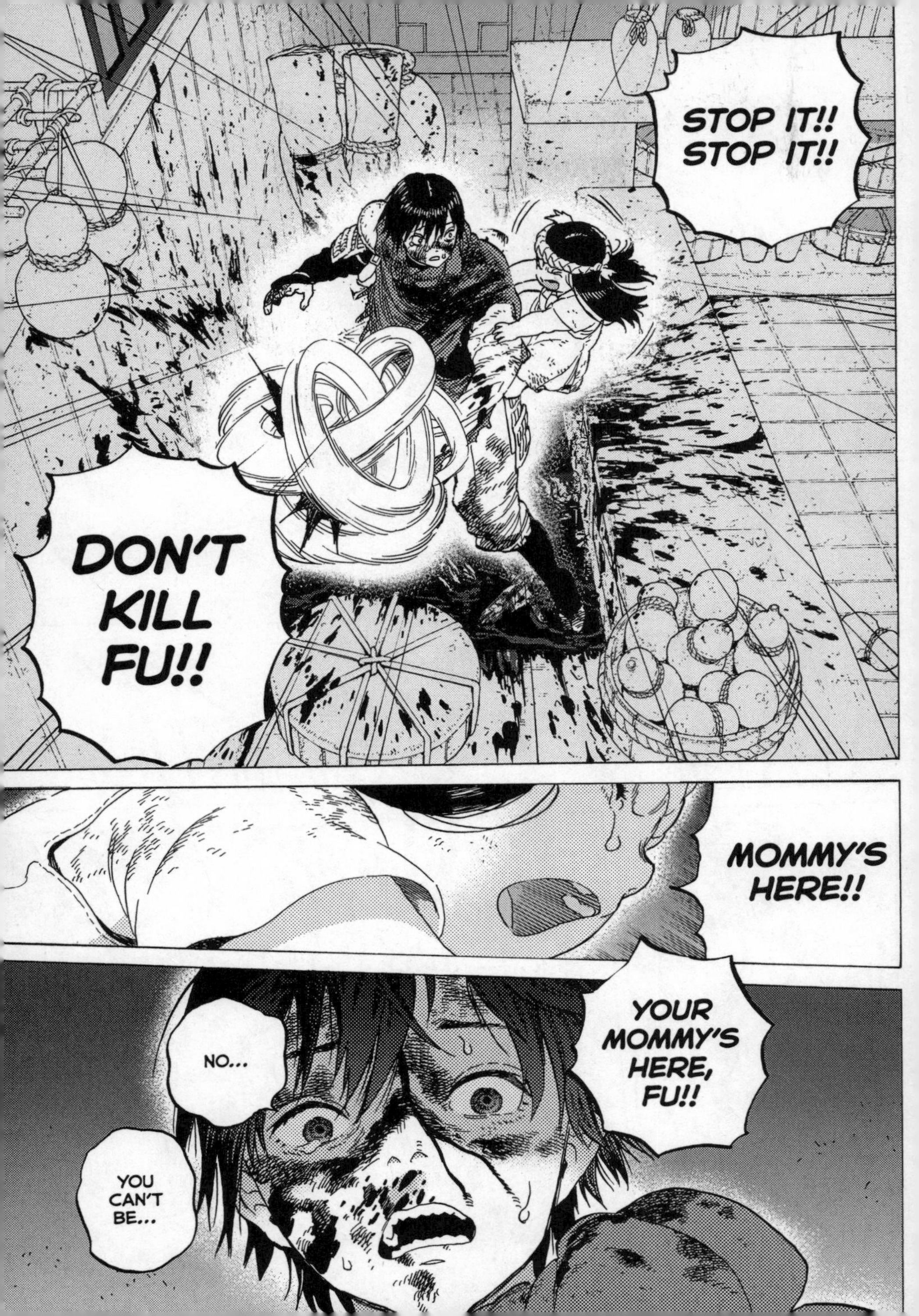
STOP IT!! STOP IT!!
DON'T KILL FU!!
MOMMY'S HERE!!
YOUR MOMMY'S HERE, FU!!
NO...
YOU CAN'T BE...

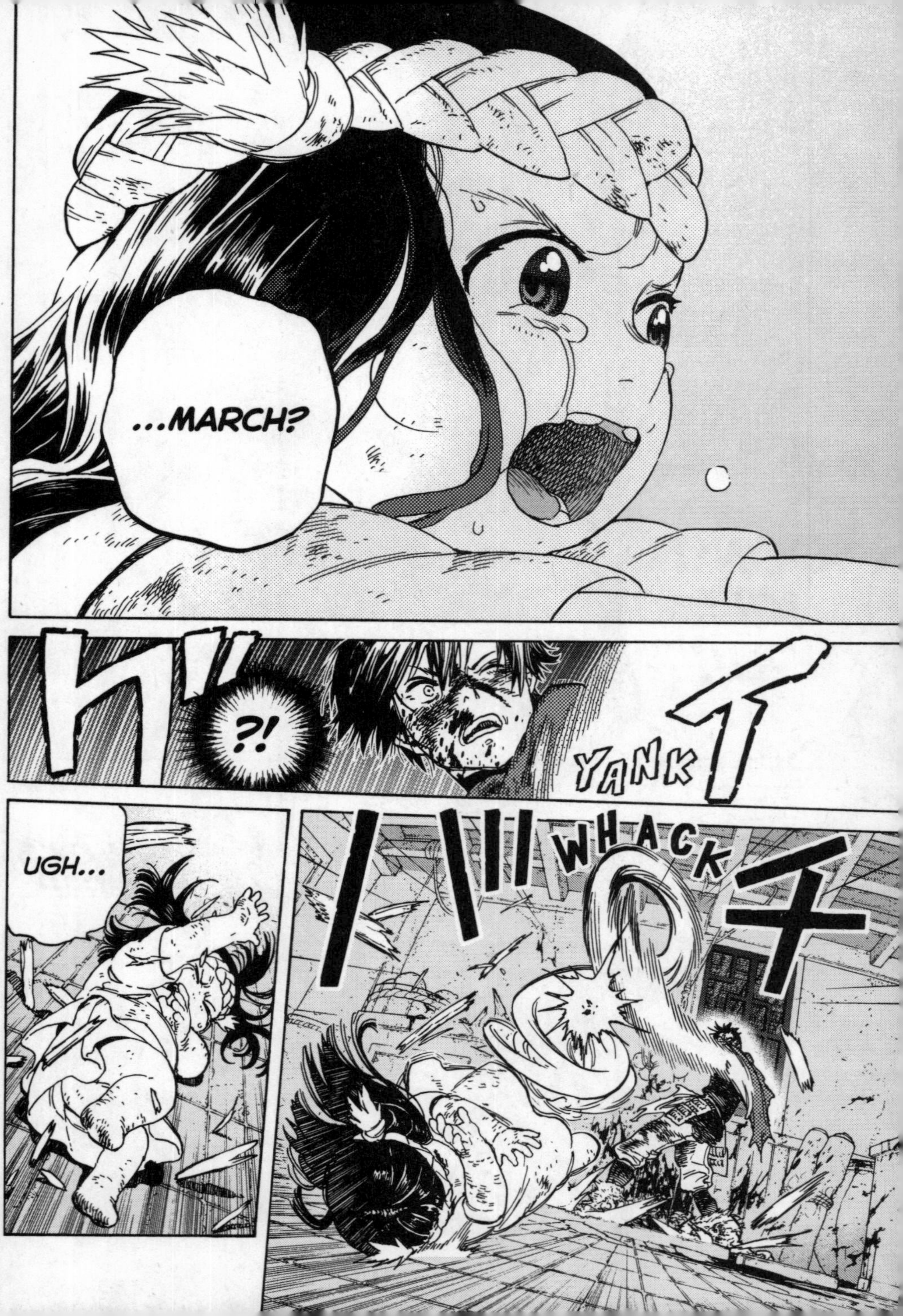
...MARCH?
YANK
?!
WHACK
UGH...

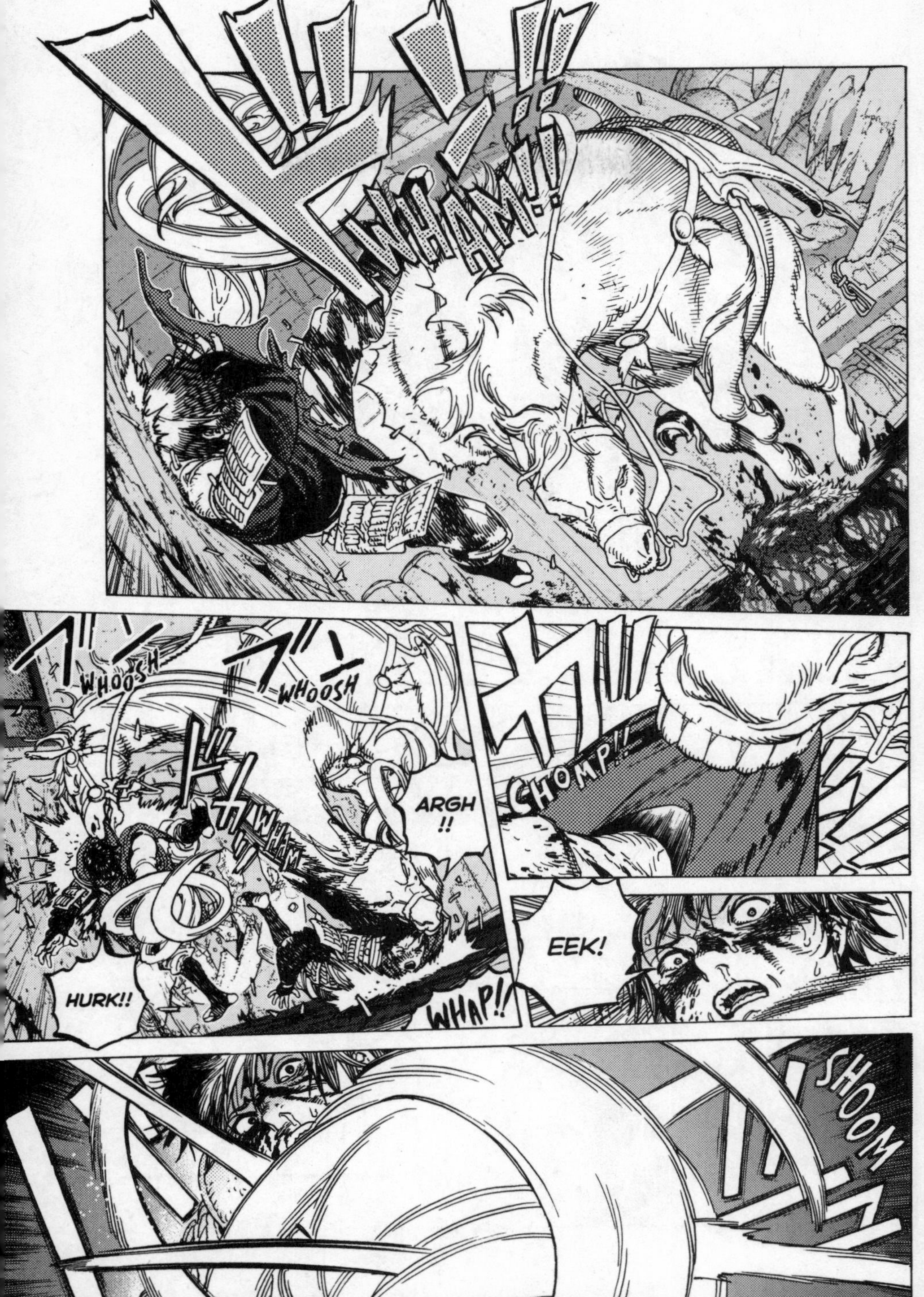

WHAM!!
CHOMP!!
EEK!
WHOOSH
ARGH!!
WHAM
WHOOSH
WHAP!!
HURK!!
SHOOM

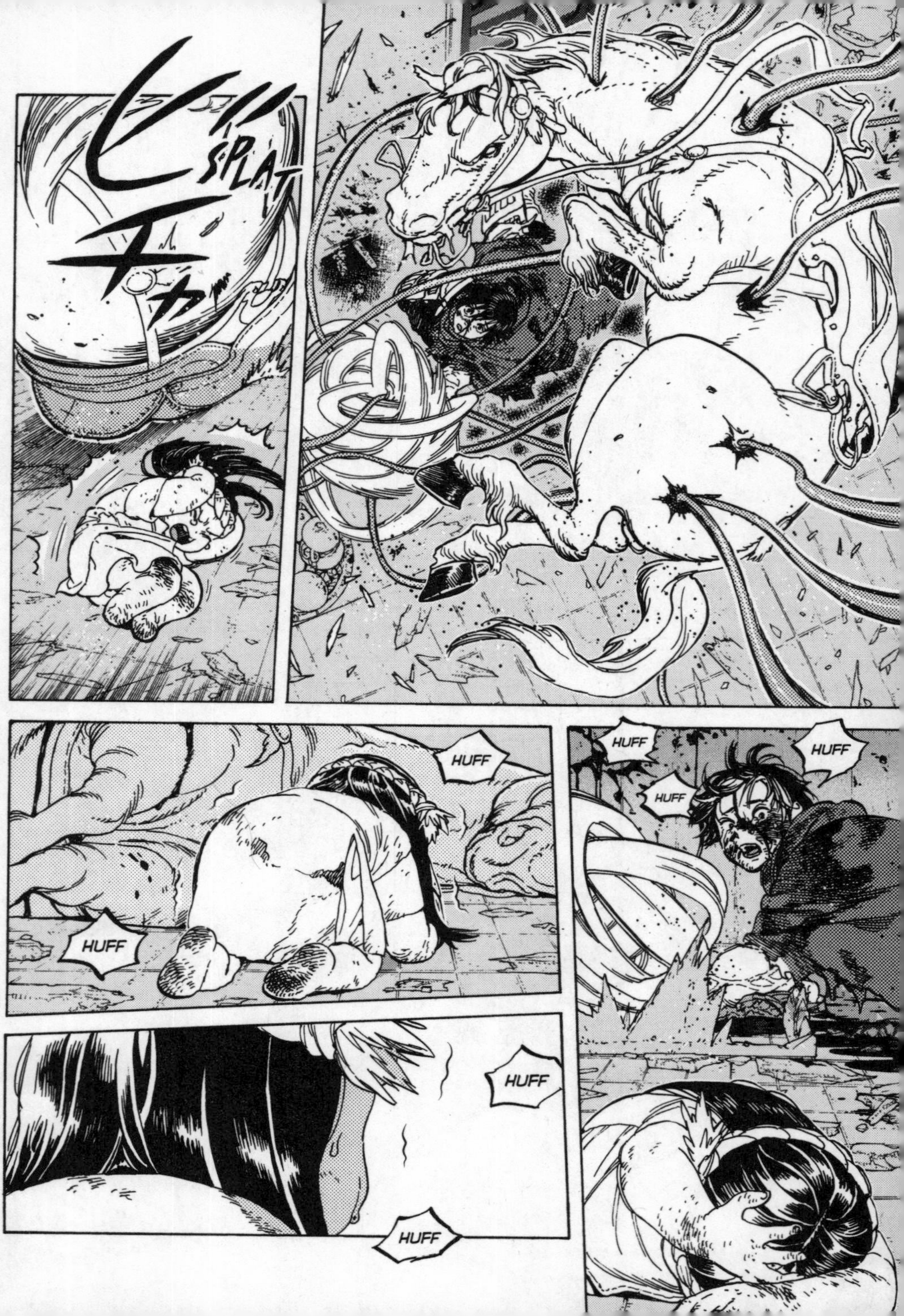
SPLAT
HUFF
HUFF
HUFF
HUFF
HUFF
HUFF
HUFF

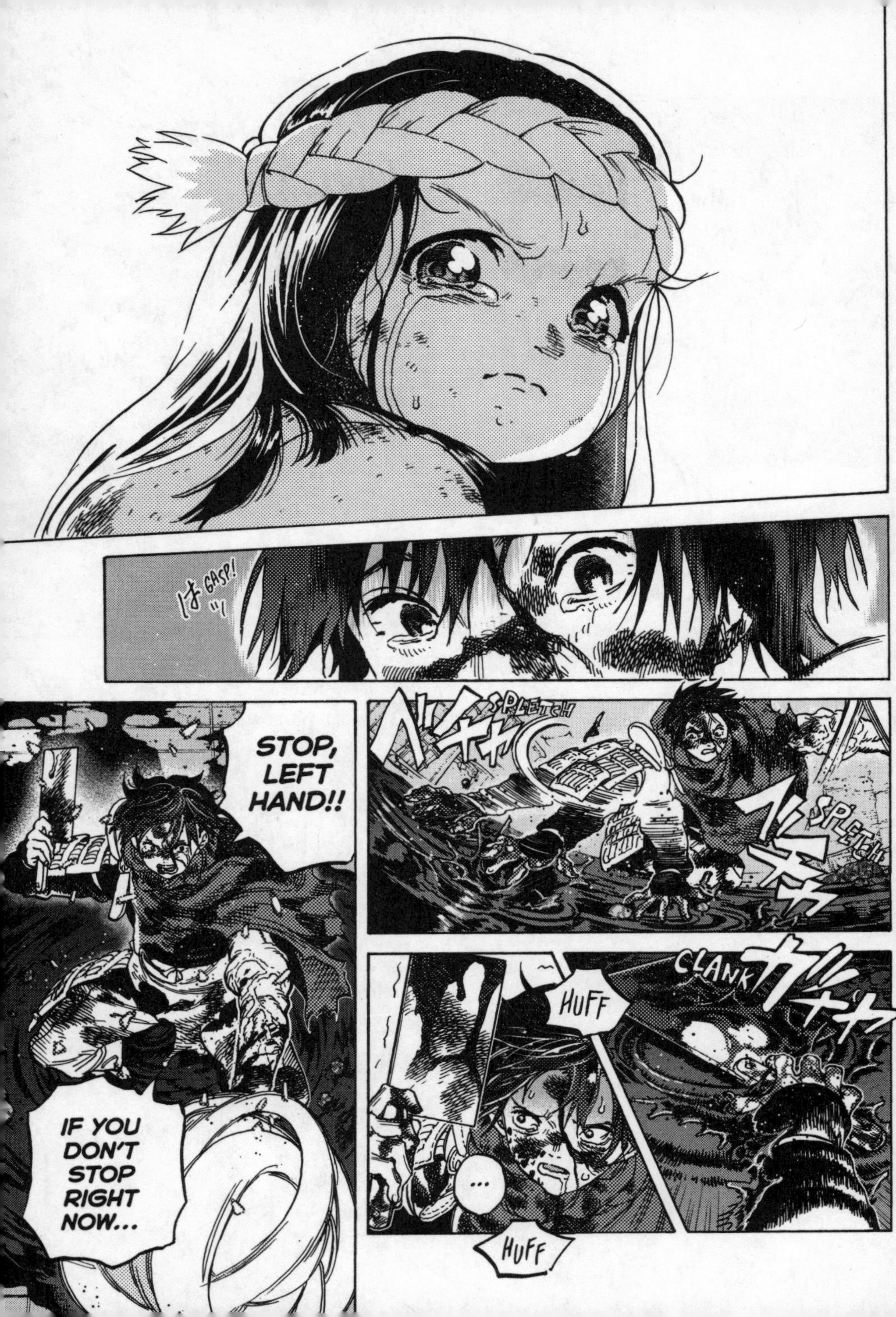
GASP!
SPLETCH
SPLETCH
CLANK
HUFF
...
HUFF
STOP, LEFT HAND!!
IF YOU DON'T STOP RIGHT NOW...

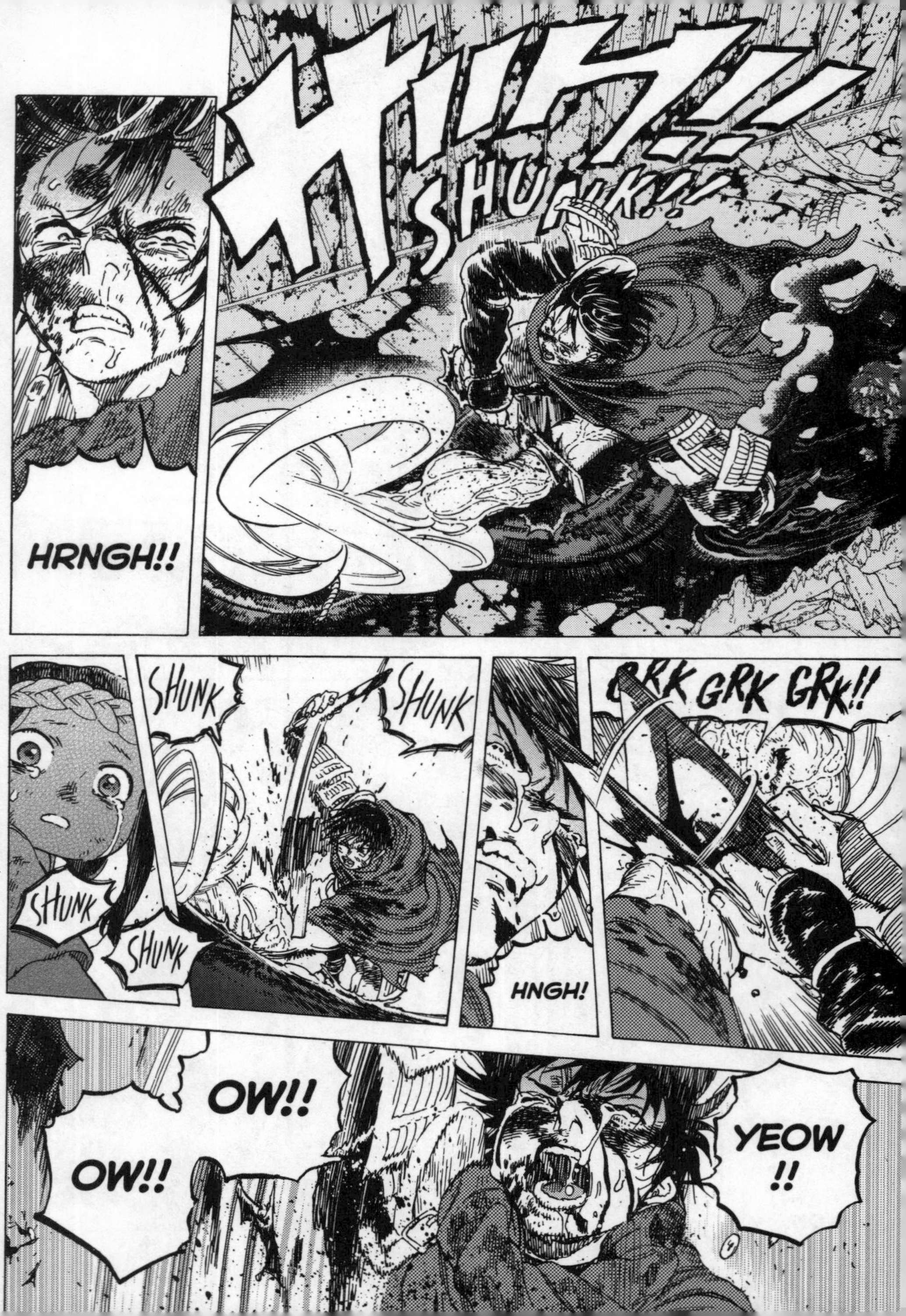

SHUNK!!
HRNGH!!
GRK GRK GRK!!
HNGH!
SHUNK
SHUNK
SHUNK
SHUNK
YEOW!!
OW!!
OW!!

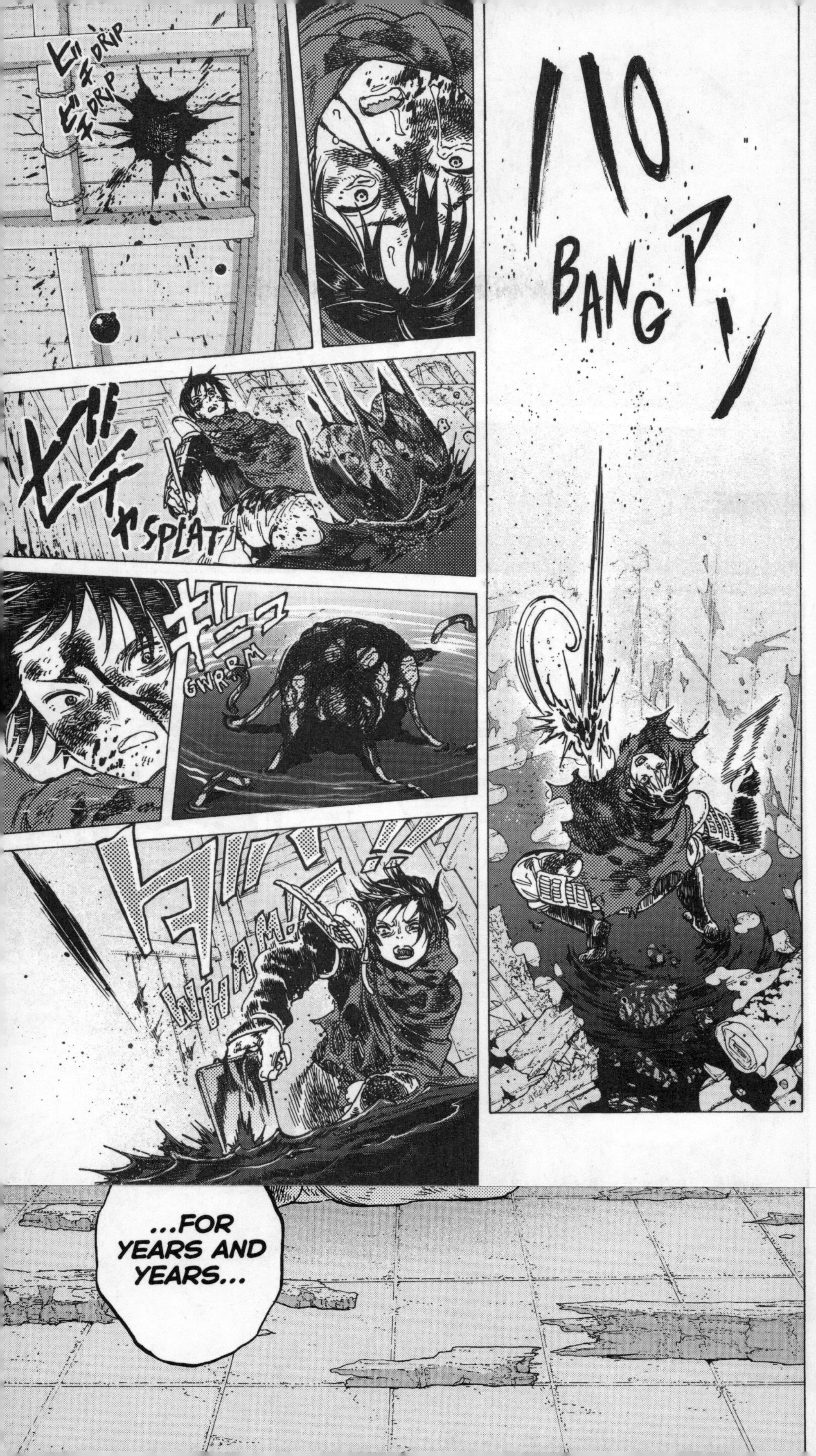
BANG
DRIP
DRIP
SPLAT
GWRRM
WHAM!
...FOR YEARS AND YEARS...

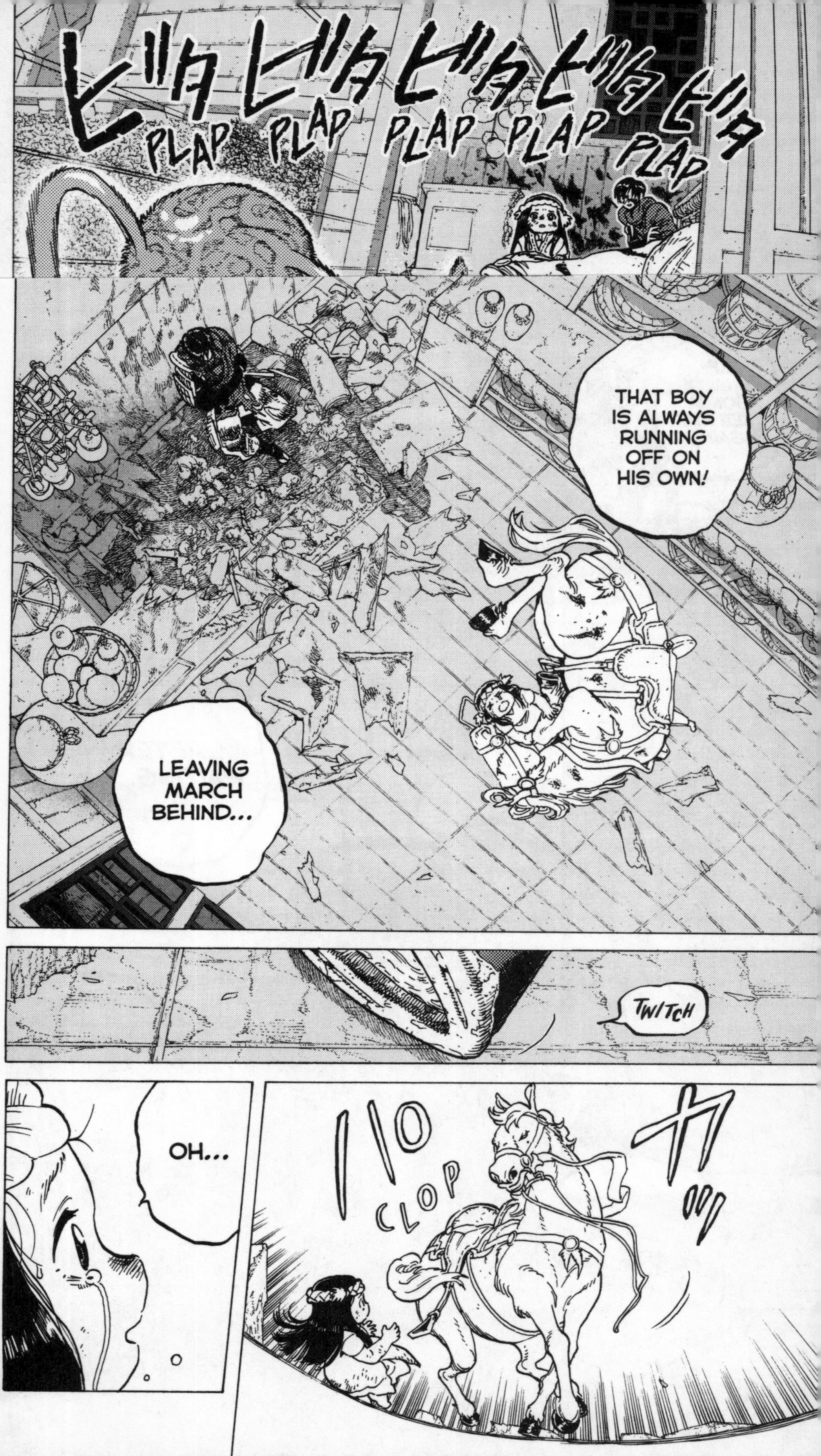
PLAP PLAP PLAP PLAP PLAP
THAT BOY IS ALWAYS RUNNING OFF ON HIS OWN!
LEAVING MARCH BEHIND...
TWITCH
CLOP
OH...

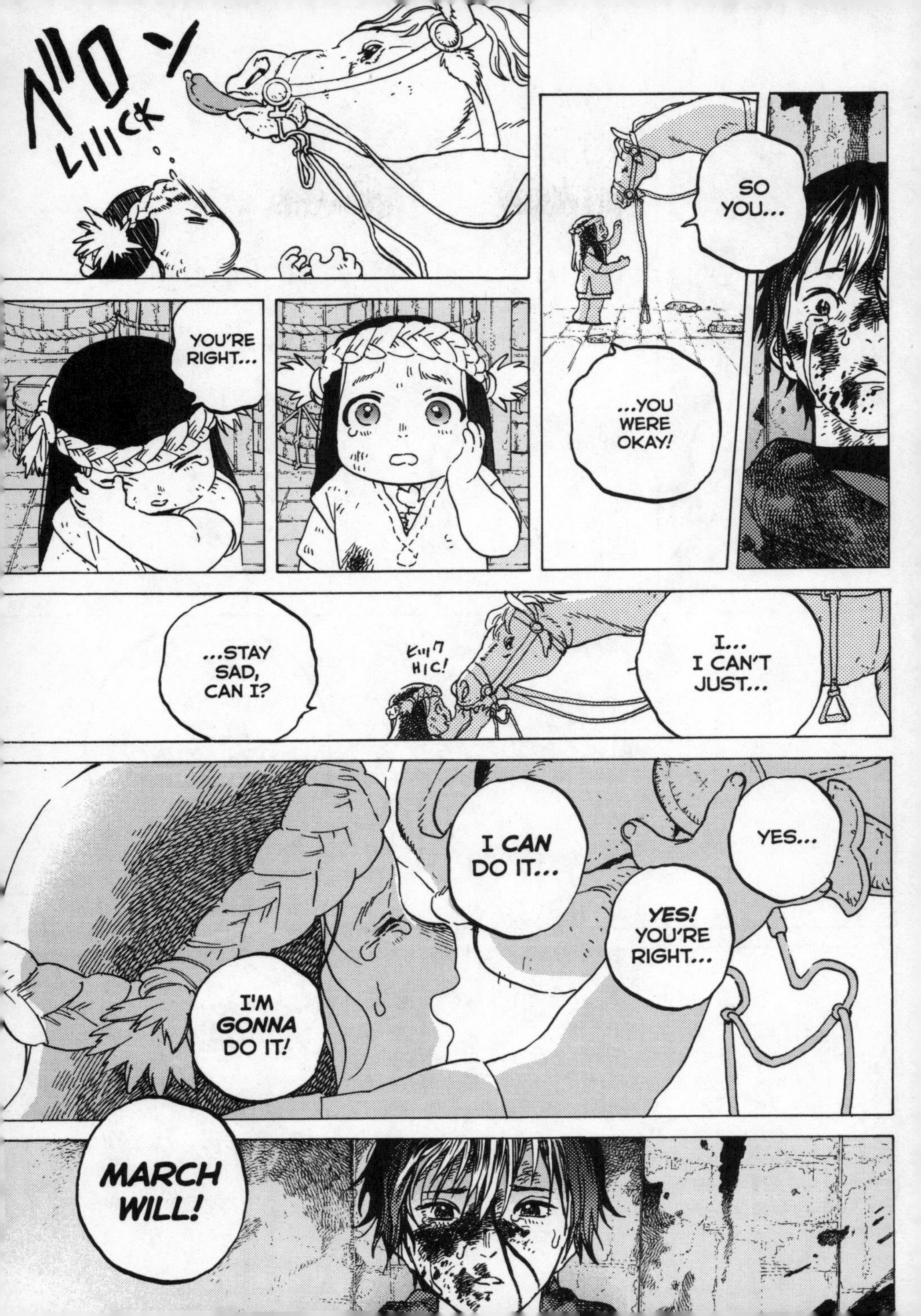
SO YOU...
...YOU WERE OKAY!
ベロン
LIIICK
YOU'RE RIGHT...
I... I CAN'T JUST...
ヒック
HIC!
...STAY SAD, CAN I?
YES...
YES! YOU'RE RIGHT...
I CAN DO IT...
I'M GONNA DO IT!
MARCH WILL!

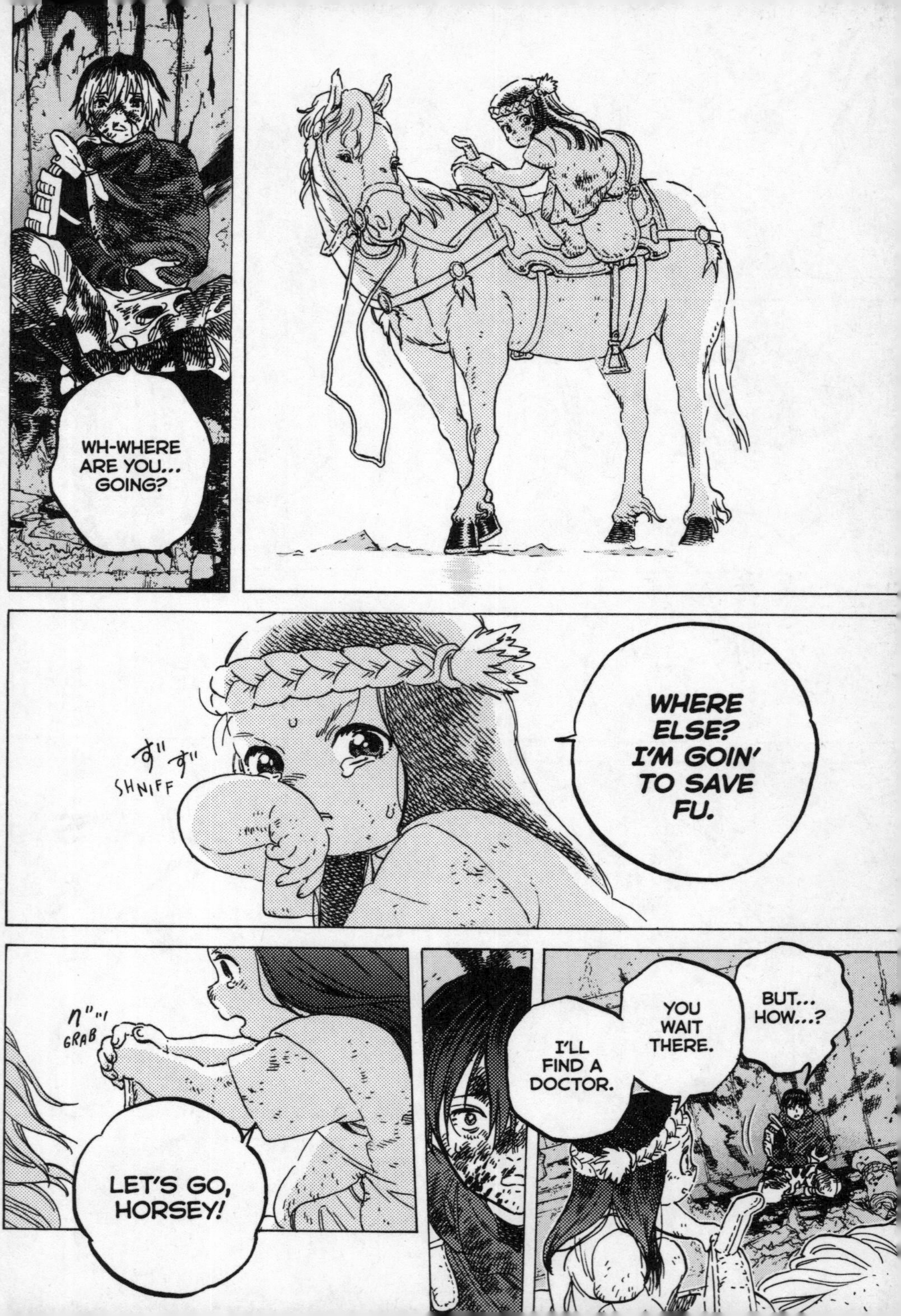
WH-WHERE ARE YOU... GOING?
ずず
SHNIFF
WHERE ELSE? I'M GOIN' TO SAVE FU.
BUT... HOW...?
YOU WAIT THERE.
I'LL FIND A DOCTOR.
GRAB
LET'S GO, HORSEY!

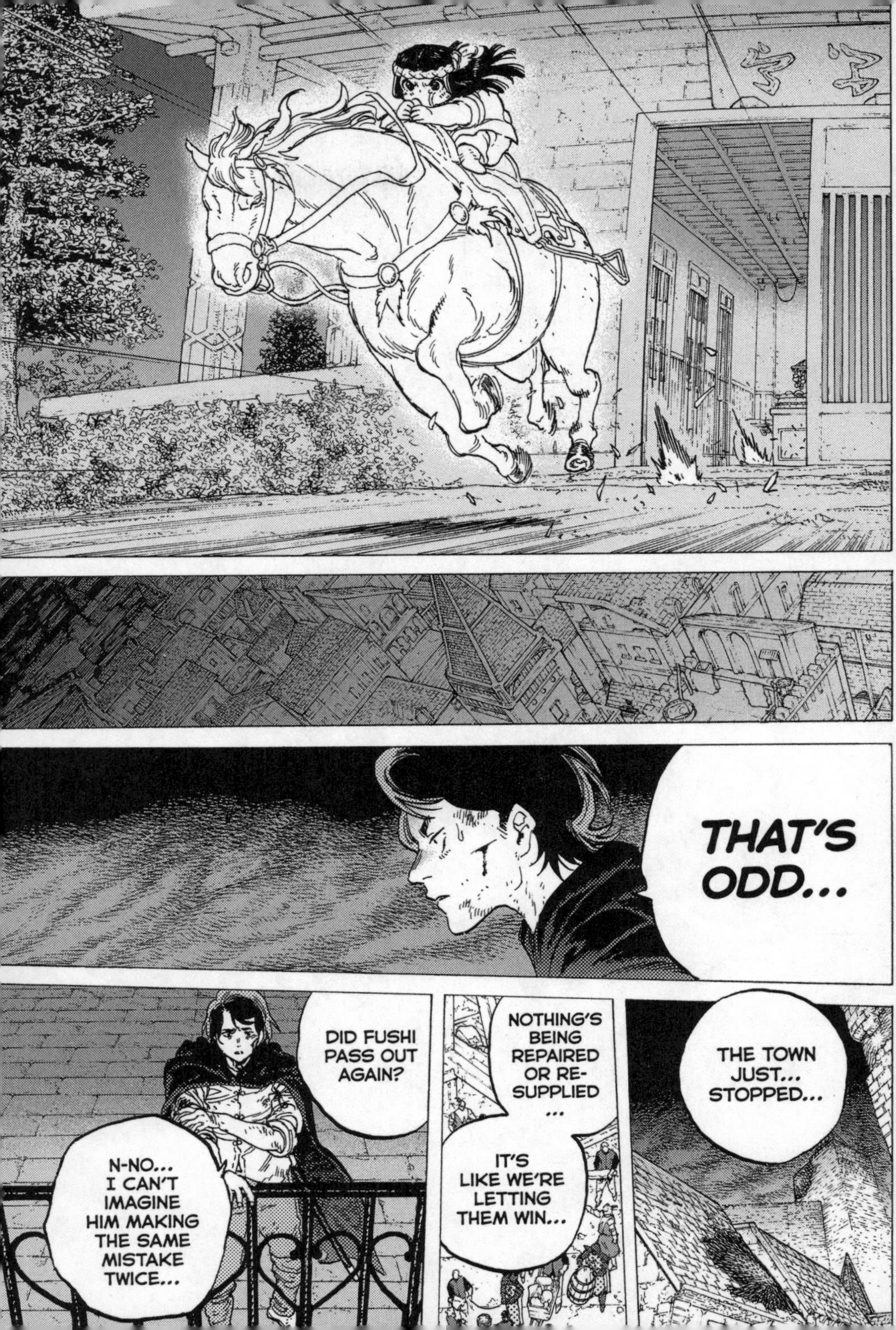
THAT'S ODD...
THE TOWN JUST... STOPPED...
NOTHING'S BEING REPAIRED OR RE-SUPPLIED ...
IT'S LIKE WE'RE LETTING THEM WIN...
DID FUSHI PASS OUT AGAIN?
N-NO... I CAN'T IMAGINE HIM MAKING THE SAME MISTAKE TWICE...

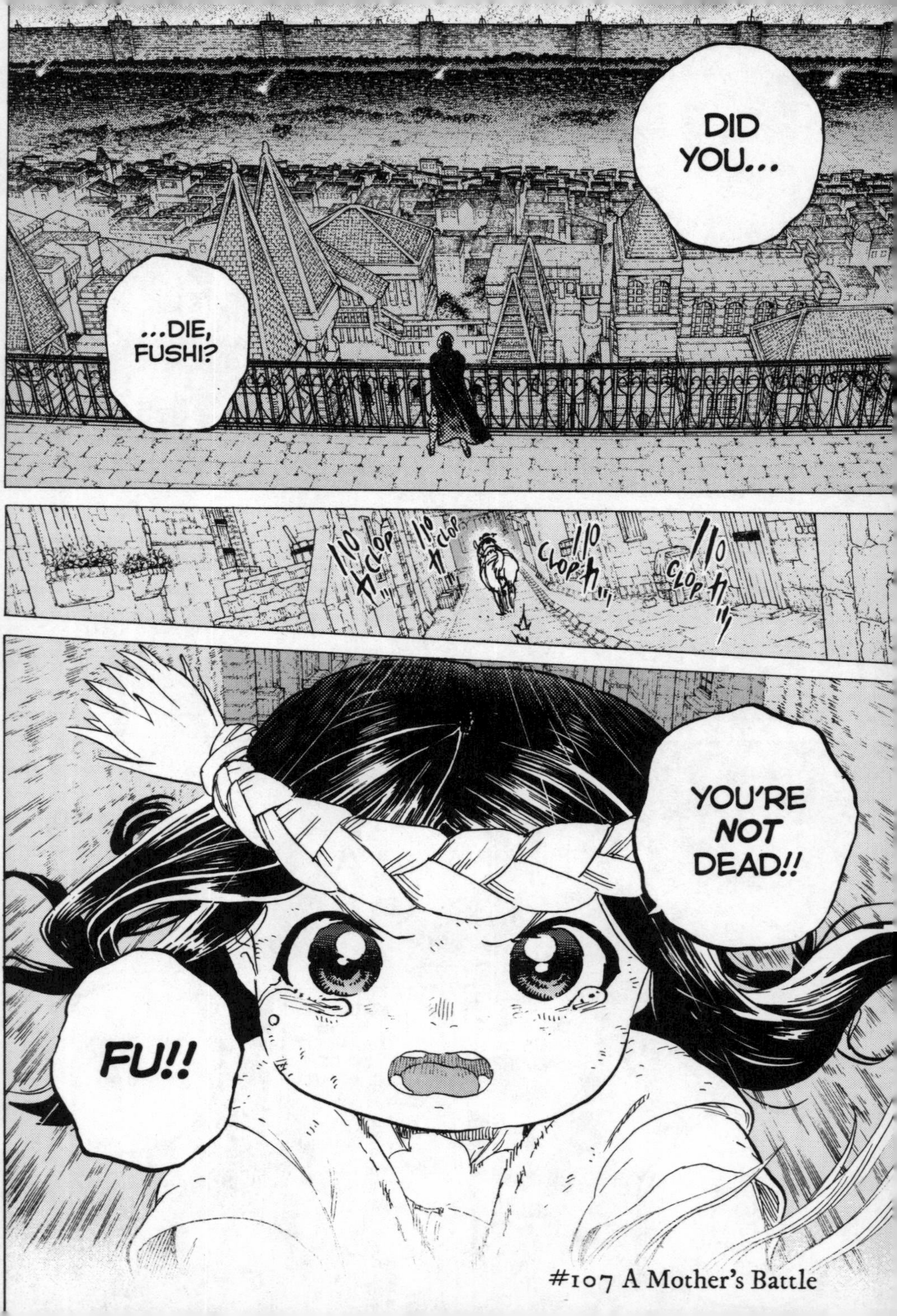
DID YOU...
...DIE, FUSHI?
CLOP
CLOP
CLOP
CLOP
YOU'RE *NOT* DEAD!!
FU!!

#107 A Mother's Battle

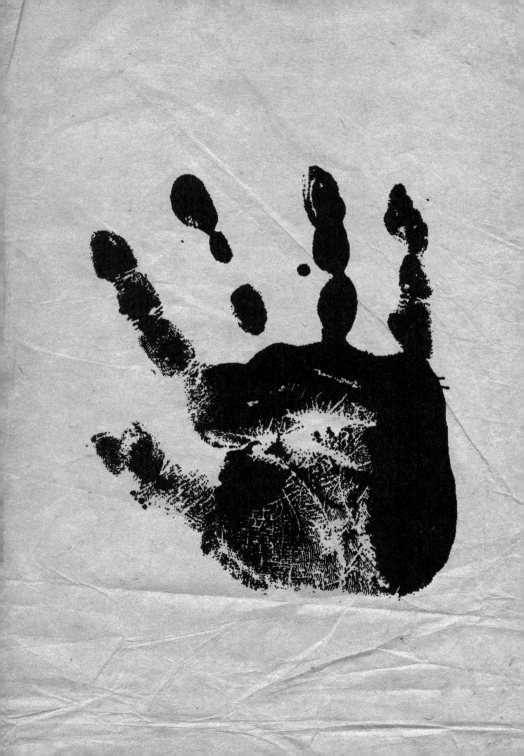

The City of Regrowth

The homes that were destroyed

were rebuilt faster than an arrow's flight.

However, nothing new grew there.

And things that do not change, may as well be dead.
They do not deserve to exist.

A LETTER TO HIS EMINENCE, THE HIGH CLERIC,
FROM A FAITHFUL BELIEVER

#108 Quickening

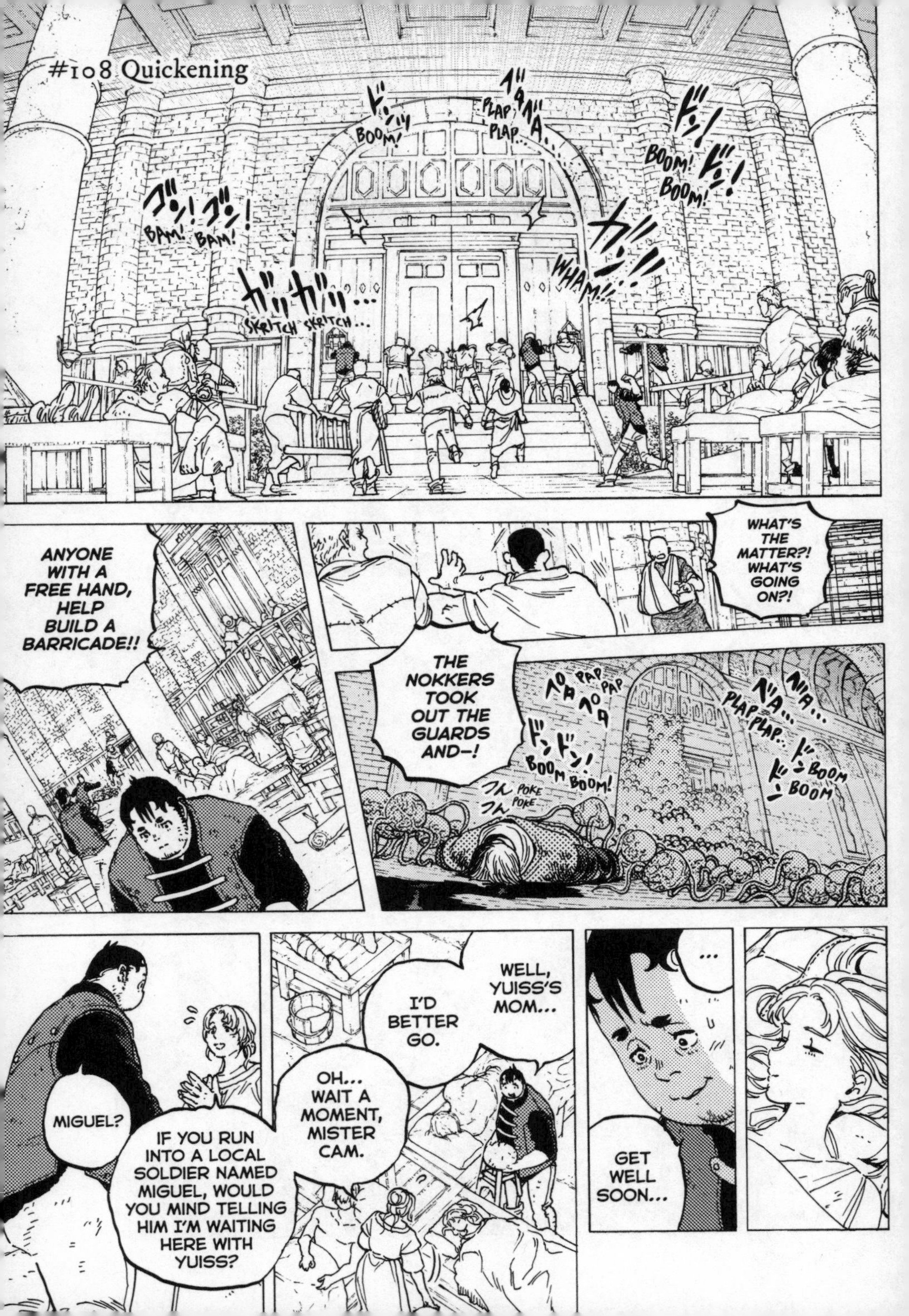
BOOM!
BOOM! BOOM!
PLAP PLAP...
BOOM!
WHAM!!
BAM! BAM!
SKRITCH SKRITCH...
WHAT'S THE MATTER?! WHAT'S GOING ON?!
THE NOKKERS TOOK OUT THE GUARDS AND—!
PLAP PLAP...
PAP PAP
BOOM BOOM
BOOM BOOM!
POKE POKE
ANYONE WITH A FREE HAND, HELP BUILD A BARRICADE!!
...
GET WELL SOON...
WELL, YUISS'S MOM...
I'D BETTER GO.
OH... WAIT A MOMENT, MISTER CAM.
MIGUEL?
IF YOU RUN INTO A LOCAL SOLDIER NAMED MIGUEL, WOULD YOU MIND TELLING HIM I'M WAITING HERE WITH YUISS?

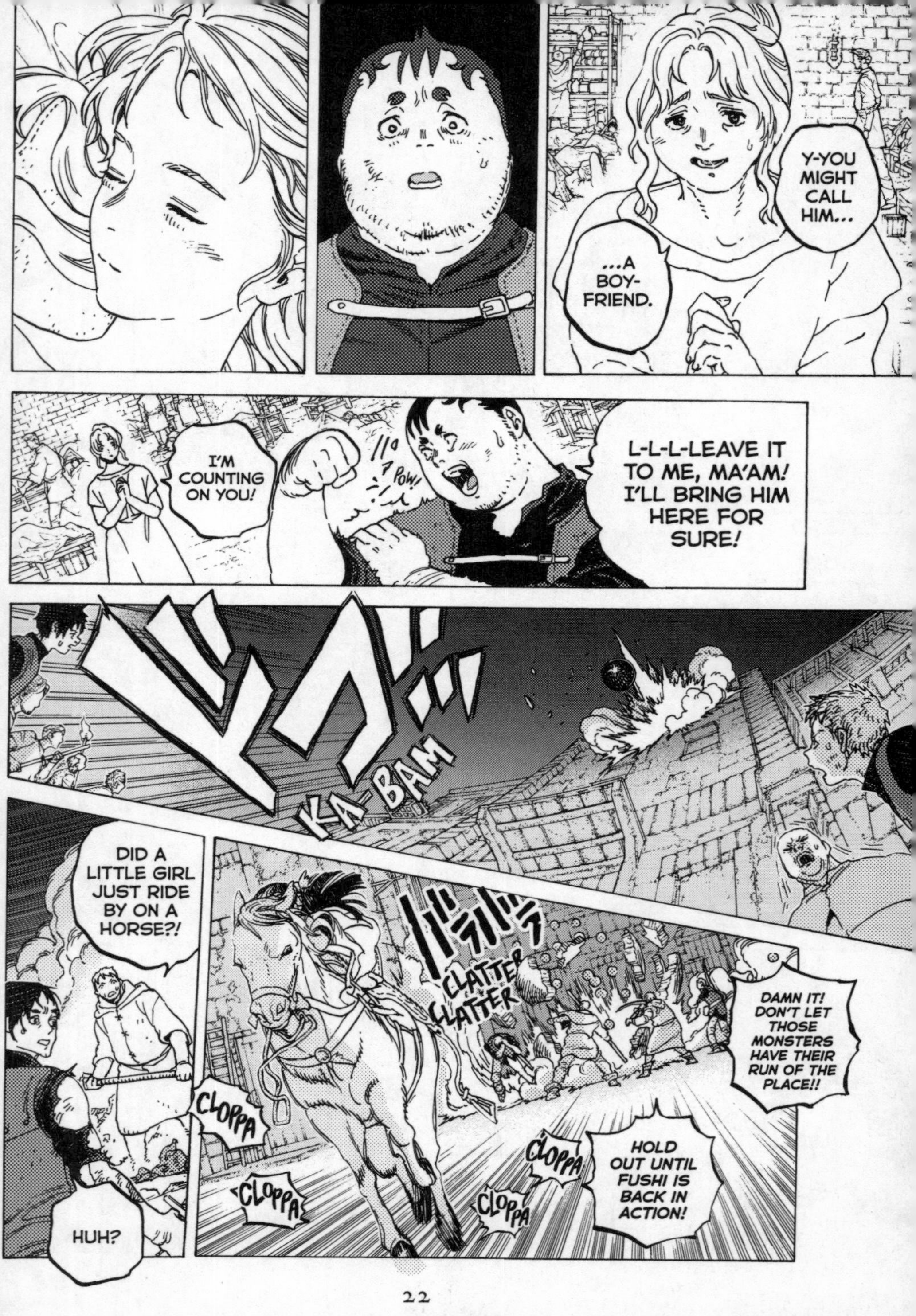
Y-YOU MIGHT CALL HIM...
...A BOY-FRIEND.
L-L-L-LEAVE IT TO ME, MA'AM! I'LL BRING HIM HERE FOR SURE!
POW!
I'M COUNTING ON YOU!
KA-BAM
DAMN IT! DON'T LET THOSE MONSTERS HAVE THEIR RUN OF THE PLACE!!
CLATTER CLATTER
HOLD OUT UNTIL FUSHI IS BACK IN ACTION!
CLOPPA
CLOPPA
CLOPPA
CLOPPA
DID A LITTLE GIRL JUST RIDE BY ON A HORSE?!
HUH?

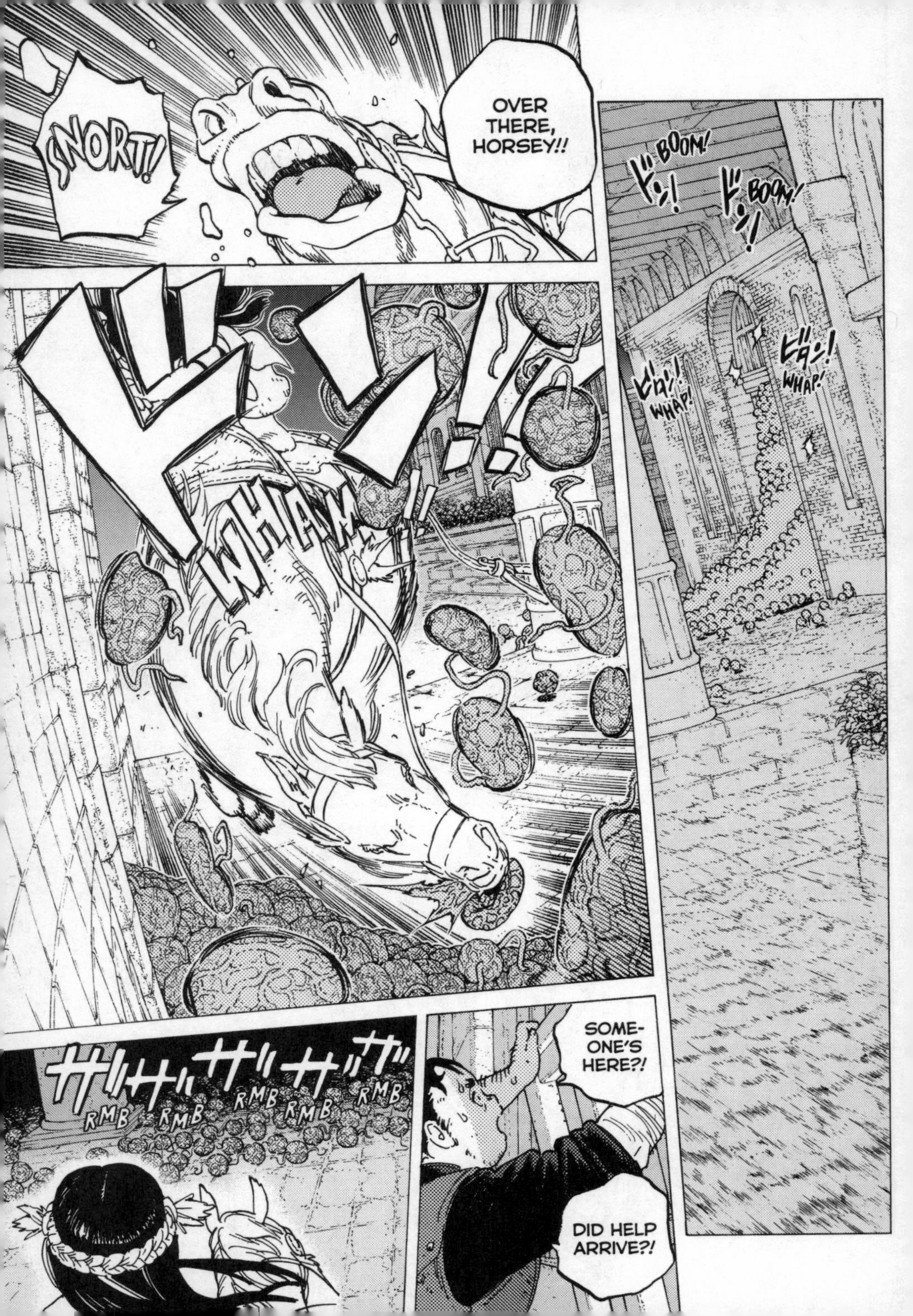
ドン! BOOM!
ドン! BOOM!
ビタン! WHAP!
ビタン! WHAP!
OVER THERE, HORSEY!!
SNORT!
WHAM
SOME-ONE'S HERE?!
DID HELP ARRIVE?!
サササササ RMB RMB RMB RMB RMB

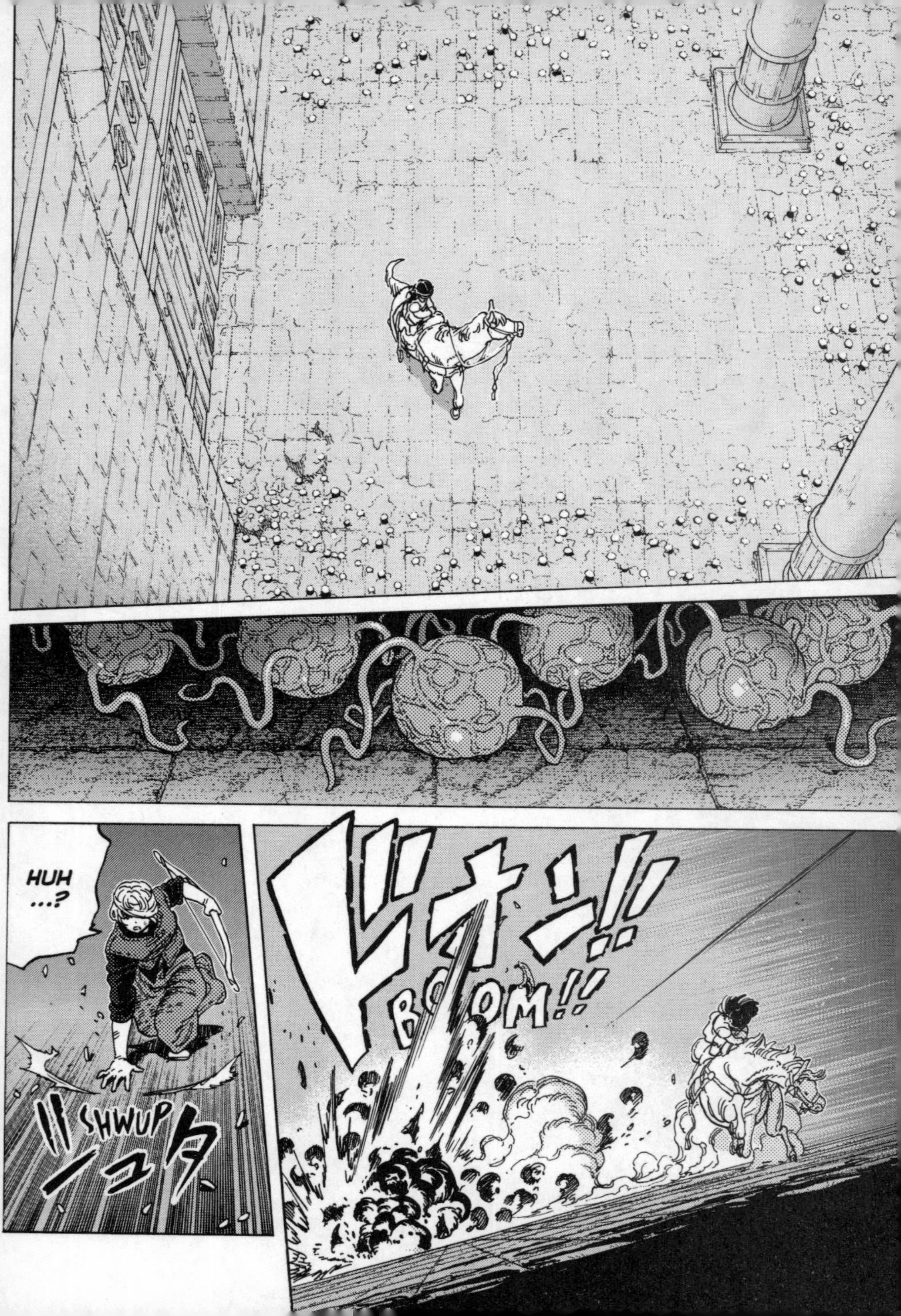
ドオン!!
BOOM!!
HUH ...?
SHWUP
シュタ

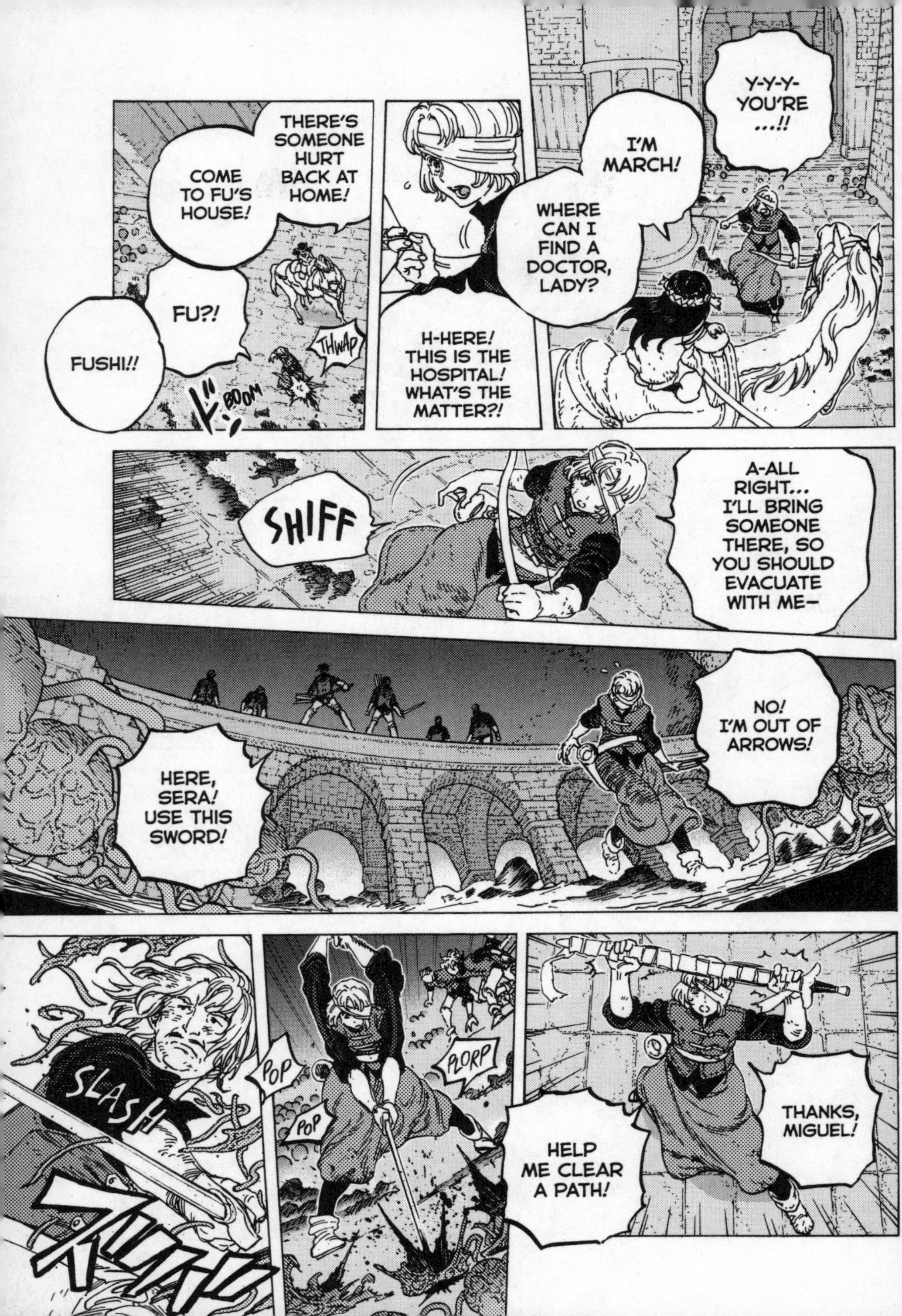
Y-Y-Y-YOU'RE ...!!
I'M MARCH!
WHERE CAN I FIND A DOCTOR, LADY?
H-HERE! THIS IS THE HOSPITAL! WHAT'S THE MATTER?!
THERE'S SOMEONE HURT BACK AT HOME!
COME TO FU'S HOUSE!
FU?!
FUSHI!!
THWAP
BOOM
A-ALL RIGHT... I'LL BRING SOMEONE THERE, SO YOU SHOULD EVACUATE WITH ME—
SHIFF
NO! I'M OUT OF ARROWS!
HERE, SERA! USE THIS SWORD!
THANKS, MIGUEL!
HELP ME CLEAR A PATH!
PLORP
POP
POP
SLASH

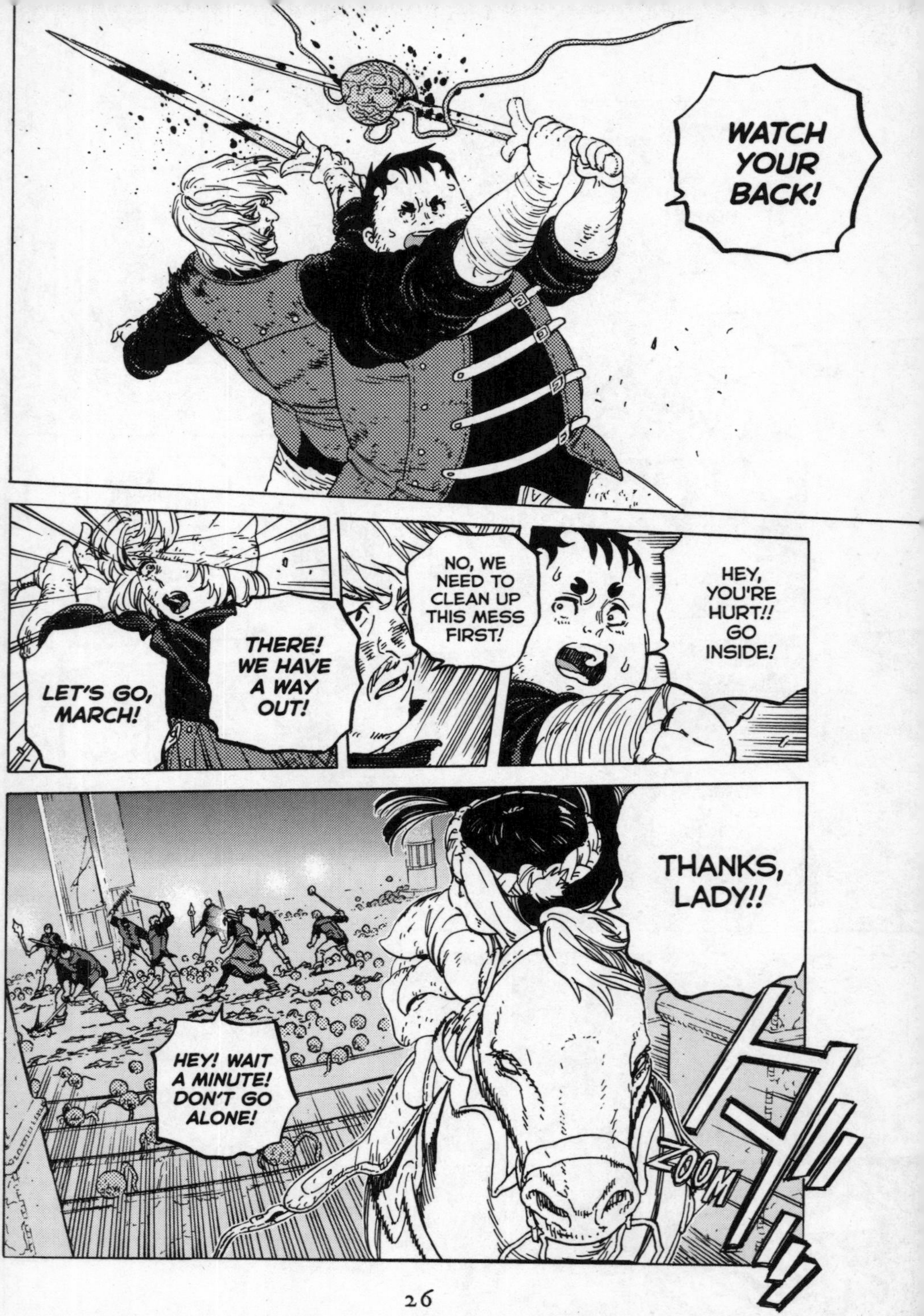
WATCH YOUR BACK!
HEY, YOU'RE HURT!! GO INSIDE!
NO, WE NEED TO CLEAN UP THIS MESS FIRST!
THERE! WE HAVE A WAY OUT!
LET'S GO, MARCH!
THANKS, LADY!!
ZOOM
HEY! WAIT A MINUTE! DON'T GO ALONE!

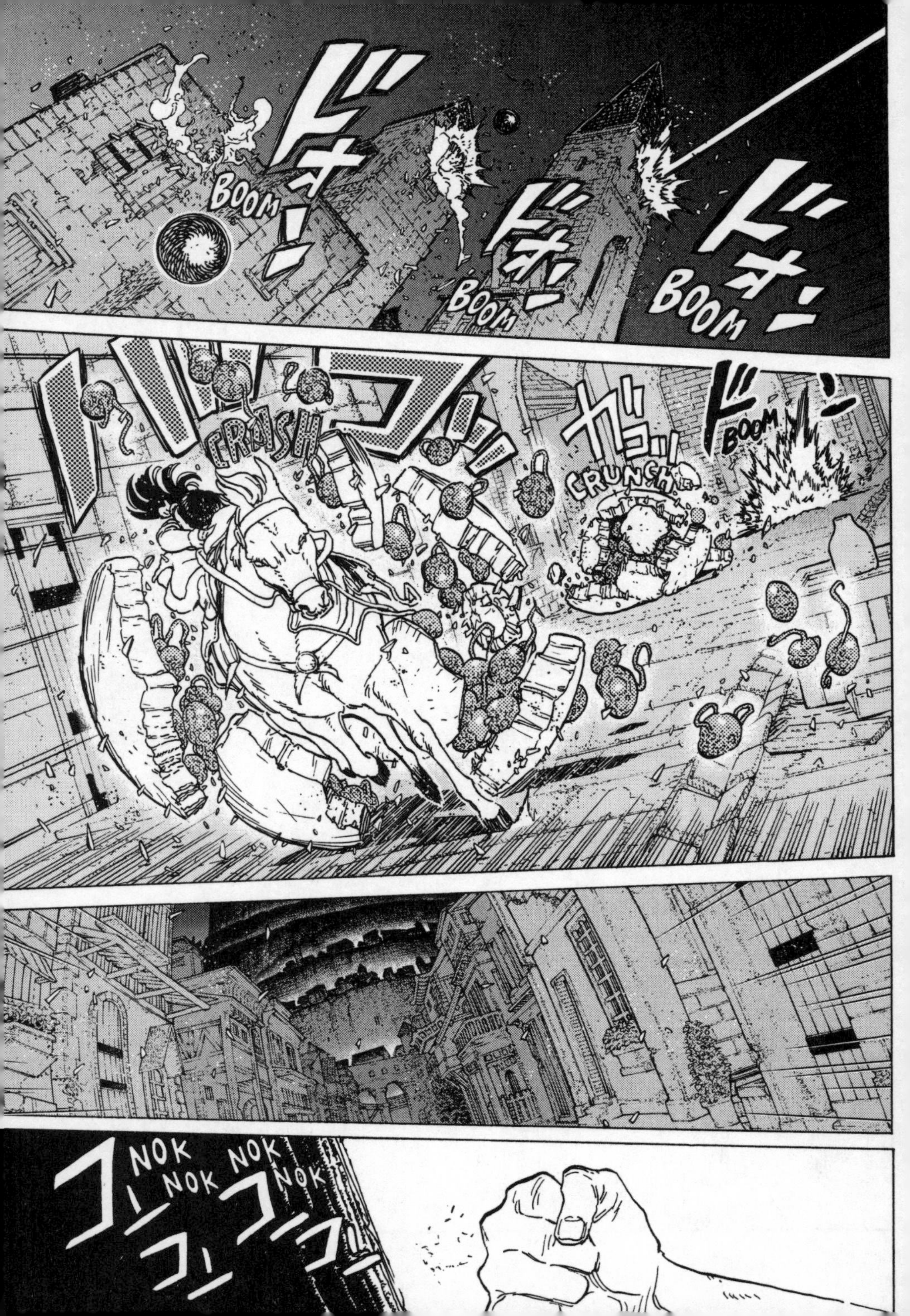
ドオン
BOOM
ドオン
BOOM
ドォ！
BOOM
ドン
BOOM
ガゴッ
CRUNCH
バコッ
CRASH
コン コン コン コン
NOK NOK NOK NOK

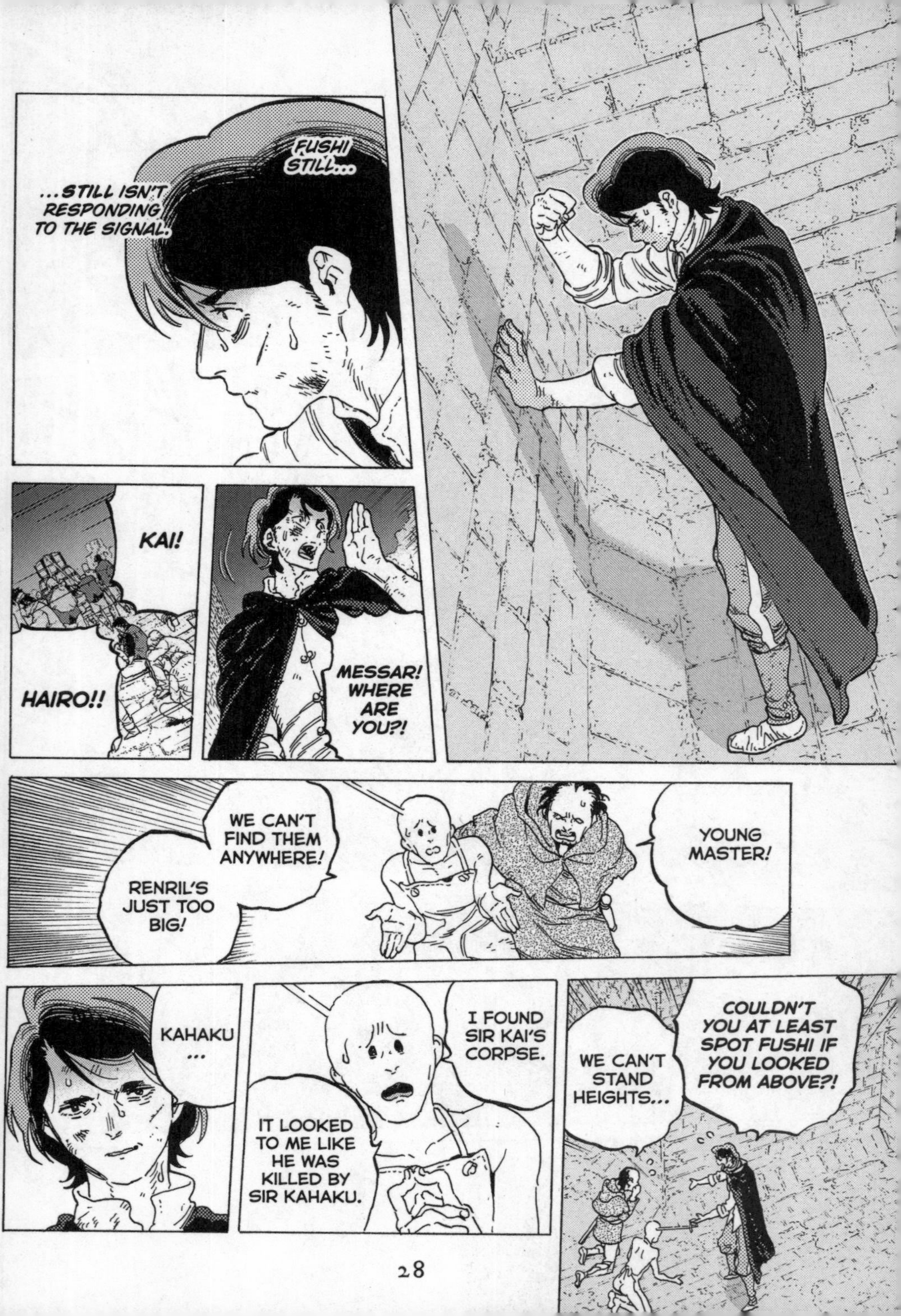
FUSHI STILL...
...STILL ISN'T RESPONDING TO THE SIGNAL.
MESSAR! WHERE ARE YOU?!
KAI!
HAIRO!!
YOUNG MASTER!
WE CAN'T FIND THEM ANYWHERE!
RENRIL'S JUST TOO BIG!
COULDN'T YOU AT LEAST SPOT FUSHI IF YOU LOOKED FROM ABOVE?!
WE CAN'T STAND HEIGHTS...
I FOUND SIR KAI'S CORPSE.
IT LOOKED TO ME LIKE HE WAS KILLED BY SIR KAHAKU.
KAHAKU ...

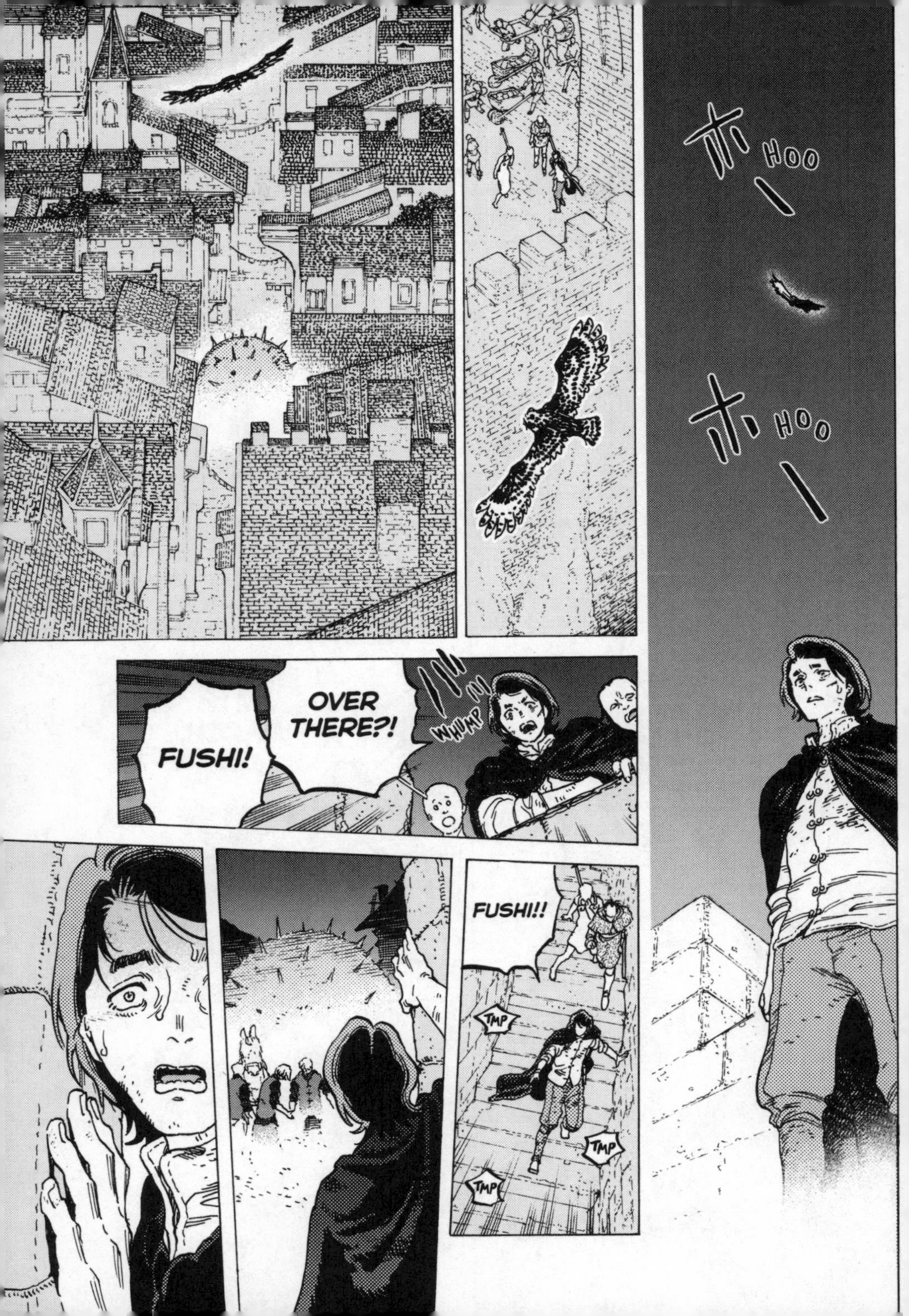

ホー HOO
ホー HOO
WHUMP
OVER THERE?!
FUSHI!
FUSHI!!
TMP
TMP
TMP

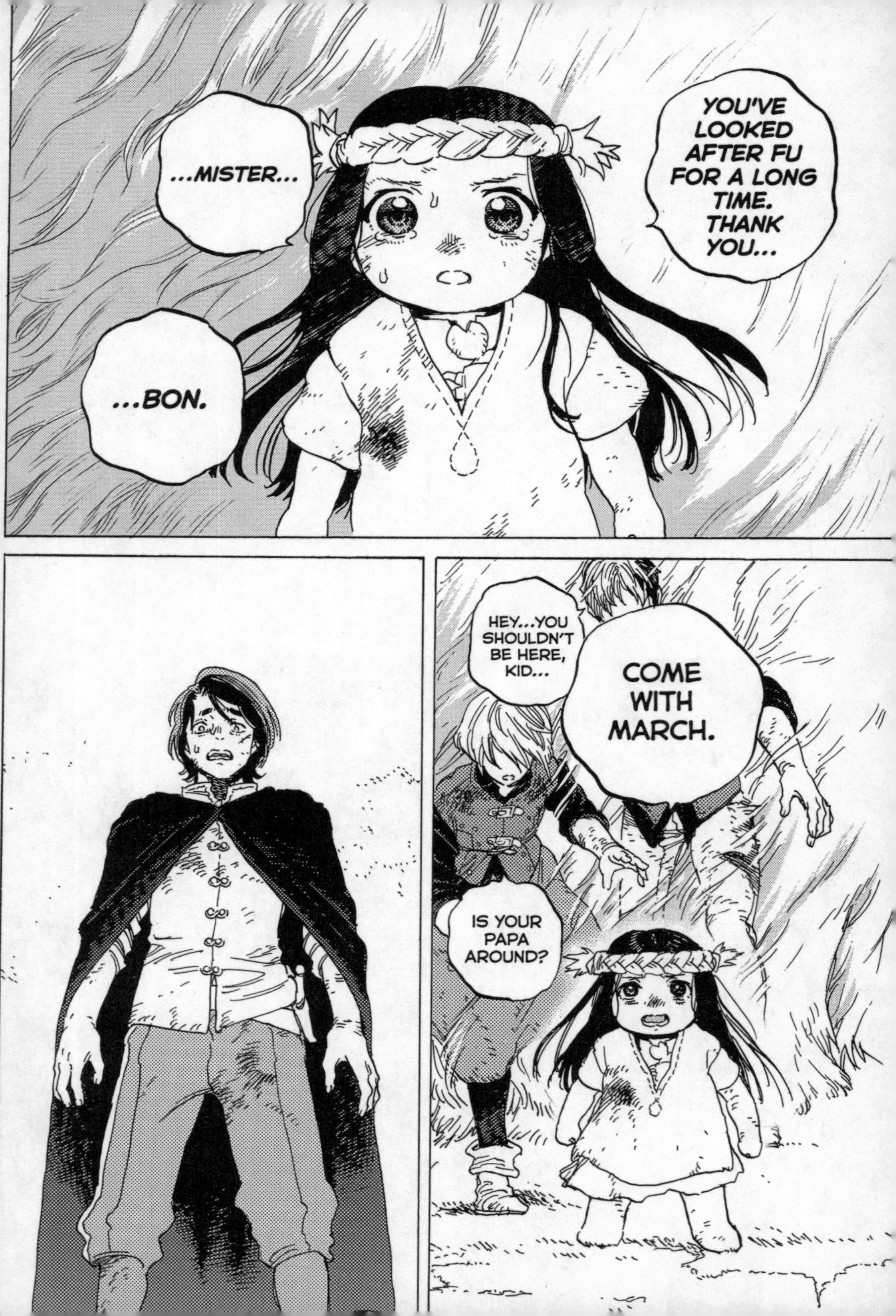
YOU'VE LOOKED AFTER FU FOR A LONG TIME. THANK YOU...
...MISTER...
...BON.
COME WITH MARCH.
HEY...YOU SHOULDN'T BE HERE, KID...
IS YOUR PAPA AROUND?

#109 Empty Cradle

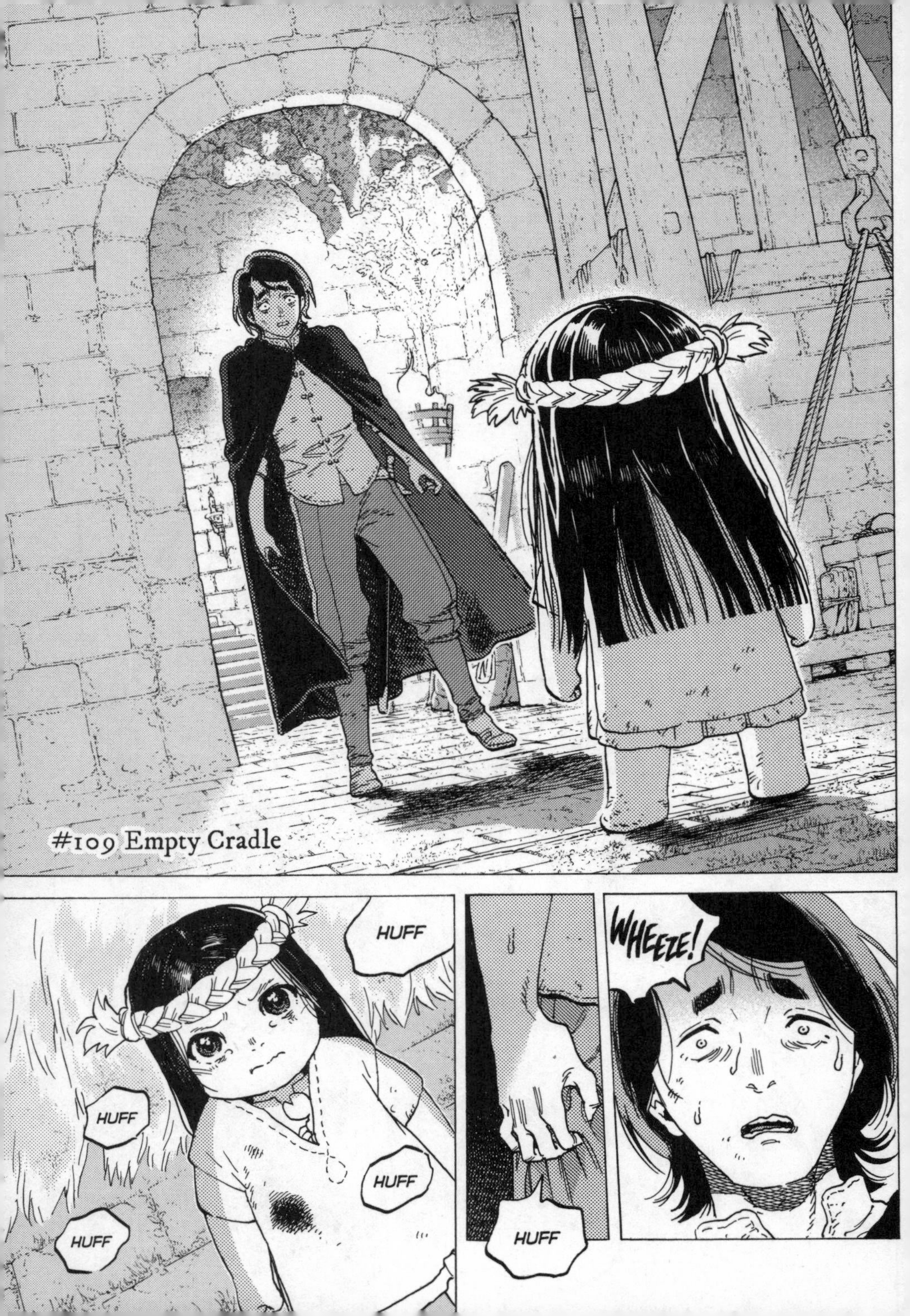
WHEEZE!
HUFF
HUFF
HUFF
HUFF
HUFF

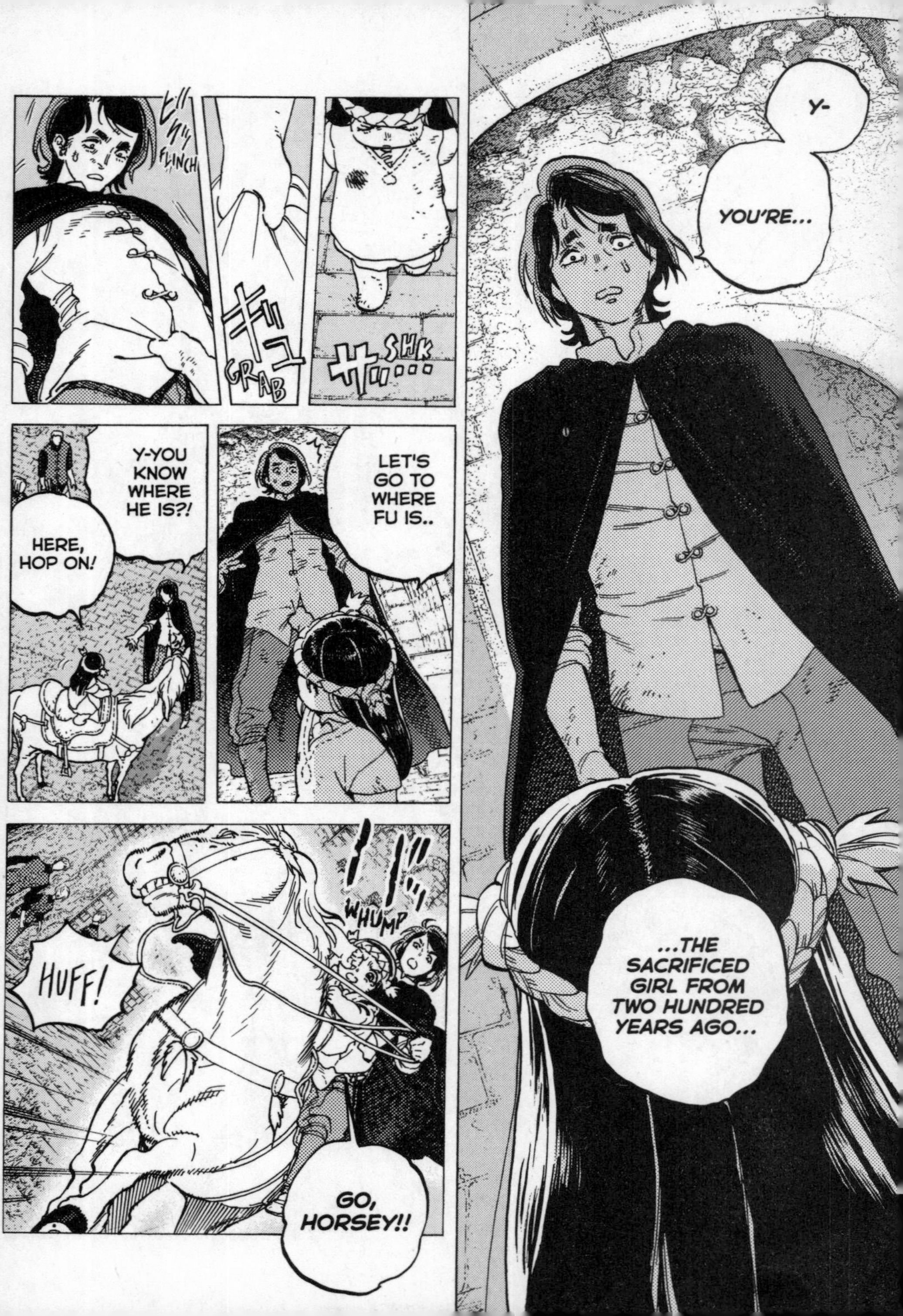
Y-
YOU'RE...
...THE SACRIFICED GIRL FROM TWO HUNDRED YEARS AGO...
SHK
GRAB
FLINCH
LET'S GO TO WHERE FU IS..
Y-YOU KNOW WHERE HE IS?!
HERE, HOP ON!
WHUMP
HUFF!
GO, HORSEY!!

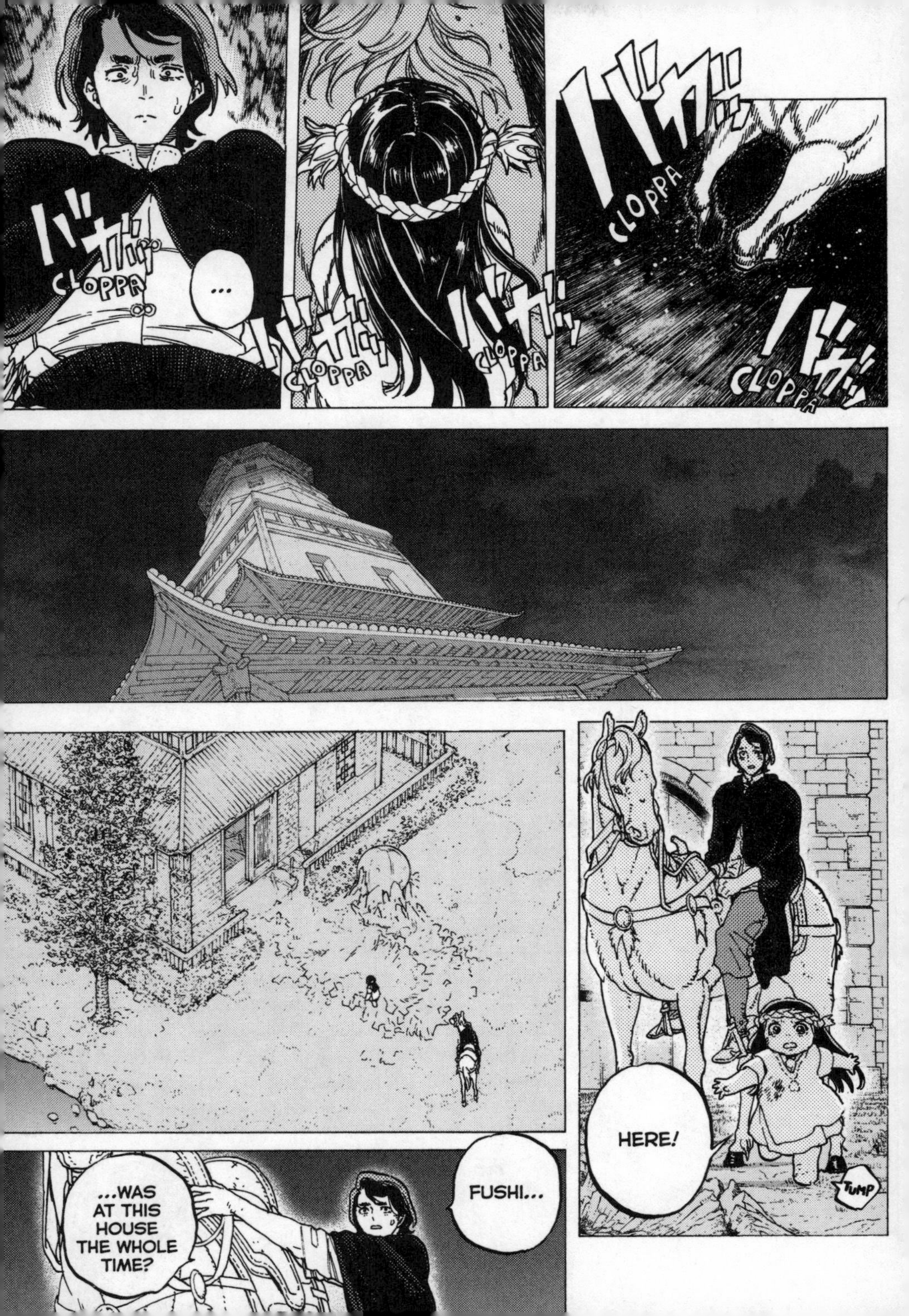
CLOPPA
CLOPPA
CLOPPA
CLOPPA
CLOPPA
...
HERE!
TUMP
FUSHI...
...WAS AT THIS HOUSE THE WHOLE TIME?

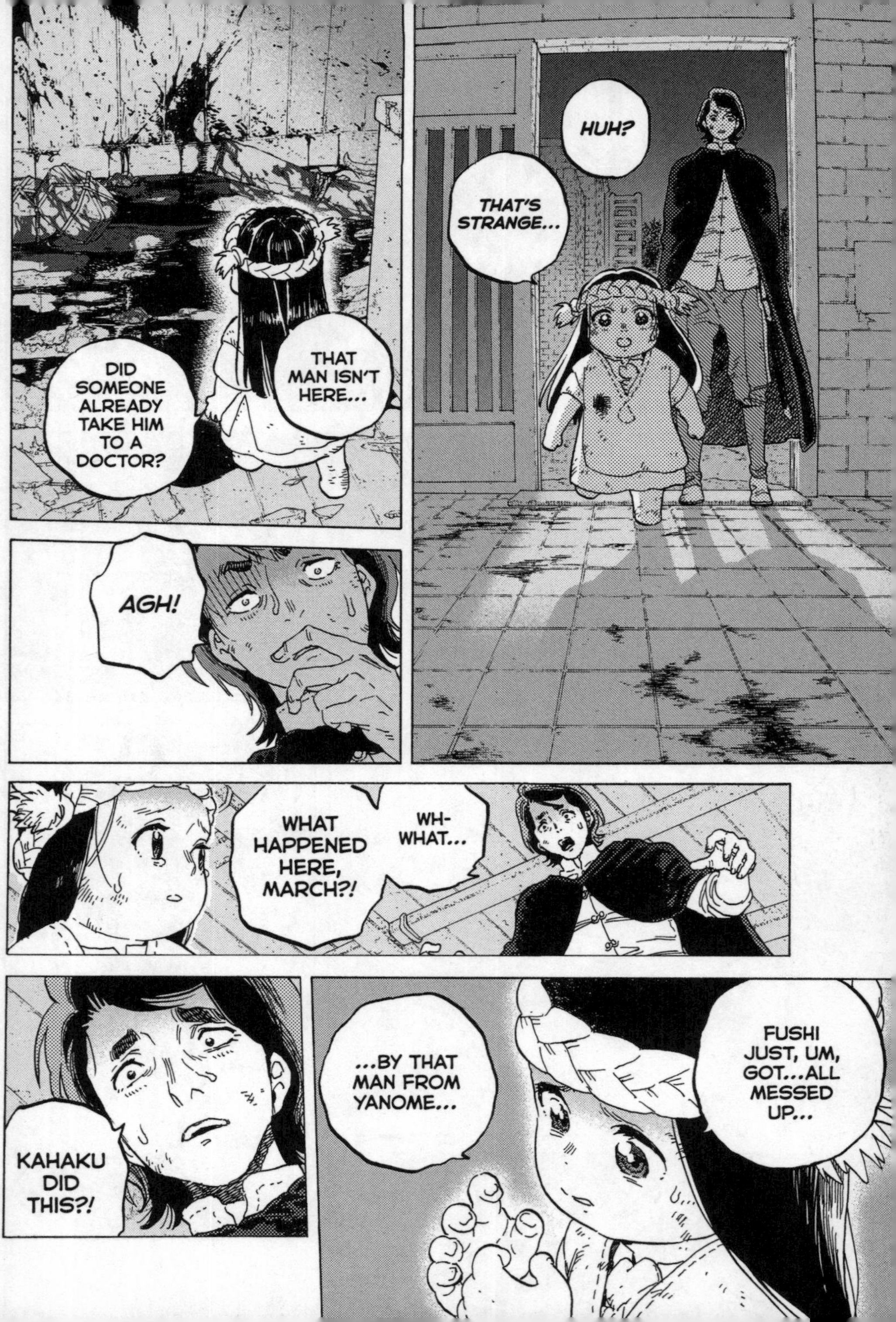
HUH?
THAT'S STRANGE...
THAT MAN ISN'T HERE...
DID SOMEONE ALREADY TAKE HIM TO A DOCTOR?
AGH!
WH- WHAT...
WHAT HAPPENED HERE, MARCH?!
FUSHI JUST, UM, GOT...ALL MESSED UP...
...BY THAT MAN FROM YANOME...
KAHAKU DID THIS?!

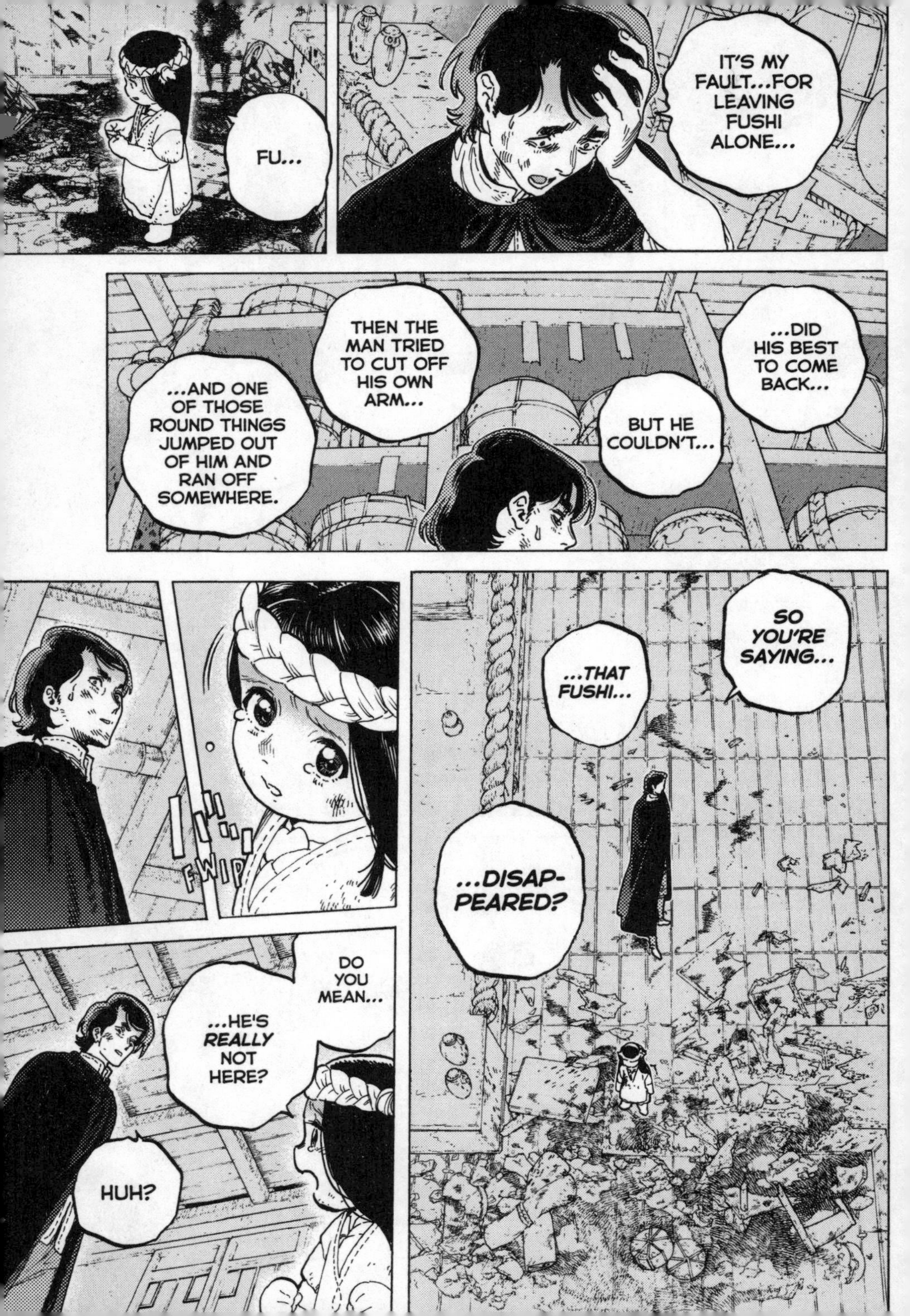
IT'S MY FAULT...FOR LEAVING FUSHI ALONE...
FU...
...DID HIS BEST TO COME BACK...
BUT HE COULDN'T...
THEN THE MAN TRIED TO CUT OFF HIS OWN ARM...
...AND ONE OF THOSE ROUND THINGS JUMPED OUT OF HIM AND RAN OFF SOMEWHERE.
SO *YOU'RE* SAYING...
...THAT FUSHI...
...DISAPPEARED?
FWIP
DO YOU MEAN...
...HE'S *REALLY* NOT HERE?
HUH?

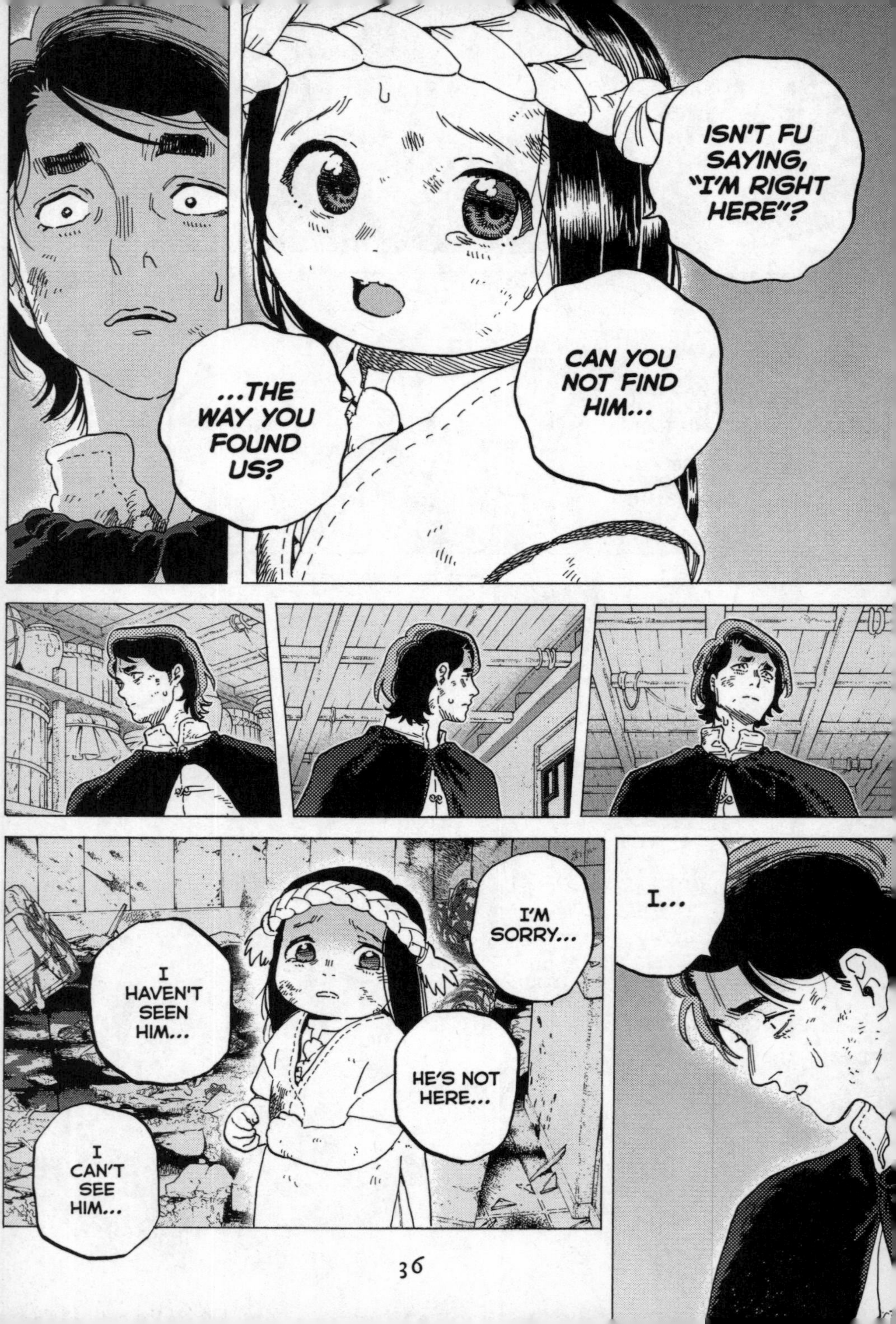
ISN'T FU SAYING, "I'M RIGHT HERE"?
CAN YOU NOT FIND HIM...
...THE WAY YOU FOUND US?
I...
I'M SORRY...
I HAVEN'T SEEN HIM...
HE'S NOT HERE...
I CAN'T SEE HIM...

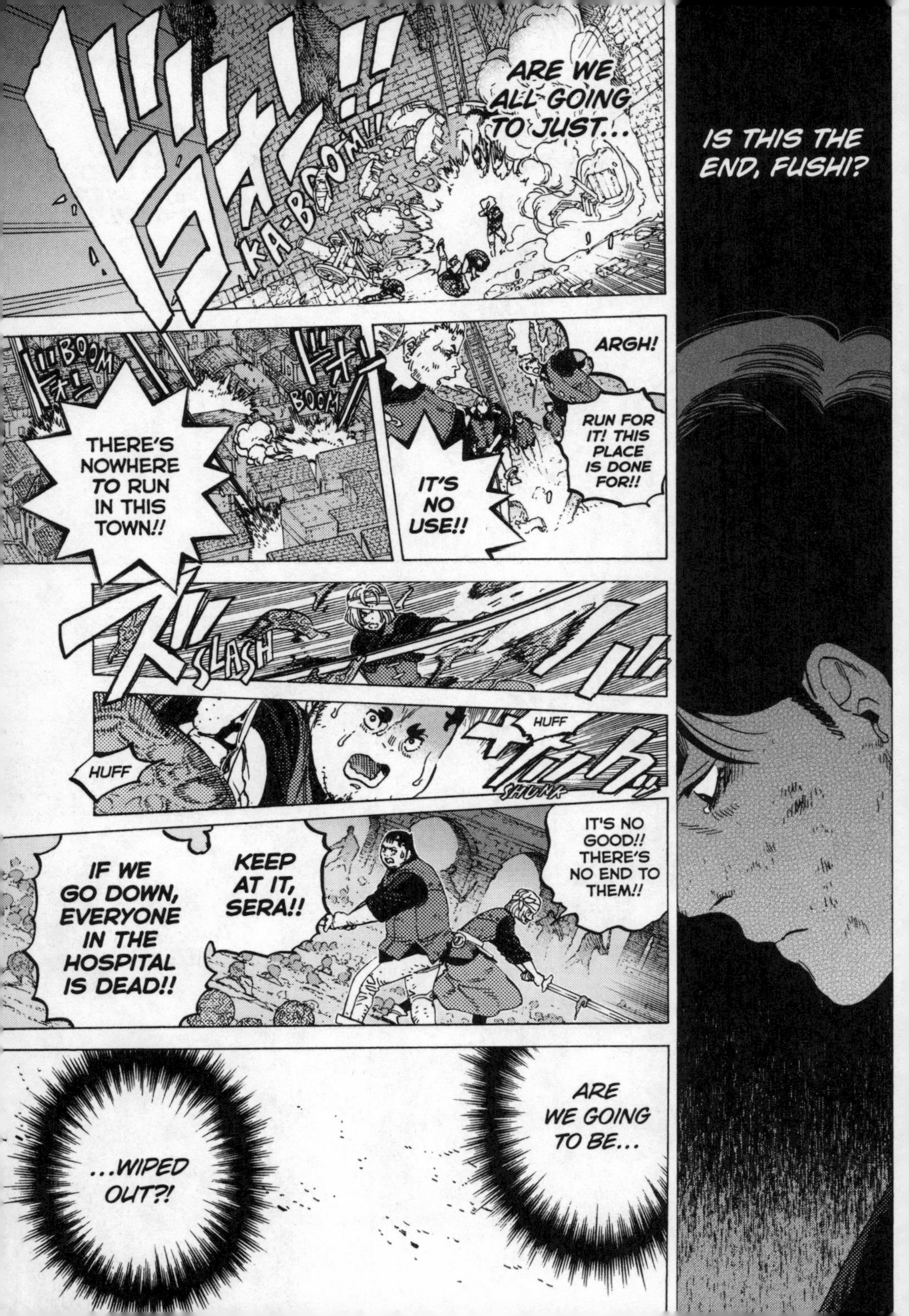
IS THIS THE END, FUSHI?
ARE WE ALL GOING TO JUST...
KA-BOOM!!
ARGH!
RUN FOR IT! THIS PLACE IS DONE FOR!!
IT'S NO USE!!
BOOM
BOOM
THERE'S NOWHERE TO RUN IN THIS TOWN!!
SLASH
HUFF
HUFF
IT'S NO GOOD!! THERE'S NO END TO THEM!!
KEEP AT IT, SERA!!
IF WE GO DOWN, EVERYONE IN THE HOSPITAL IS DEAD!!
ARE WE GOING TO BE...
...WIPED OUT?!

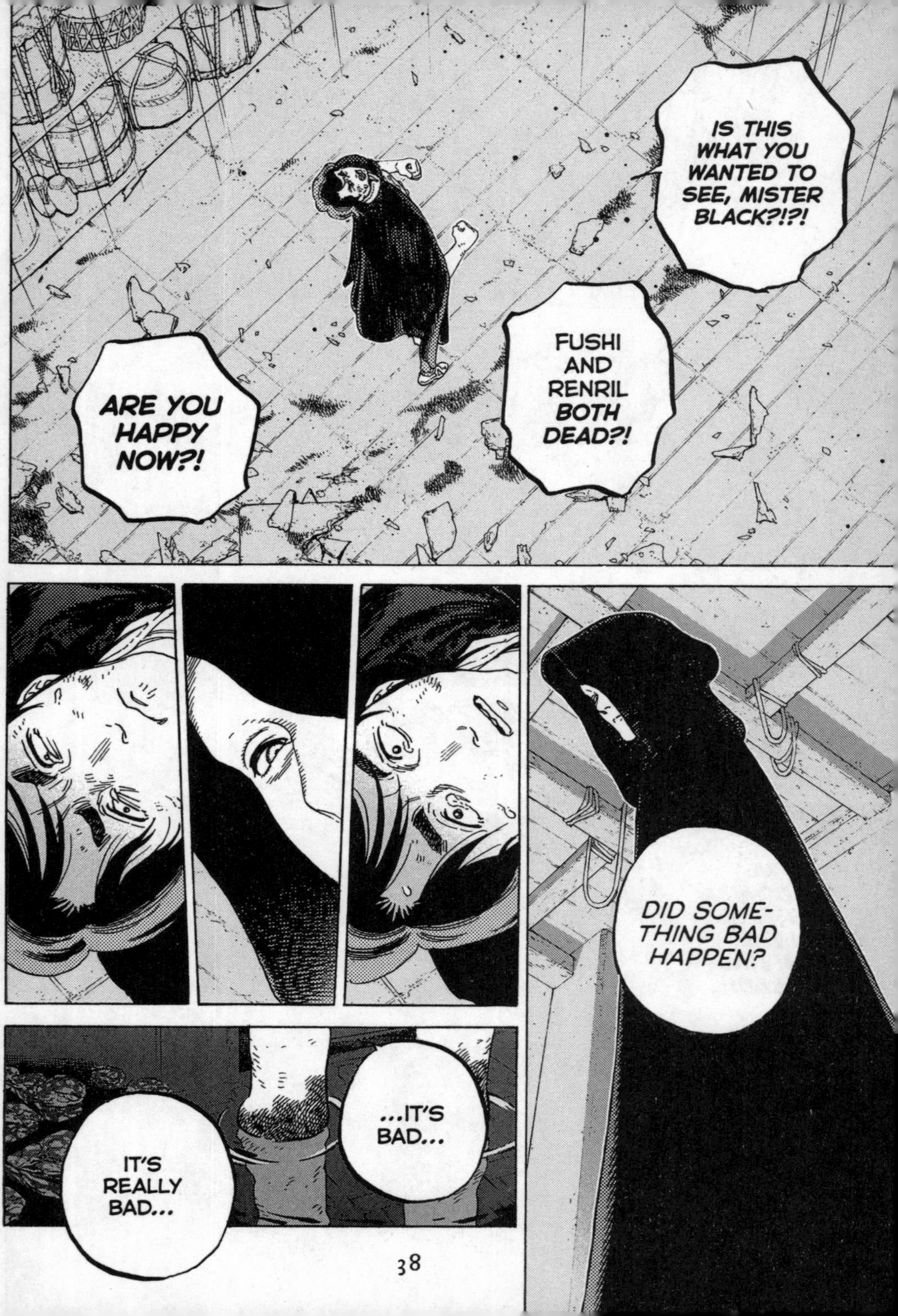
IS THIS WHAT YOU WANTED TO SEE, MISTER BLACK?!?!
FUSHI AND RENRIL BOTH DEAD?!
ARE YOU HAPPY NOW?!
DID SOME-THING BAD HAPPEN?
...IT'S BAD...
IT'S REALLY BAD...

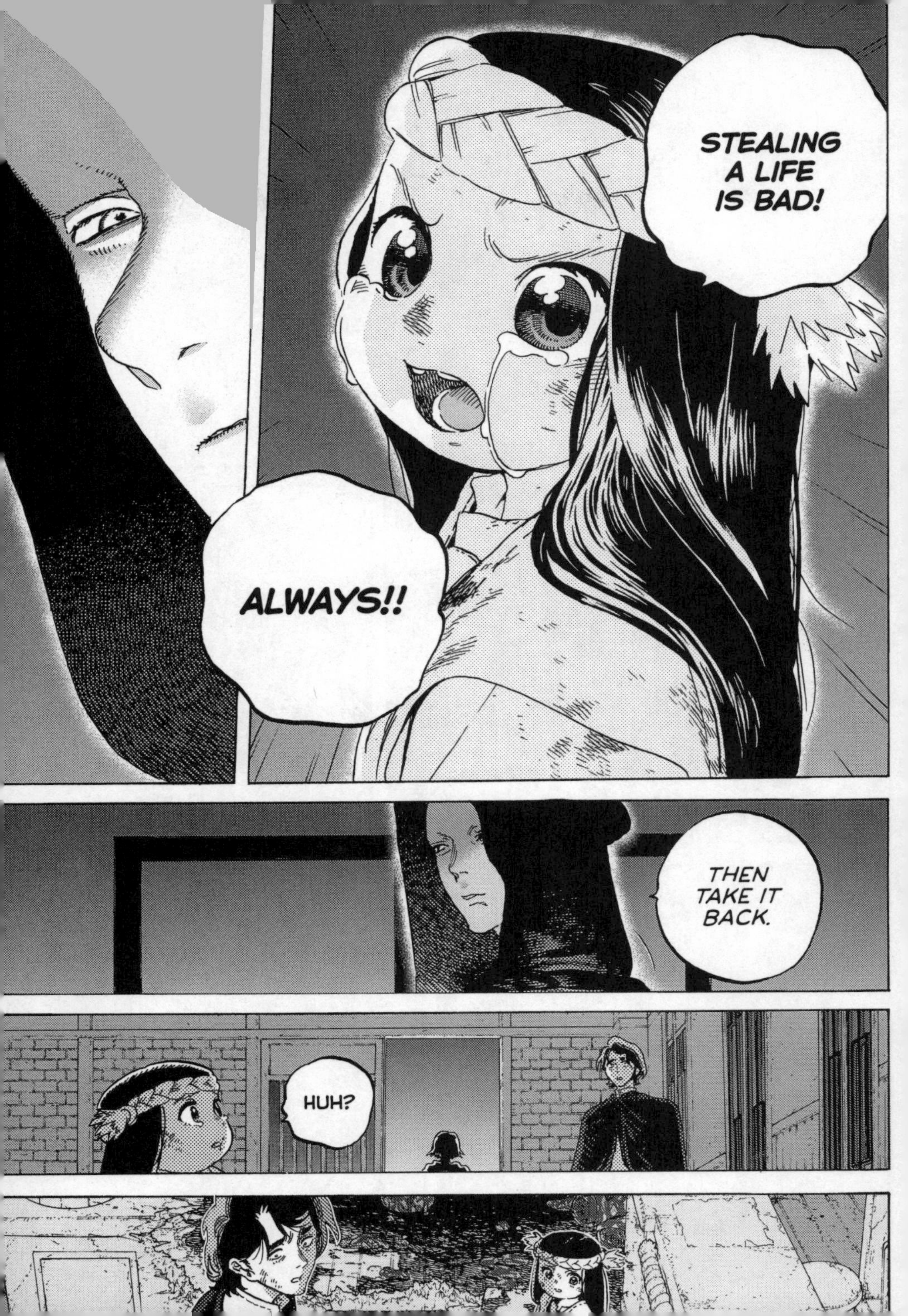
STEALING A LIFE IS BAD!
ALWAYS!!
THEN TAKE IT BACK.
HUH?

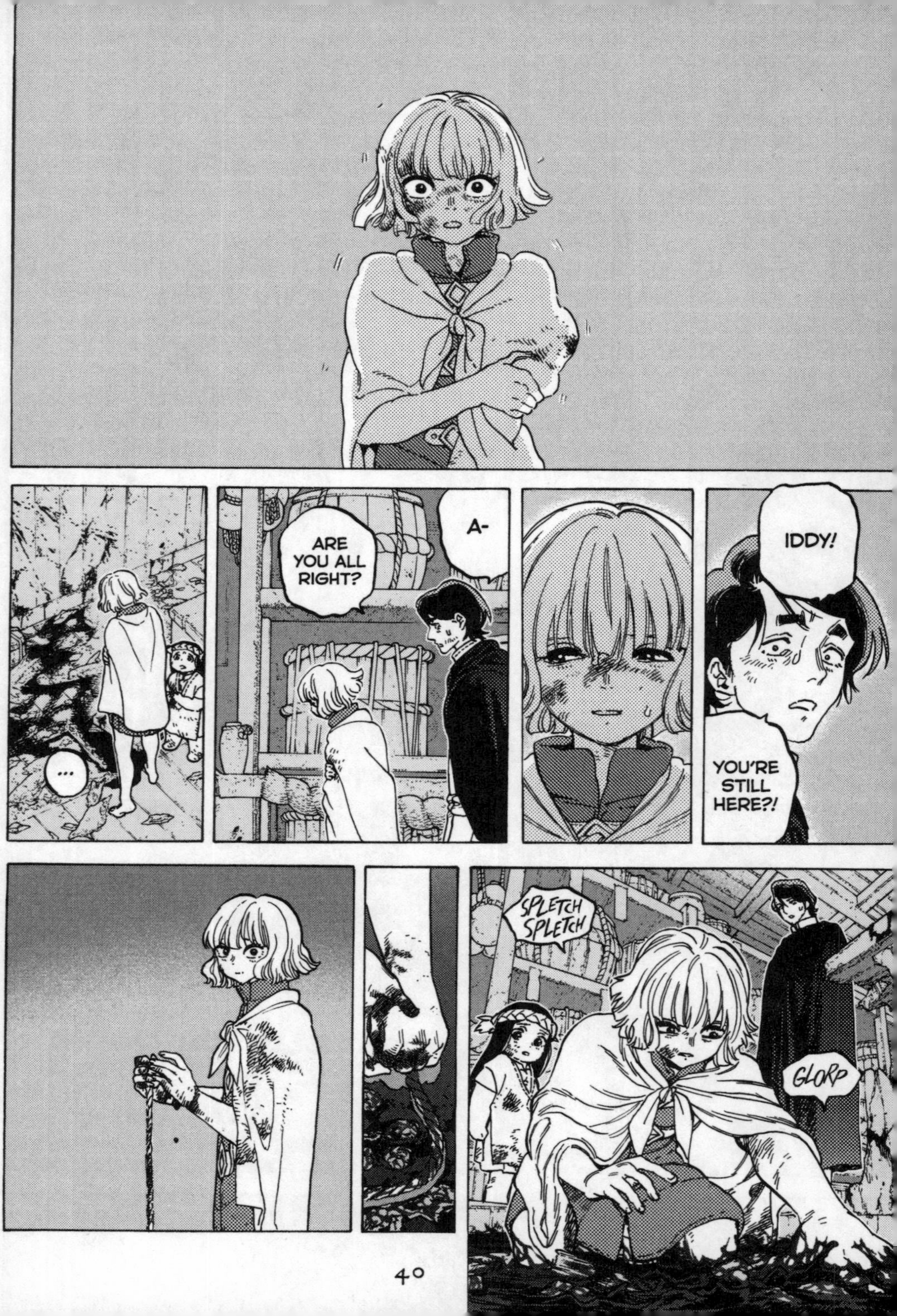
IDDY!
YOU'RE STILL HERE?!
A-
ARE YOU ALL RIGHT?
...
SPLETCH SPLETCH
GLORP

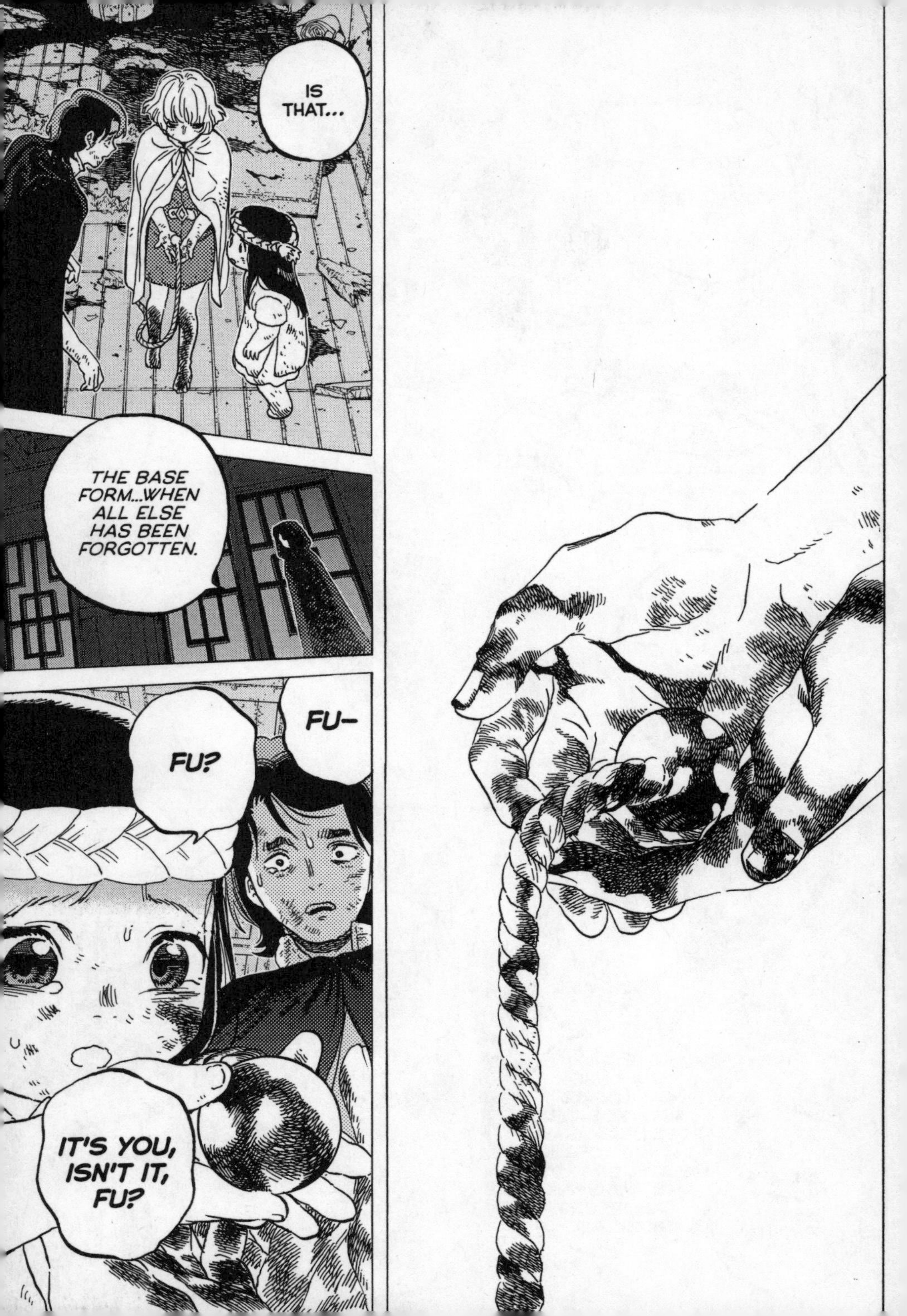
IS THAT...
THE BASE FORM...WHEN ALL ELSE HAS BEEN FORGOTTEN.
FU-
FU?
IT'S YOU, ISN'T IT, FU?

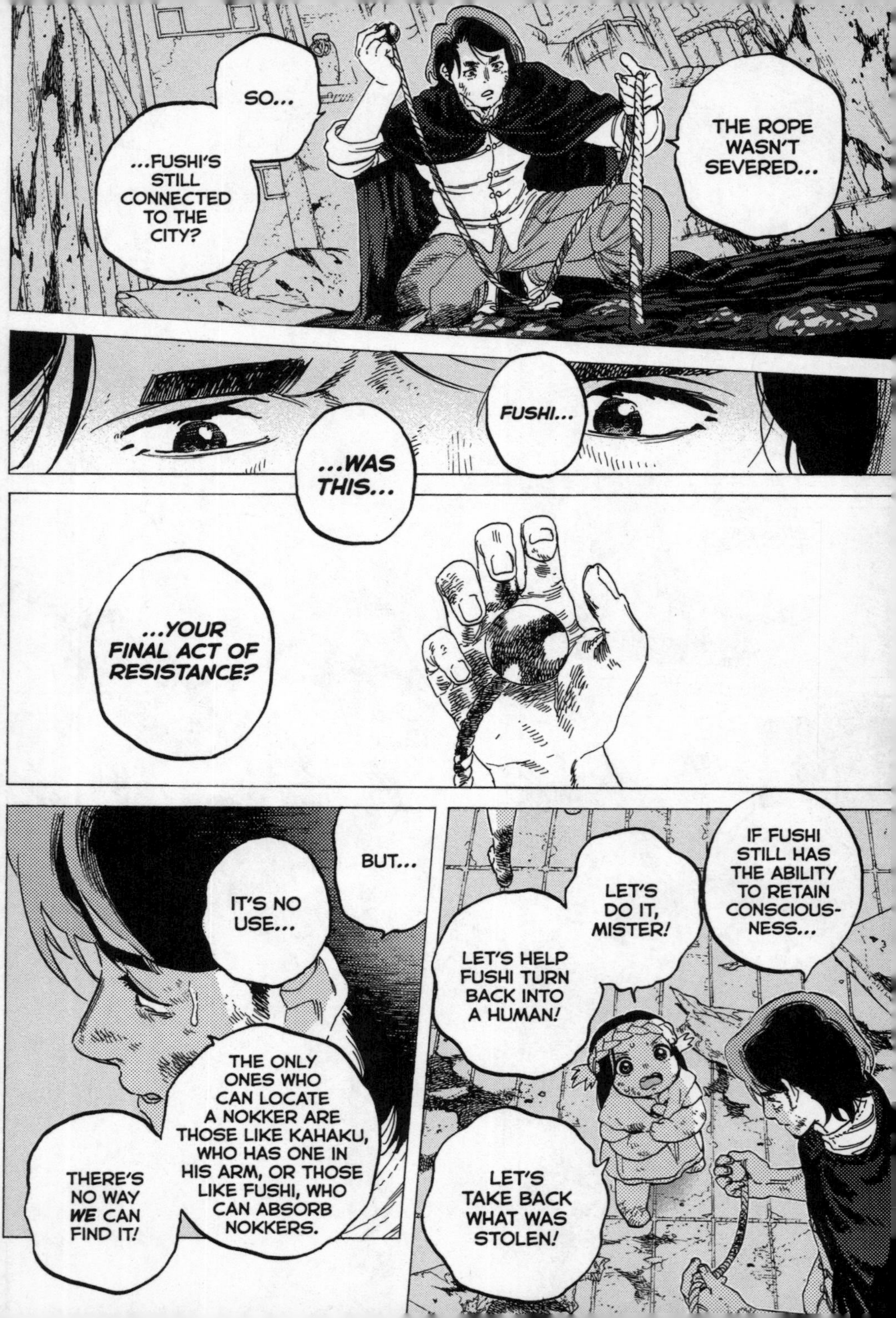
THE ROPE WASN'T SEVERED...
SO...
...FUSHI'S STILL CONNECTED TO THE CITY?
FUSHI...
...WAS THIS...
...YOUR FINAL ACT OF RESISTANCE?
IF FUSHI STILL HAS THE ABILITY TO RETAIN CONSCIOUS-NESS...
LET'S DO IT, MISTER!
LET'S HELP FUSHI TURN BACK INTO A HUMAN!
LET'S TAKE BACK WHAT WAS STOLEN!
BUT...
IT'S NO USE...
THE ONLY ONES WHO CAN LOCATE A NOKKER ARE THOSE LIKE KAHAKU, WHO HAS ONE IN HIS ARM, OR THOSE LIKE FUSHI, WHO CAN ABSORB NOKKERS.
THERE'S NO WAY *WE* CAN FIND IT!

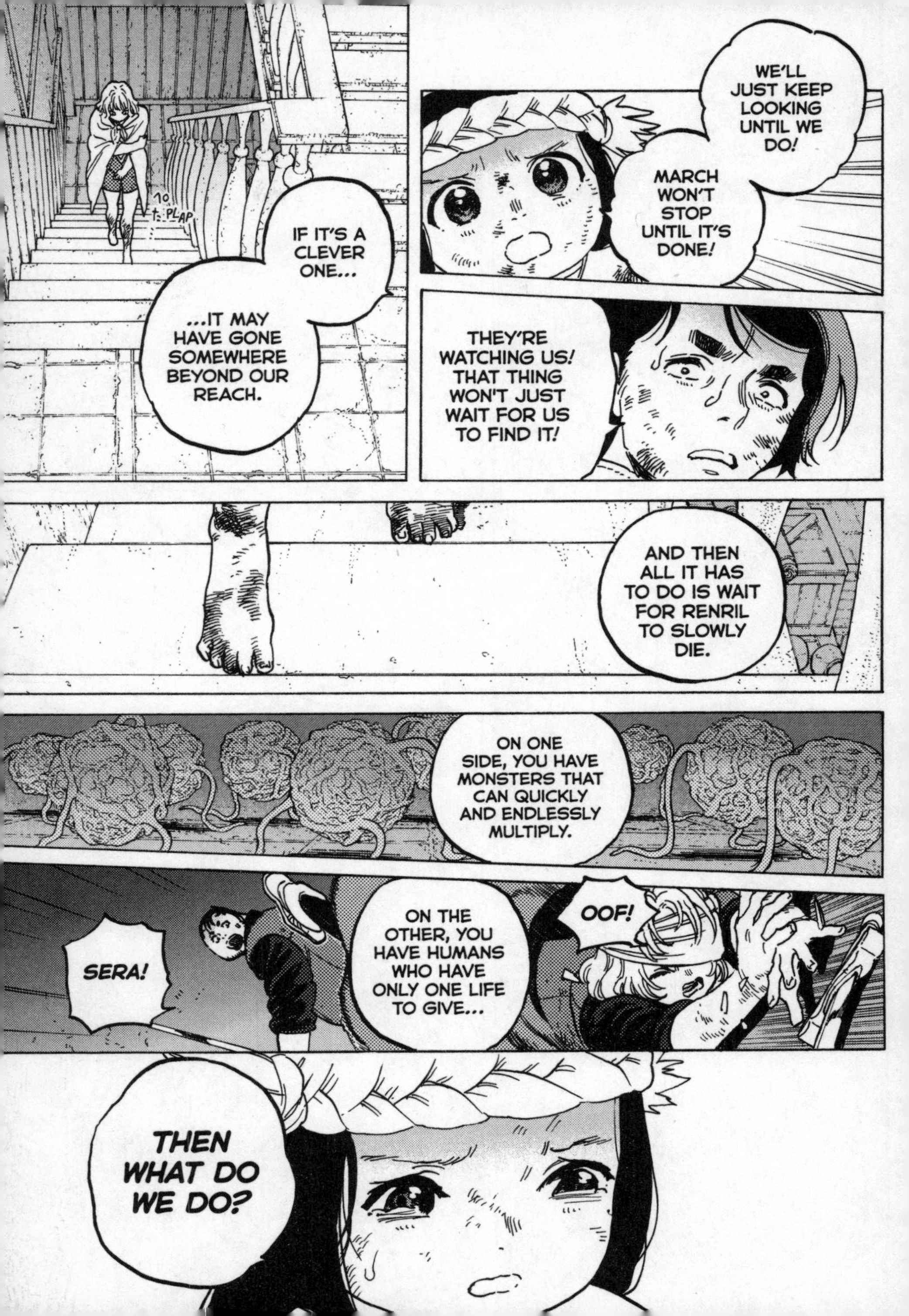
WE'LL JUST KEEP LOOKING UNTIL WE DO!
MARCH WON'T STOP UNTIL IT'S DONE!
THEY'RE WATCHING US! THAT THING WON'T JUST WAIT FOR US TO FIND IT!
IF IT'S A CLEVER ONE...
...IT MAY HAVE GONE SOMEWHERE BEYOND OUR REACH.
PLAP
AND THEN ALL IT HAS TO DO IS WAIT FOR RENRIL TO SLOWLY DIE.
ON ONE SIDE, YOU HAVE MONSTERS THAT CAN QUICKLY AND ENDLESSLY MULTIPLY.
OOF!
ON THE OTHER, YOU HAVE HUMANS WHO HAVE ONLY ONE LIFE TO GIVE...
SERA!
THEN WHAT DO WE DO?

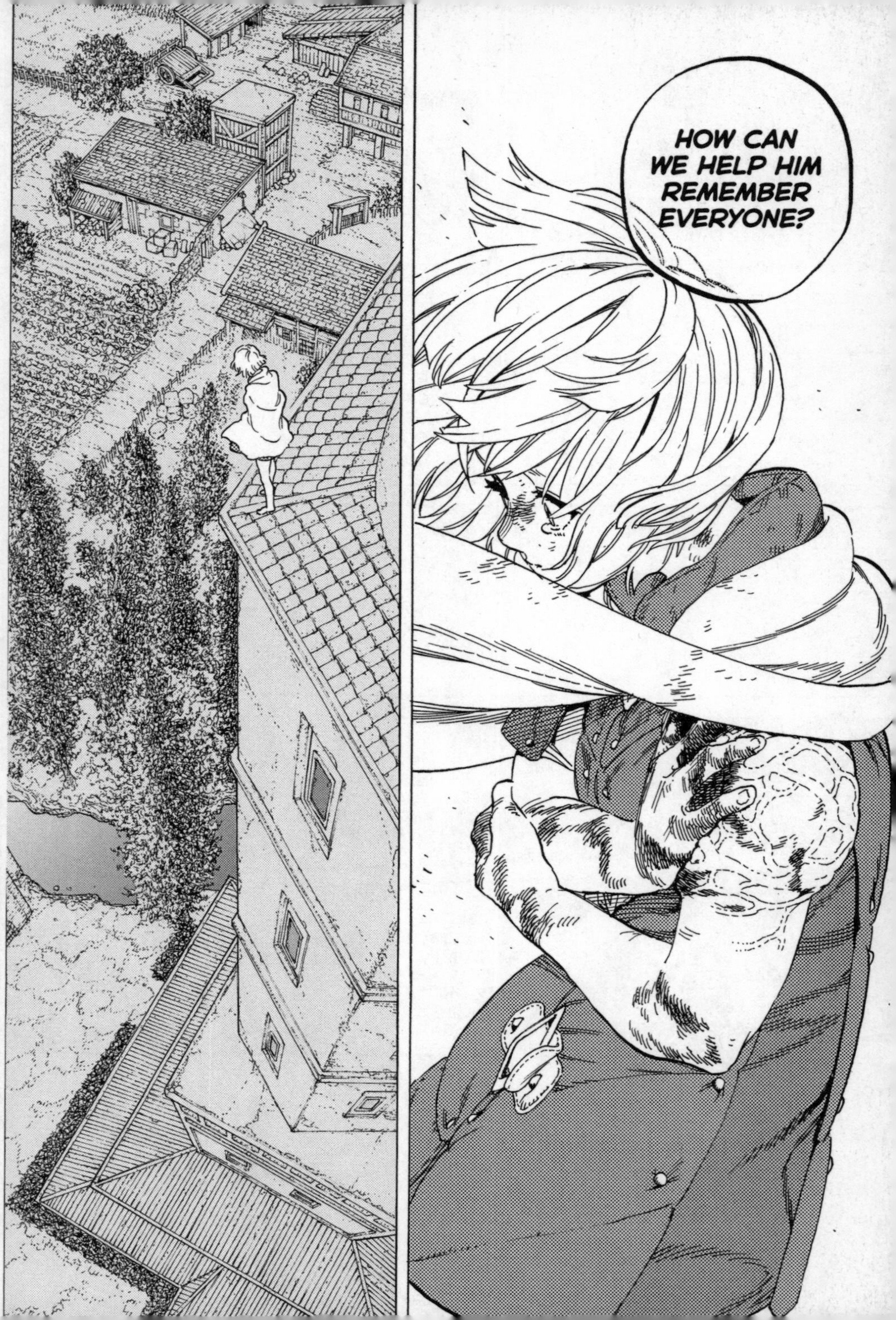
HOW CAN WE HELP HIM REMEMBER EVERYONE?

#110 The Price of a Vessel

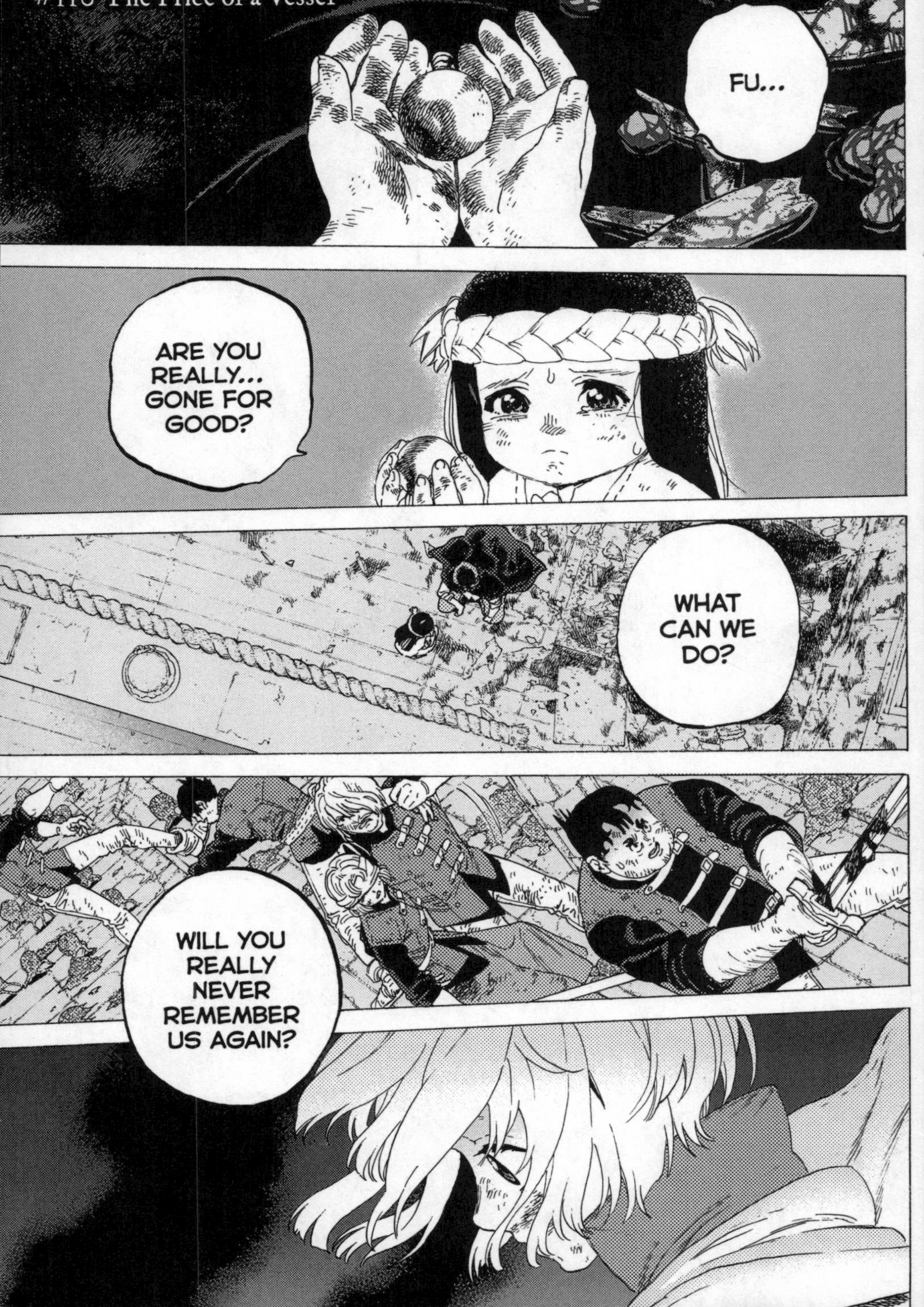
FU...
ARE YOU REALLY... GONE FOR GOOD?
WHAT CAN WE DO?
WILL YOU REALLY NEVER REMEMBER US AGAIN?

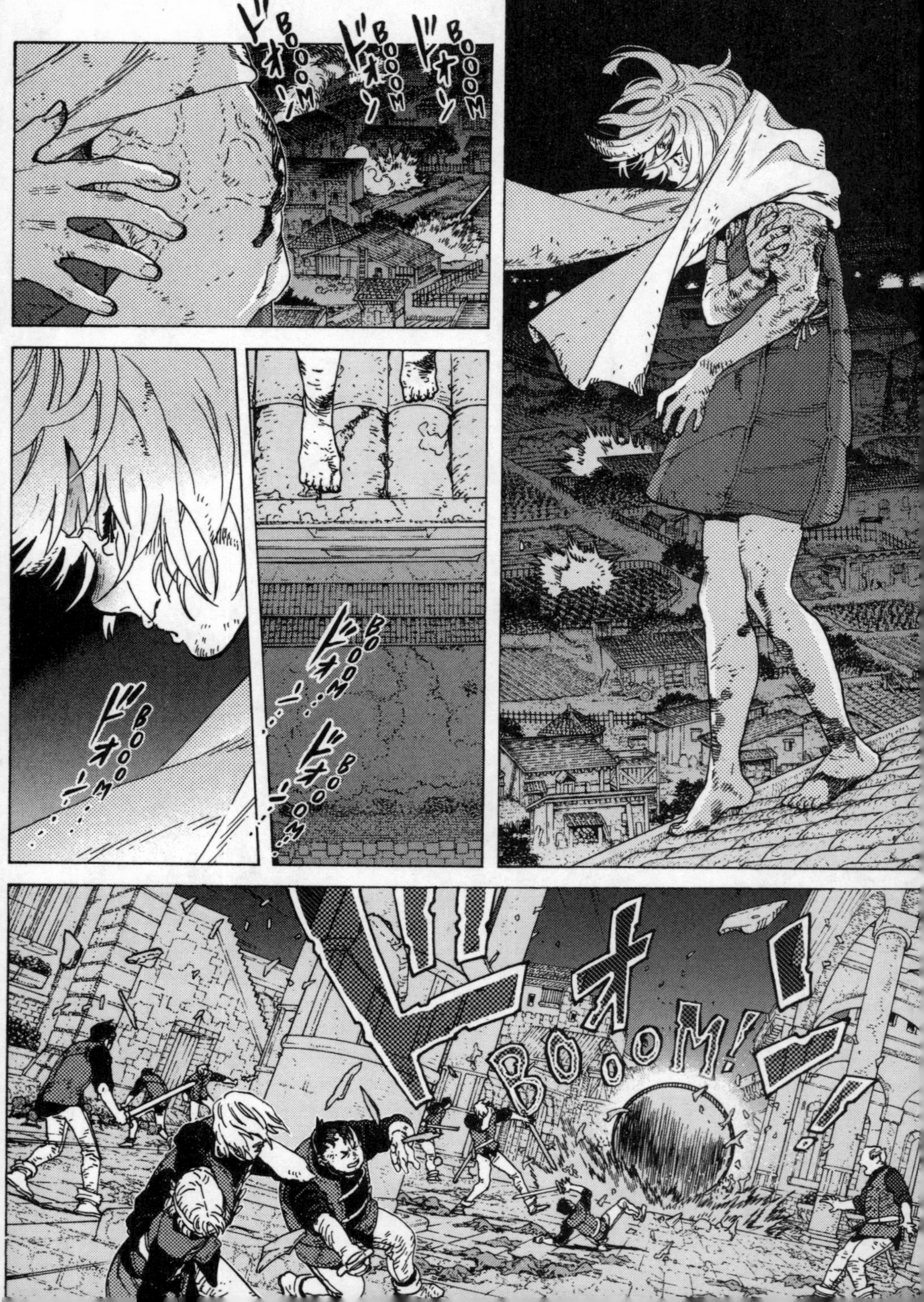
ドォーン BOOOM
ドォーン BOOOM
ドォーン BOOOM
ドォー… BOOOM
ドォー… BOOOM
ドォー… BOOOM
ドォーン!! BOOOM!

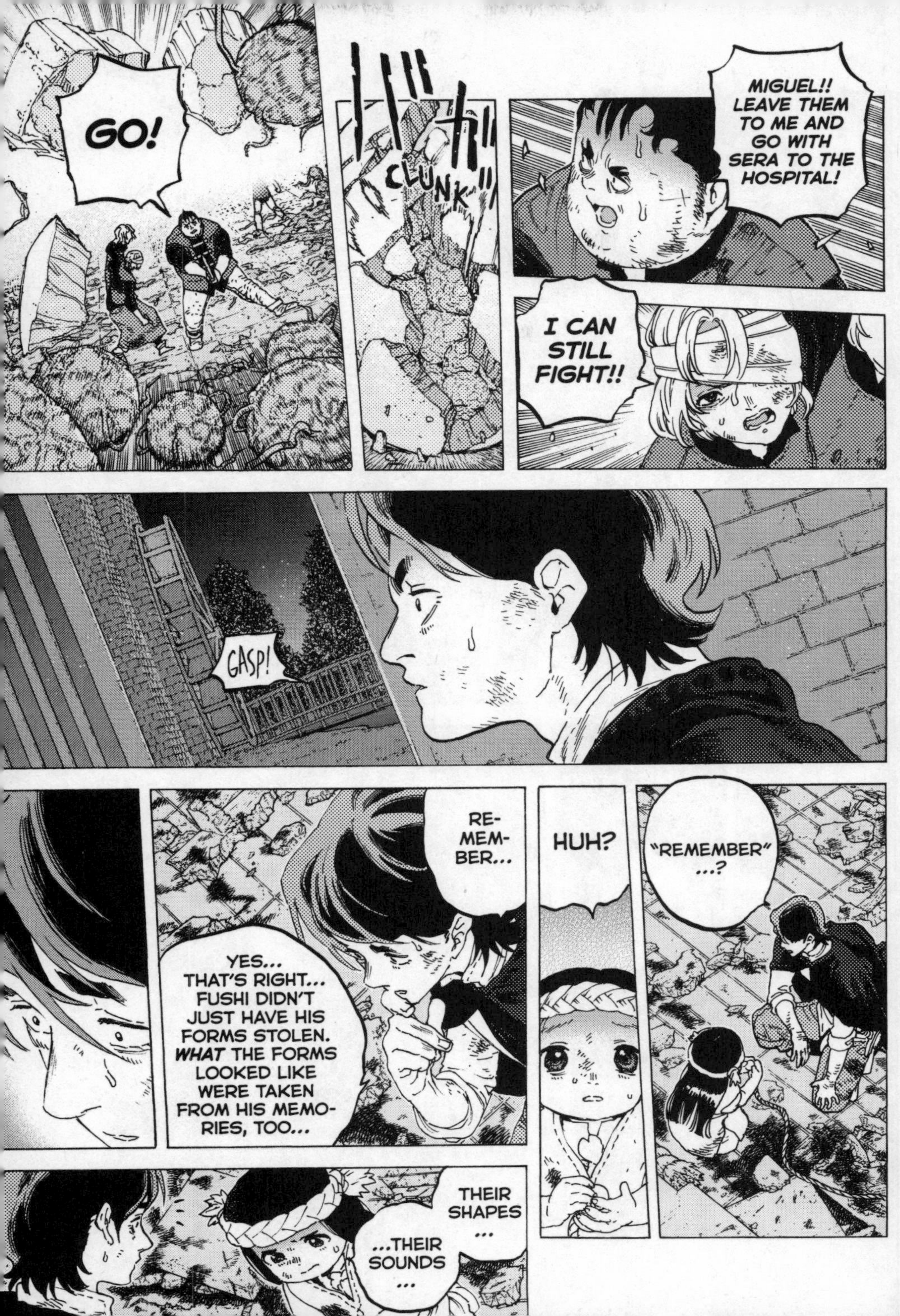
MIGUEL!! LEAVE THEM TO ME AND GO WITH SERA TO THE HOSPITAL!
I CAN STILL FIGHT!!
CLUNK
GO!
GASP!
"REMEMBER" ...?
HUH?
RE-MEM-BER...
YES... THAT'S RIGHT... FUSHI DIDN'T JUST HAVE HIS FORMS STOLEN. *WHAT* THE FORMS LOOKED LIKE WERE TAKEN FROM HIS MEMO-RIES, TOO...
THEIR SHAPES ...
...THEIR SOUNDS ...

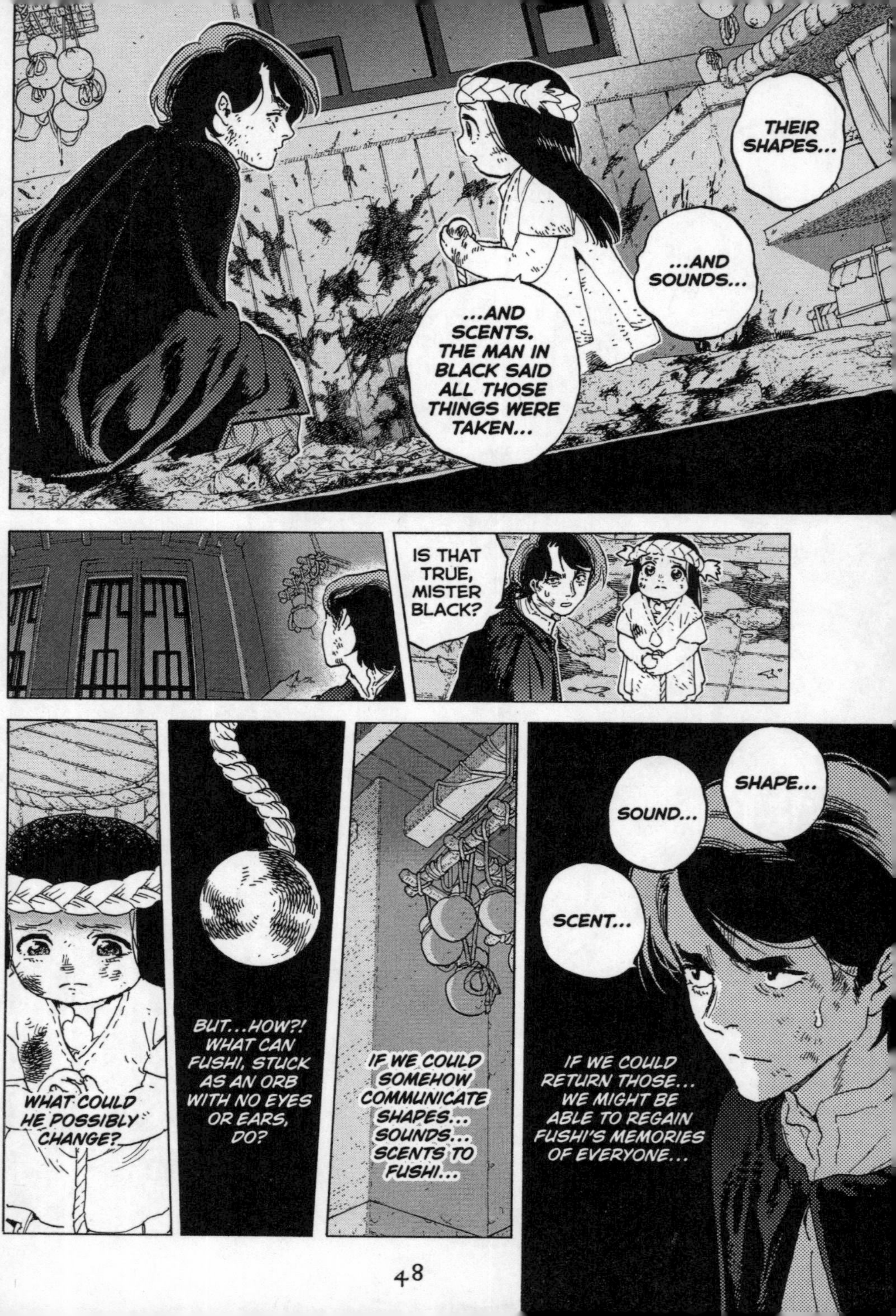
THEIR SHAPES...
...AND SOUNDS...
...AND SCENTS. THE MAN IN BLACK SAID ALL THOSE THINGS WERE TAKEN...
IS THAT TRUE, MISTER BLACK?
SHAPE...
SOUND...
SCENT...
IF WE COULD RETURN THOSE... WE MIGHT BE ABLE TO REGAIN FUSHI'S MEMORIES OF EVERYONE...
IF WE COULD SOMEHOW COMMUNICATE SHAPES... SOUNDS... SCENTS TO FUSHI...
BUT...HOW?! WHAT CAN FUSHI, STUCK AS AN ORB WITH NO EYES OR EARS, DO?
WHAT COULD HE POSSIBLY CHANGE?

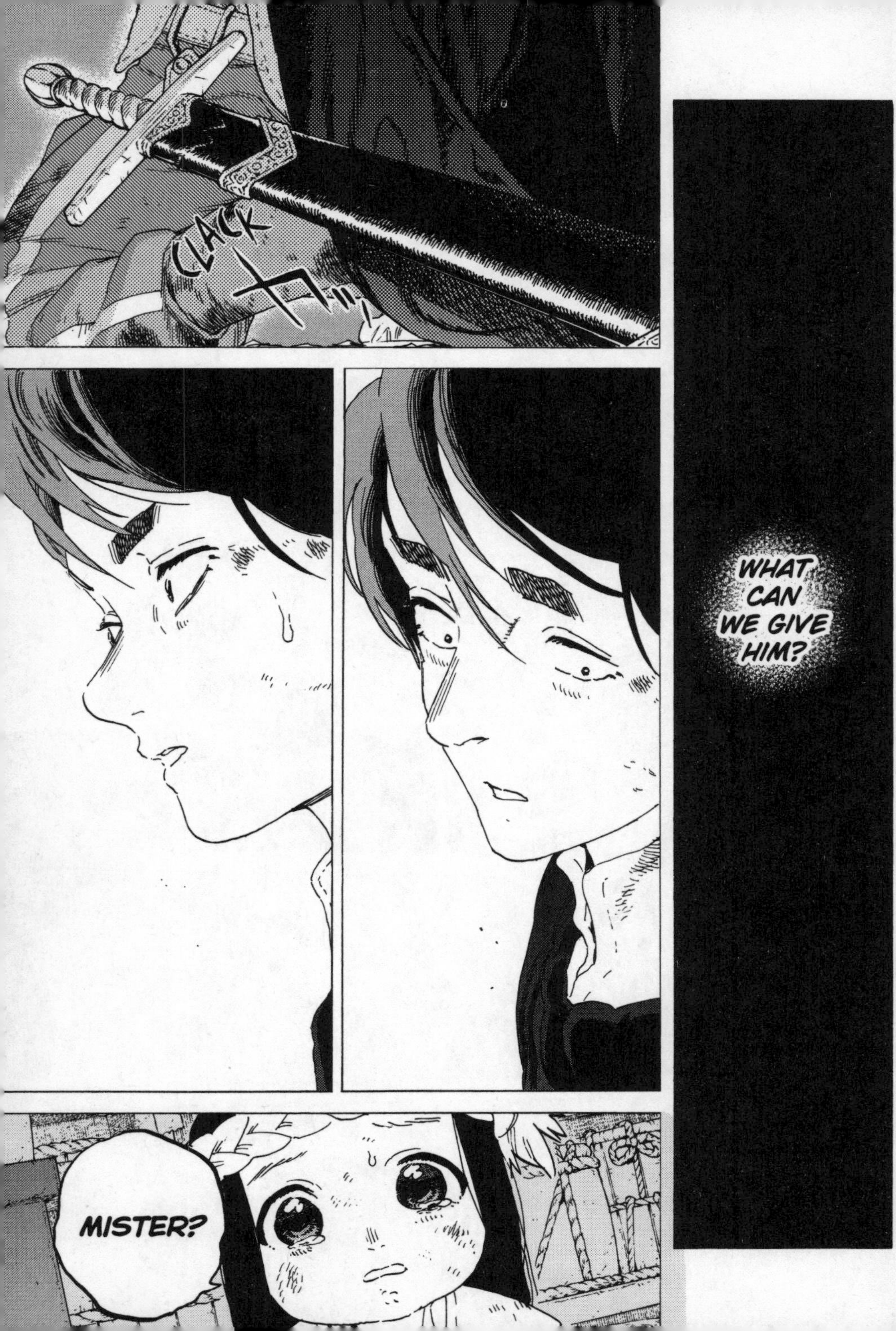
CLACK
WHAT CAN WE GIVE HIM?
MISTER?

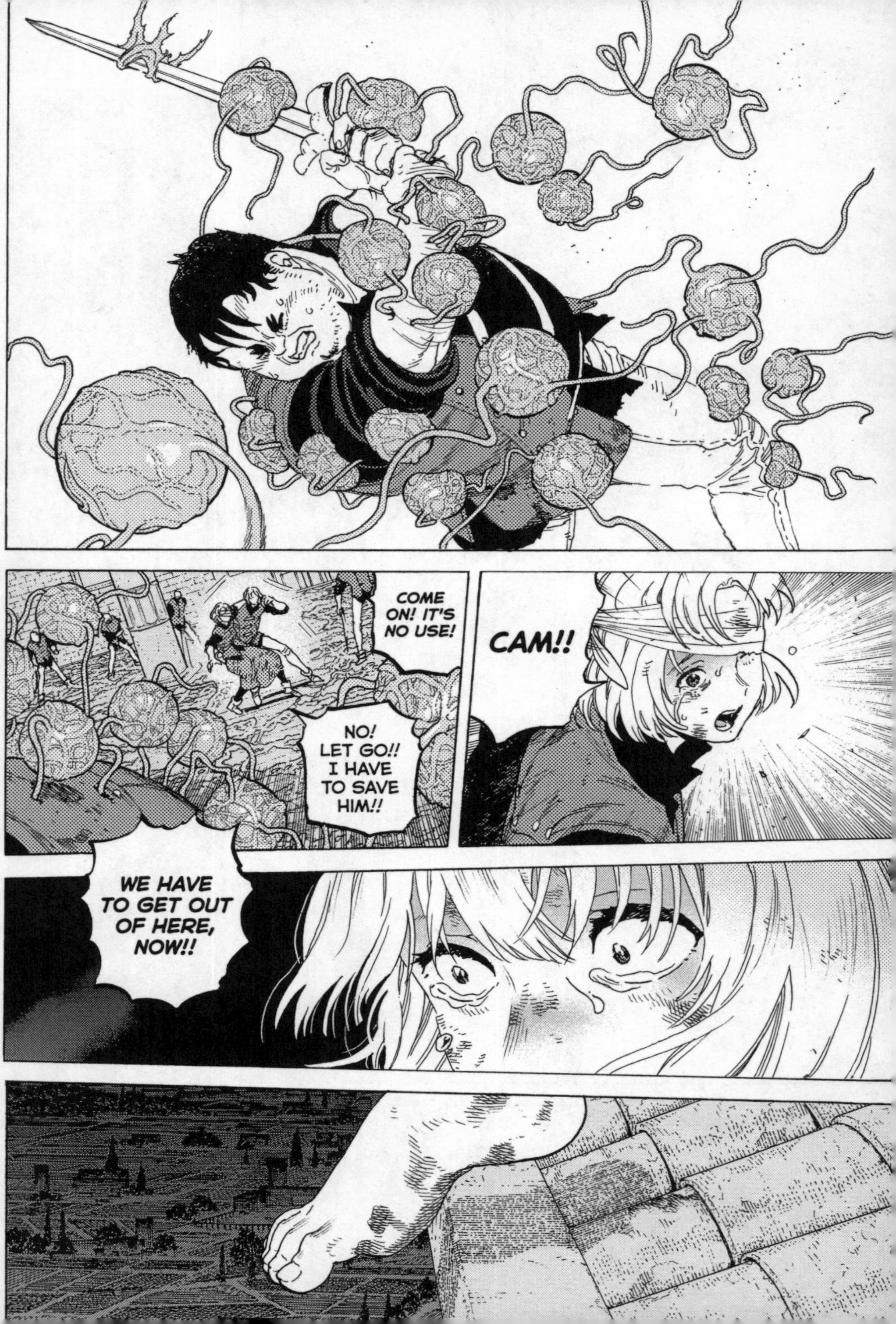
CAM!!
COME ON! IT'S NO USE!
NO! LET GO!! I HAVE TO SAVE HIM!!
WE HAVE TO GET OUT OF HERE, NOW!!

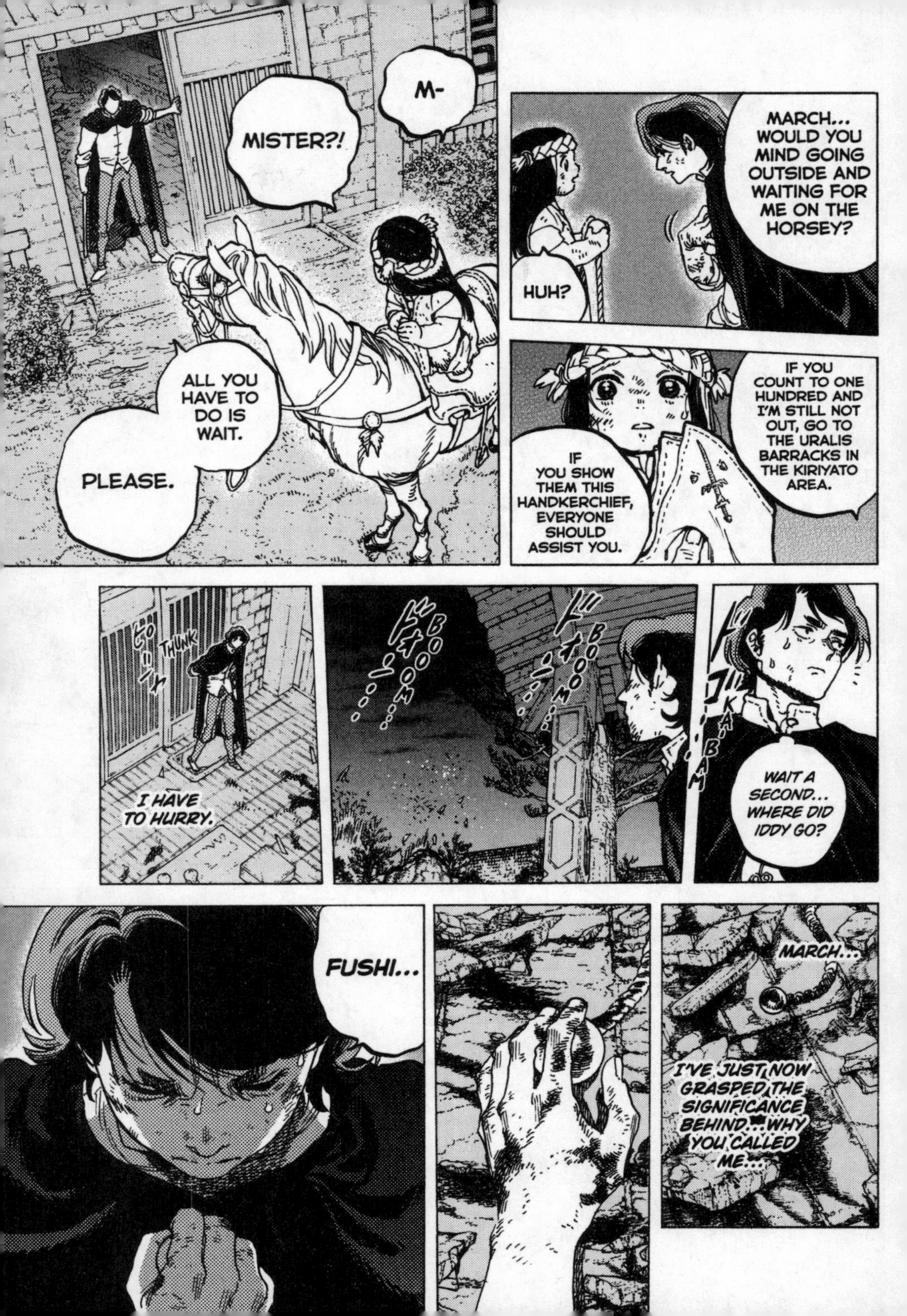
MARCH... WOULD YOU MIND GOING OUTSIDE AND WAITING FOR ME ON THE HORSEY?
HUH?
IF YOU COUNT TO ONE HUNDRED AND I'M STILL NOT OUT, GO TO THE URALIS BARRACKS IN THE KIRIYATO AREA.
IF YOU SHOW THEM THIS HANDKERCHIEF, EVERYONE SHOULD ASSIST YOU.
M-
MISTER?!
ALL YOU HAVE TO DO IS WAIT.
PLEASE.
KA...BAM
WAIT A SECOND... WHERE DID IDDY GO?
BOOOM...
BOOOM...
THUNK
I HAVE TO HURRY.
MARCH...
I'VE JUST NOW GRASPED THE SIGNIFICANCE BEHIND... WHY YOU CALLED ME...
FUSHI...

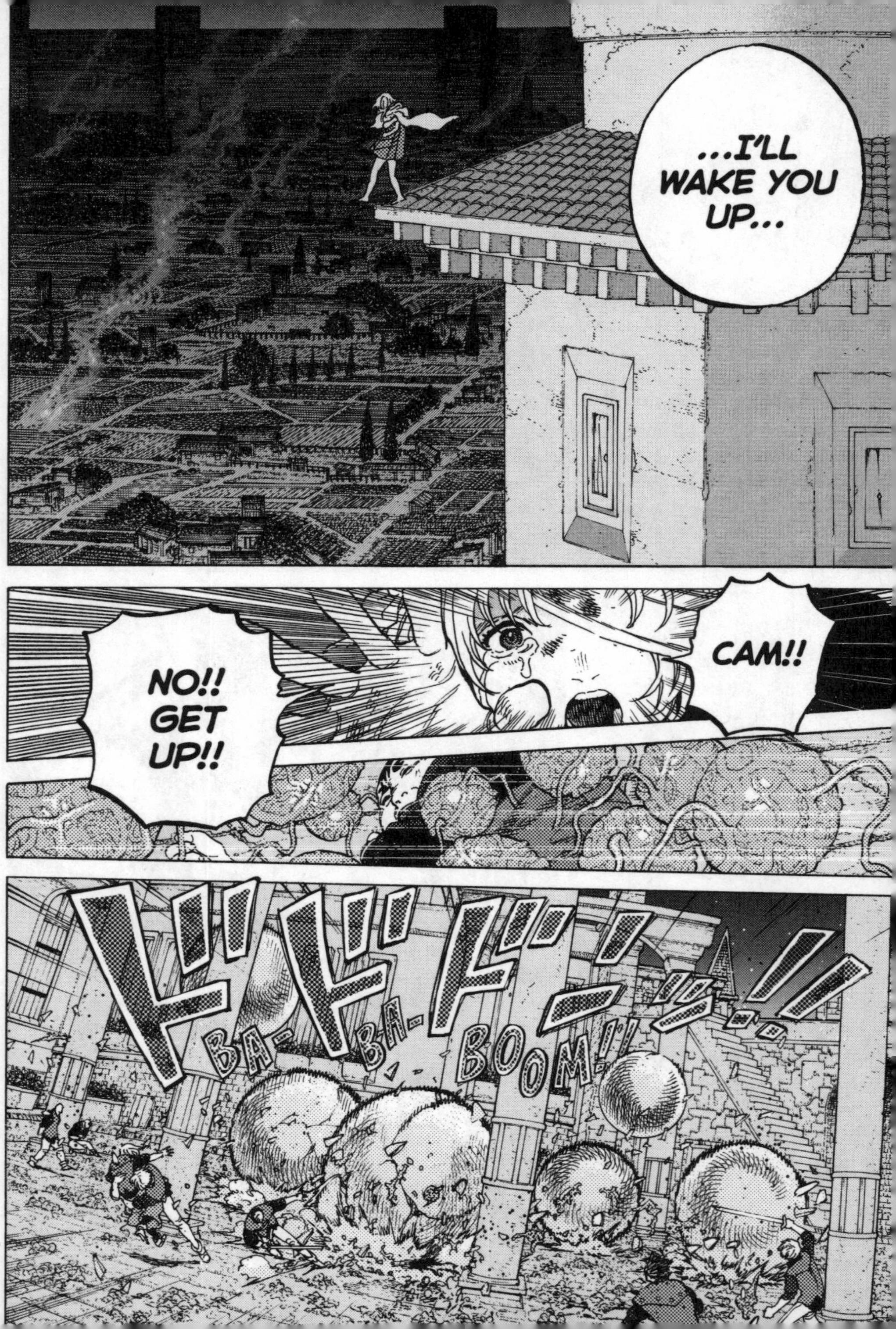
...I'LL WAKE YOU UP...
CAM!!
NO!! GET UP!!
BA-BA-BOOM!!

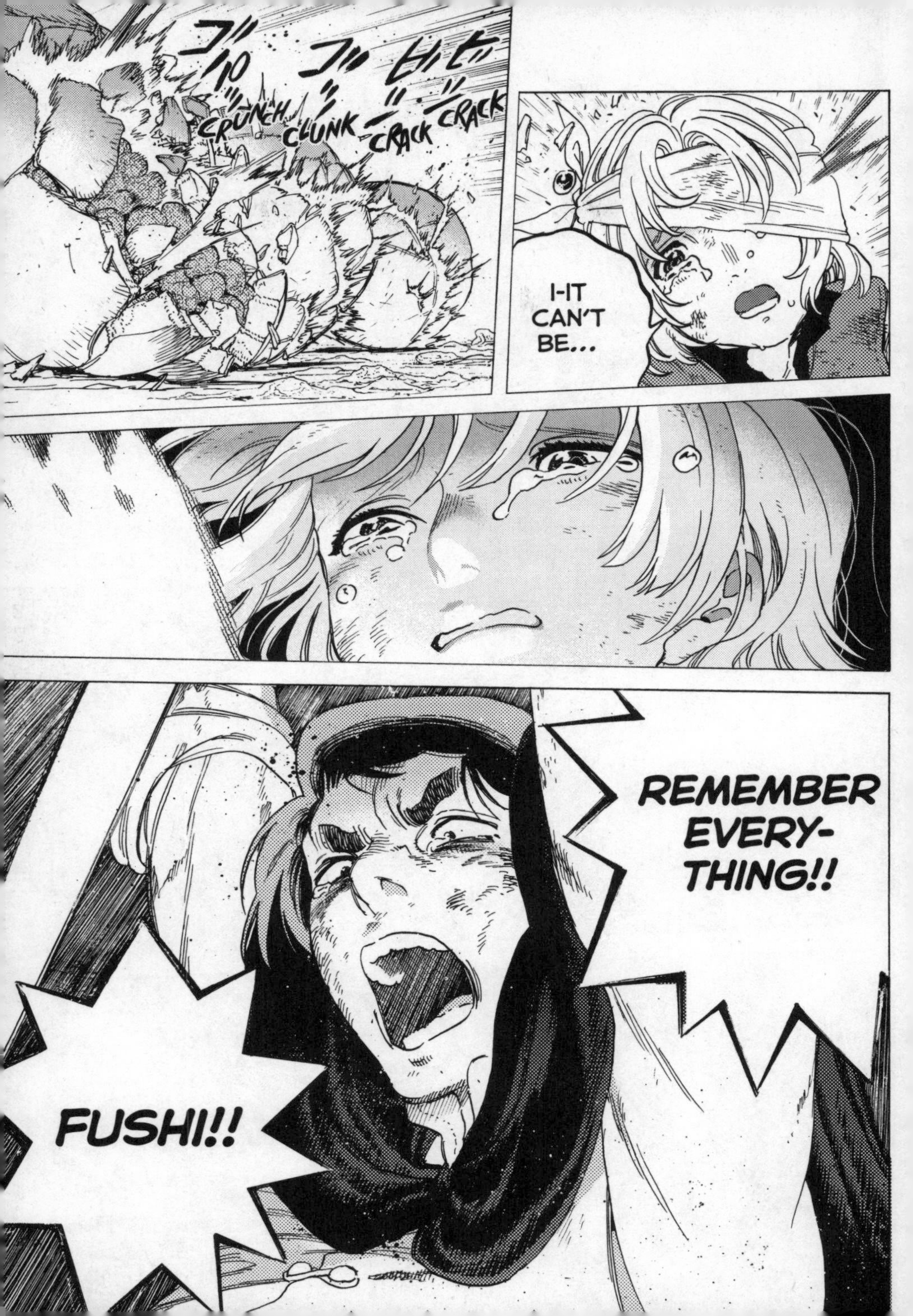
I-IT CAN'T BE...
CRUNCH
CLUNK
CRACK
CRACK
REMEMBER EVERY-THING!!
FUSHI!!

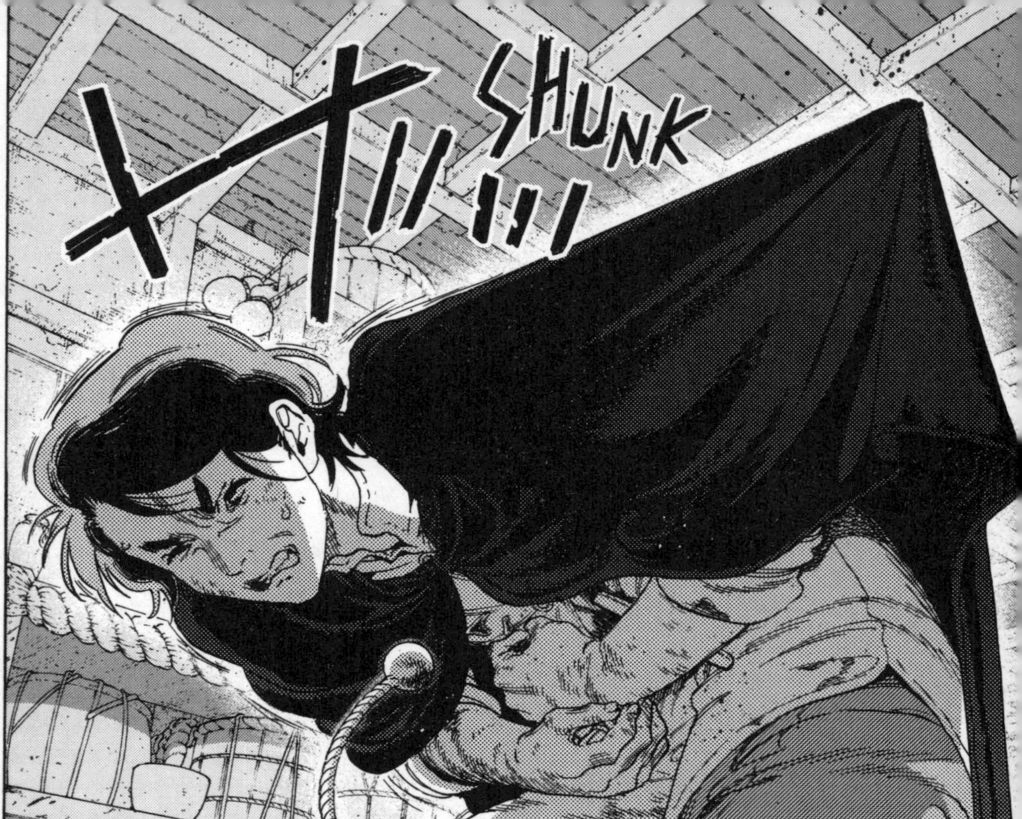
SHUNK
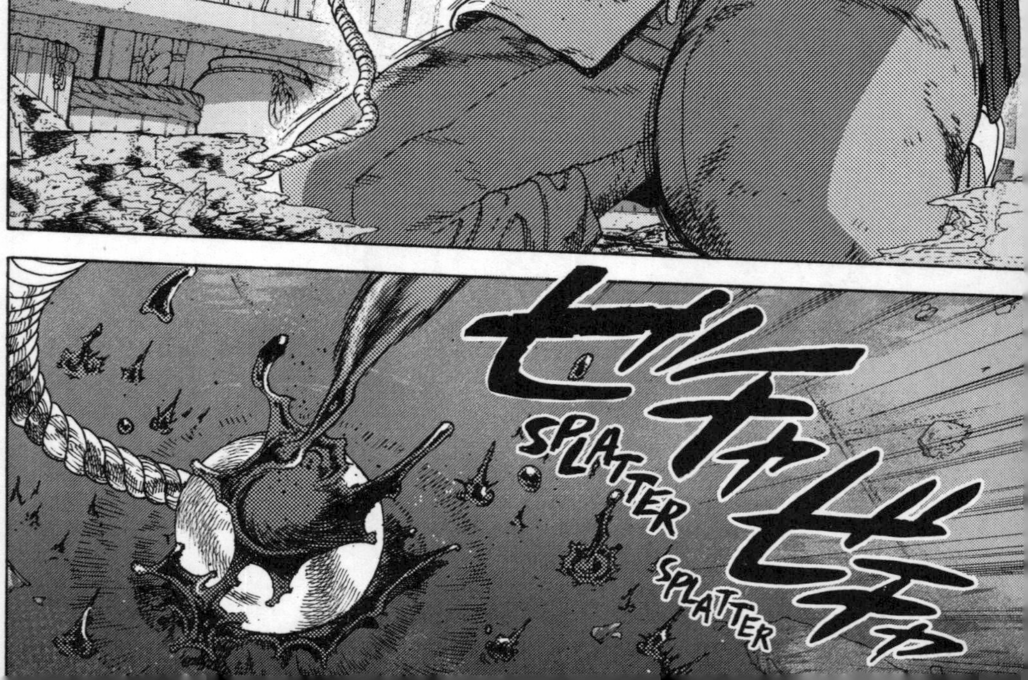
SPLATTER
SPLATTER

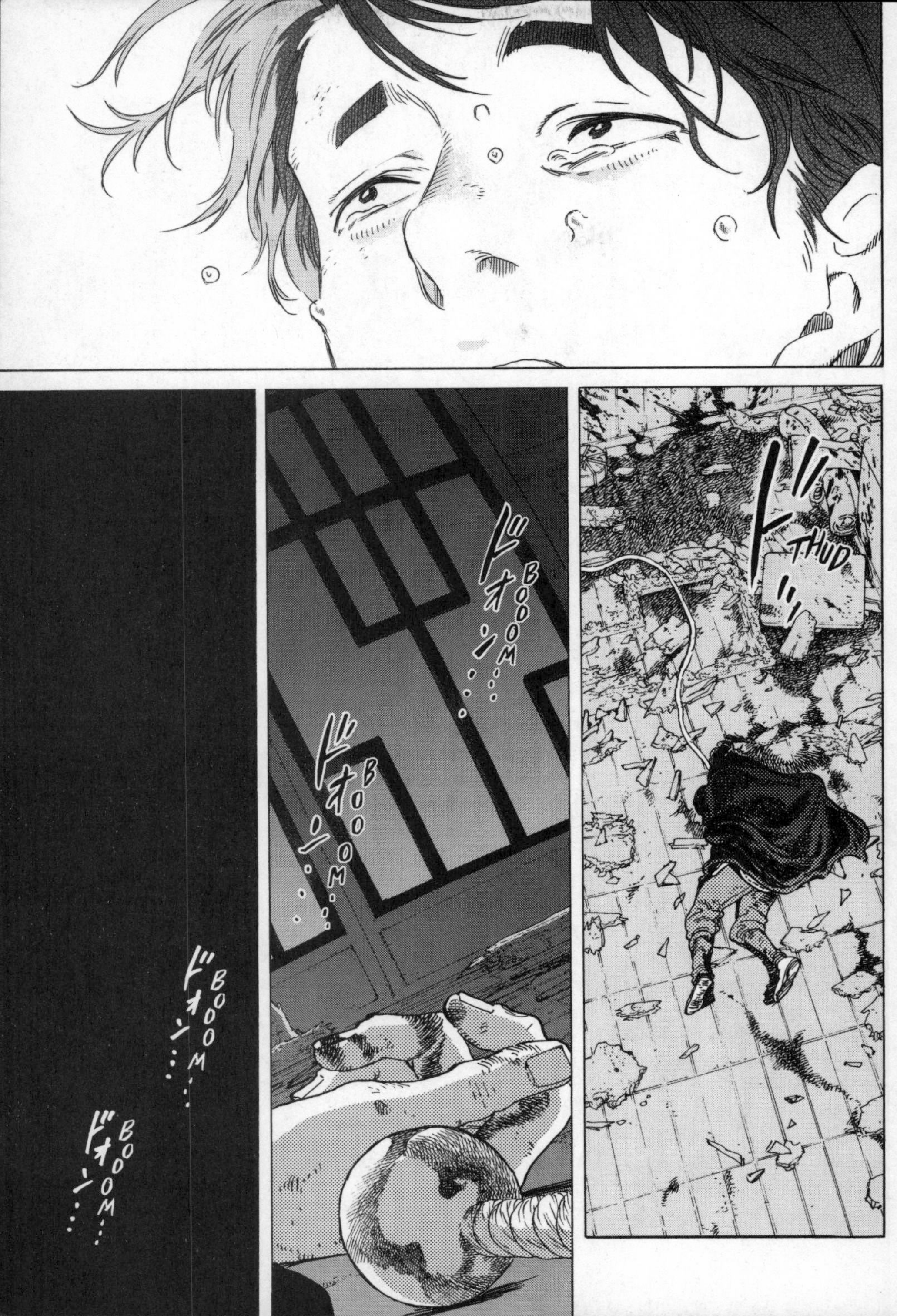

ドッ
THUD
ドォン…
BOOOM...
ドォン…
BOOOM...
ドォン…
BOOOM...
ドォン…
BOOOM...

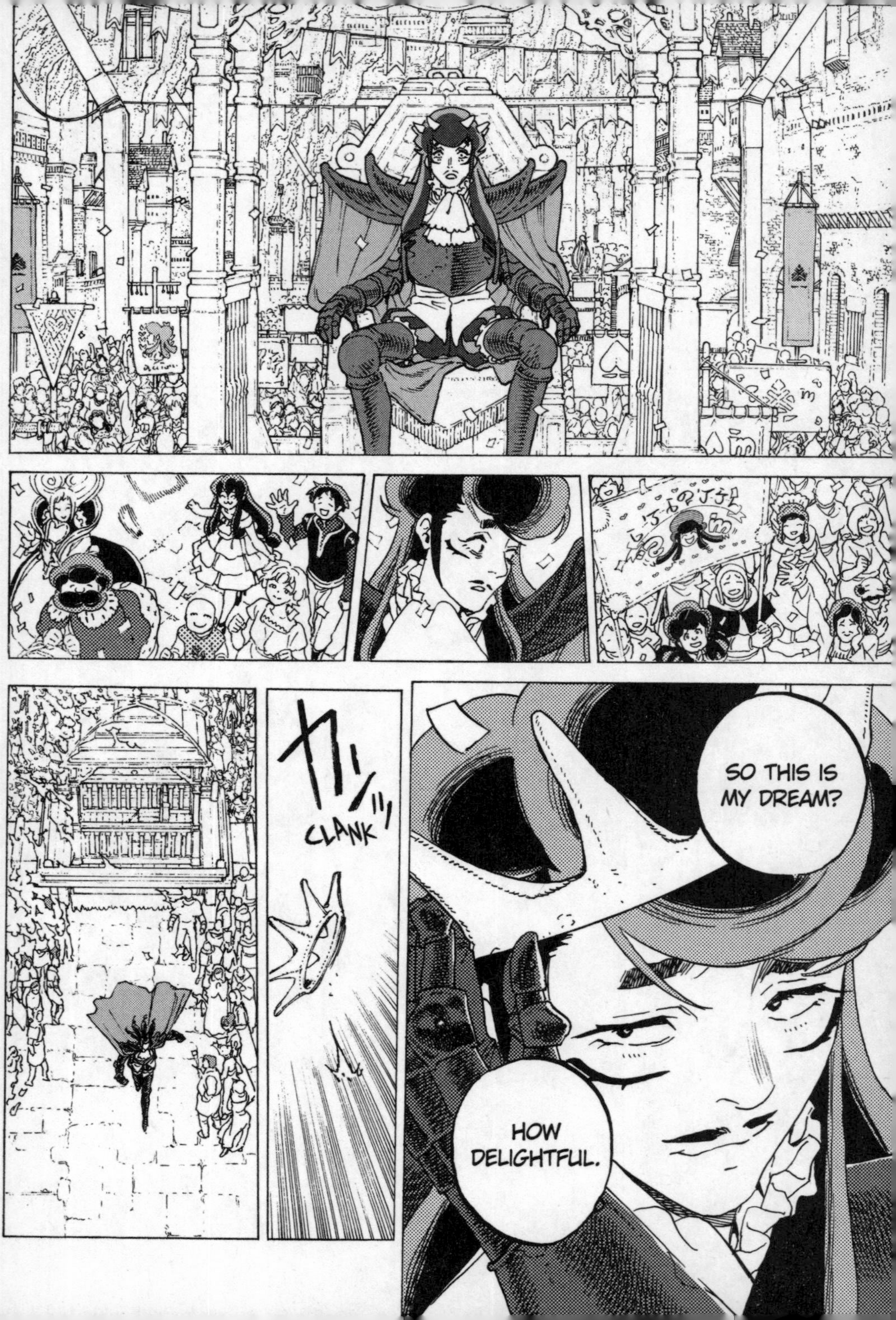
SO THIS IS MY DREAM?
HOW DELIGHTFUL.
カン
CLANK

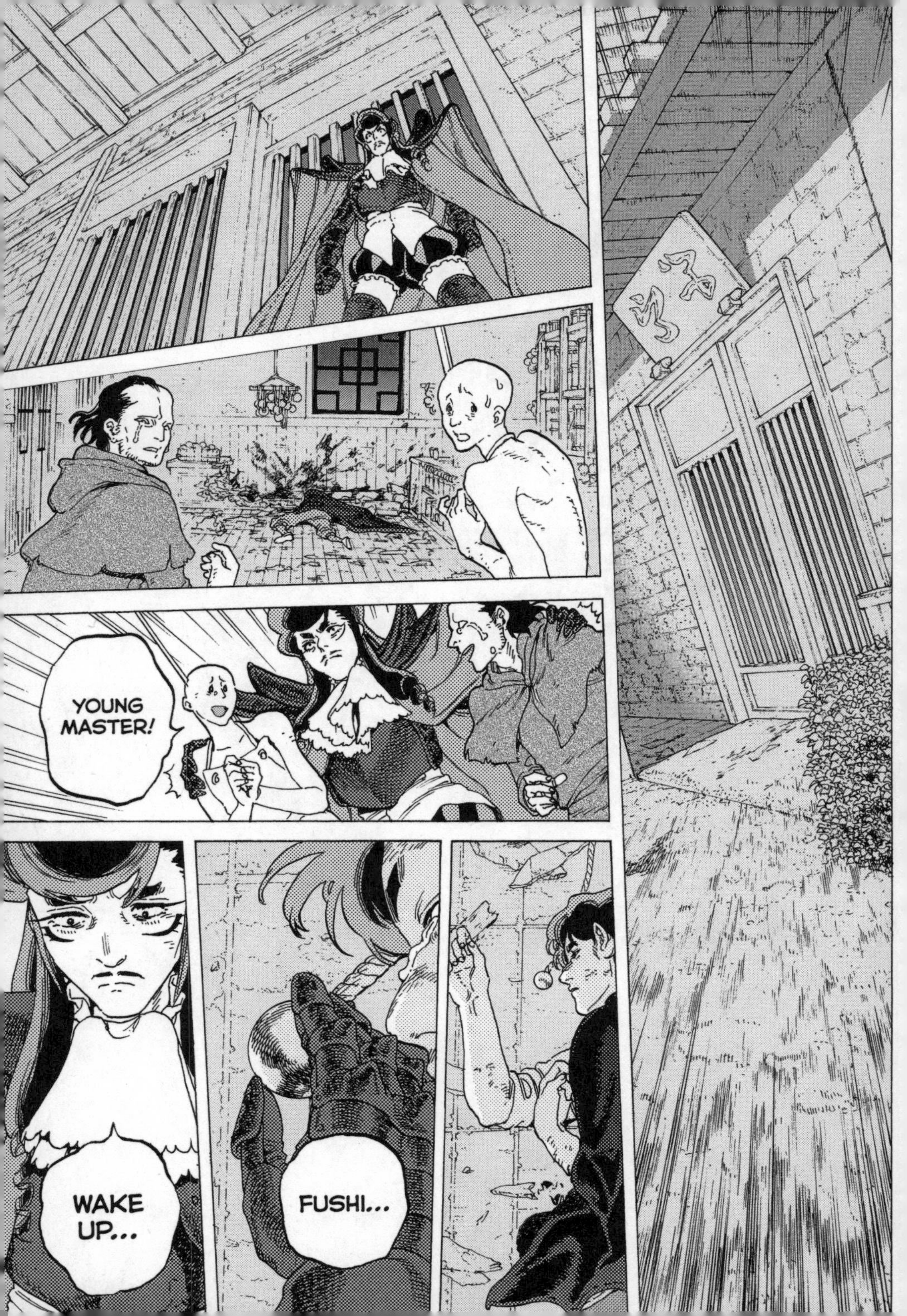
YOUNG MASTER!
FUSHI...
WAKE UP...

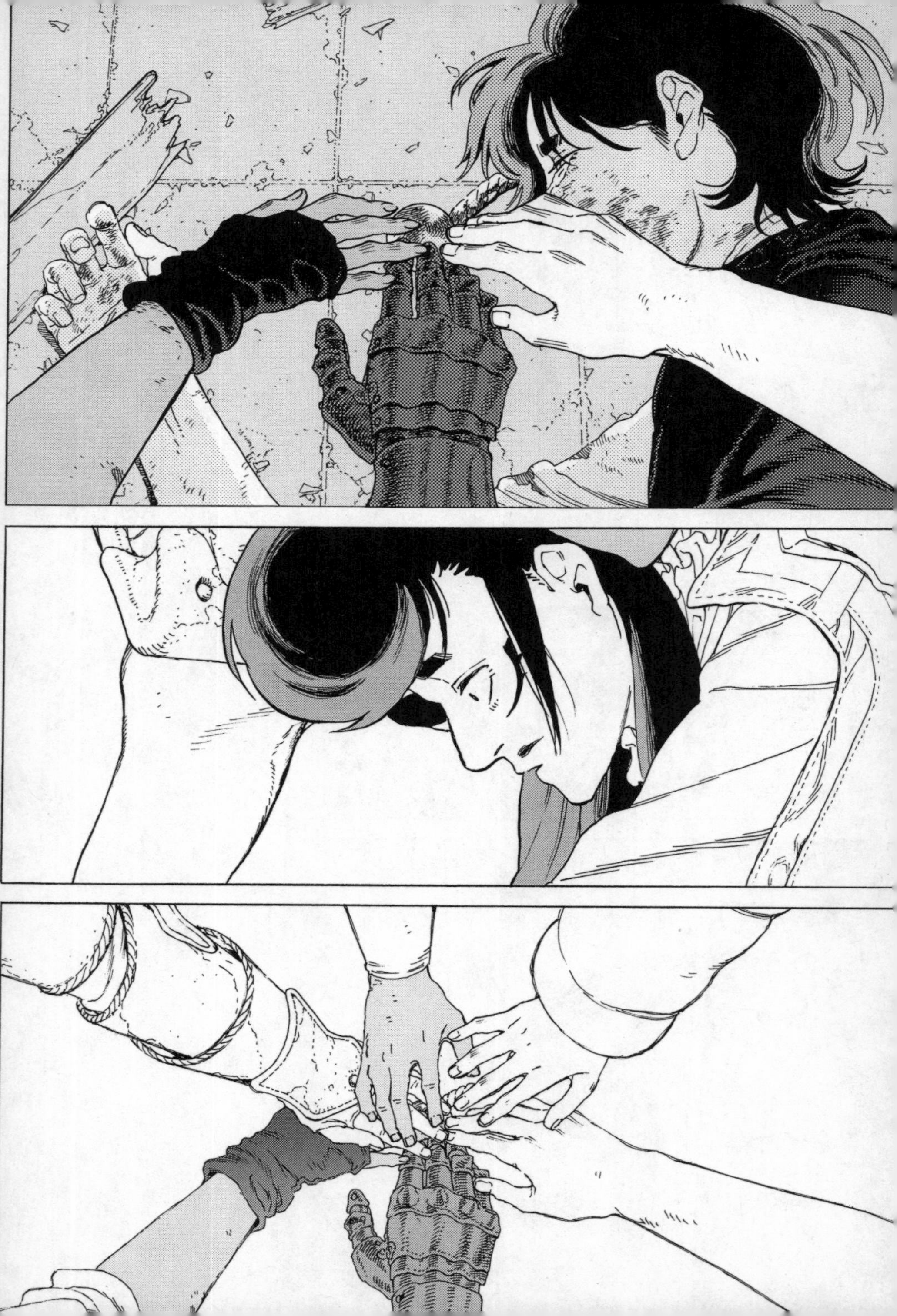

TO YOUR ETERNITY

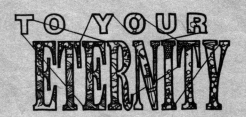

TO YOUR ETERNITY

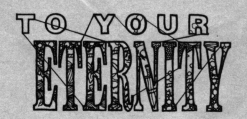

#111 Daybreak

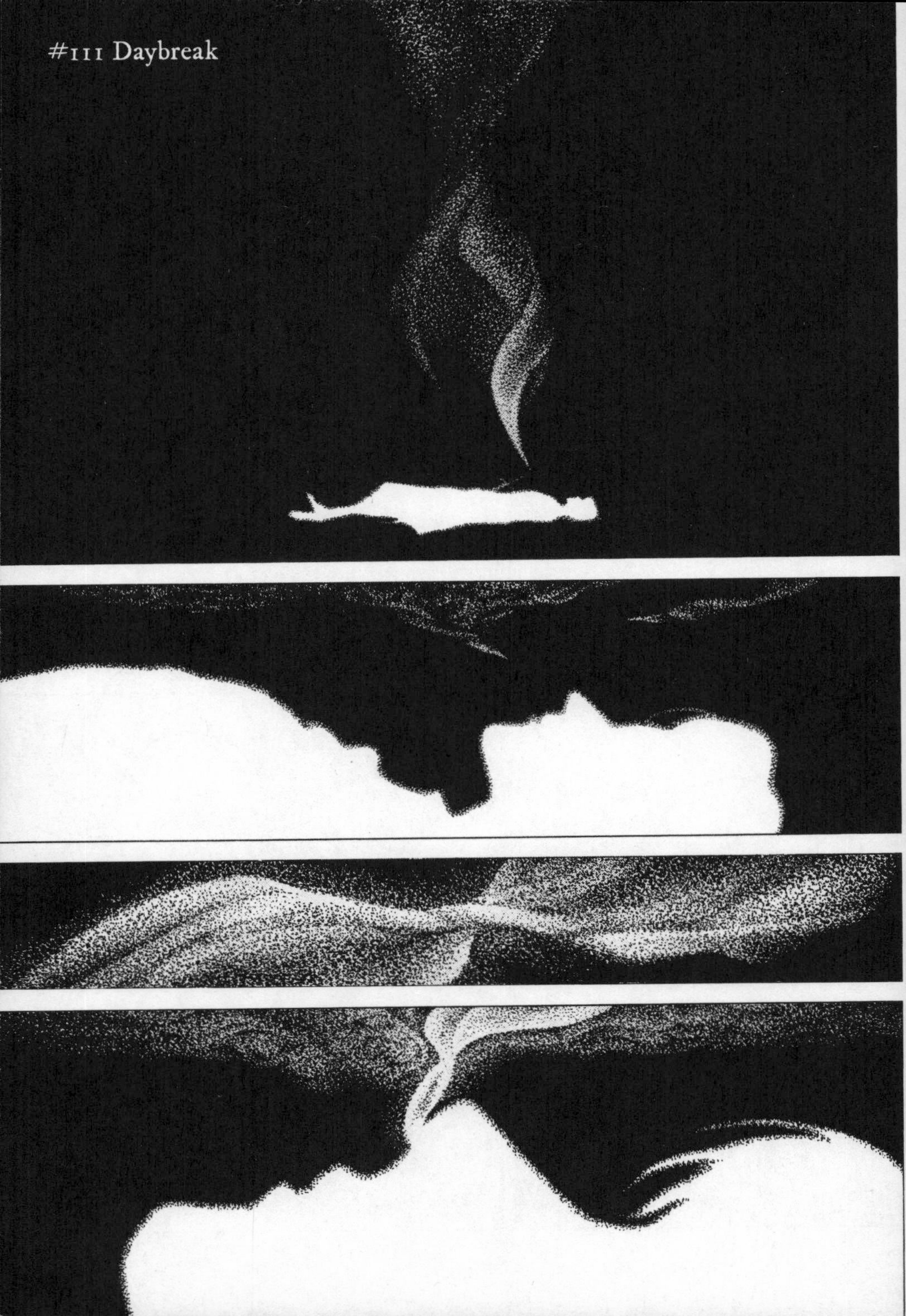

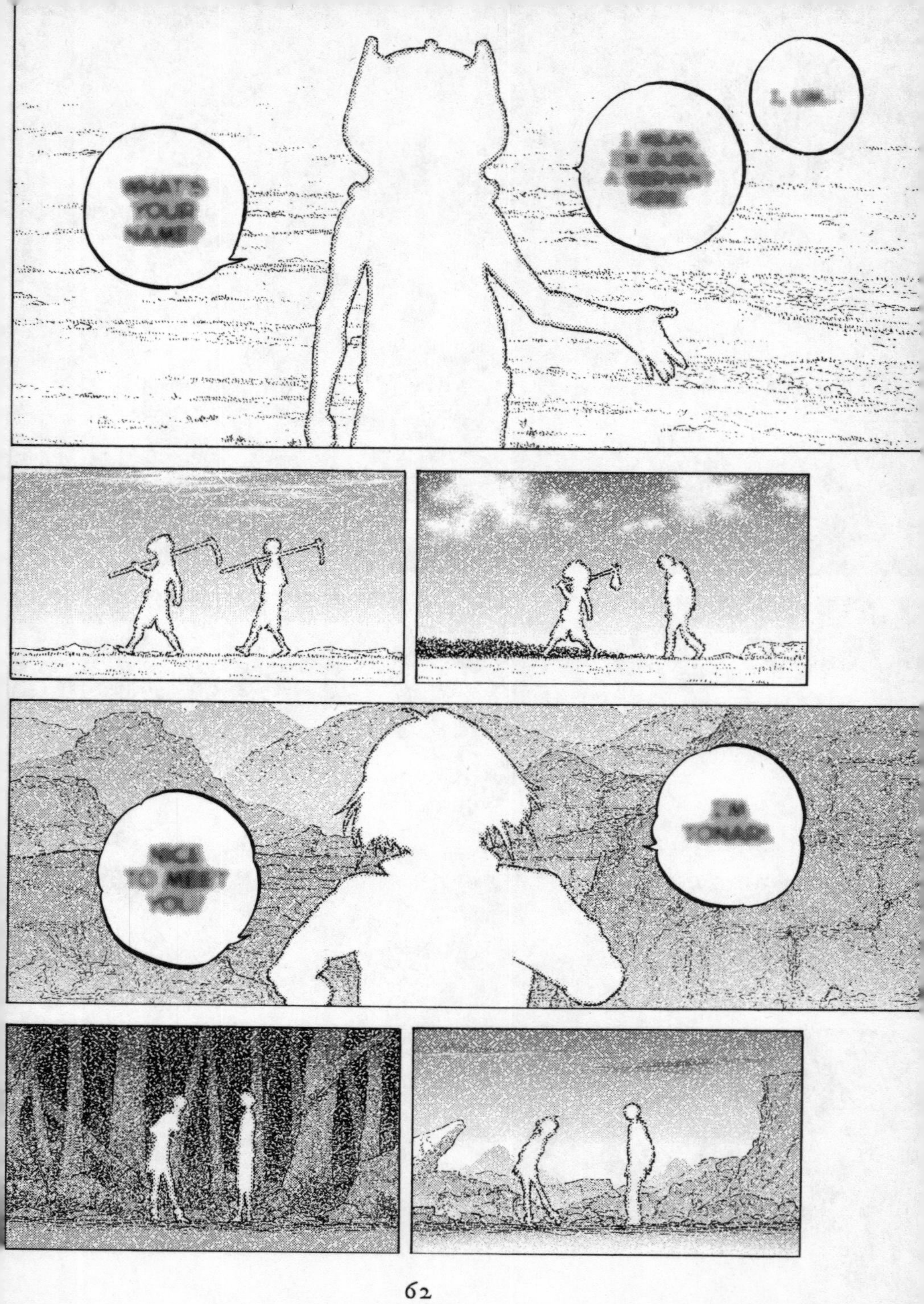

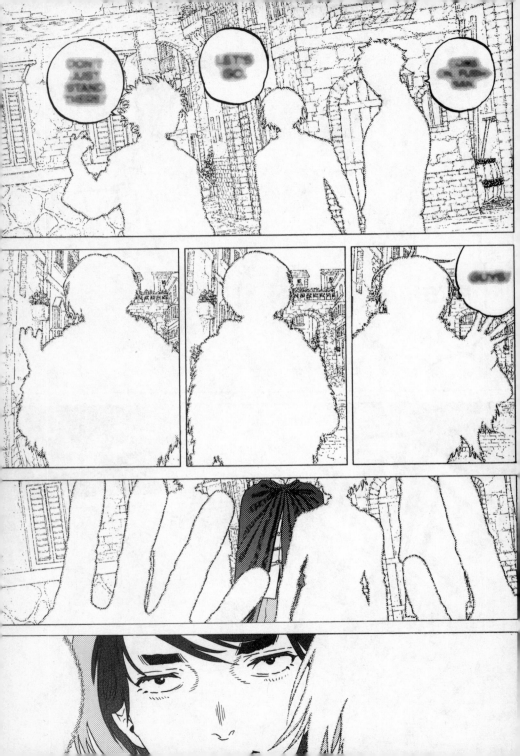

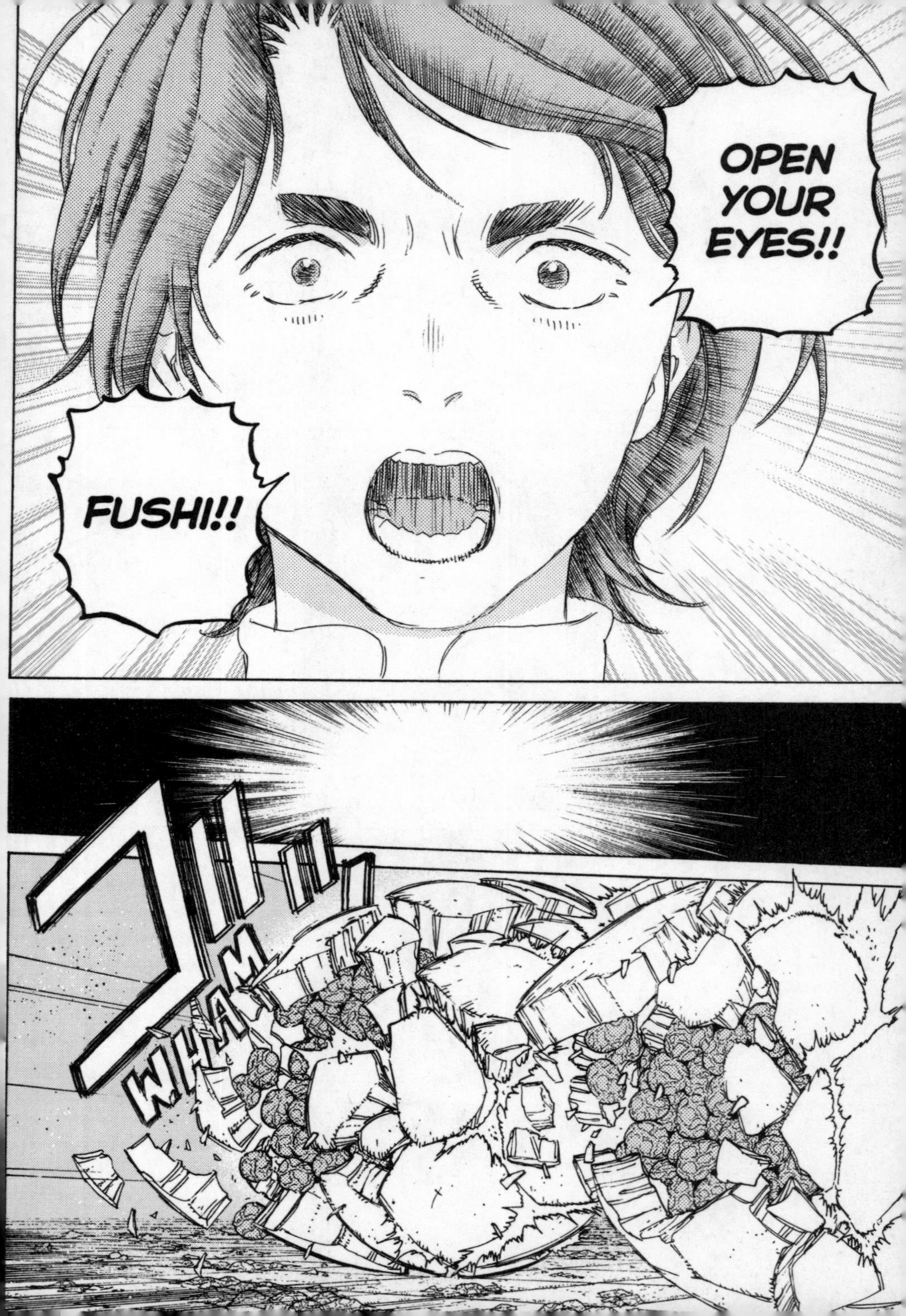
OPEN YOUR EYES!!
FUSHI!!
WHAM

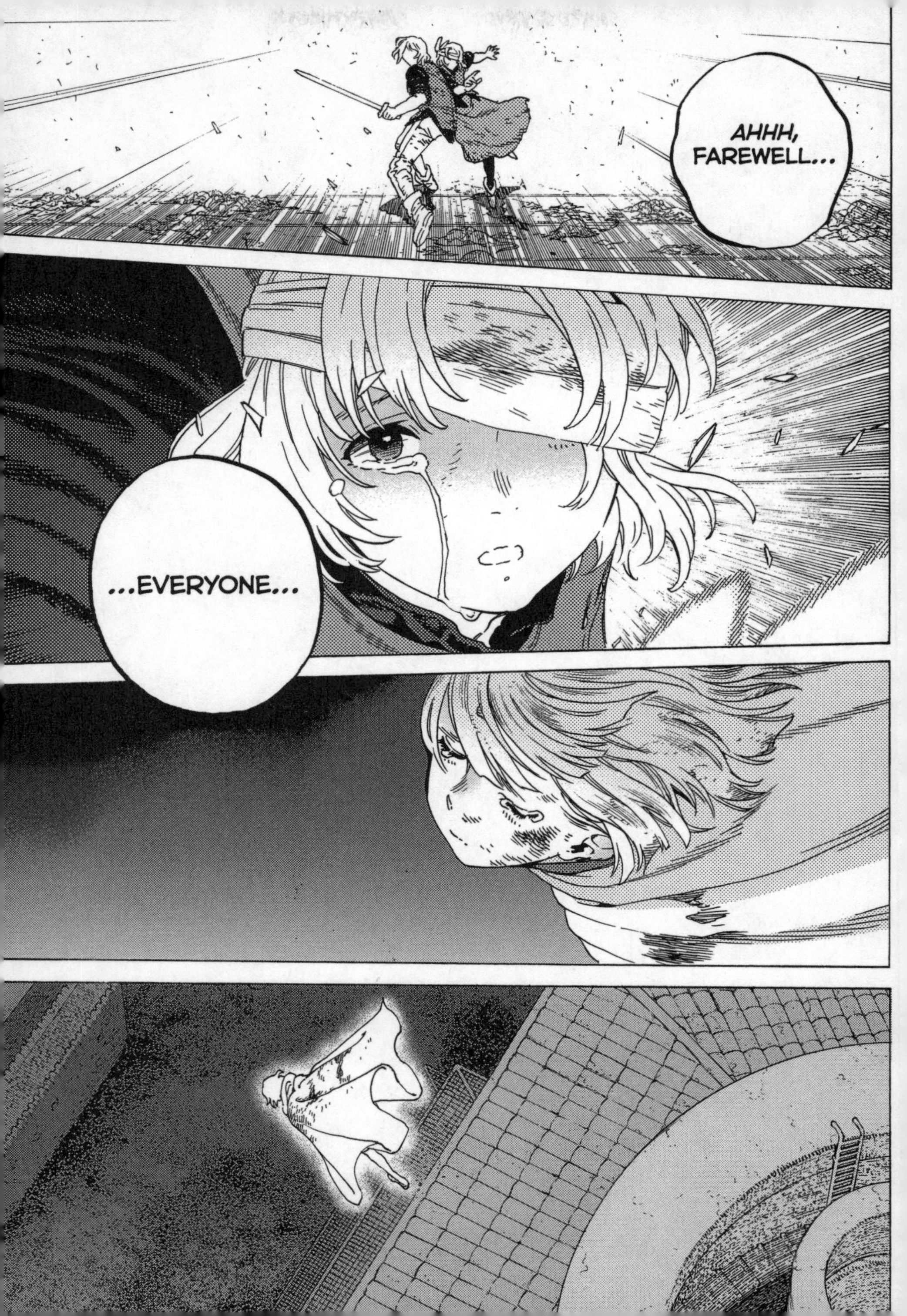
AHHH, FAREWELL...
...EVERYONE...

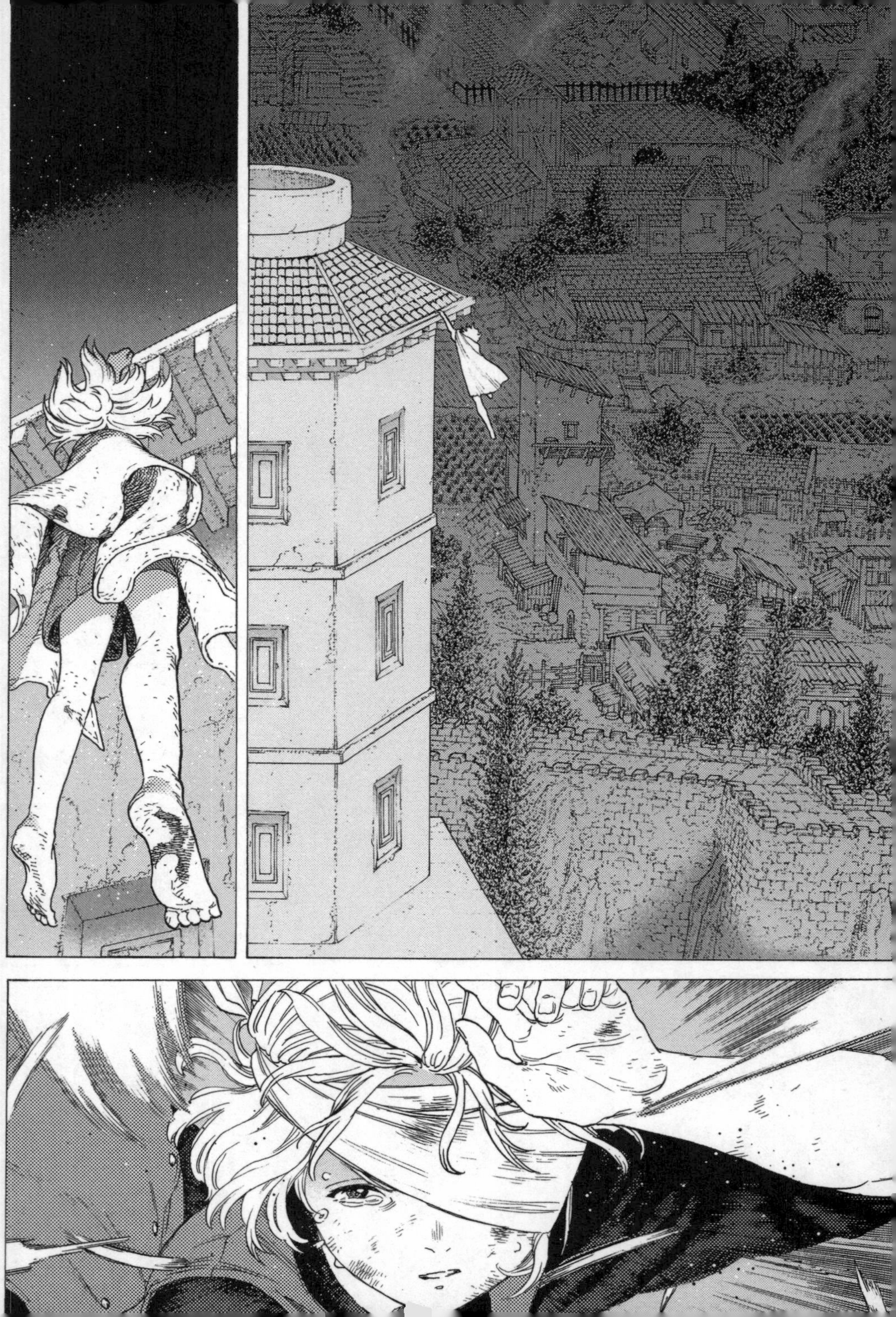

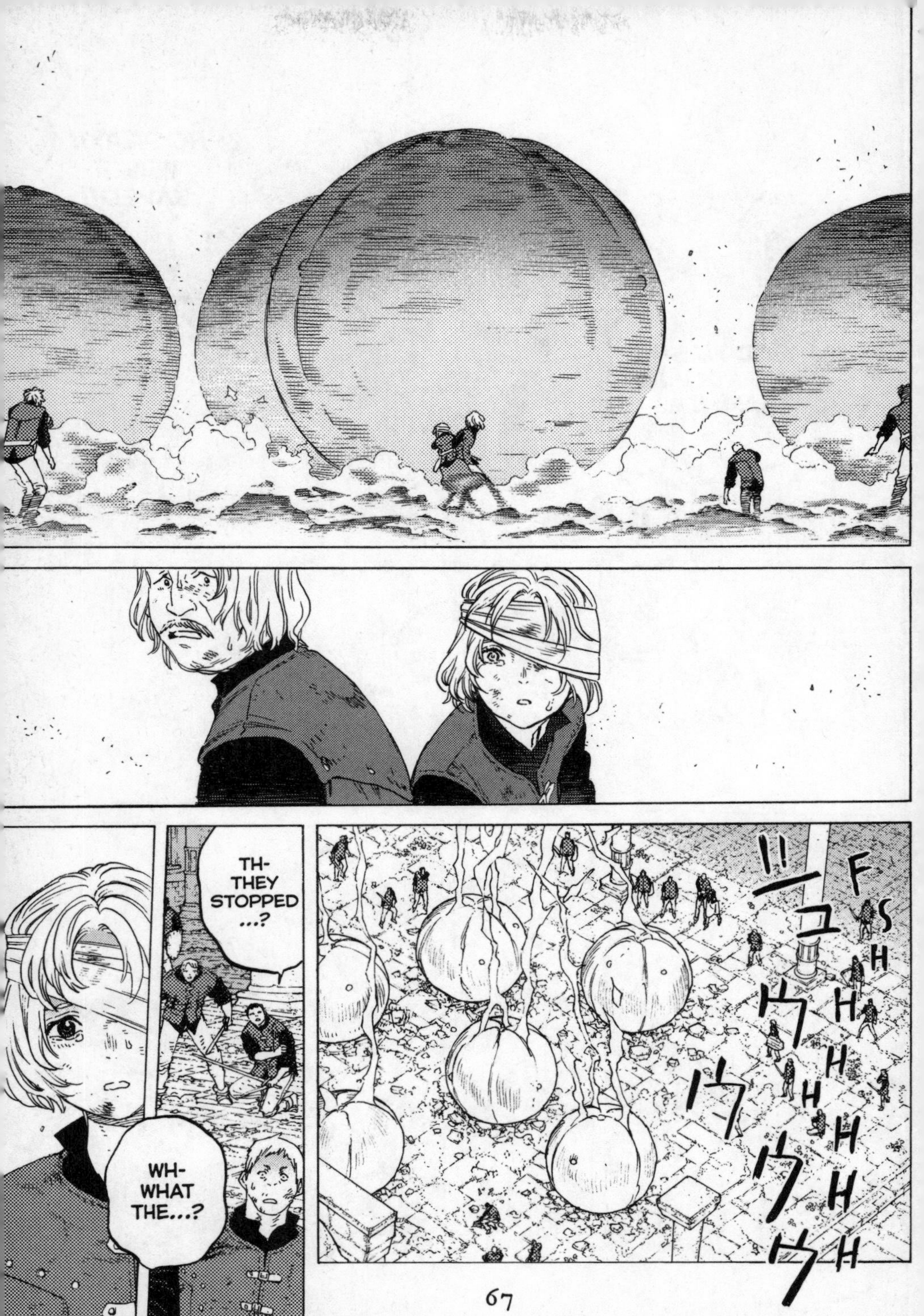
FSHHHHHHHH
TH- THEY STOPPED ...?
WH- WHAT THE...?

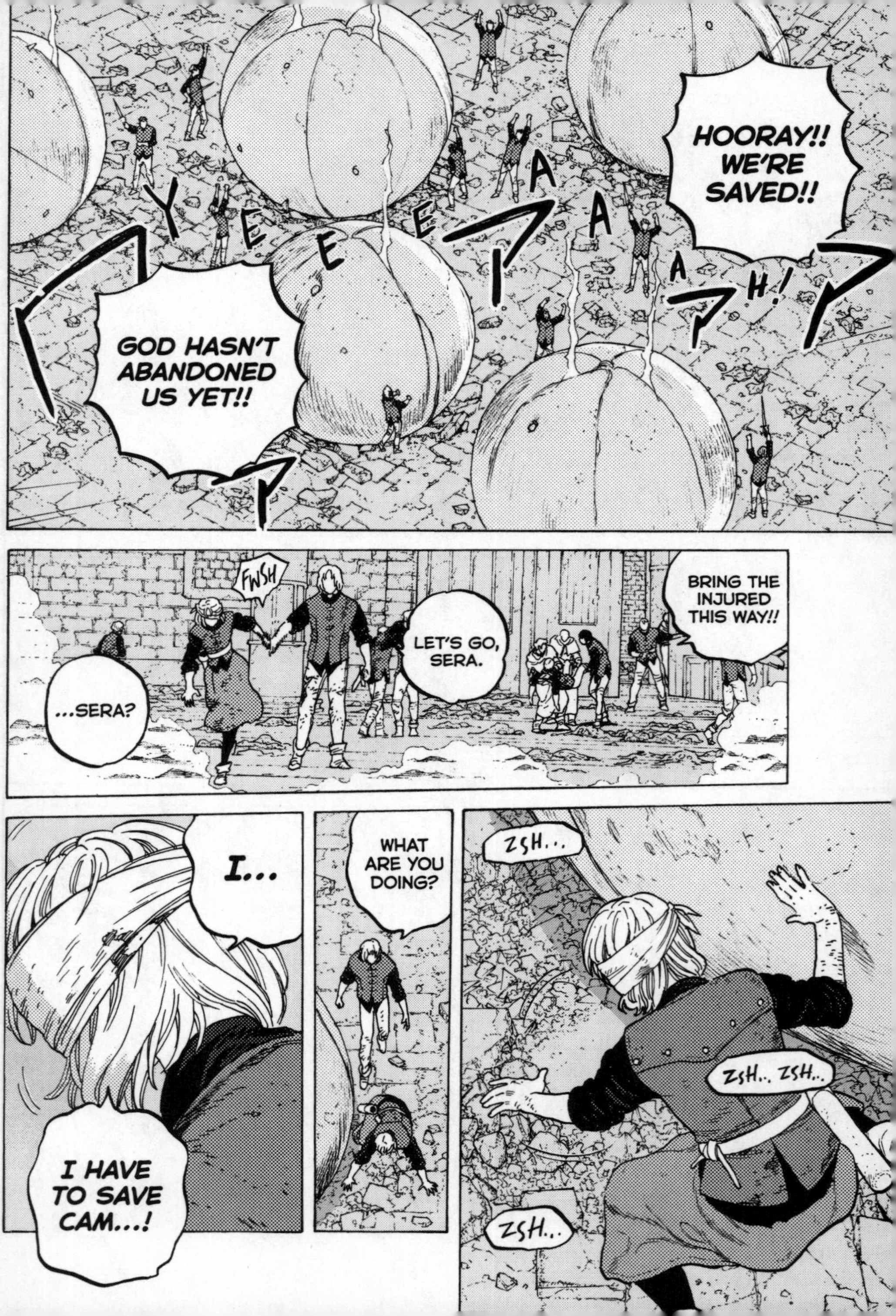
HOORAY!! WE'RE SAVED!!
YEEEAAAH!
GOD HASN'T ABANDONED US YET!!
BRING THE INJURED THIS WAY!!
LET'S GO, SERA.
FWSH
...SERA?
ZSH...
ZSH... ZSH...
ZSH...
WHAT ARE YOU DOING?
I...
I HAVE TO SAVE CAM...!

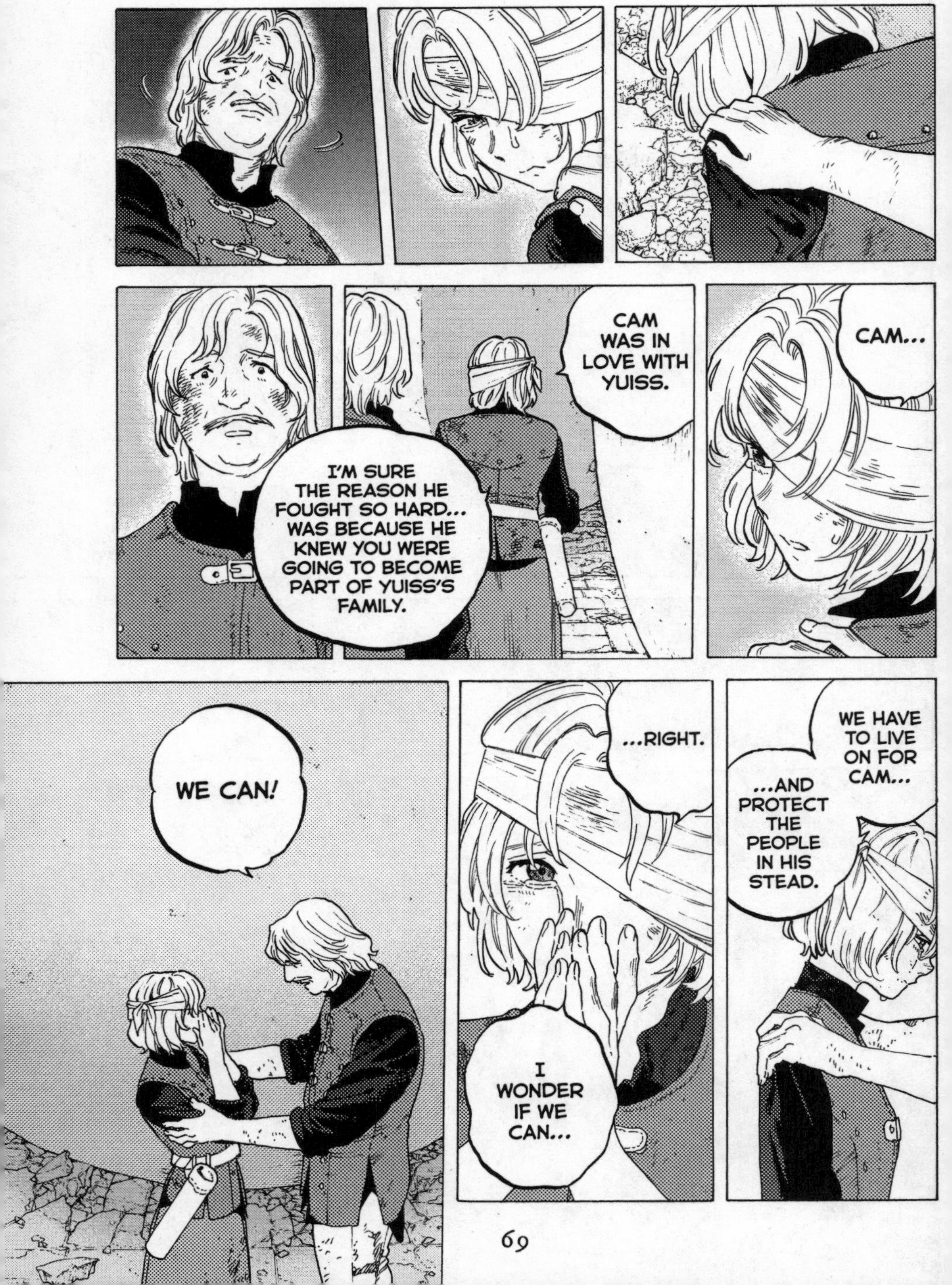
CAM...
CAM WAS IN LOVE WITH YUISS.
I'M SURE THE REASON HE FOUGHT SO HARD... WAS BECAUSE HE KNEW YOU WERE GOING TO BECOME PART OF YUISS'S FAMILY.
WE HAVE TO LIVE ON FOR CAM...
...AND PROTECT THE PEOPLE IN HIS STEAD.
...RIGHT.
I WONDER IF WE CAN...
WE CAN!

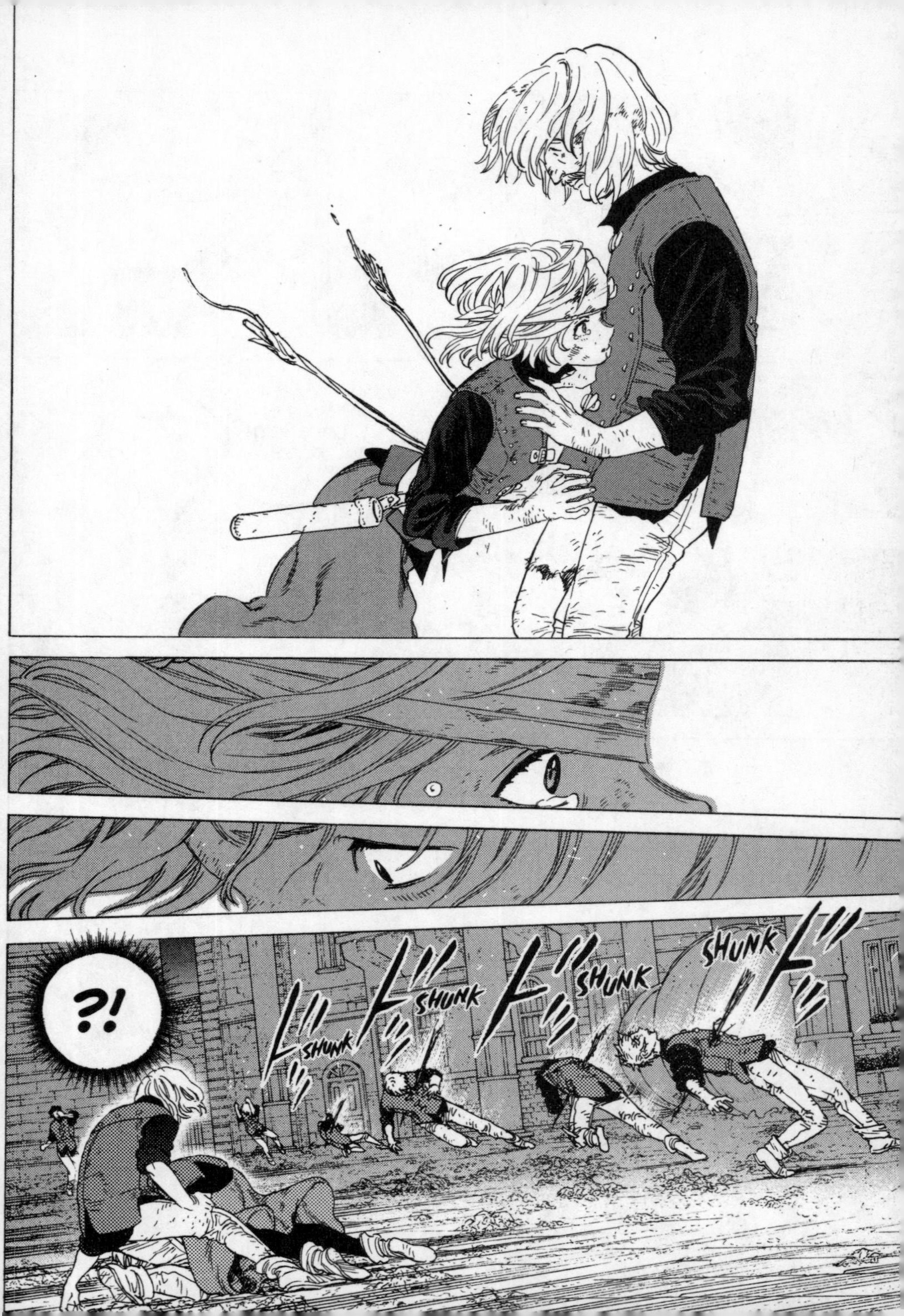
SHUNK
SHUNK
SHUNK
SHUNK
?!

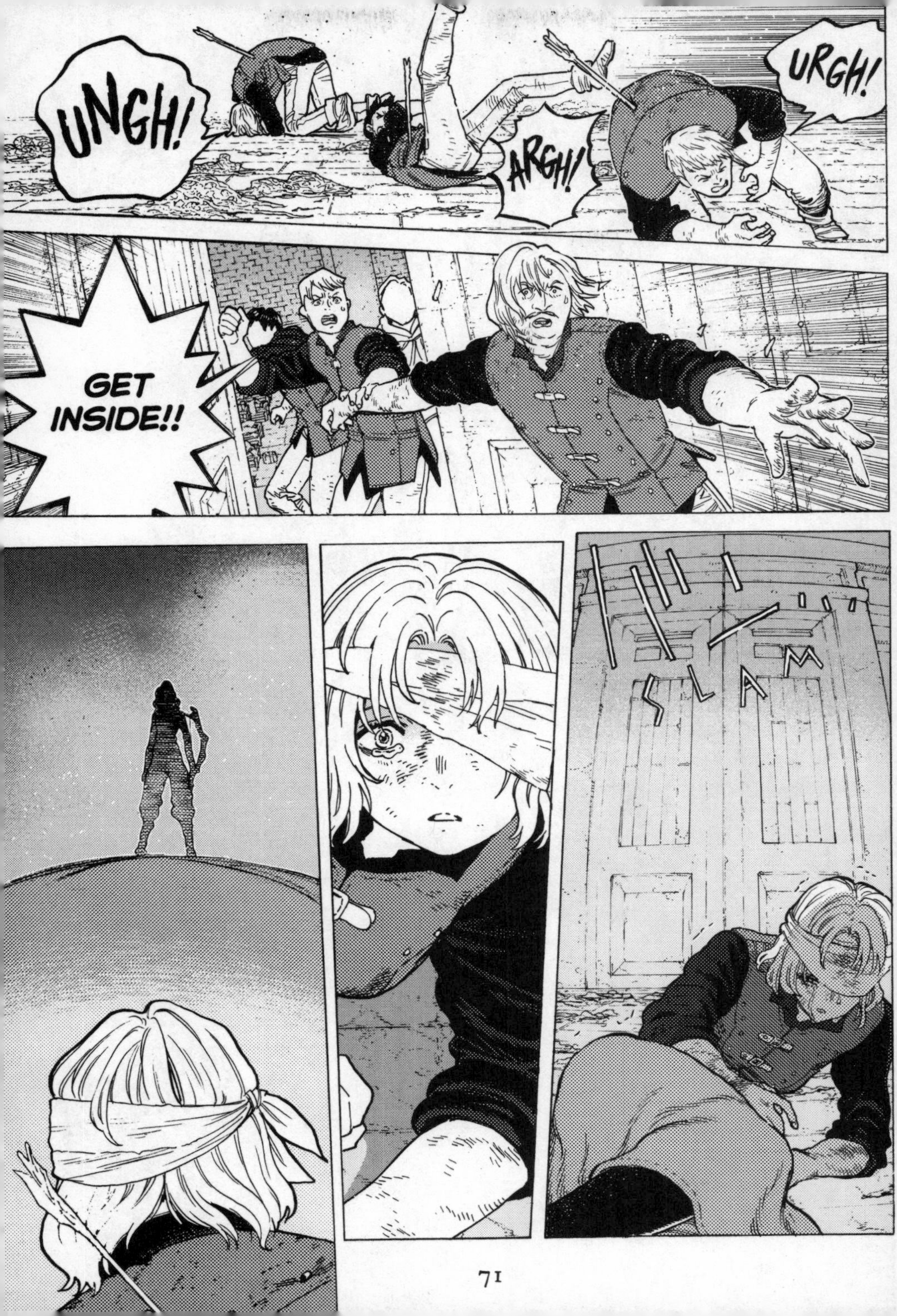
URGH!
ARGH!
UNGH!
GET INSIDE!!
SLAM

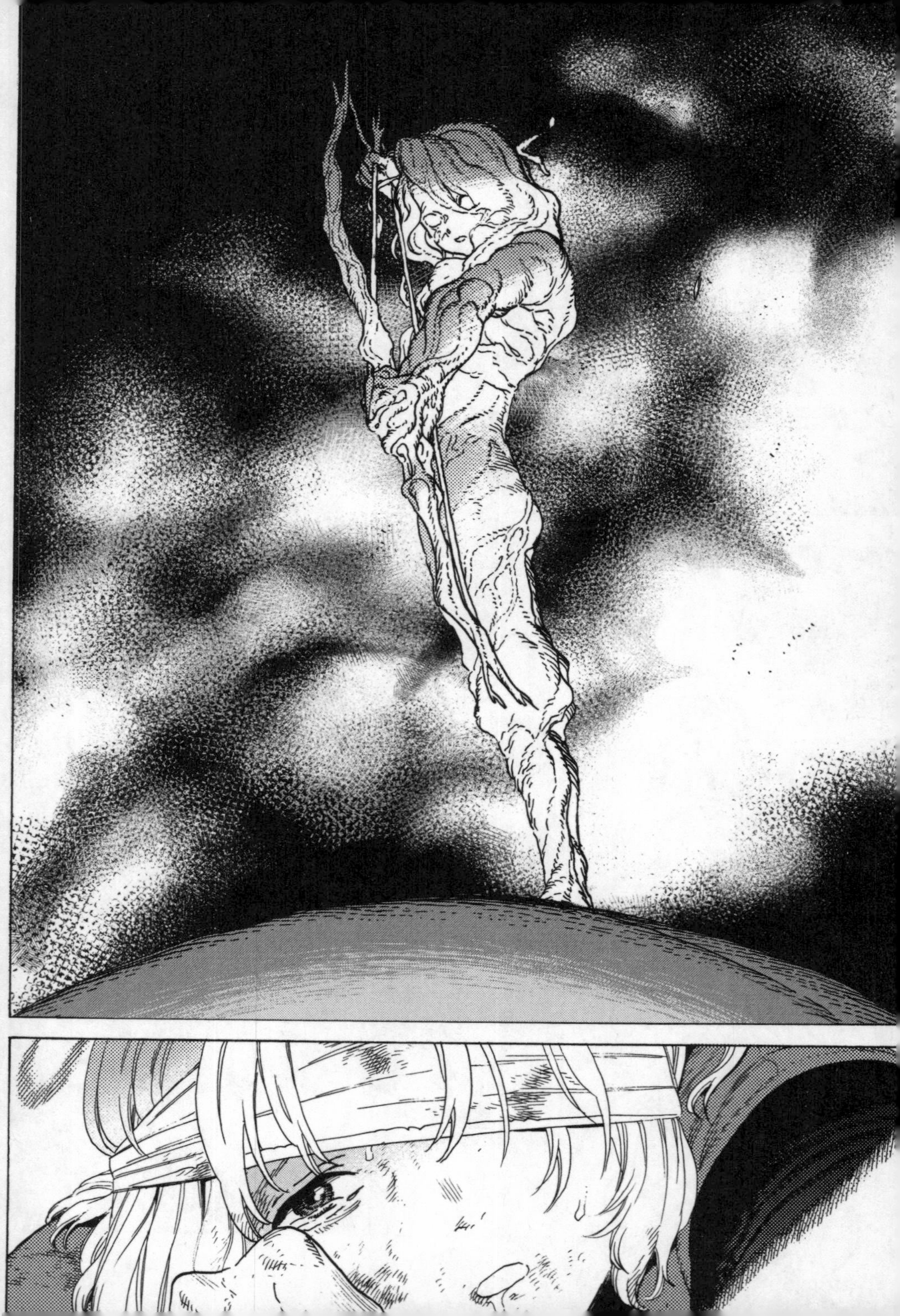

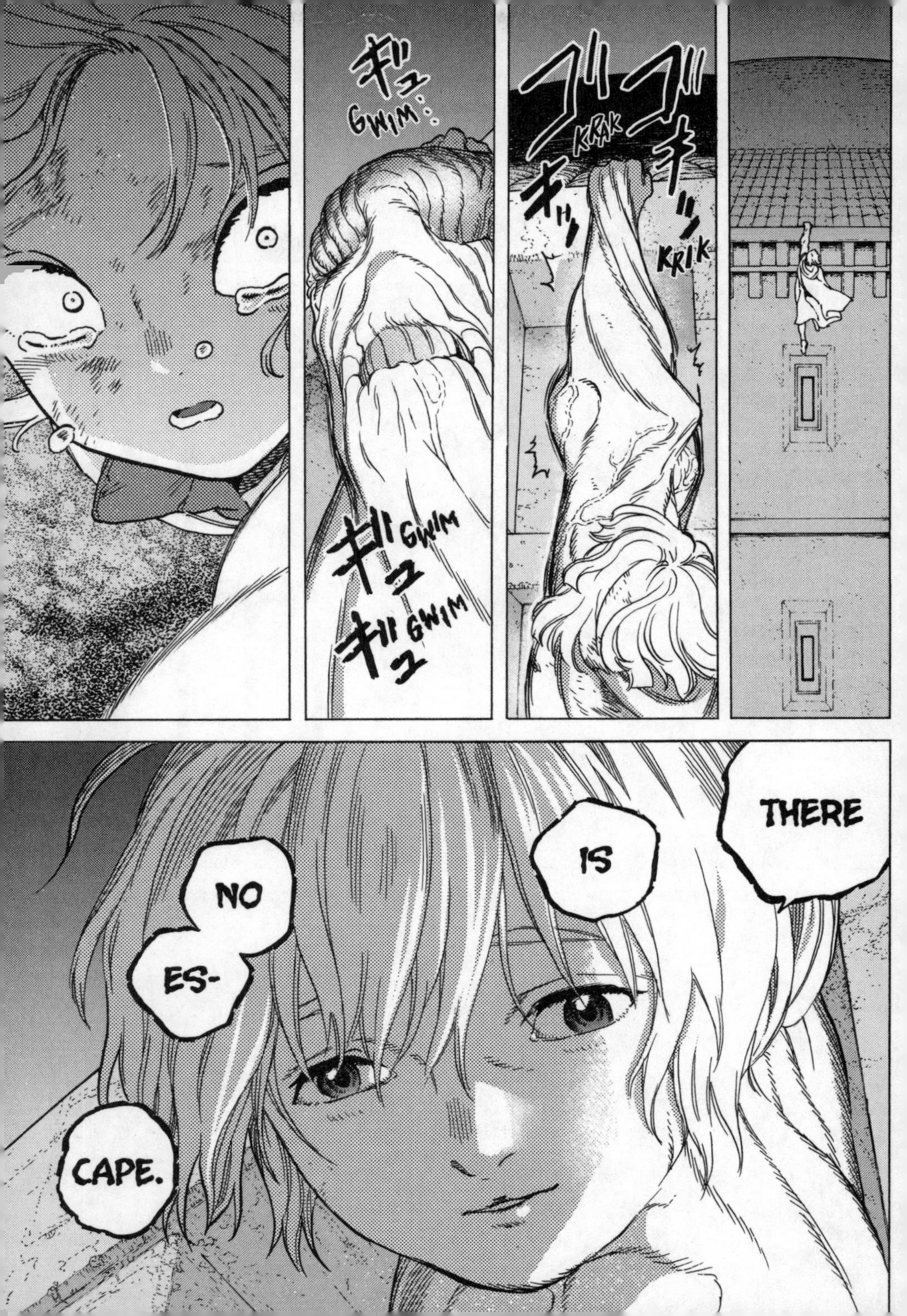
ゴリ KRAK
ゴリ
ギッ KRIK
ギッ
ギュ GWIM..
ギュ GWIM
ギュ GWIM
THERE
IS
NO
ES-
CAPE.

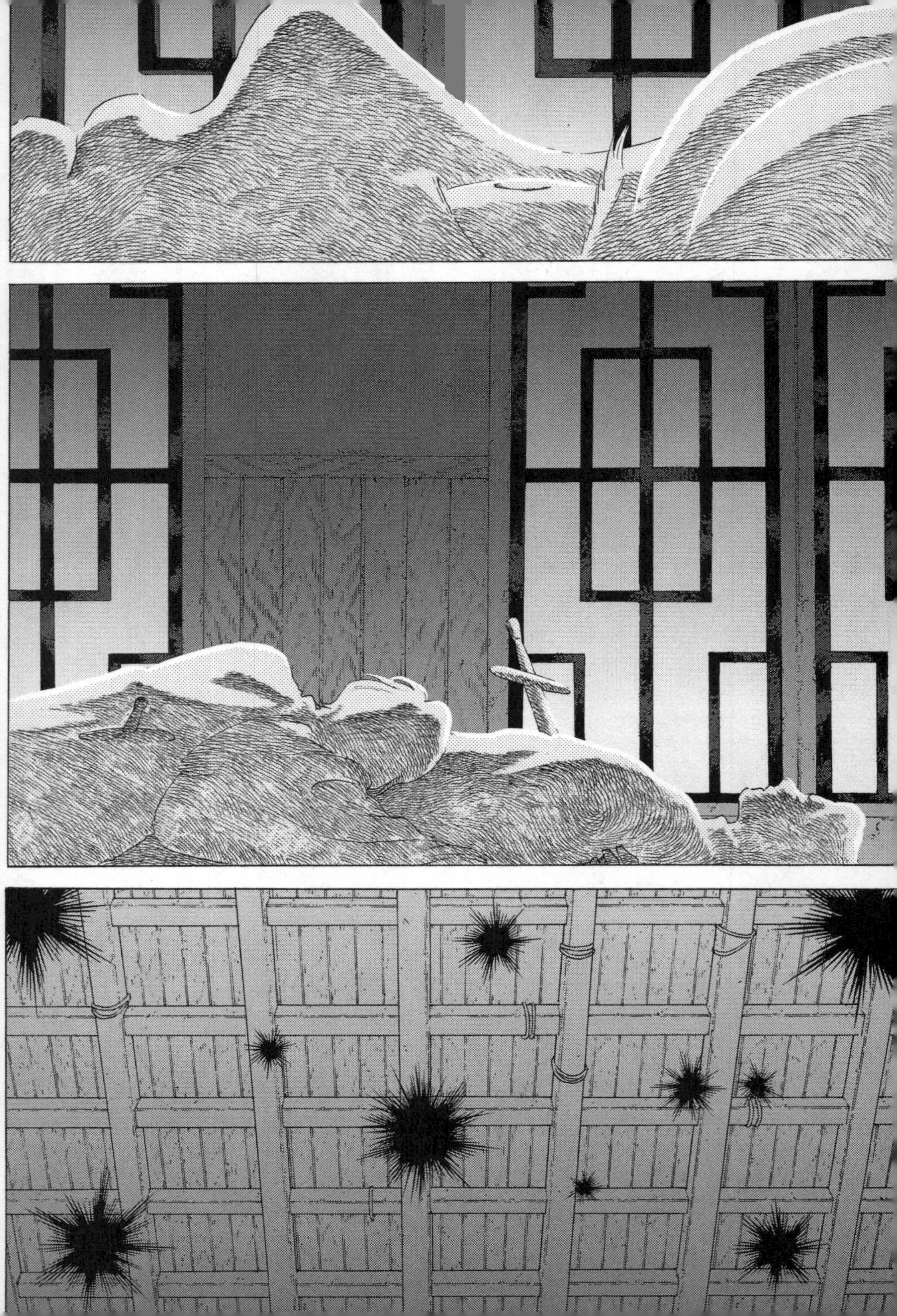

TO YOUR
ETERNITY

TO YOUR ETERNITY

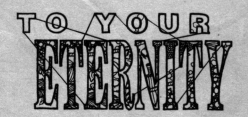

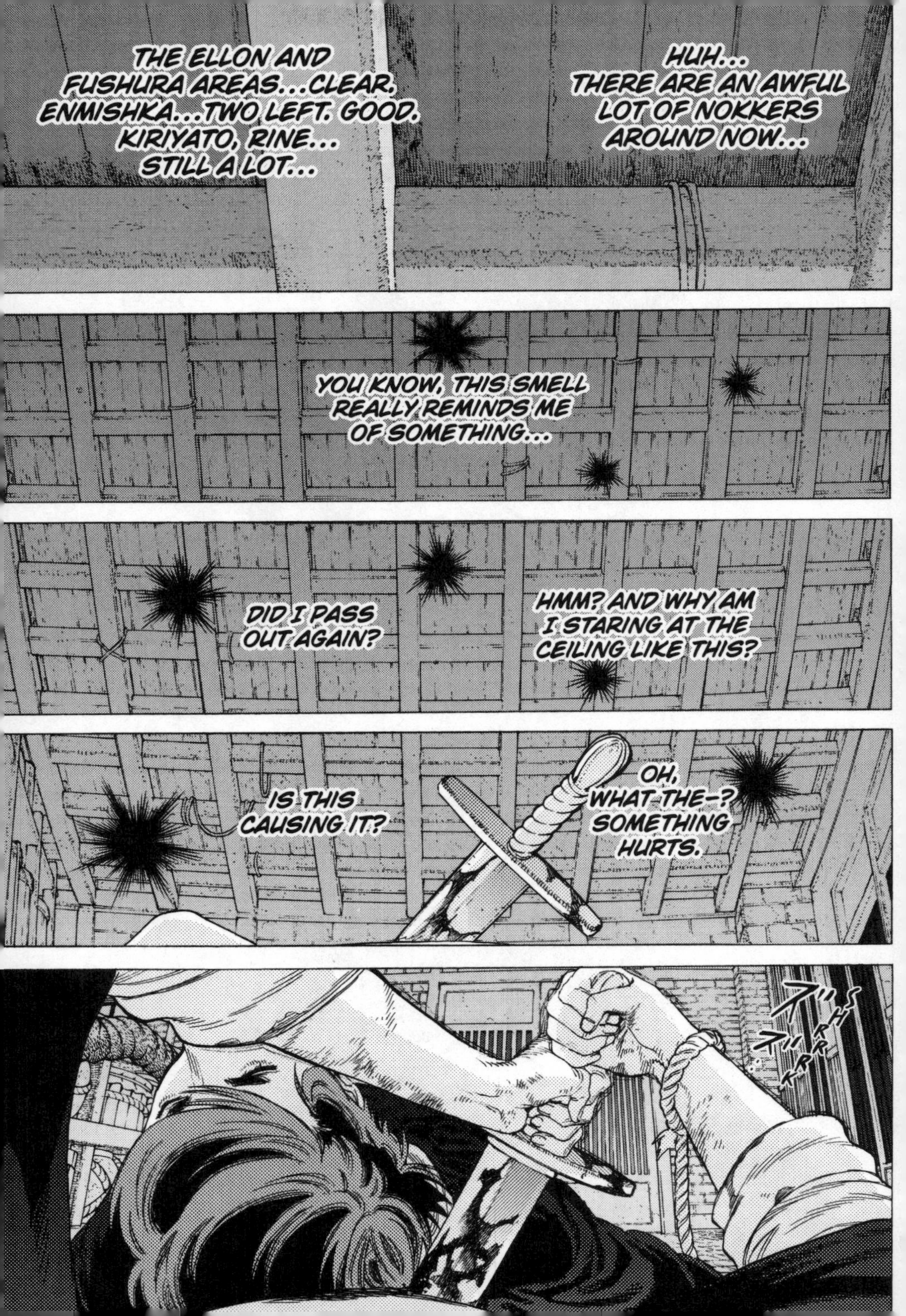
HUH... THERE ARE AN AWFUL LOT OF NOKKERS AROUND NOW...
THE ELLON AND FUSHURA AREAS...CLEAR. ENMISHKA...TWO LEFT. GOOD. KIRIYATO, RINE... STILL A LOT...
YOU KNOW, THIS SMELL REALLY REMINDS ME OF SOMETHING...
HMM? AND WHY AM I STARING AT THE CEILING LIKE THIS?
DID I PASS OUT AGAIN?
OH, WHAT THE-? SOMETHING HURTS.
IS THIS CAUSING IT?
ズリ ズリ
SHRRRRK

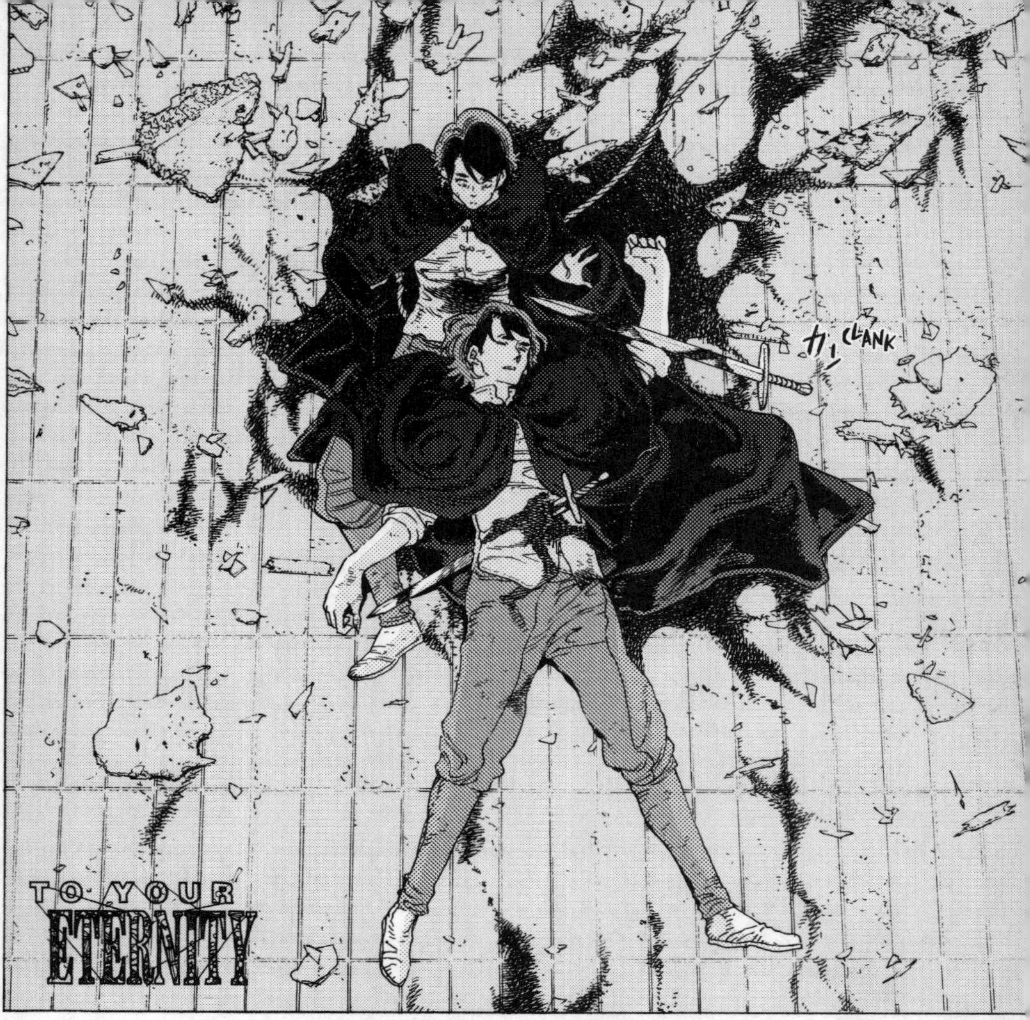

ガ
CLANK
TO YOUR ETERNITY

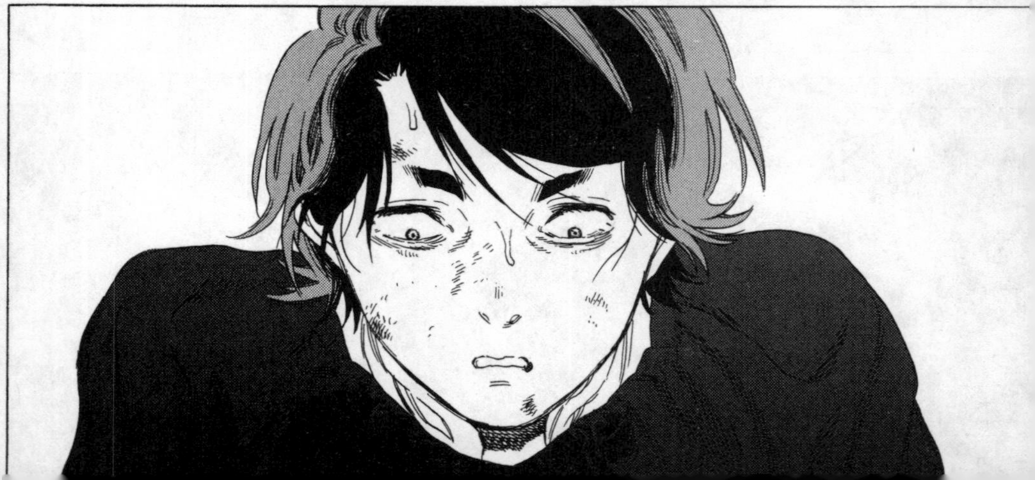

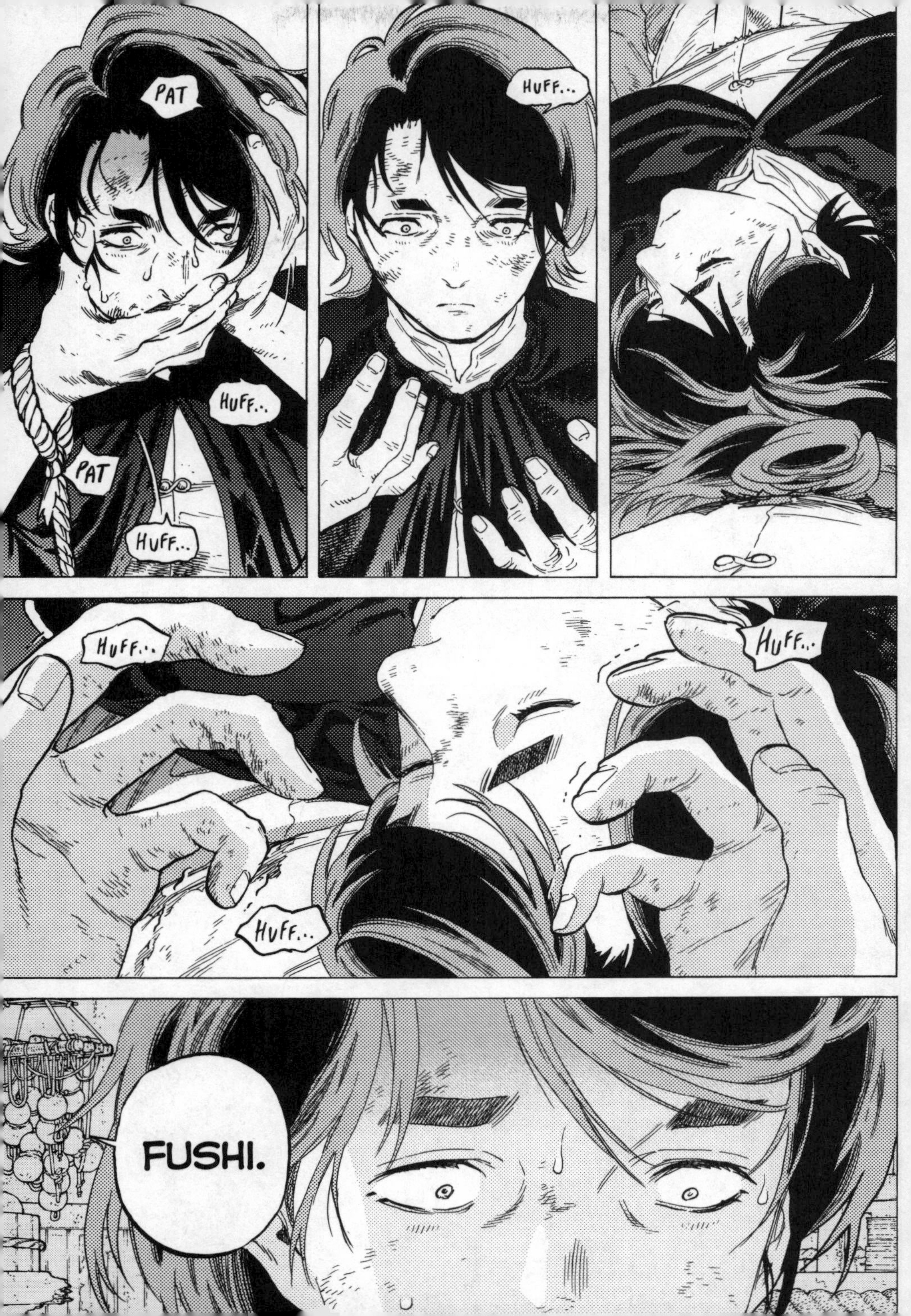
HUFF...
PAT
HUFF...
PAT
HUFF...
HUFF...
HUFF...
HUFF...
FUSHI.

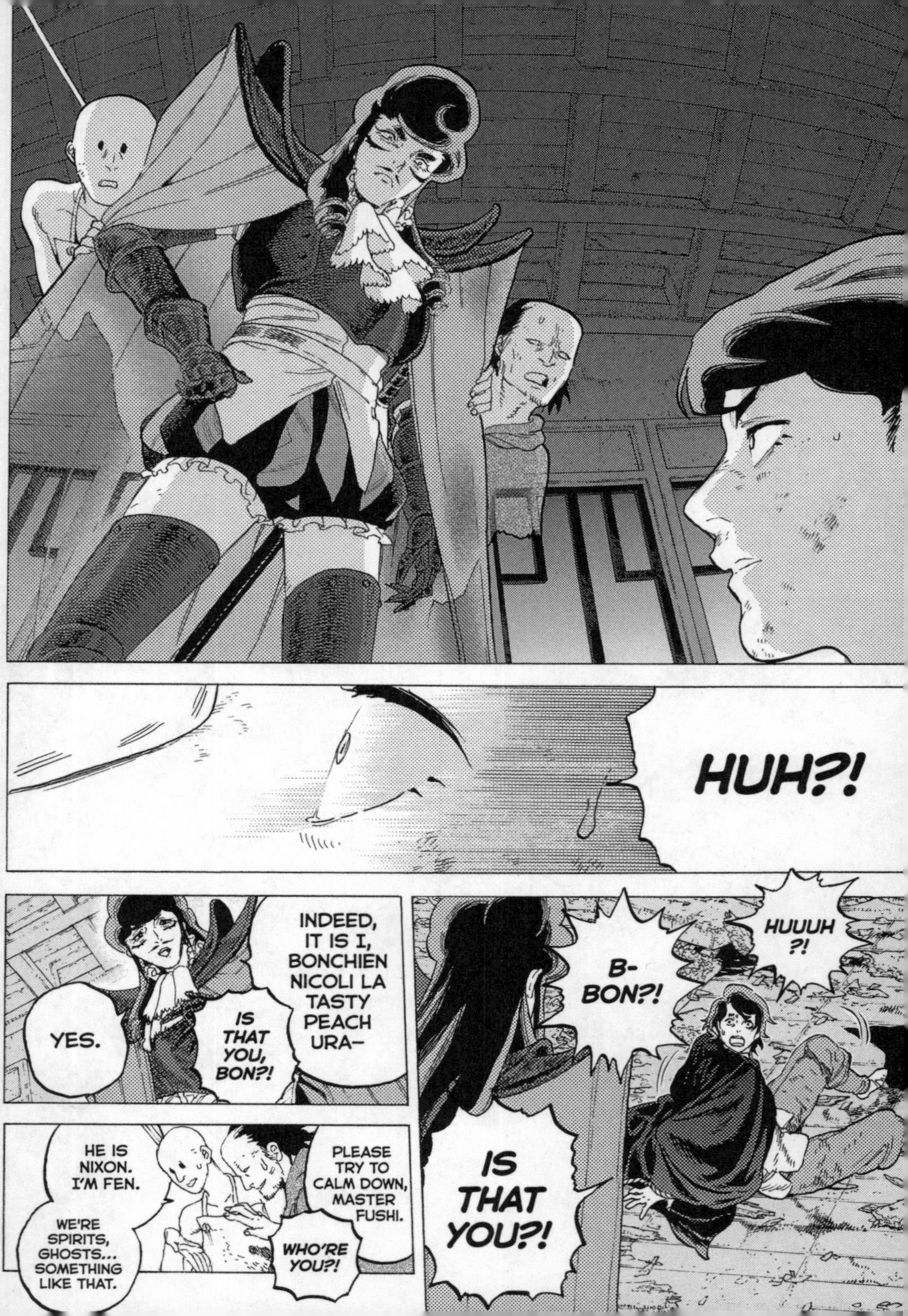
HUH?!
HUUUH ?!
B- BON?!
IS THAT YOU?!
INDEED, IT IS I, BONCHIEN NICOLI LA TASTY PEACH URA–
IS THAT YOU, BON?!
YES.
PLEASE TRY TO CALM DOWN, MASTER FUSHI.
HE IS NIXON. I'M FEN.
WHO'RE YOU?!
WE'RE SPIRITS, GHOSTS... SOMETHING LIKE THAT.

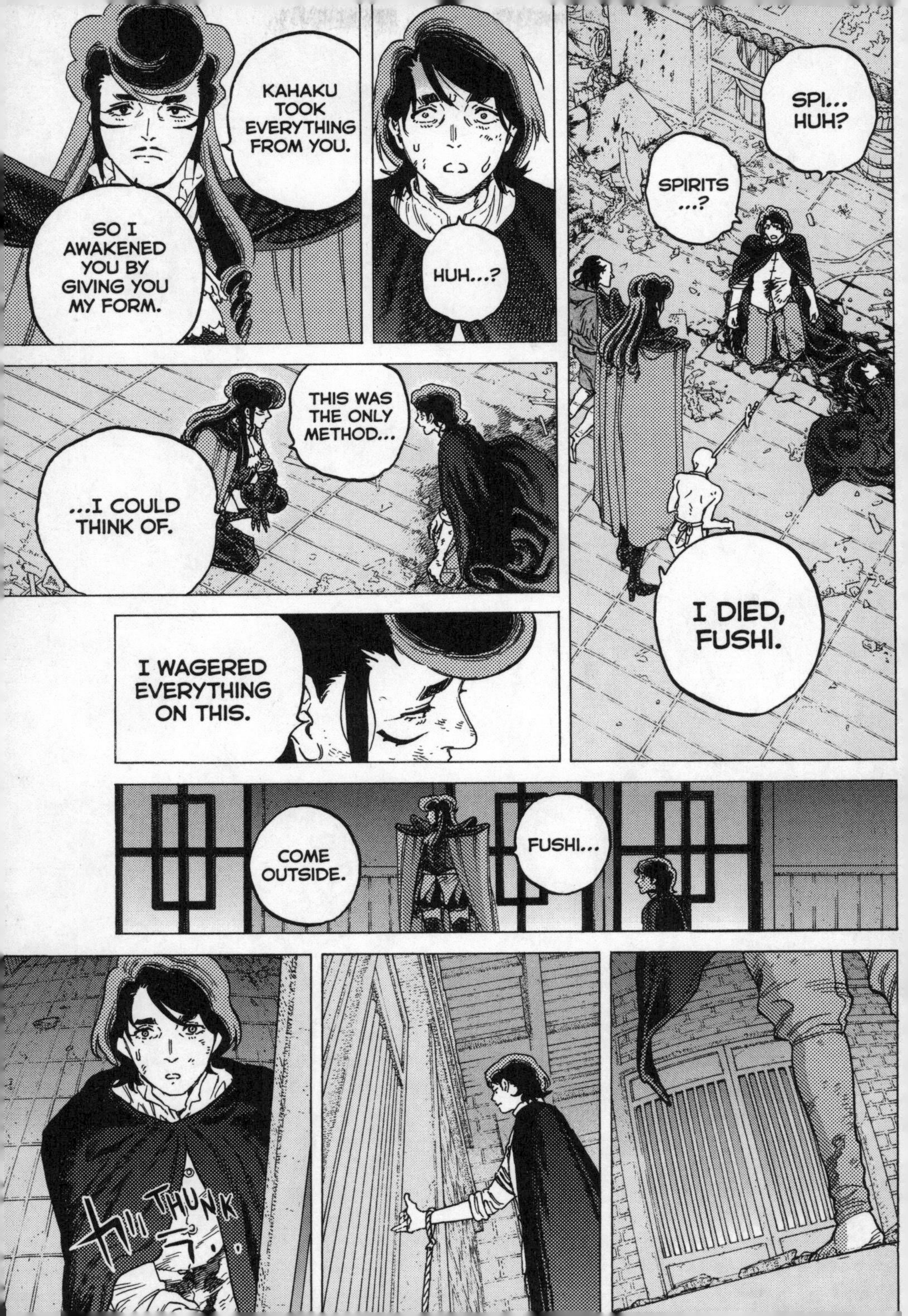
SPI... HUH?
SPIRITS ...?
I DIED, FUSHI.
KAHAKU TOOK EVERYTHING FROM YOU.
SO I AWAKENED YOU BY GIVING YOU MY FORM.
HUH...?
THIS WAS THE ONLY METHOD...
...I COULD THINK OF.
I WAGERED EVERYTHING ON THIS.
FUSHI...
COME OUTSIDE.
THUNK

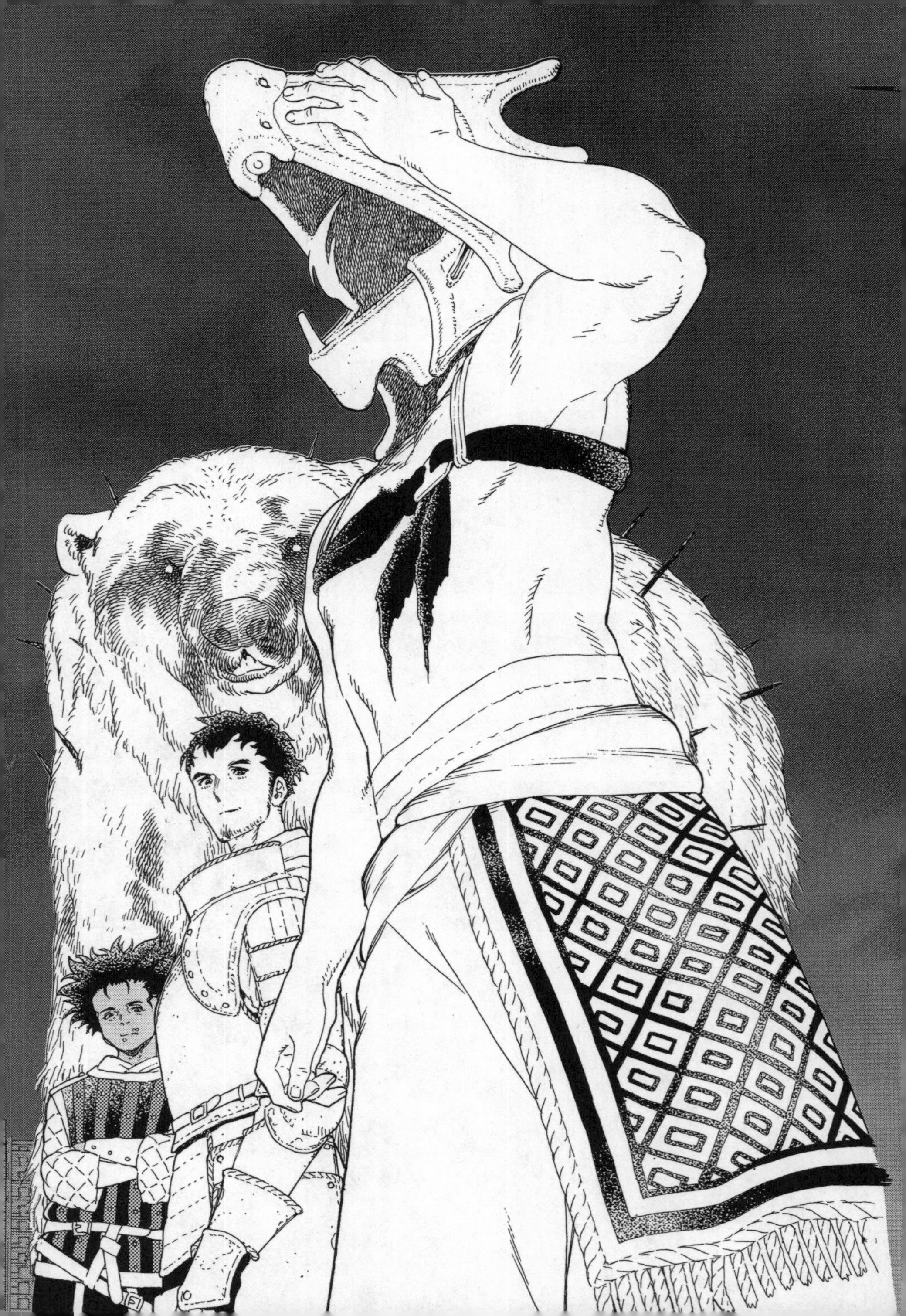

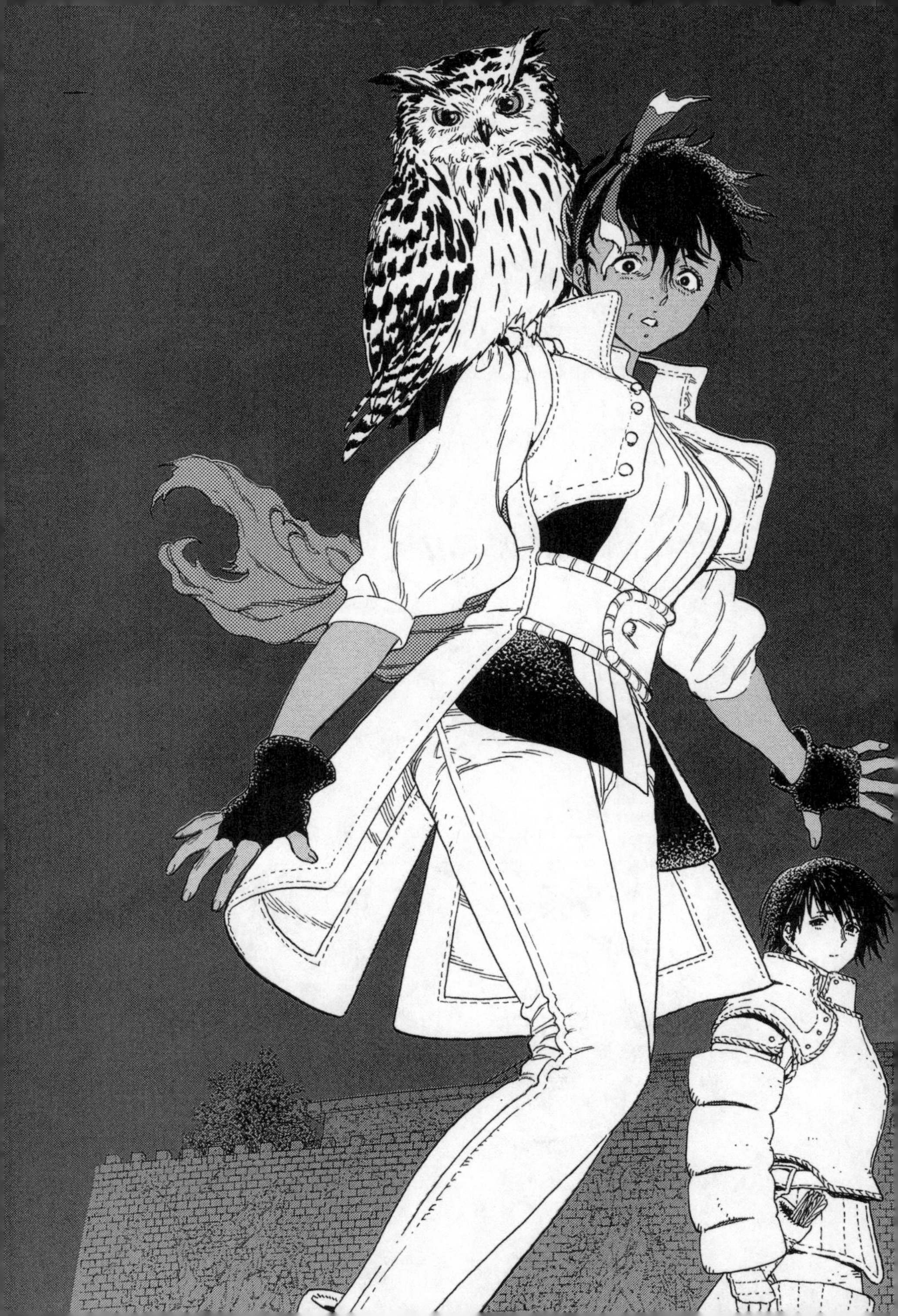

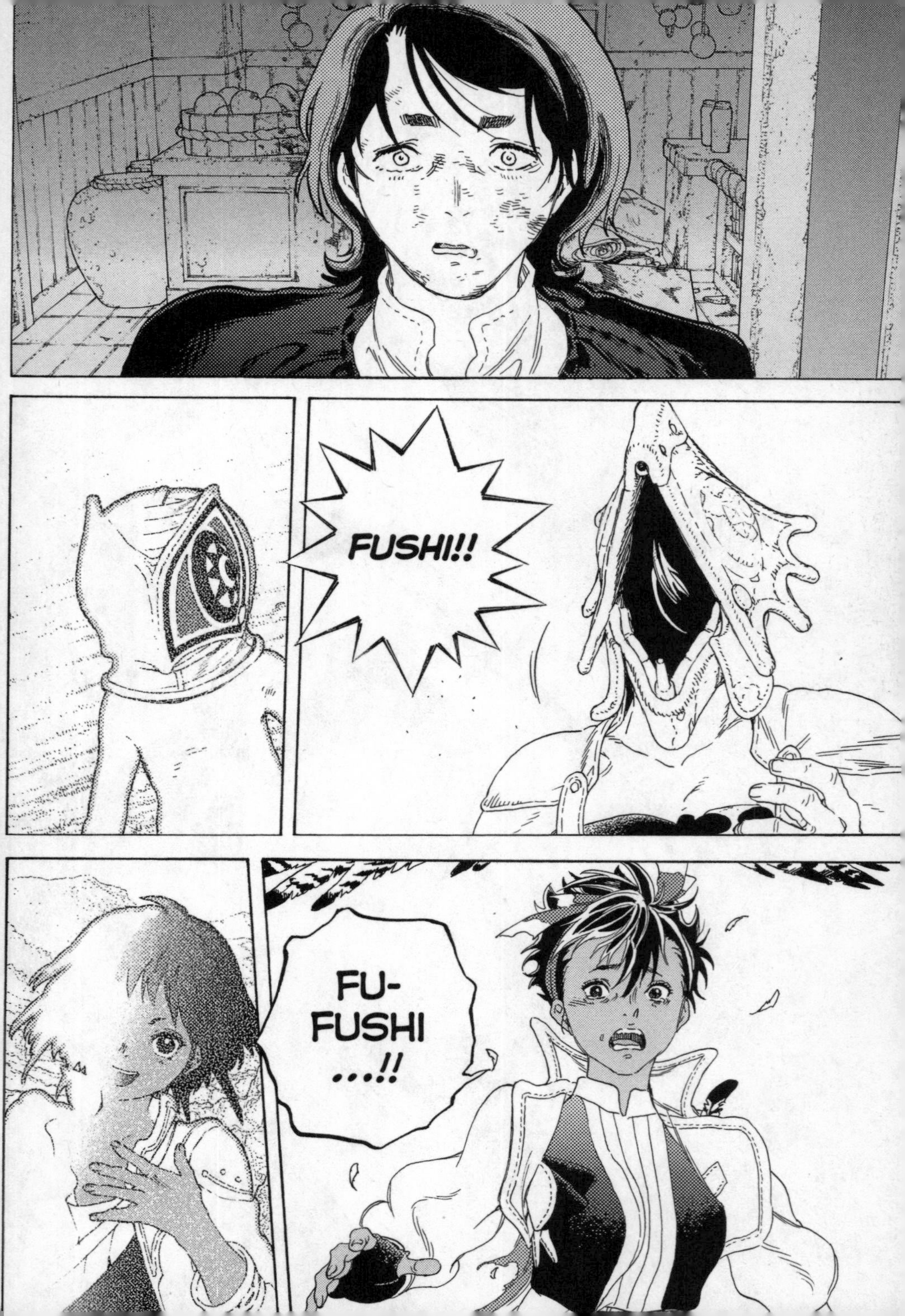
FUSHI!!
FU-FUSHI ...!!

REMEMBER US...

...FU!

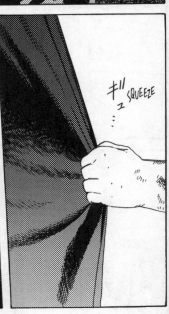

キ!! SQUEEZE

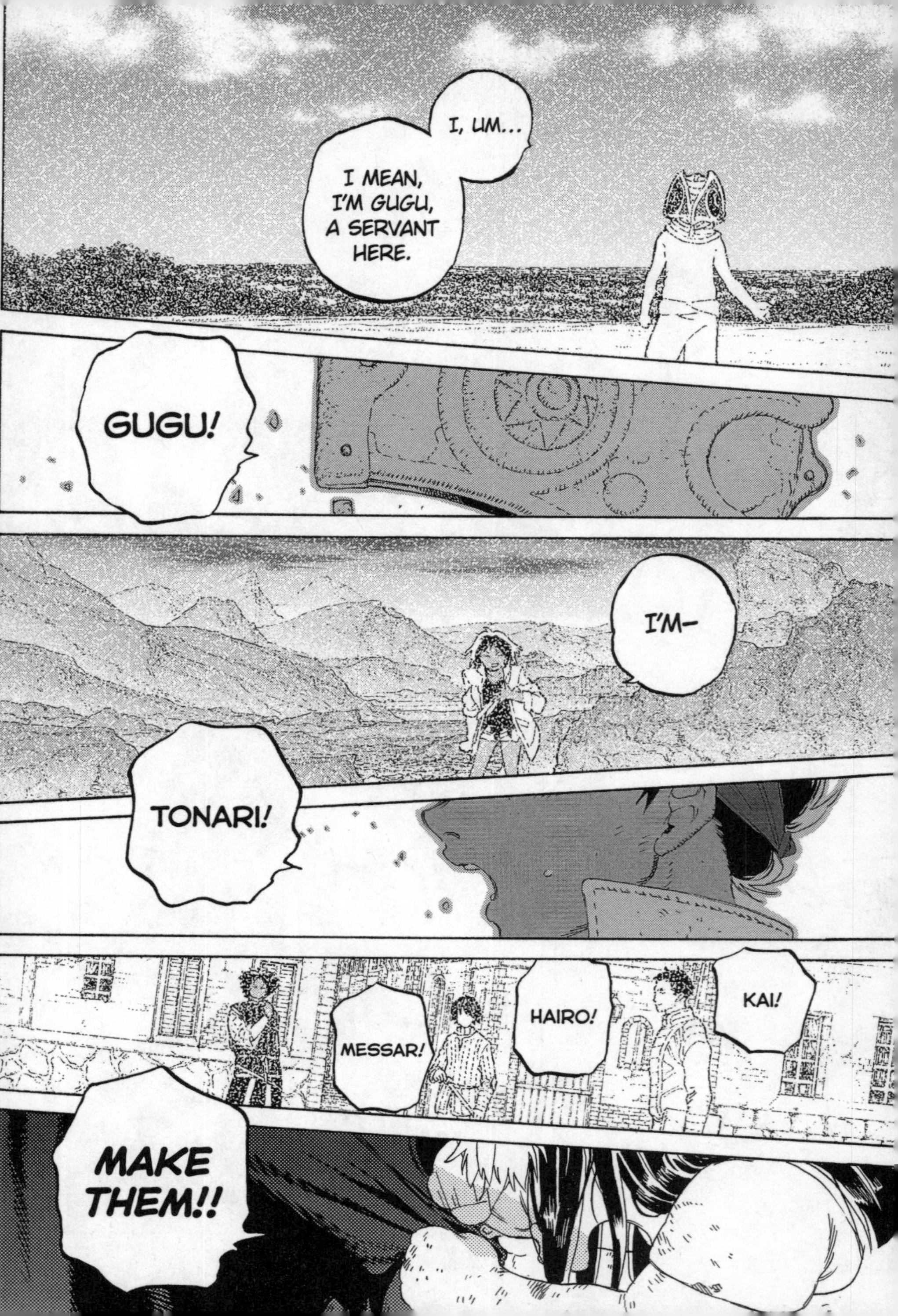
I, UM...
I MEAN, I'M GUGU, A SERVANT HERE.
GUGU!
I'M–
TONARI!
KAI!
HAIRO!
MESSAR!
MAKE THEM!!

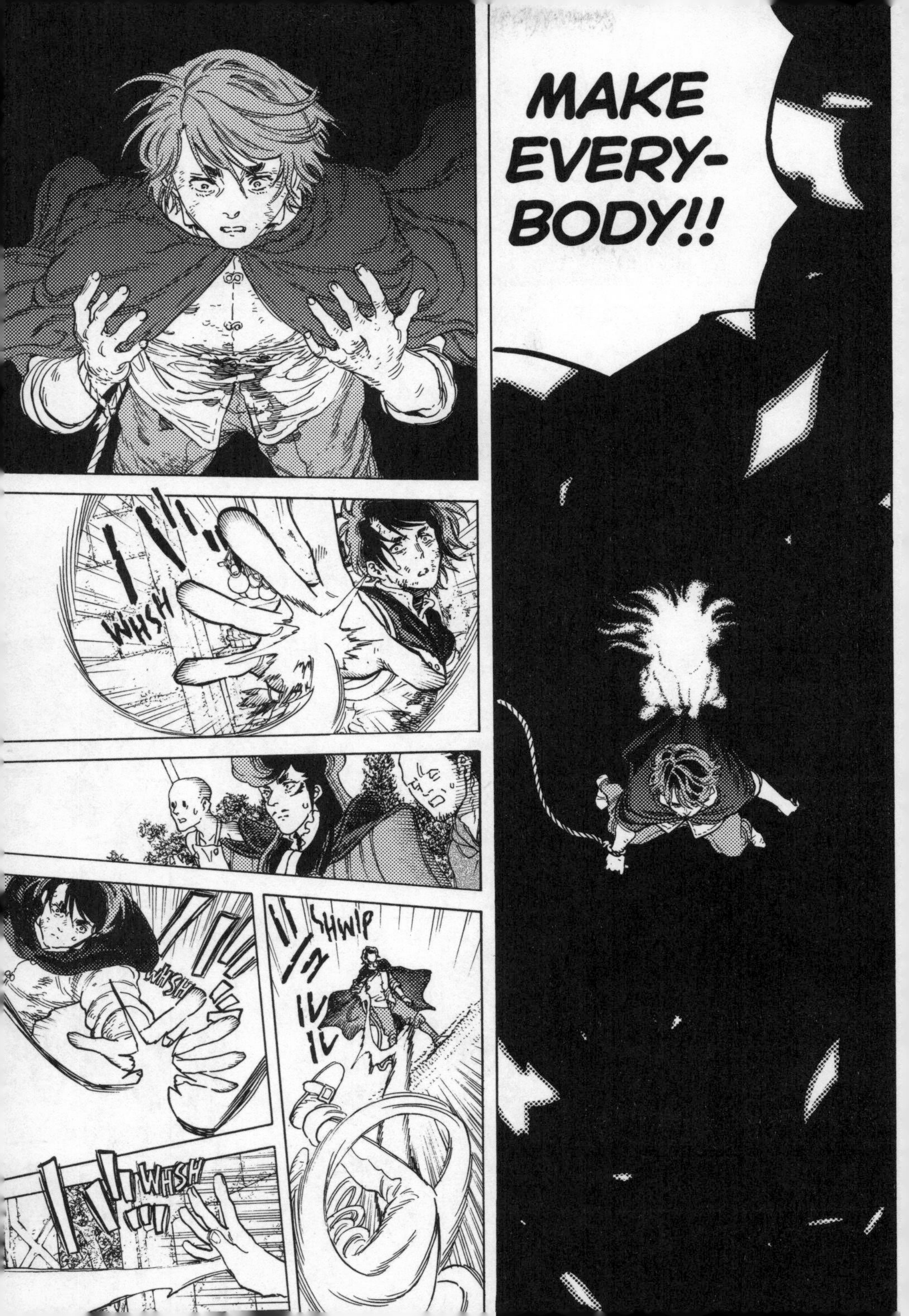
MAKE EVERY-BODY!!
WHSH
SHWIP
WHSH
WHSH

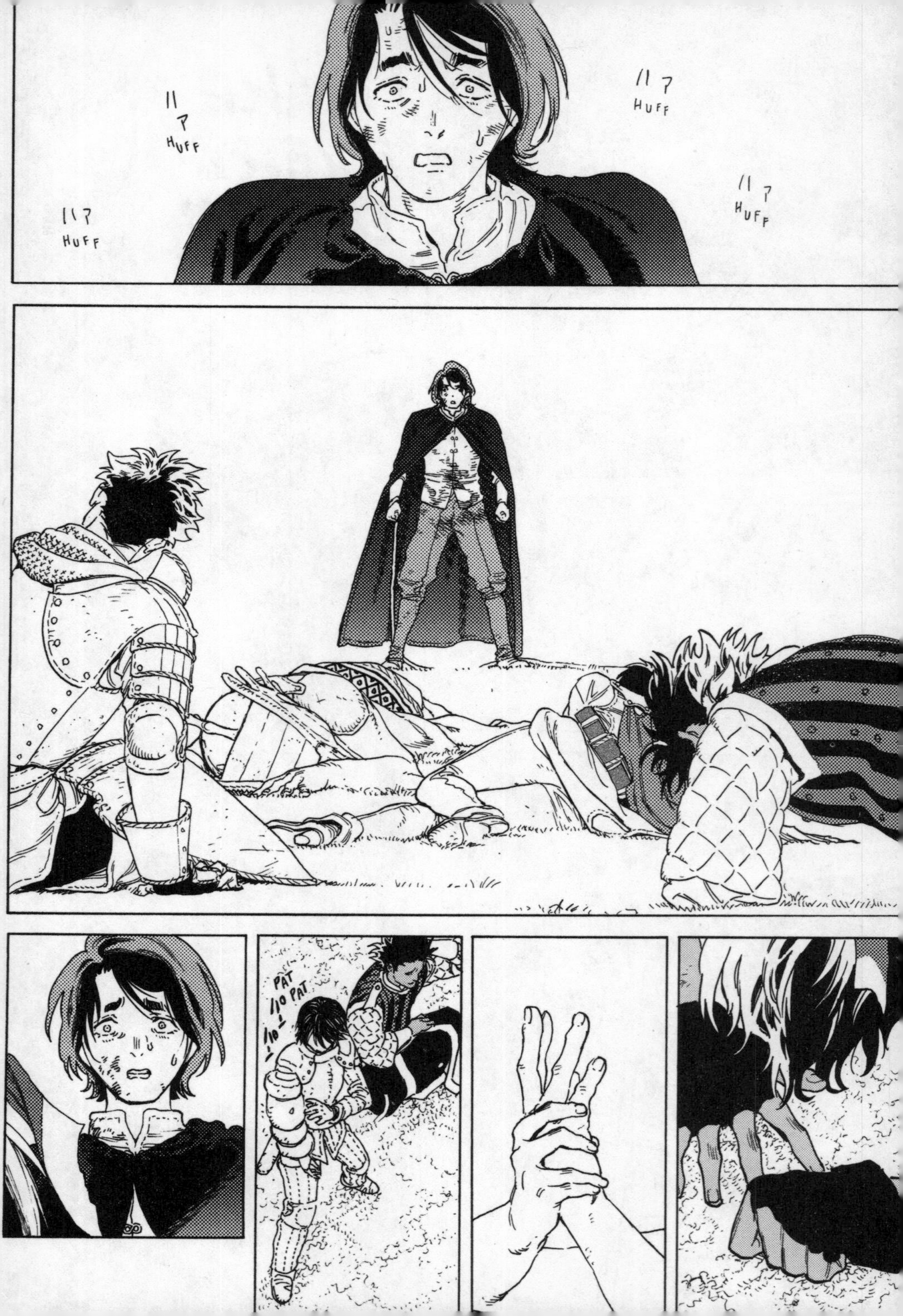

ハア
HUFF
ハア
HUFF
ハア
HUFF
ハア
HUFF
PAT
PAT

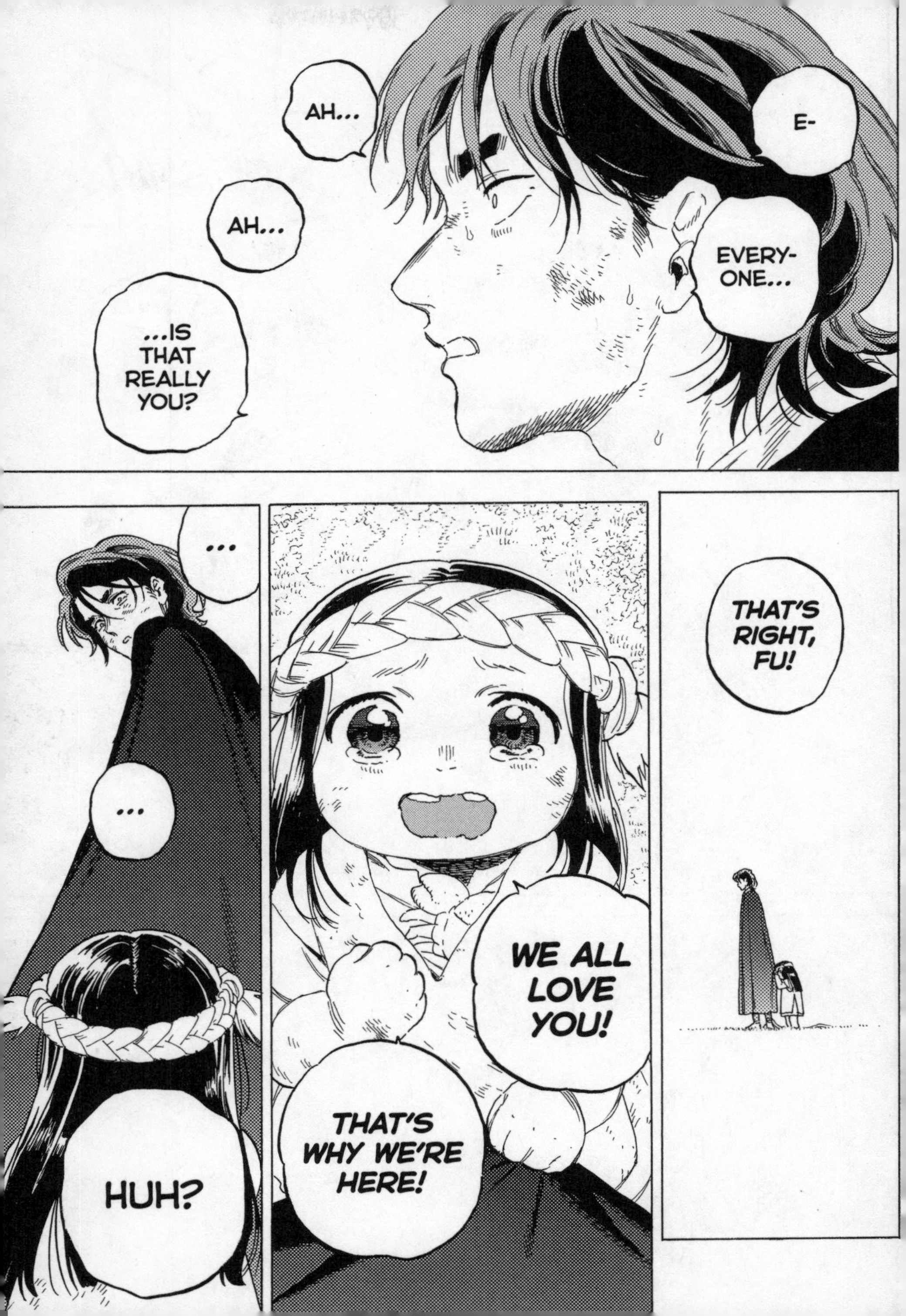
E-
EVERY-ONE...
AH...
AH...
...IS THAT REALLY YOU?
THAT'S RIGHT, FU!
WE ALL LOVE YOU!
THAT'S WHY WE'RE HERE!
...
...
HUH?

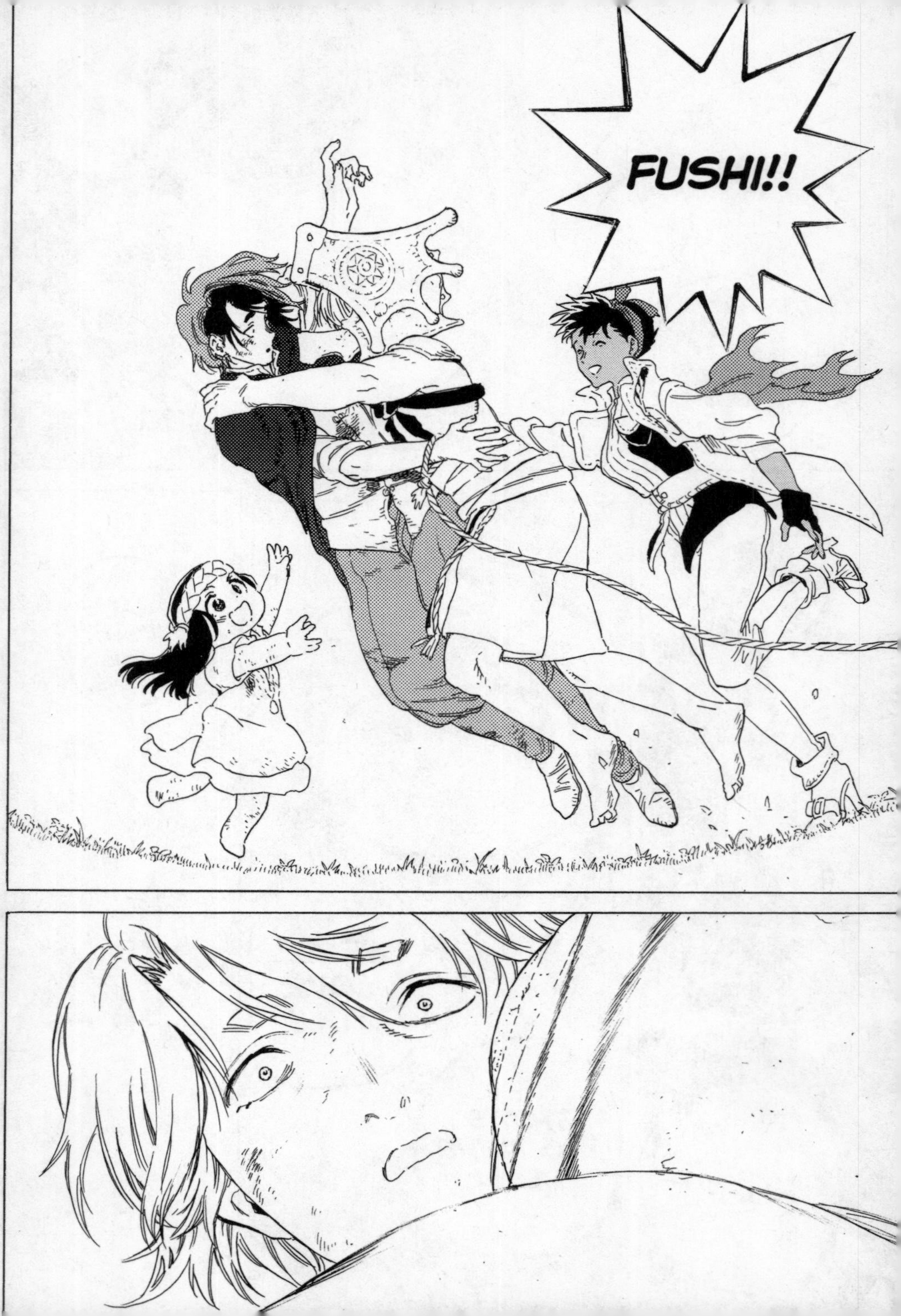
FUSHI!!

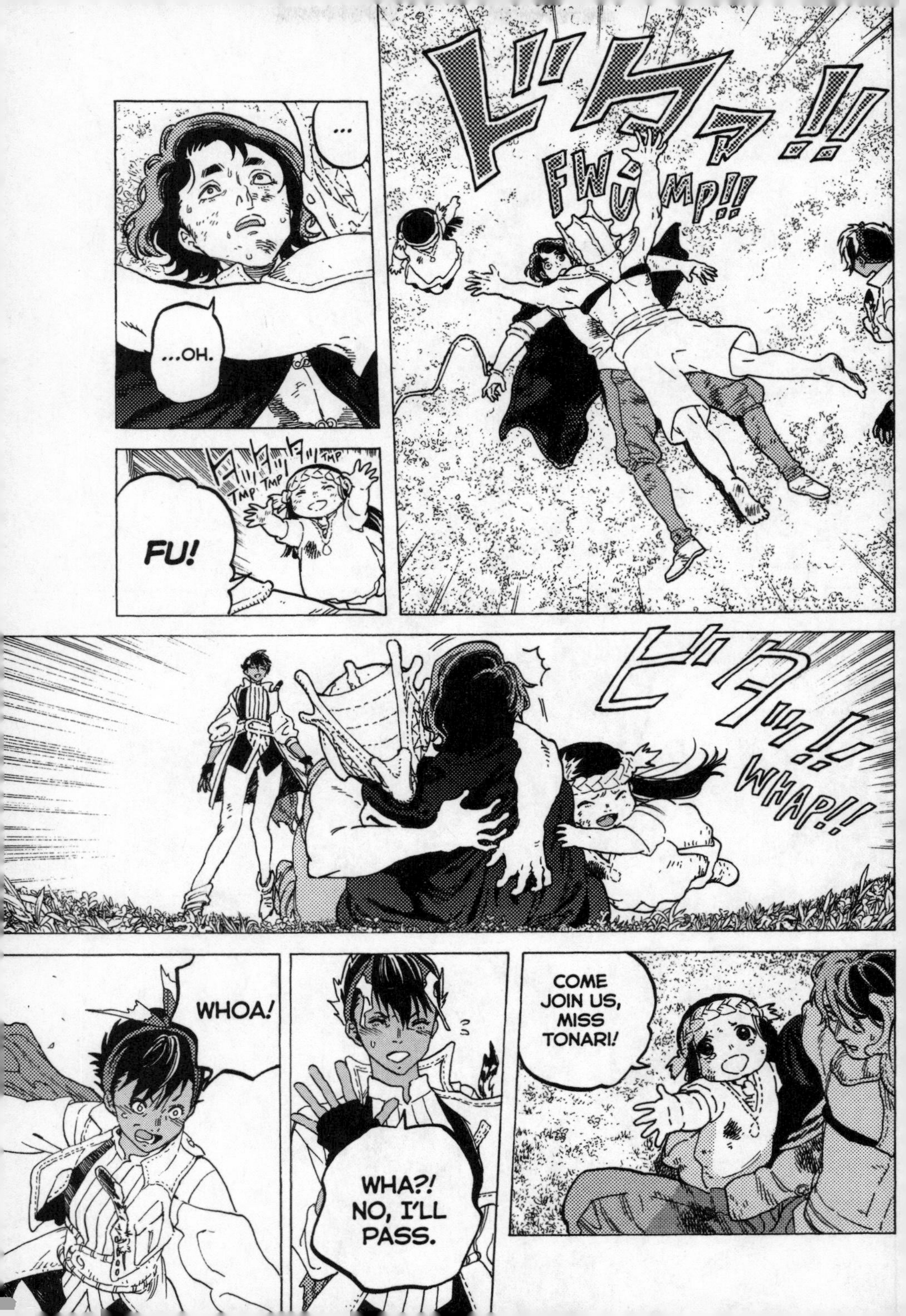
ドサァ!!
FWUMP!!
...
...OH.
タッタッタッ
TMP TMP TMP
FU!
ビタッ!!
WHAP!!
COME JOIN US, MISS TONARI!
WHA?! NO, I'LL PASS.
WHOA!

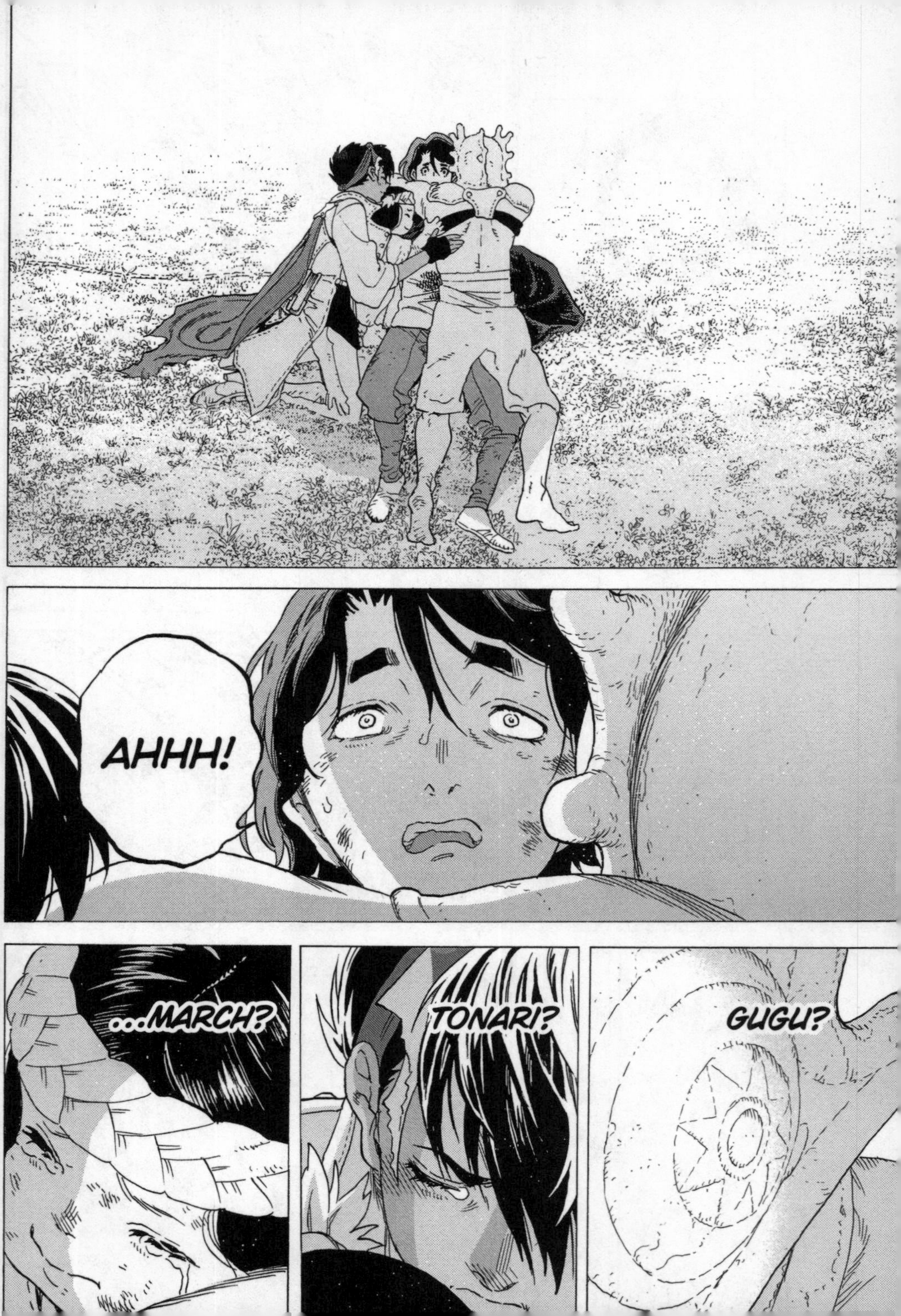
AHHH!
GUGU?
TONARI?
...MARCH?

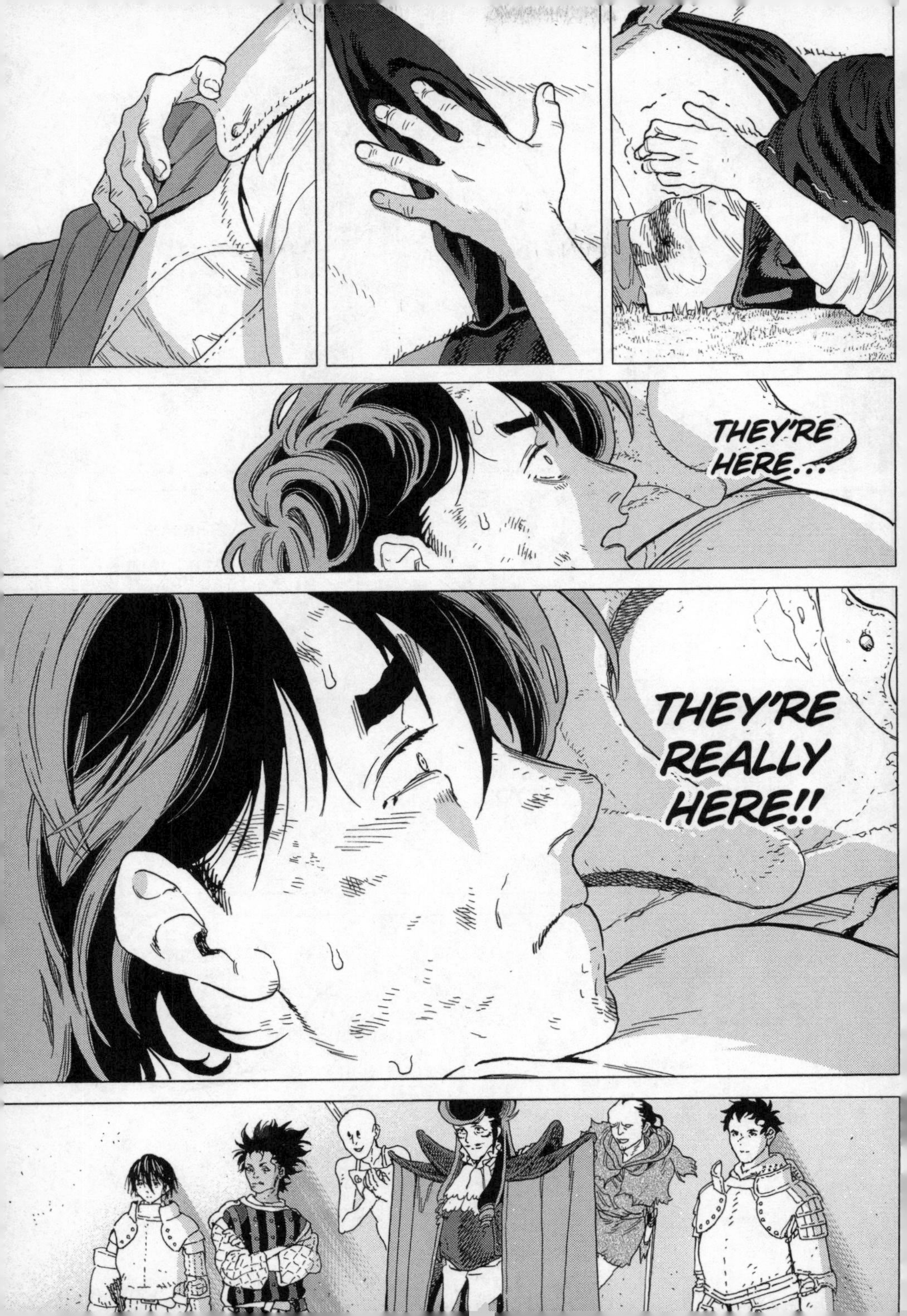
THEY'RE HERE...
THEY'RE REALLY HERE!!

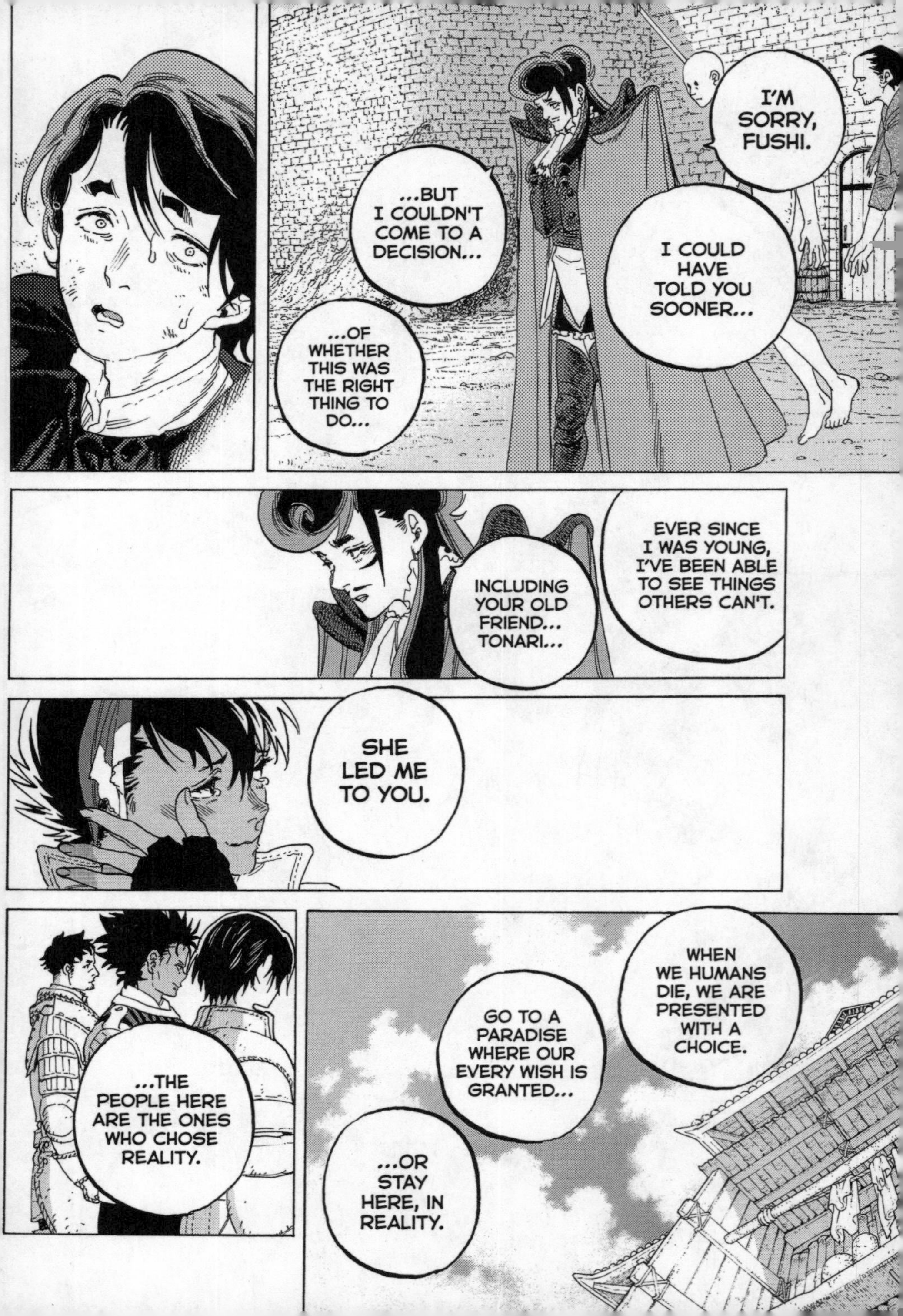
I'M SORRY, FUSHI.
I COULD HAVE TOLD YOU SOONER...
...BUT I COULDN'T COME TO A DECISION...
...OF WHETHER THIS WAS THE RIGHT THING TO DO...
EVER SINCE I WAS YOUNG, I'VE BEEN ABLE TO SEE THINGS OTHERS CAN'T.
INCLUDING YOUR OLD FRIEND... TONARI...
SHE LED ME TO YOU.
WHEN WE HUMANS DIE, WE ARE PRESENTED WITH A CHOICE.
GO TO A PARADISE WHERE OUR EVERY WISH IS GRANTED...
...OR STAY HERE, IN REALITY.
...THE PEOPLE HERE ARE THE ONES WHO CHOSE REALITY.

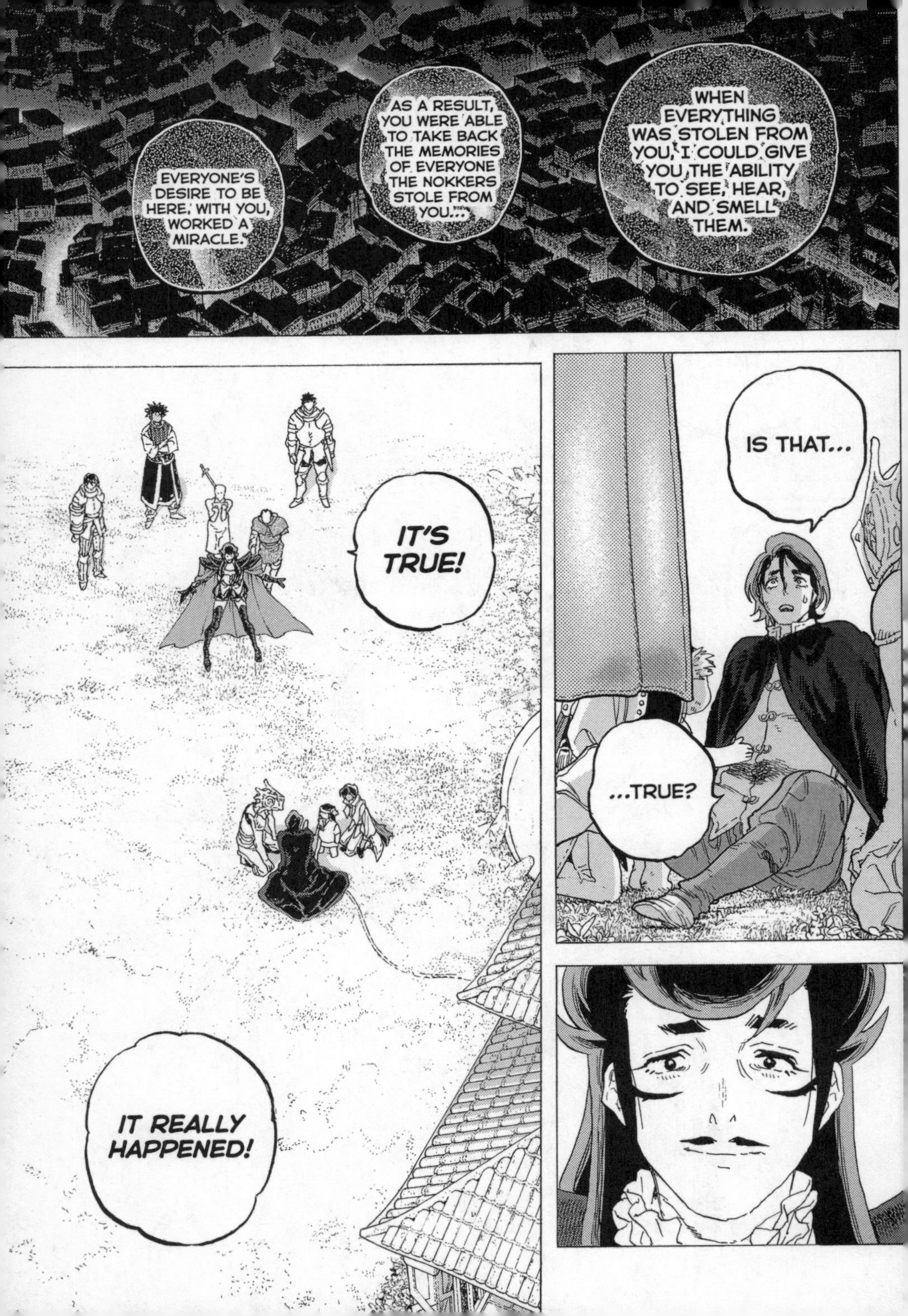
WHEN EVERYTHING WAS STOLEN FROM YOU, I COULD GIVE YOU THE ABILITY TO SEE, HEAR, AND SMELL THEM.
AS A RESULT, YOU WERE ABLE TO TAKE BACK THE MEMORIES OF EVERYONE THE NOKKERS STOLE FROM YOU...
EVERYONE'S DESIRE TO BE HERE, WITH YOU, WORKED A MIRACLE.
IS THAT...
...TRUE?
IT'S TRUE!
IT REALLY HAPPENED!

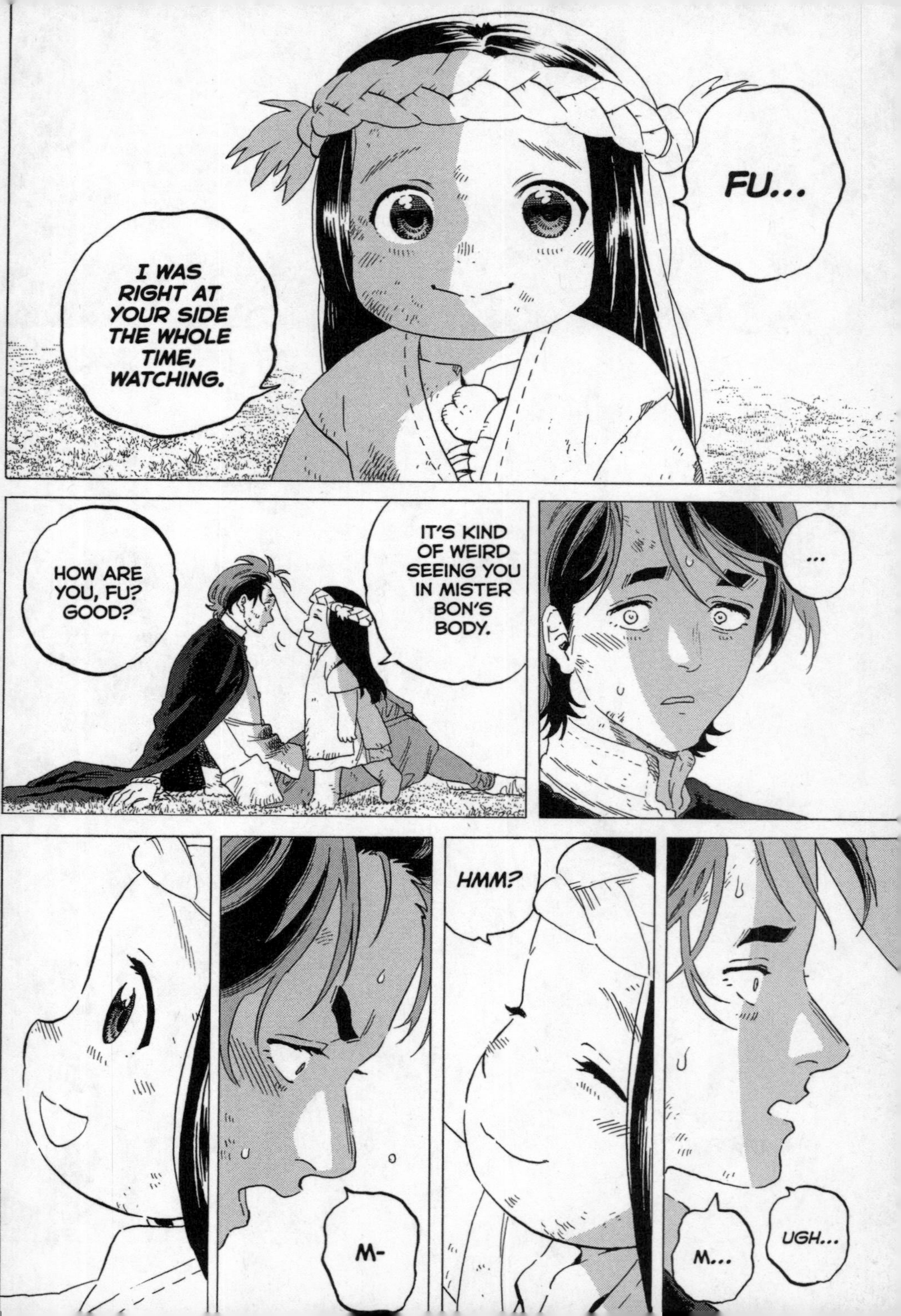
FU...
I WAS RIGHT AT YOUR SIDE THE WHOLE TIME, WATCHING.
...
IT'S KIND OF WEIRD SEEING YOU IN MISTER BON'S BODY.
HOW ARE YOU, FU? GOOD?
UGH...
HMM?
M...
M-

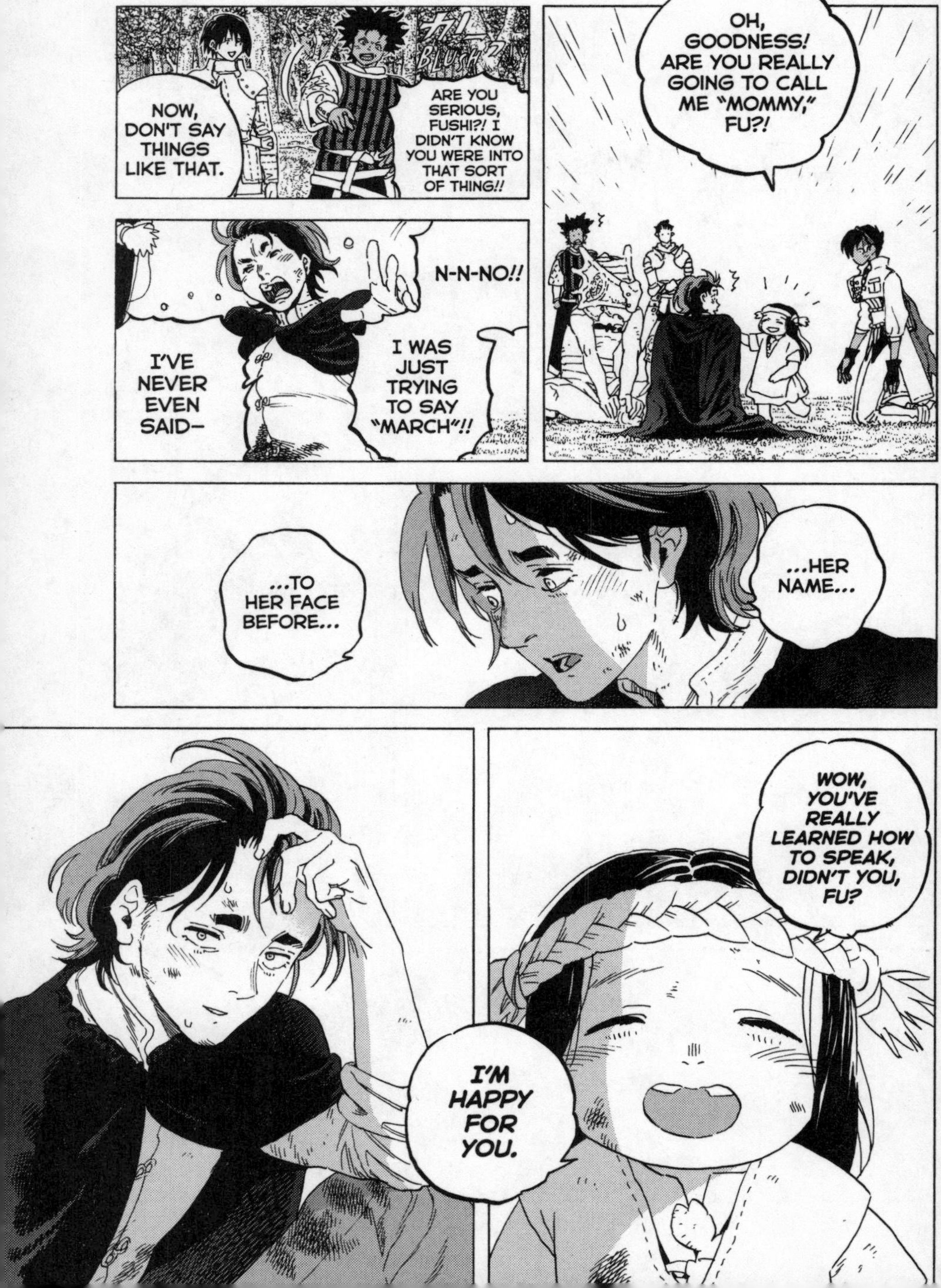
OH, GOODNESS! ARE YOU REALLY GOING TO CALL ME "MOMMY," FU?!
カー BLUSH
ARE YOU SERIOUS, FUSHI?! I DIDN'T KNOW YOU WERE INTO THAT SORT OF THING!!
NOW, DON'T SAY THINGS LIKE THAT.
N-N-NO!!
I WAS JUST TRYING TO SAY "MARCH"!!
I'VE NEVER EVEN SAID—
...HER NAME...
...TO HER FACE BEFORE...
WOW, YOU'VE REALLY LEARNED HOW TO SPEAK, DIDN'T YOU, FU?
I'M HAPPY FOR YOU.

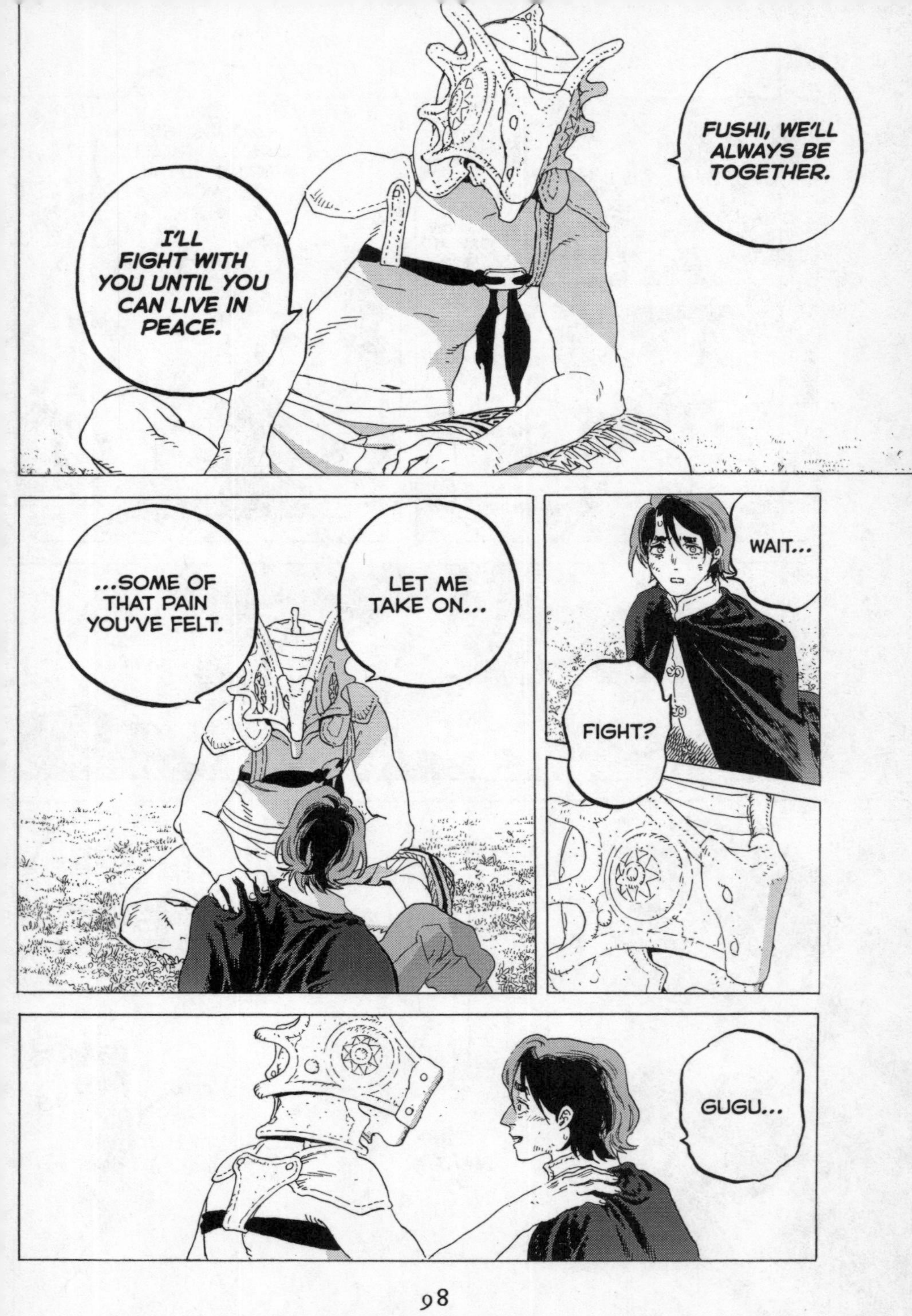
FUSHI, WE'LL ALWAYS BE TOGETHER.
I'LL FIGHT WITH YOU UNTIL YOU CAN LIVE IN PEACE.
WAIT...
FIGHT?
LET ME TAKE ON...
...SOME OF THAT PAIN YOU'VE FELT.
GUGU...

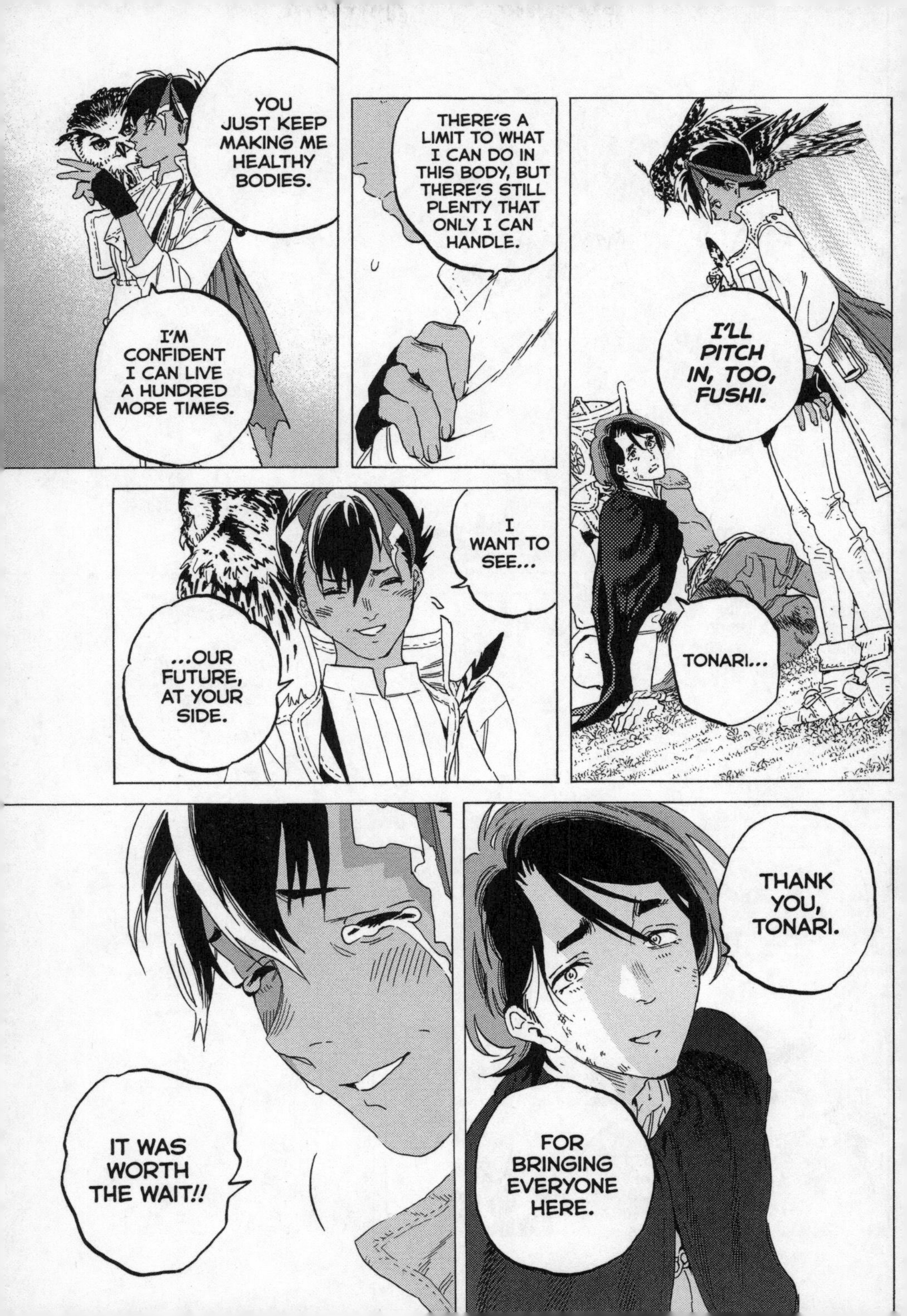
I'LL PITCH IN, TOO, FUSHI.
TONARI...
THERE'S A LIMIT TO WHAT I CAN DO IN THIS BODY, BUT THERE'S STILL PLENTY THAT ONLY I CAN HANDLE.
YOU JUST KEEP MAKING ME HEALTHY BODIES.
I'M CONFIDENT I CAN LIVE A HUNDRED MORE TIMES.
I WANT TO SEE...
...OUR FUTURE, AT YOUR SIDE.
THANK YOU, TONARI.
FOR BRINGING EVERYONE HERE.
IT WAS WORTH THE WAIT!!

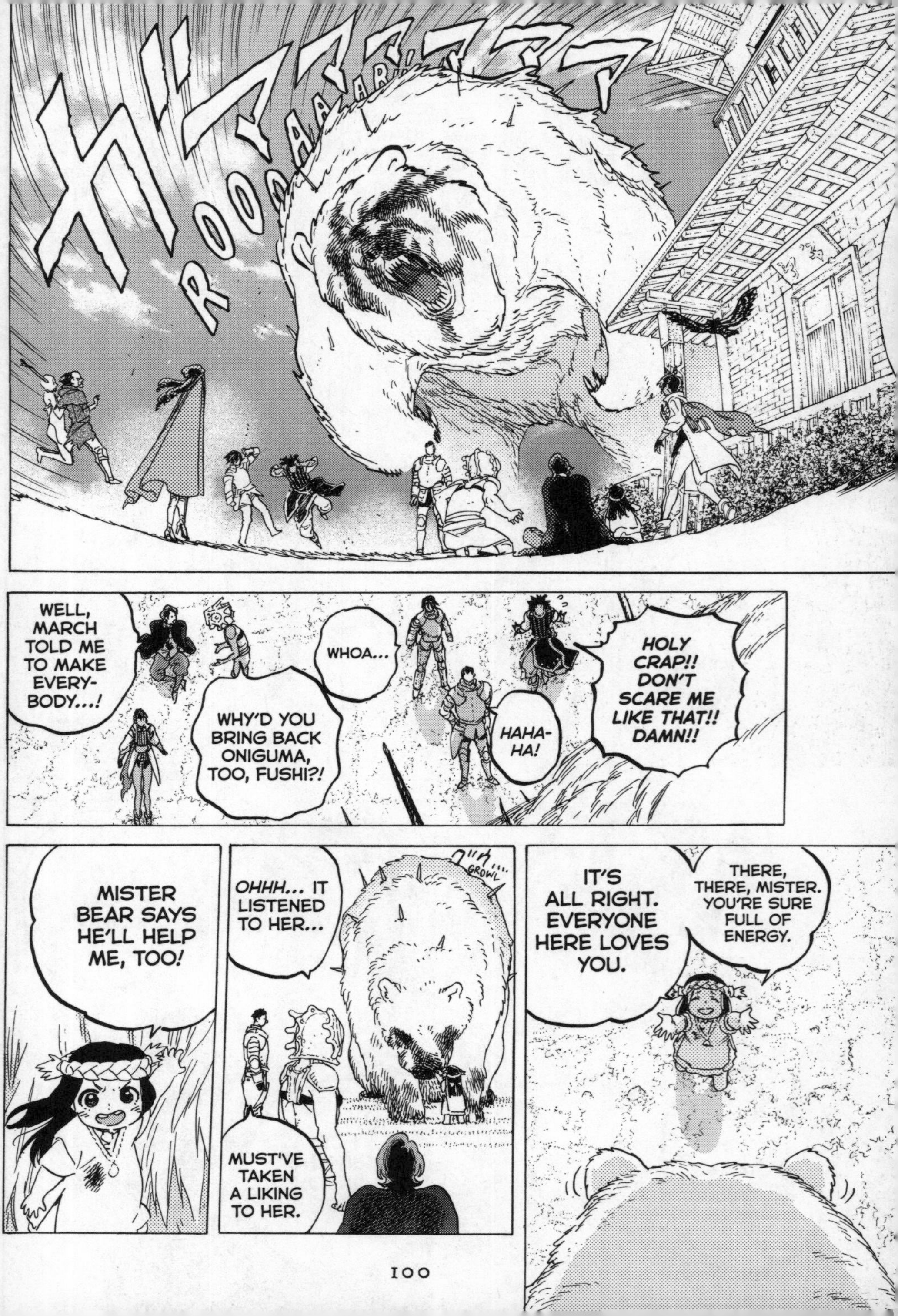
ROOOAAAR!
HOLY CRAP!! DON'T SCARE ME LIKE THAT!! DAMN!!
HAHA-HA!
WHOA...
WHY'D YOU BRING BACK ONIGUMA, TOO, FUSHI?!
WELL, MARCH TOLD ME TO MAKE EVERY-BODY...!
THERE, THERE, MISTER. YOU'RE SURE FULL OF ENERGY.
IT'S ALL RIGHT. EVERYONE HERE LOVES YOU.
GROWL...
OHHH... IT LISTENED TO HER...
MUST'VE TAKEN A LIKING TO HER.
MISTER BEAR SAYS HE'LL HELP ME, TOO!

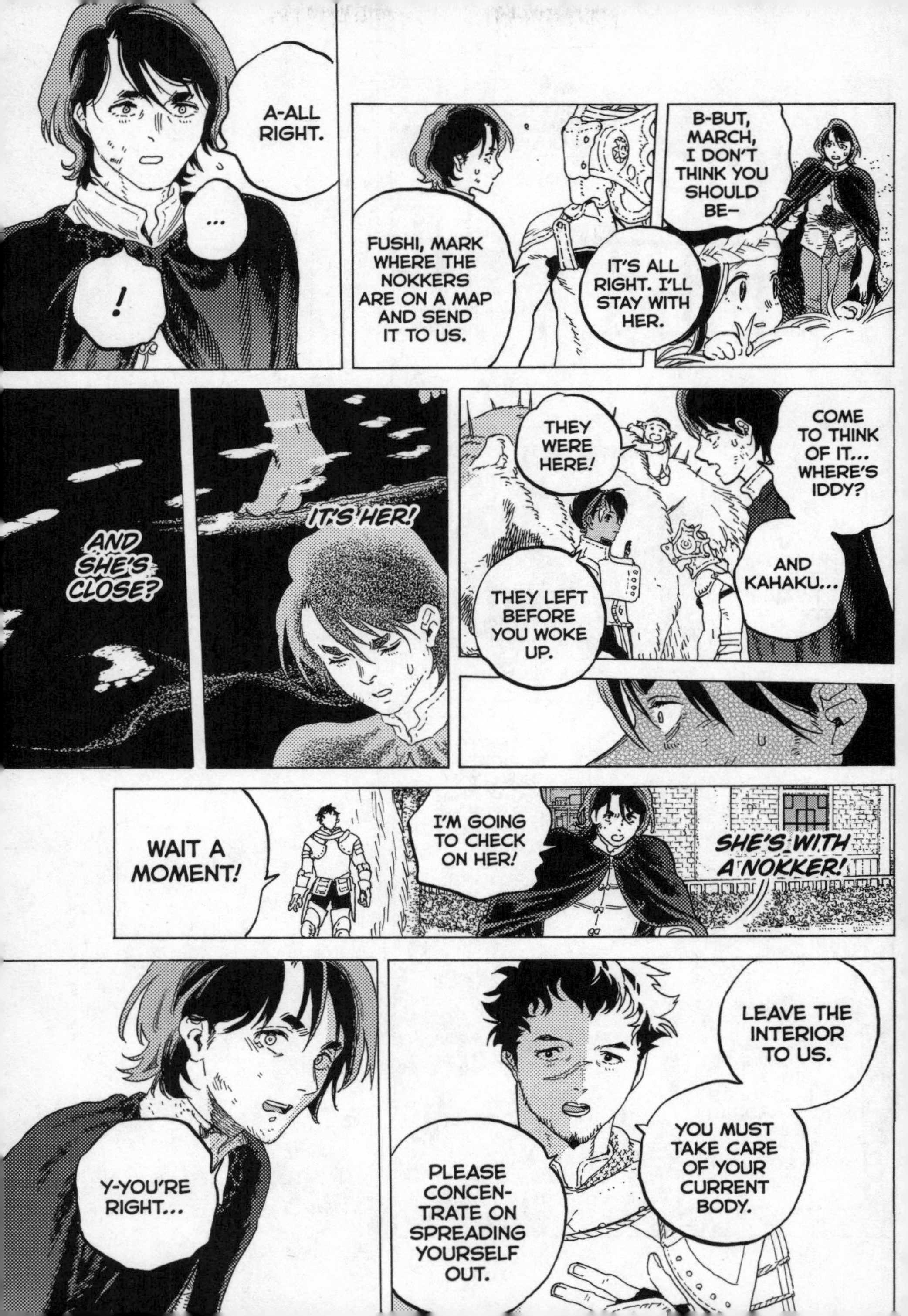
B-BUT, MARCH, I DON'T THINK YOU SHOULD BE—
IT'S ALL RIGHT. I'LL STAY WITH HER.
FUSHI, MARK WHERE THE NOKKERS ARE ON A MAP AND SEND IT TO US.
A-ALL RIGHT.
...
!
COME TO THINK OF IT... WHERE'S IDDY?
THEY WERE HERE!
AND KAHAKU...
THEY LEFT BEFORE YOU WOKE UP.
IT'S HER!
AND SHE'S CLOSE?
SHE'S WITH A NOKKER!
I'M GOING TO CHECK ON HER!
WAIT A MOMENT!
LEAVE THE INTERIOR TO US.
YOU MUST TAKE CARE OF YOUR CURRENT BODY.
PLEASE CONCENTRATE ON SPREADING YOURSELF OUT.
Y-YOU'RE RIGHT...

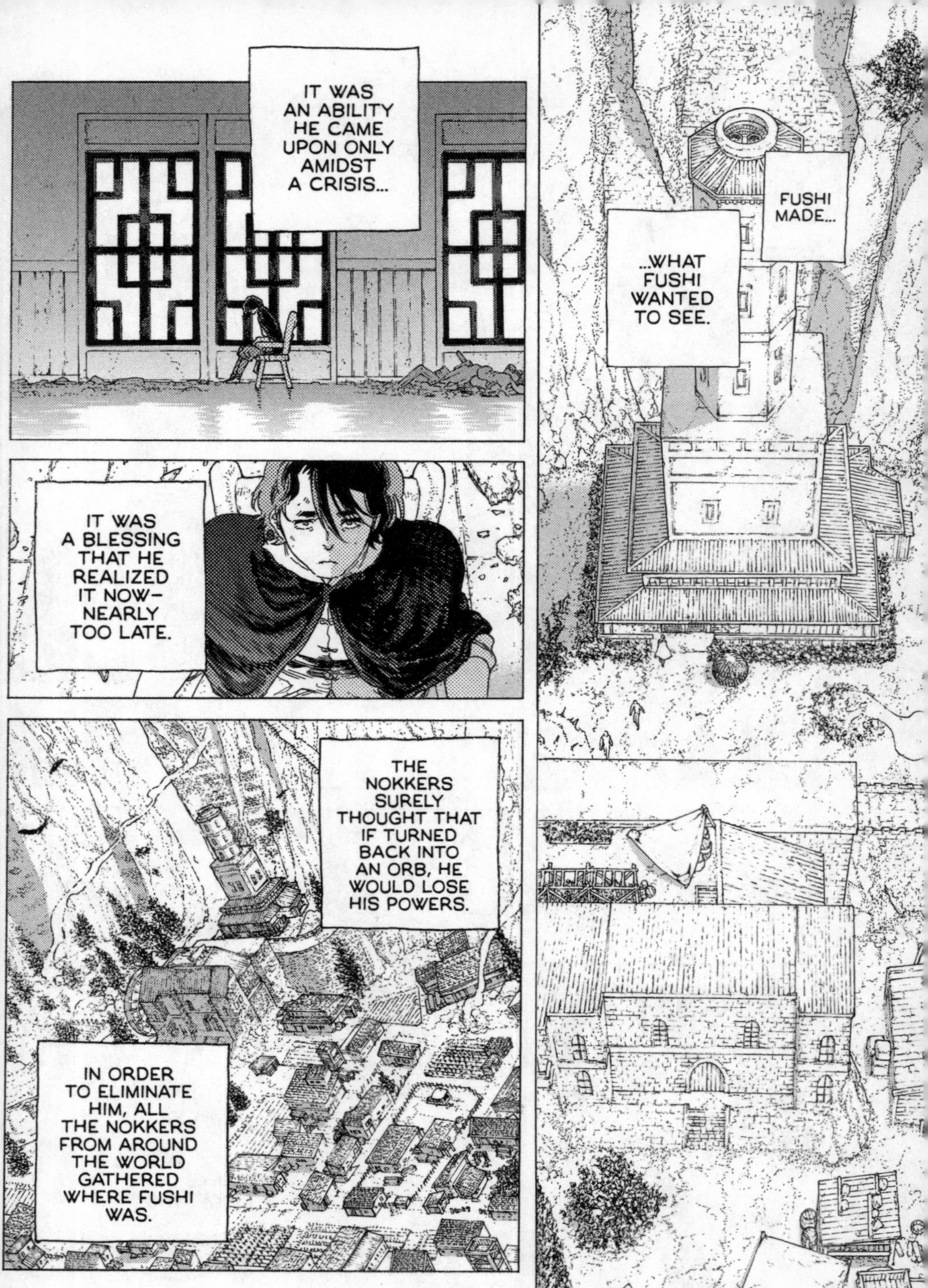
FUSHI MADE...
...WHAT FUSHI WANTED TO SEE.
IT WAS AN ABILITY HE CAME UPON ONLY AMIDST A CRISIS...
IT WAS A BLESSING THAT HE REALIZED IT NOW— NEARLY TOO LATE.
THE NOKKERS SURELY THOUGHT THAT IF TURNED BACK INTO AN ORB, HE WOULD LOSE HIS POWERS.
IN ORDER TO ELIMINATE HIM, ALL THE NOKKERS FROM AROUND THE WORLD GATHERED WHERE FUSHI WAS.

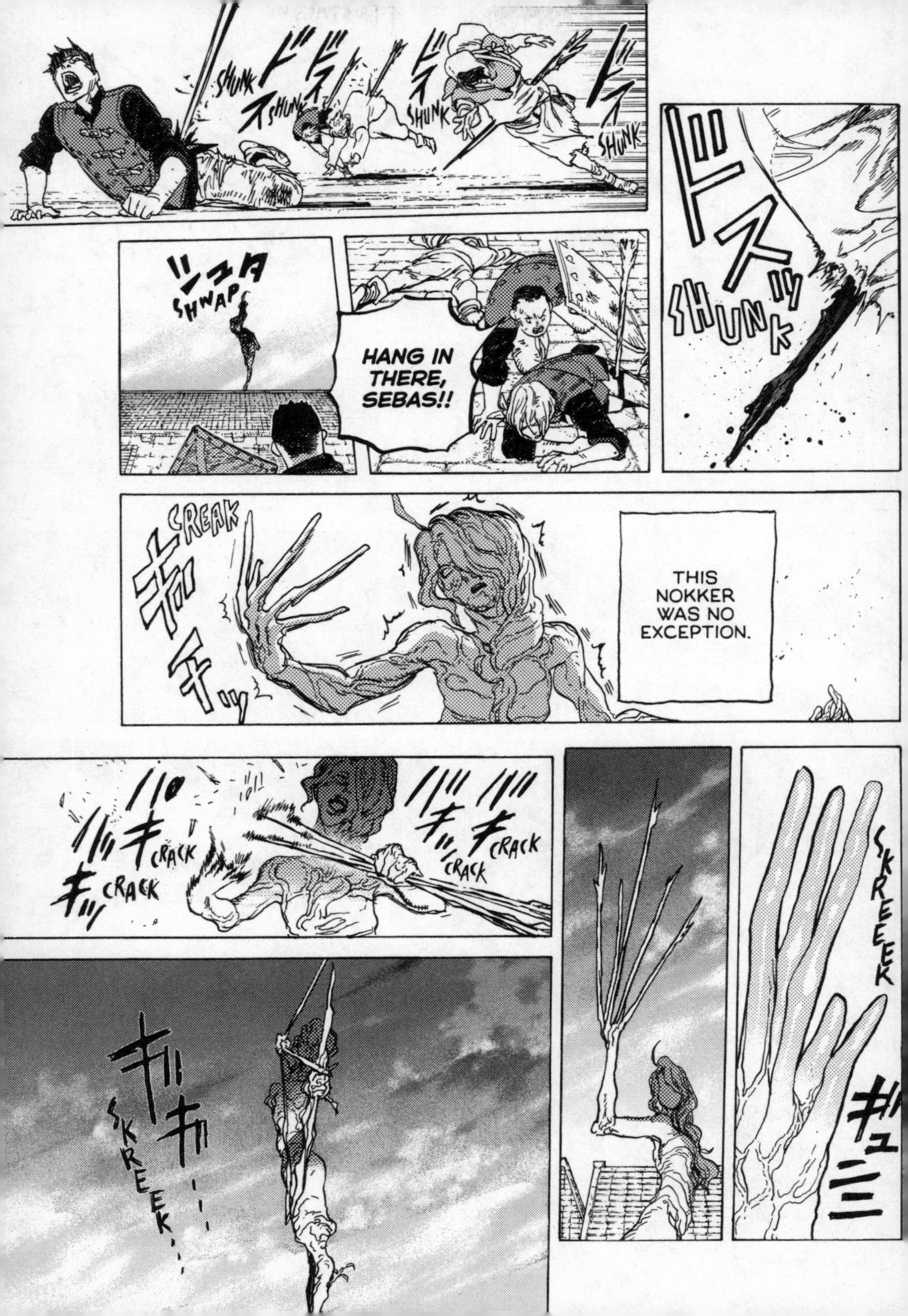

SHUNK
SHUNK
SHUNK
SHUNK
SHUNK
HANG IN THERE, SEBAS!!
SHWAP
THIS NOKKER WAS NO EXCEPTION.
CREAK
SKREEEK
CRACK
CRACK
CRACK
CRACK
SKREEEK...

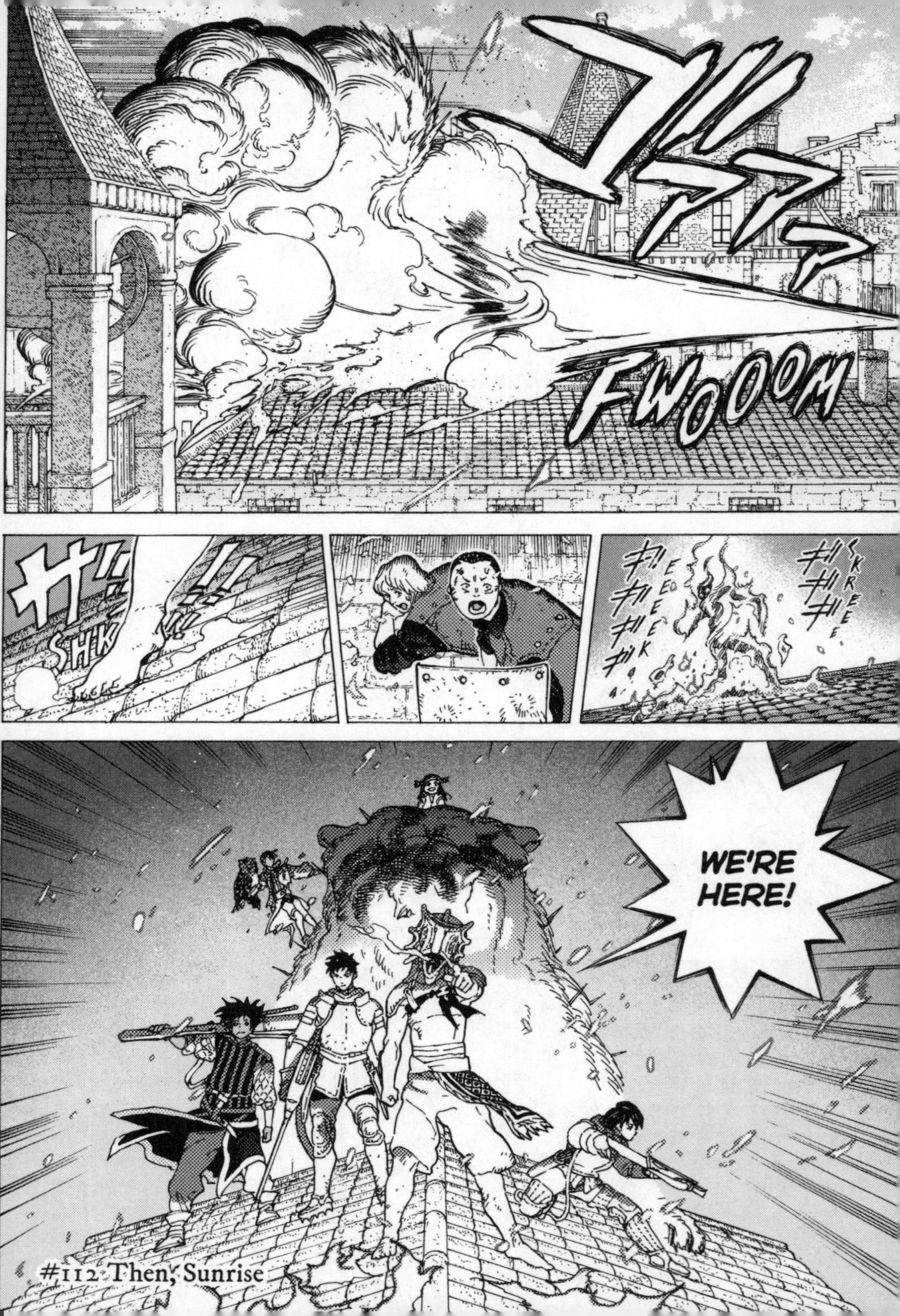
FWOOOM
SKREEE
EEEEK
SHK
WE'RE HERE!

#112 Then, Sunrise

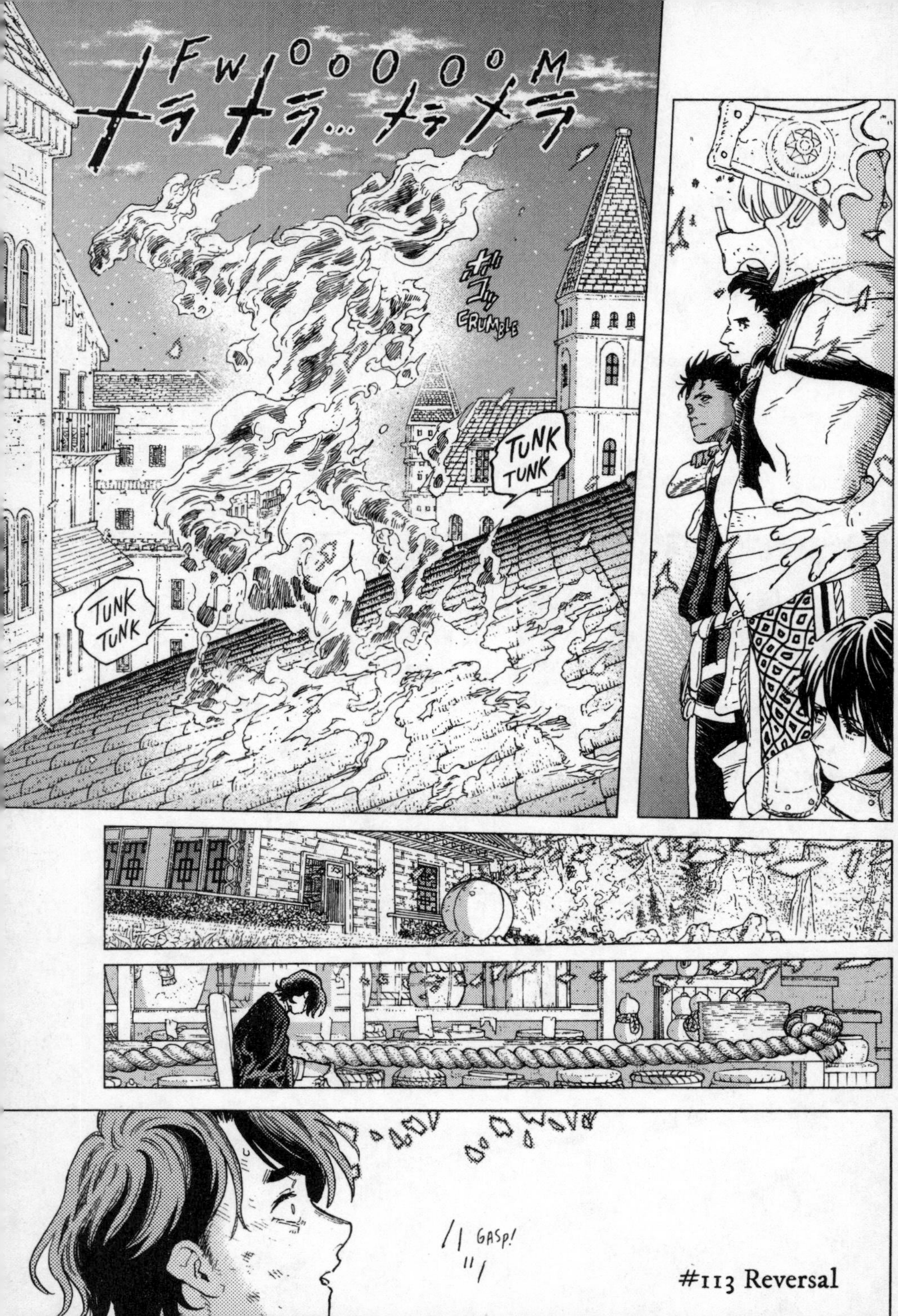
FWOOOOOM
メラメラ…メラメラ
ボゴッ
CRUMBLE
TUNK TUNK
TUNK TUNK
GASP!

#113 Reversal

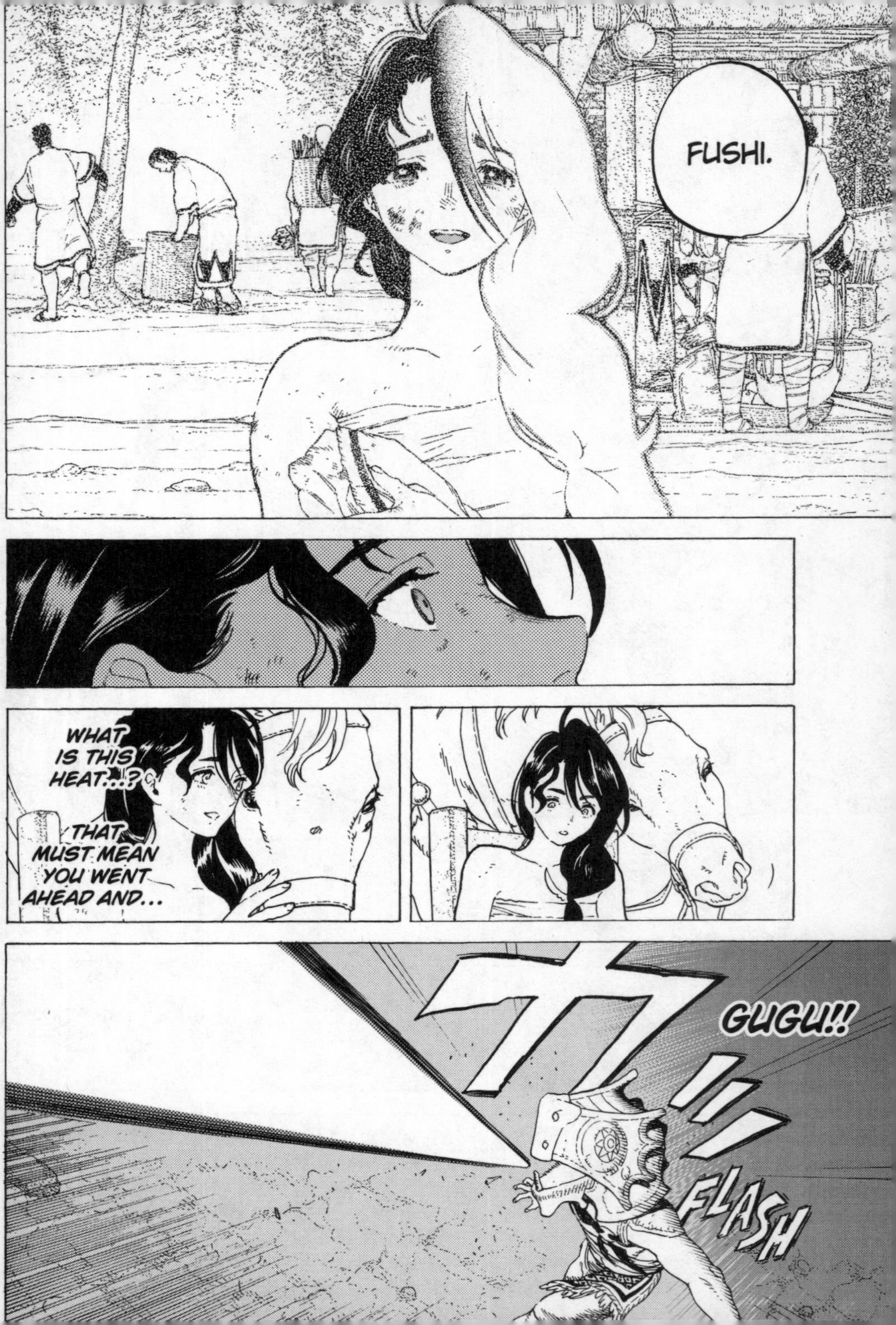
FUSHI.
WHAT IS THIS HEAT...?
THAT MUST MEAN YOU WENT AHEAD AND...
GUGU!!
FLASH

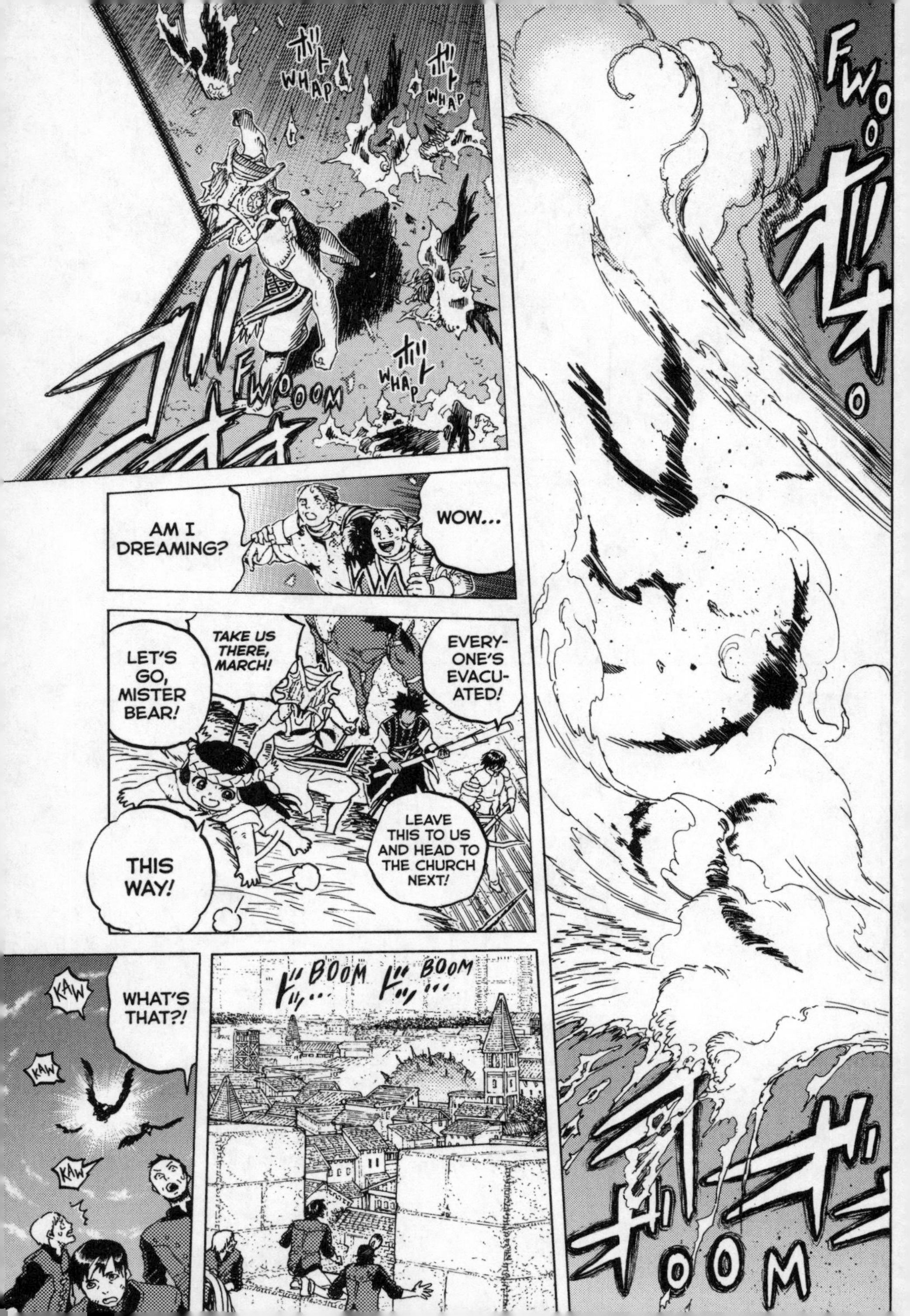
FWOOOO
OOM
WHAP
WHAP
FWOOOM
WHAP
WOW...
AM I DREAMING?
EVERY-ONE'S EVACU-ATED!
TAKE US THERE, MARCH!
LET'S GO, MISTER BEAR!
LEAVE THIS TO US AND HEAD TO THE CHURCH NEXT!
THIS WAY!
BOOM
BOOM
WHAT'S THAT?!
KAW
KAW
KAW

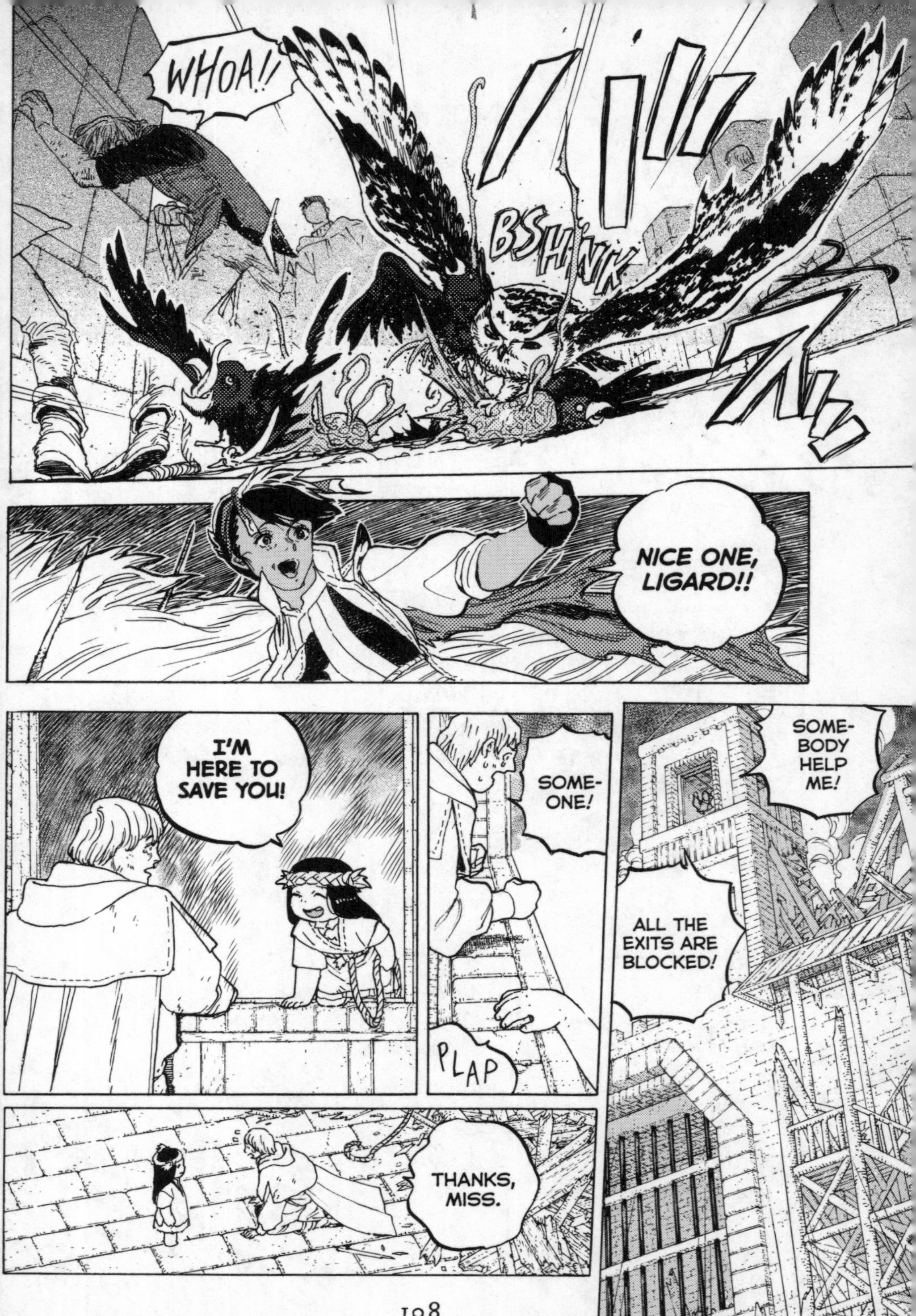

WHOA!!
BSHINK
NICE ONE, LIGARD!!
SOME-BODY HELP ME!
ALL THE EXITS ARE BLOCKED!
SOME-ONE!
PLAP
I'M HERE TO SAVE YOU!
THANKS, MISS.

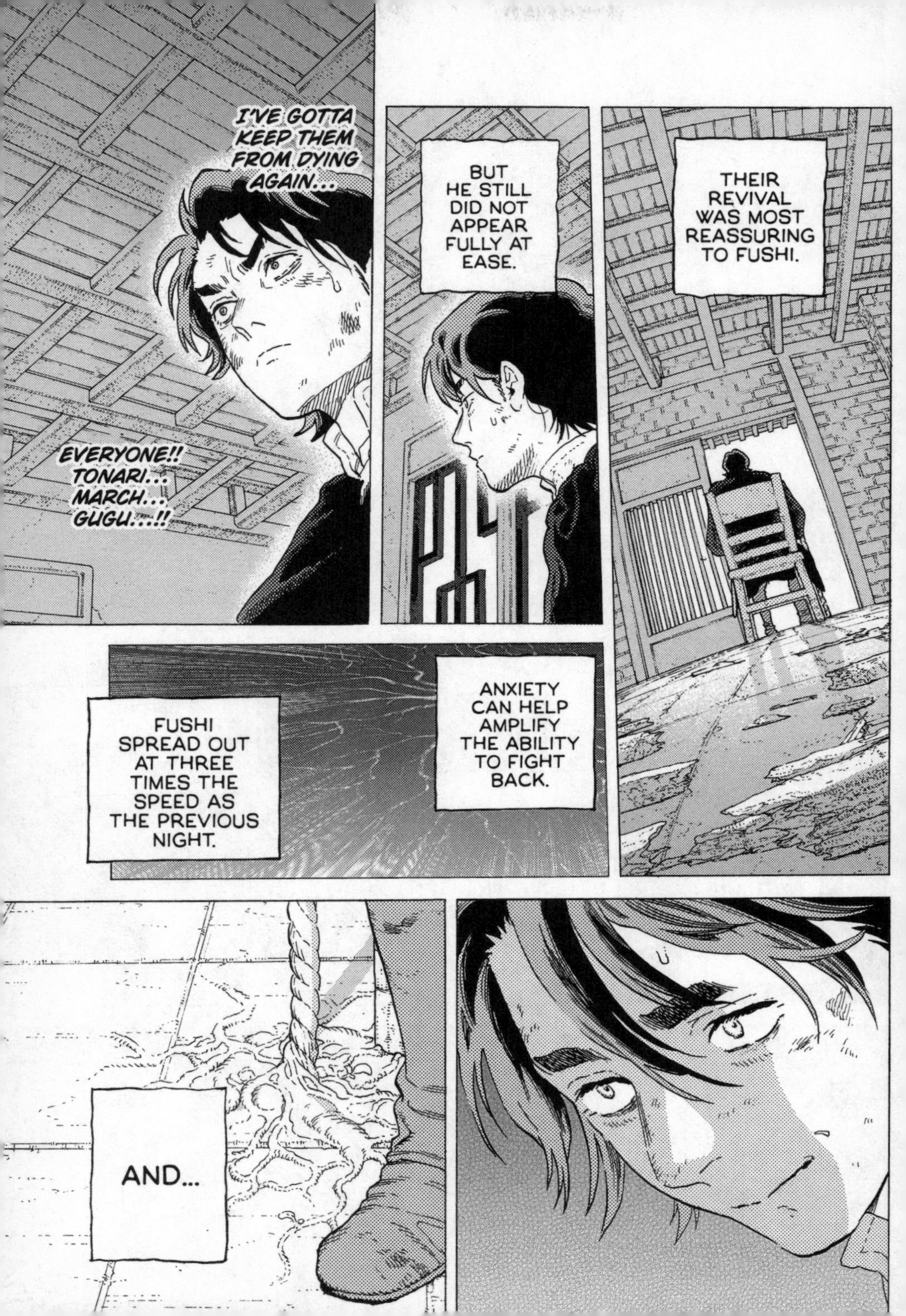
THEIR REVIVAL WAS MOST REASSURING TO FUSHI.
BUT HE STILL DID NOT APPEAR FULLY AT EASE.
I'VE GOTTA KEEP THEM FROM DYING AGAIN...
EVERYONE!! TONARI... MARCH... GUGU...!!
ANXIETY CAN HELP AMPLIFY THE ABILITY TO FIGHT BACK.
FUSHI SPREAD OUT AT THREE TIMES THE SPEED AS THE PREVIOUS NIGHT.
AND...

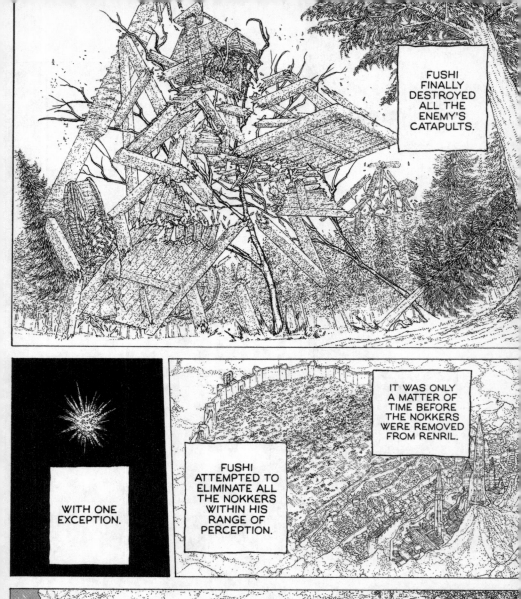

FUSHI FINALLY DESTROYED ALL THE ENEMY'S CATAPULTS.

IT WAS ONLY A MATTER OF TIME BEFORE THE NOKKERS WERE REMOVED FROM RENRIL.

FUSHI ATTEMPTED TO ELIMINATE ALL THE NOKKERS WITHIN HIS RANGE OF PERCEPTION.

WITH ONE EXCEPTION.

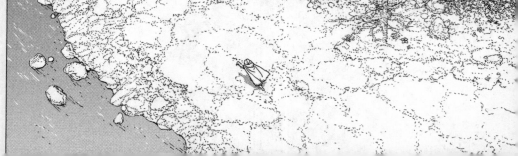

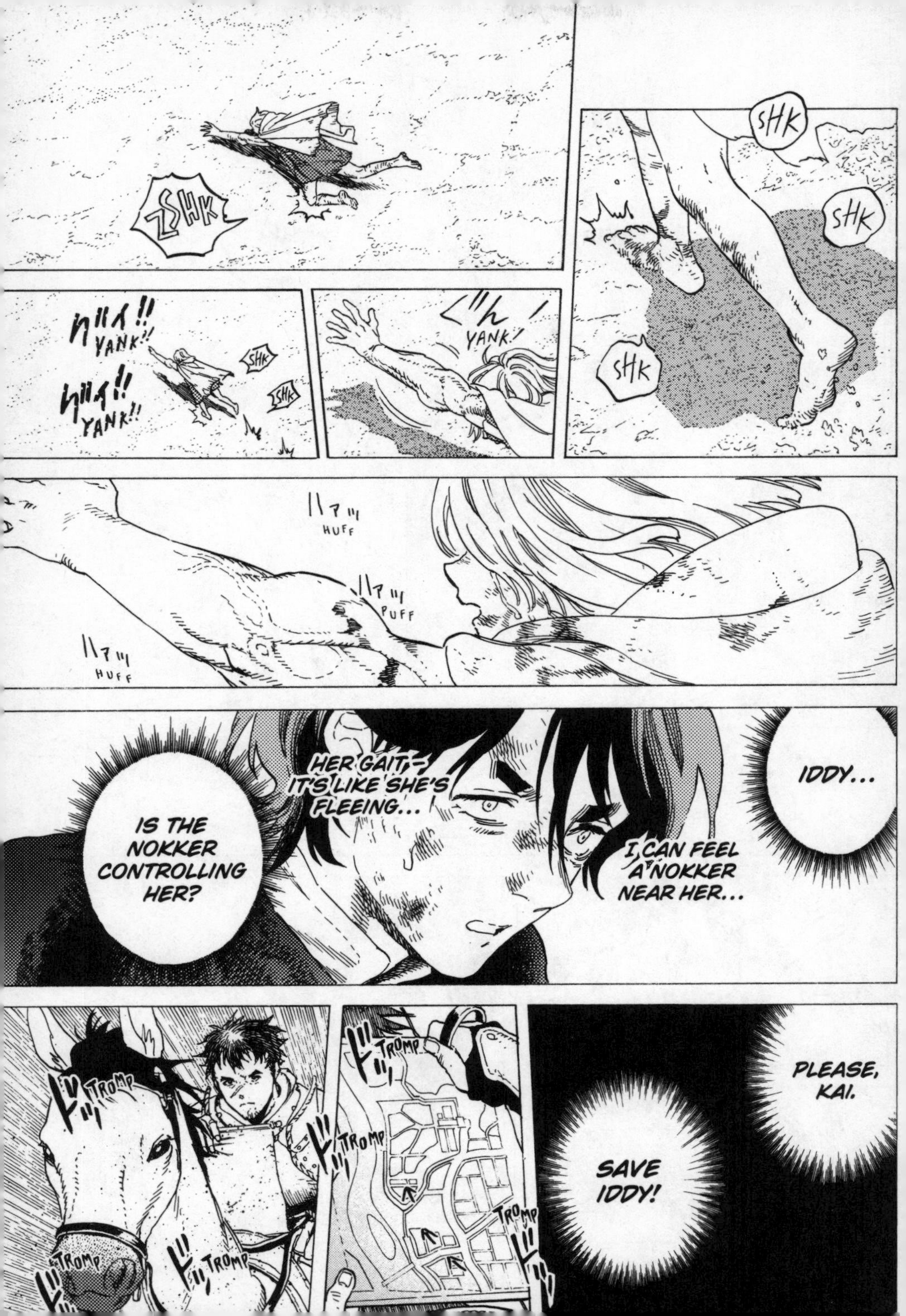
SHK
SHK
SHK
ZSHK
ぐいん
YANK!
グイ!!
YANK!!
グイ!!
YANK!!
SHK
SHK
ハァッ
HUFF
ハァッ
PUFF
ハァッ
HUFF
IDDY...
I CAN FEEL A NOKKER NEAR HER...
HER GAIT, IT'S LIKE SHE'S FLEEING...
IS THE NOKKER CONTROLLING HER?
PLEASE, KAI.
SAVE IDDY!
TROMP
TROMP
TROMP
TROMP
TROMP
TROMP
TROMP

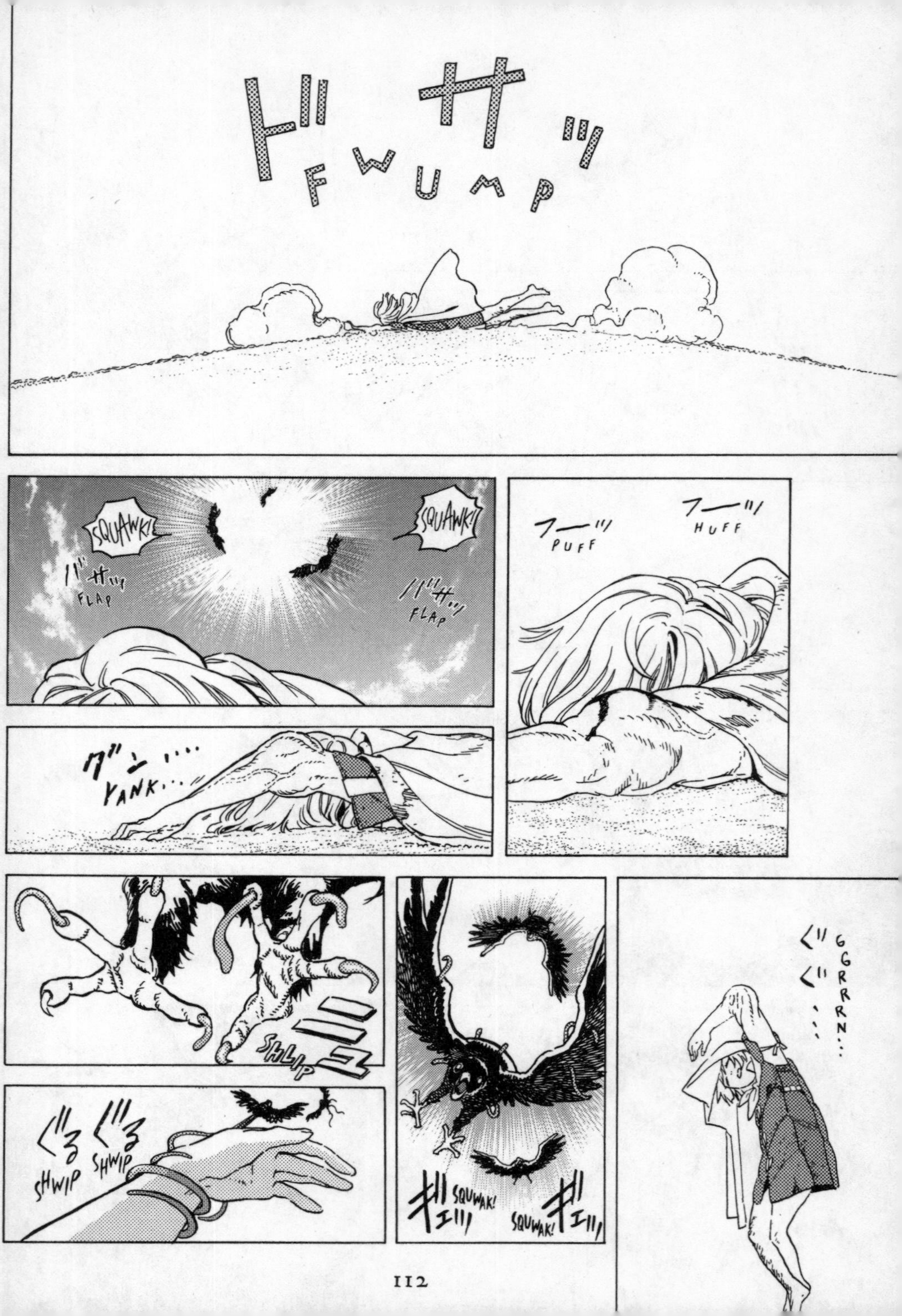
ドサッ
FWUMP
フーッ
HUFF
フーッ
PUFF
SQUAWK!
バサッ
FLAP
SQUAWK!
バサッ
FLAP
グン…
YANK…
ぐぐ…
GGRRRN…
ギエーッ
SQUWAK!
ギエーッ
SQUWAK!
SHLIP
ぐる ぐる
SHWIP SHWIP

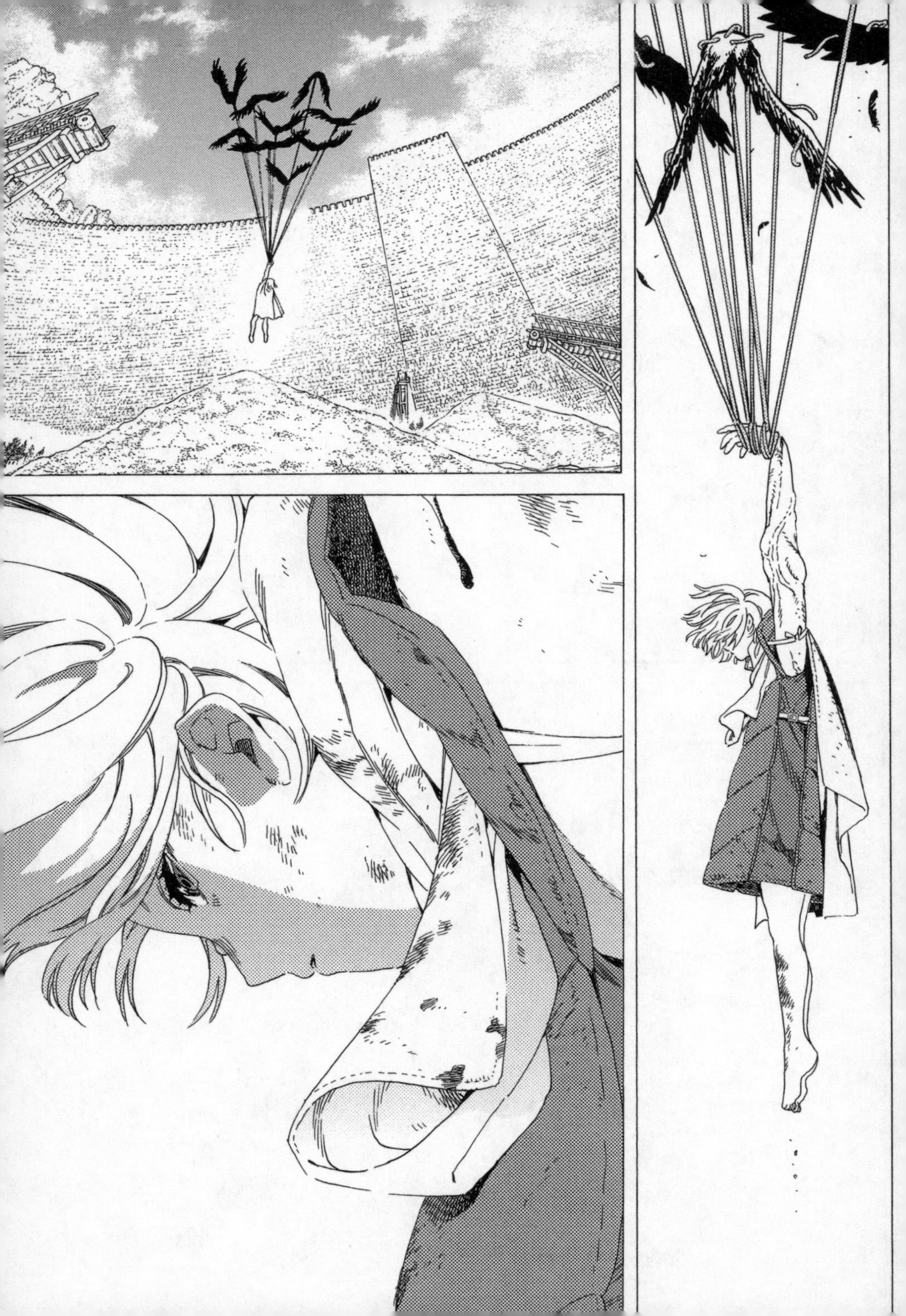

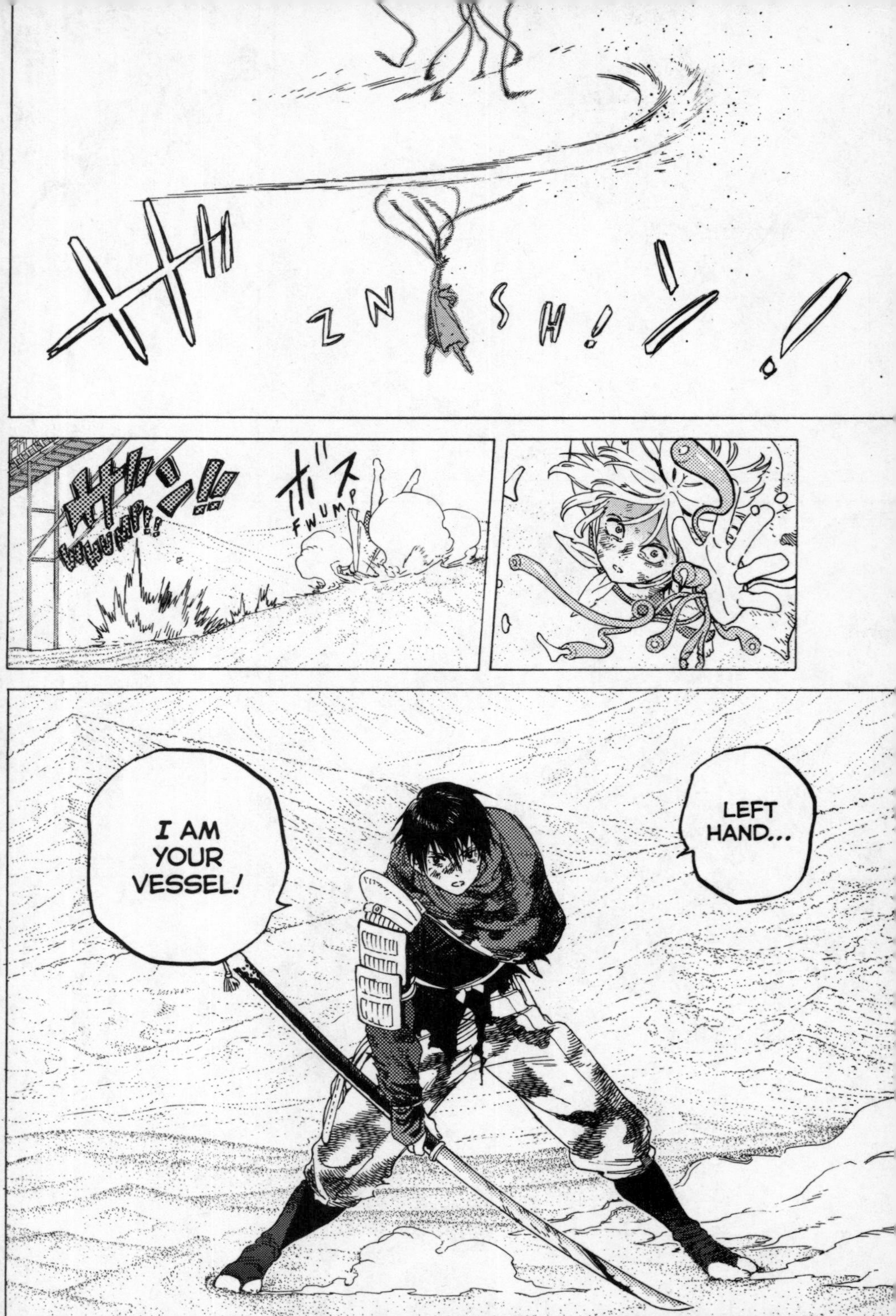
ZNSH!!
ボス
FWUMP
ガシャン!!
WHUMP!!
LEFT HAND...
I AM YOUR VESSEL!

NOW,
COME
HOME
TO ME!

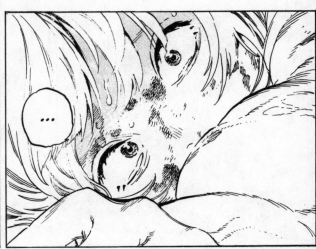

...

TWITCH

CRACK

CRACK

....!

....!!

GWUMP

GWUMP

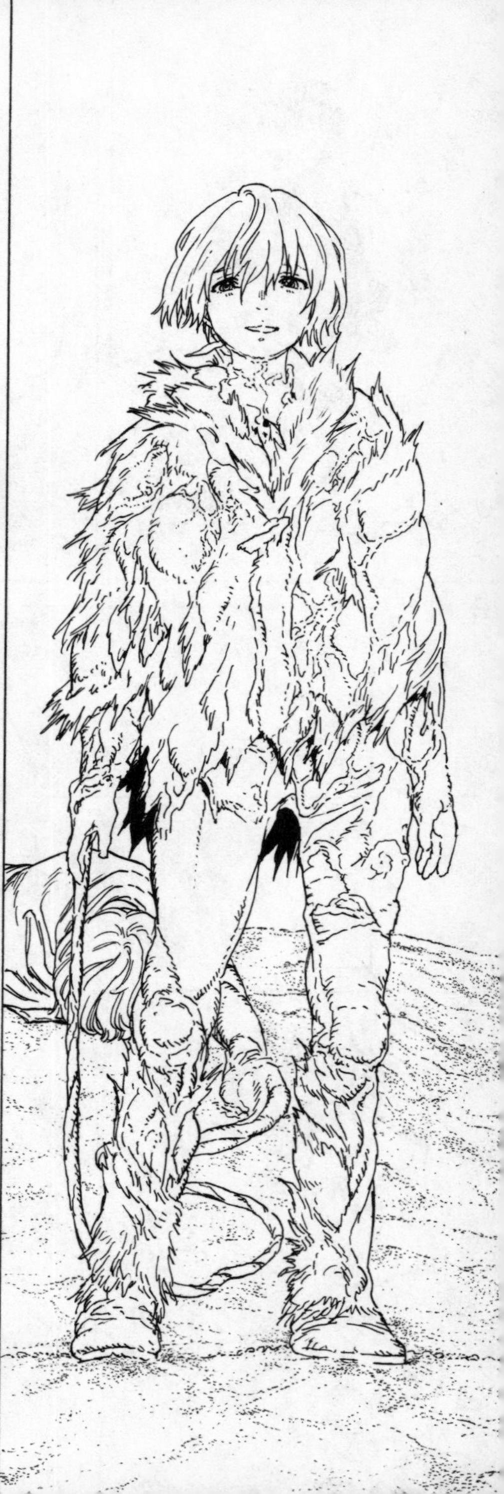

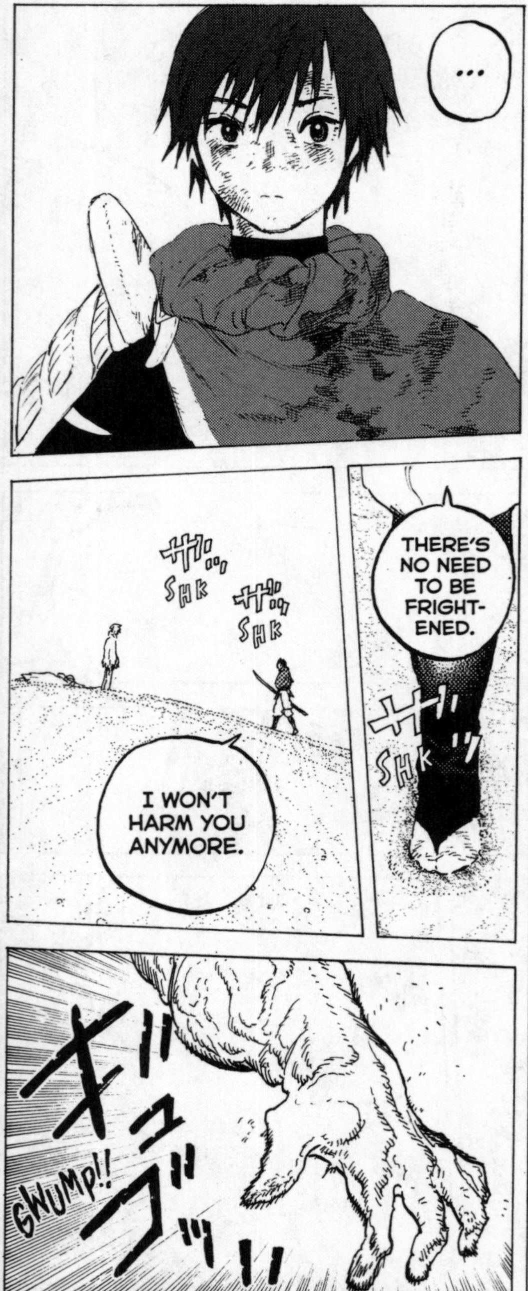

...
THERE'S NO NEED TO BE FRIGHTENED.
SHK
SHK
SHK
I WON'T HARM YOU ANYMORE.
GWUMP!!

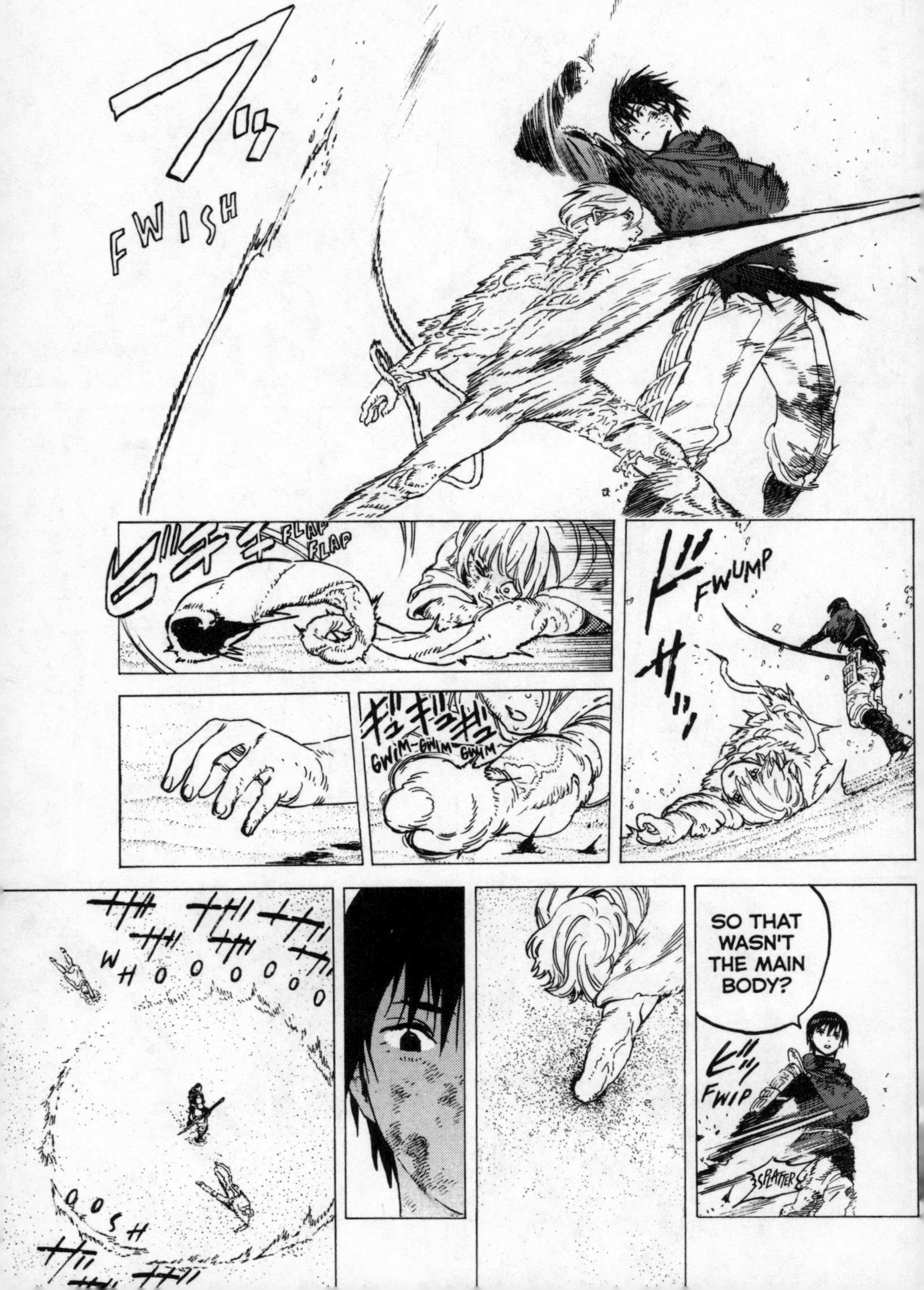
FWISH
FWUMP
FLAP FLAP
GWIM-GWIM GWIM
SO THAT WASN'T THE MAIN BODY?
FWIP
SPLATTER
WHOOOOOOO
OOSH

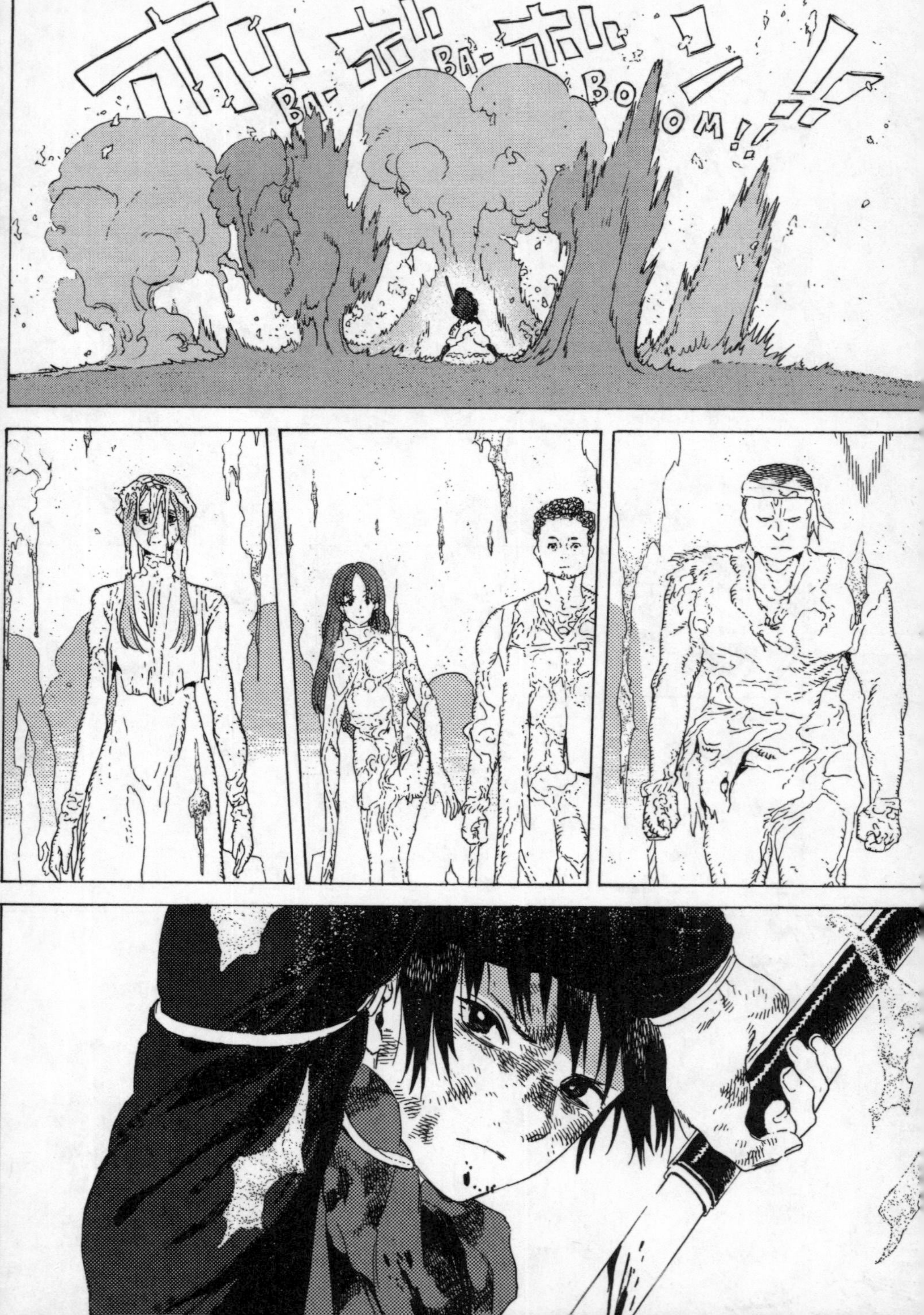
BA- BA- BOOM!!

#114 Dust and Demigods

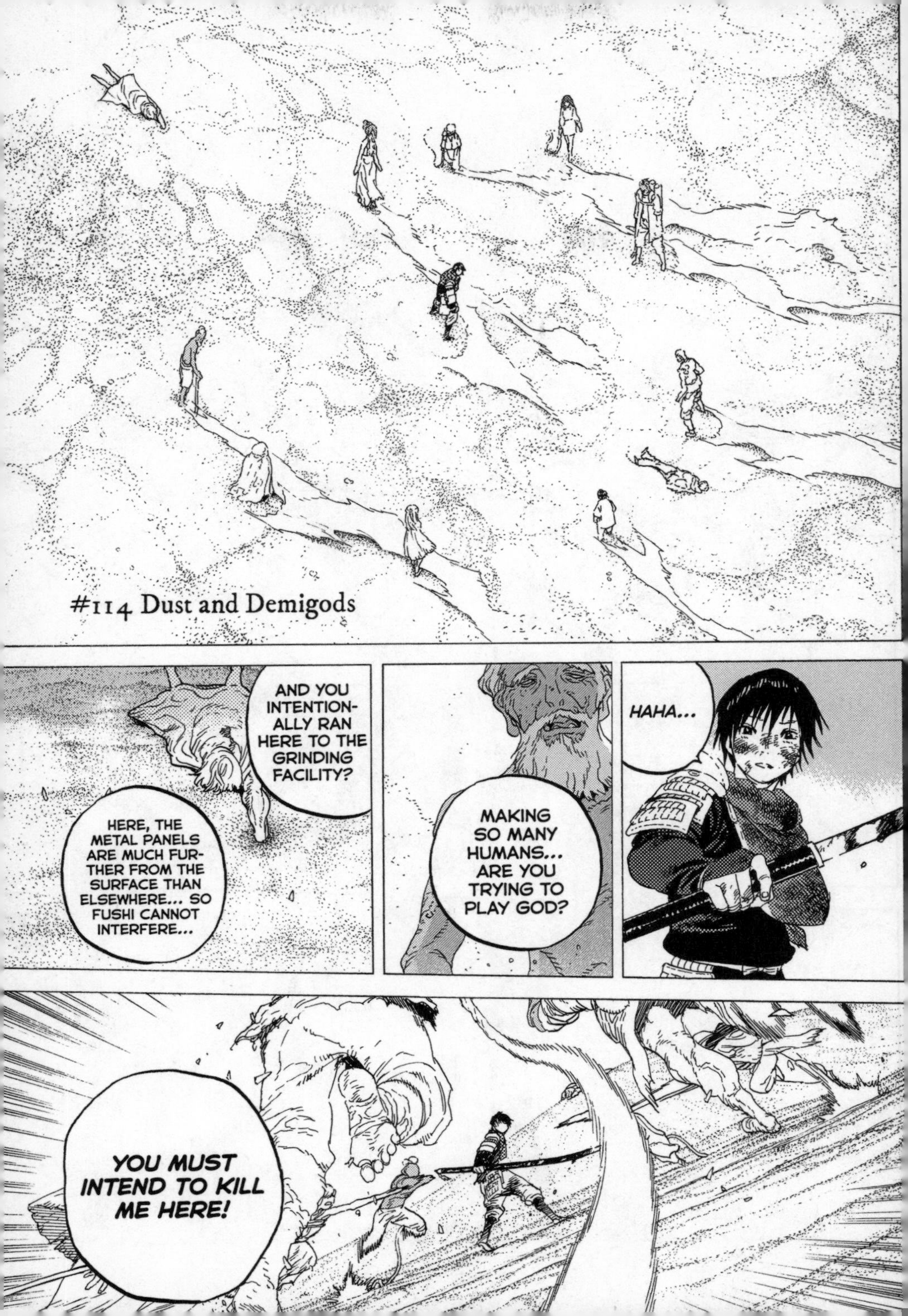
HAHA...
MAKING SO MANY HUMANS... ARE YOU TRYING TO PLAY GOD?
AND YOU INTENTIONALLY RAN HERE TO THE GRINDING FACILITY?
HERE, THE METAL PANELS ARE MUCH FURTHER FROM THE SURFACE THAN ELSEWHERE... SO FUSHI CANNOT INTERFERE...
YOU MUST INTEND TO KILL ME HERE!

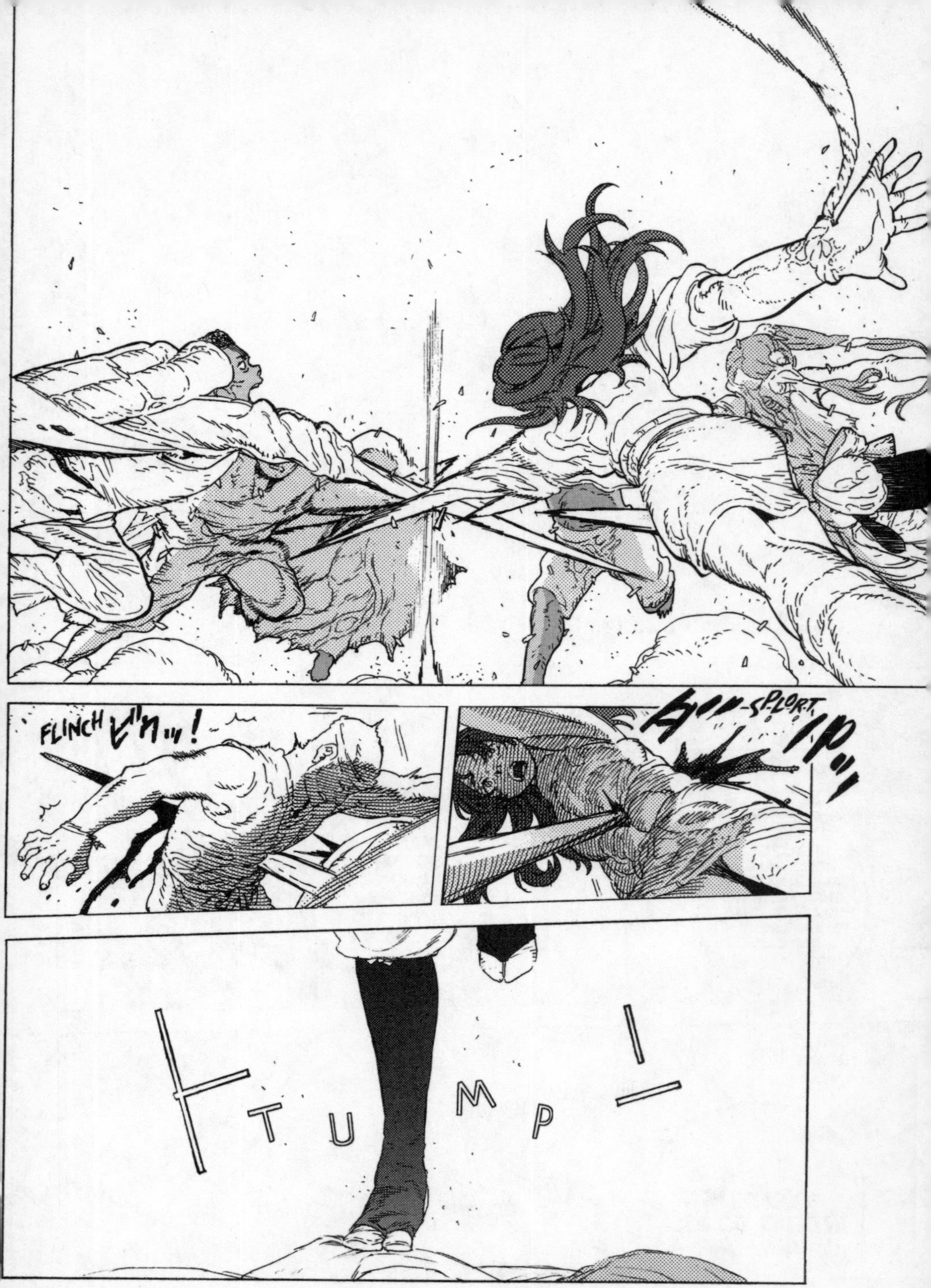
SPLORT
FLINCH ビクッ!
TUMP

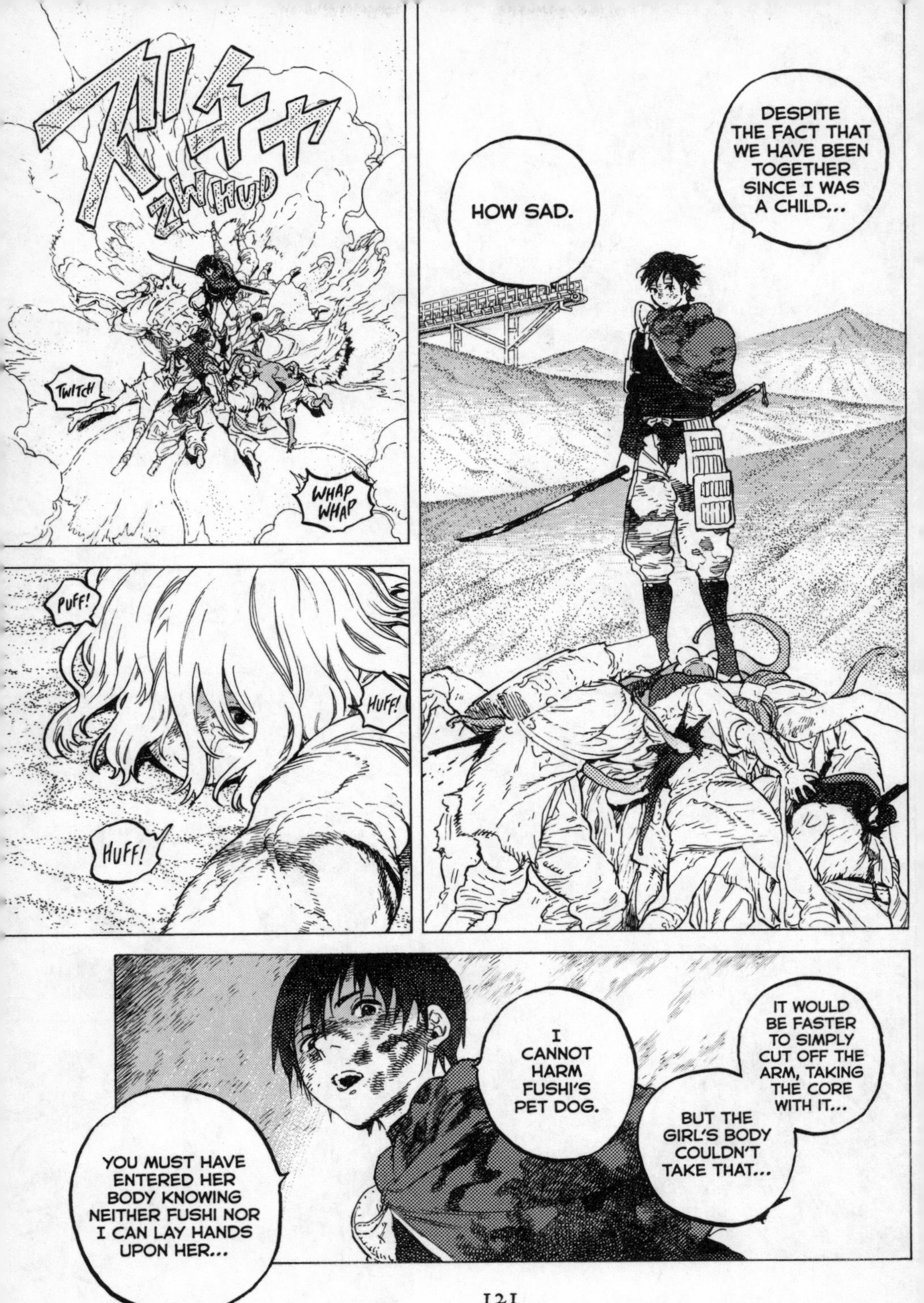
DESPITE THE FACT THAT WE HAVE BEEN TOGETHER SINCE I WAS A CHILD...
HOW SAD.
ZWHUD
TWITCH
WHAP WHAP
PUFF!
HUFF!
HUFF!
IT WOULD BE FASTER TO SIMPLY CUT OFF THE ARM, TAKING THE CORE WITH IT...
BUT THE GIRL'S BODY COULDN'T TAKE THAT...
I CANNOT HARM FUSHI'S PET DOG.
YOU MUST HAVE ENTERED HER BODY KNOWING NEITHER FUSHI NOR I CAN LAY HANDS UPON HER...

WHAM

WHACK!!

GRAB

WHOOSH

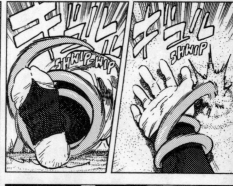

SHWIPSHWIP

SHWIP

SHLICH

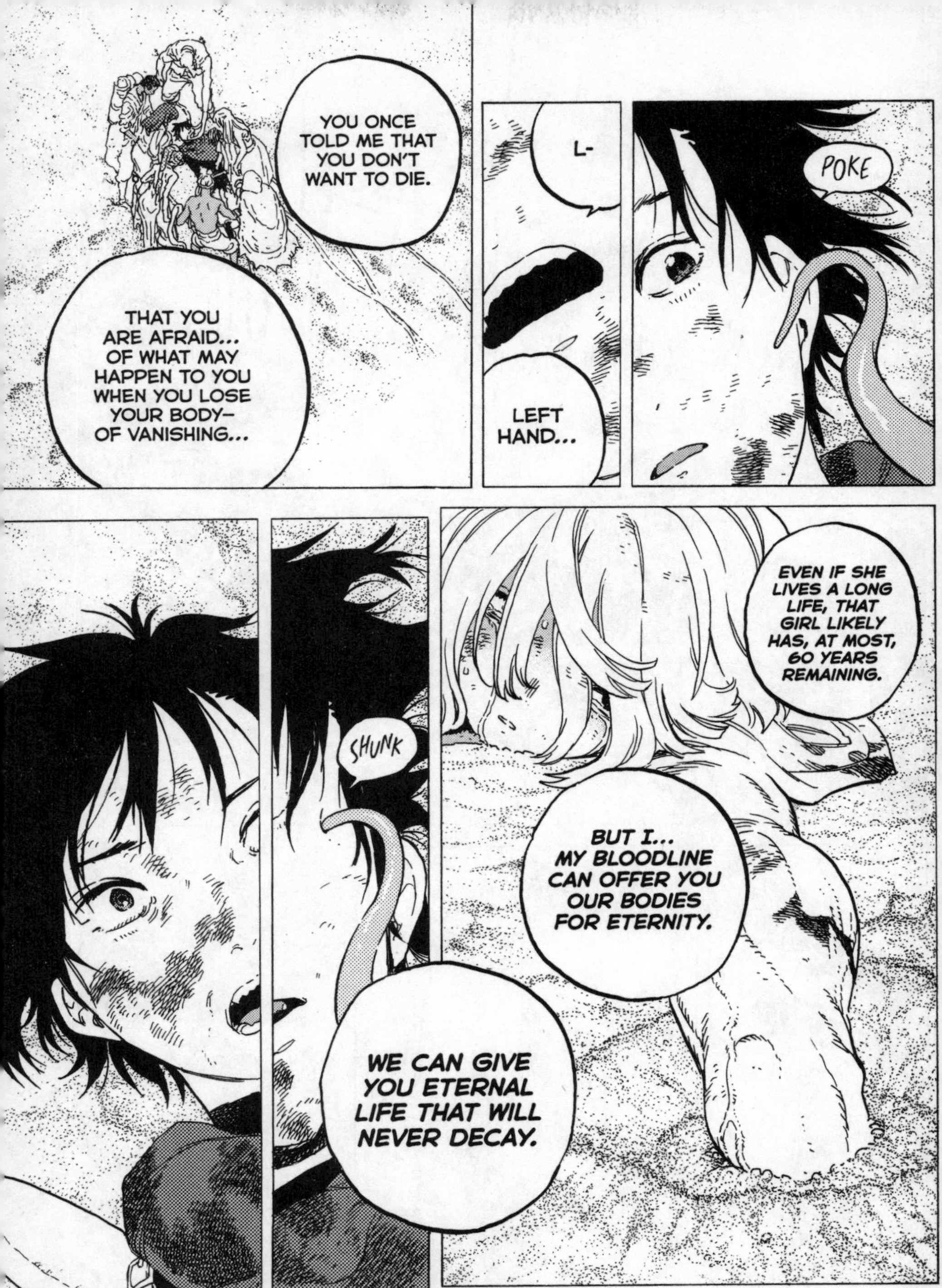
POKE
L-
LEFT HAND...
YOU ONCE TOLD ME THAT YOU DON'T WANT TO DIE.
THAT YOU ARE AFRAID... OF WHAT MAY HAPPEN TO YOU WHEN YOU LOSE YOUR BODY— OF VANISHING...
EVEN IF SHE LIVES A LONG LIFE, THAT GIRL LIKELY HAS, AT MOST, 60 YEARS REMAINING.
BUT I... MY BLOODLINE CAN OFFER YOU OUR BODIES FOR ETERNITY.
SHUNK
WE CAN GIVE YOU ETERNAL LIFE THAT WILL NEVER DECAY.

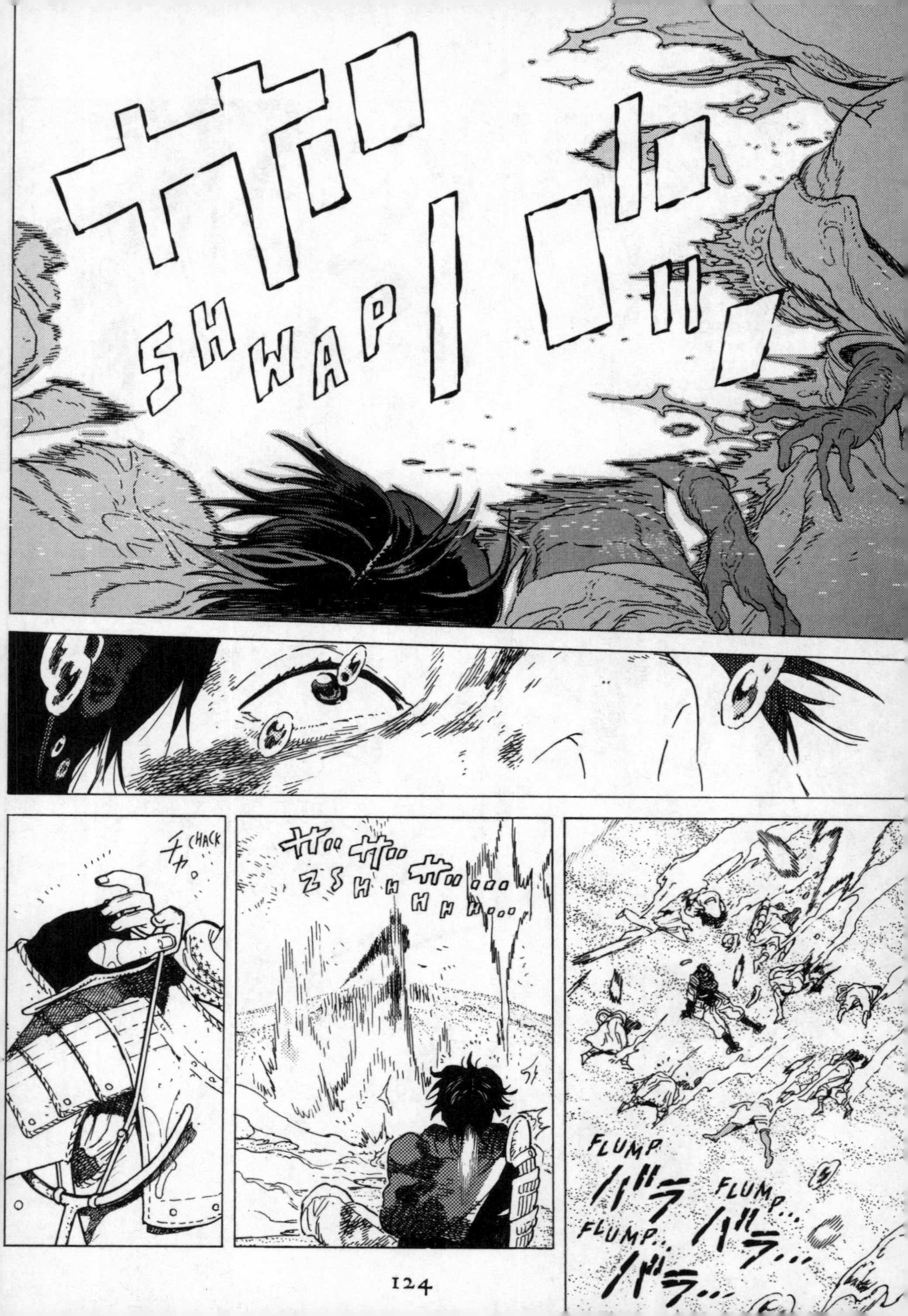
SHWAP
FLUMP
バラ
FLUMP...
バラ...
FLUMP...
バラ...
ZSHHHHHH...
CHACK
チャ。

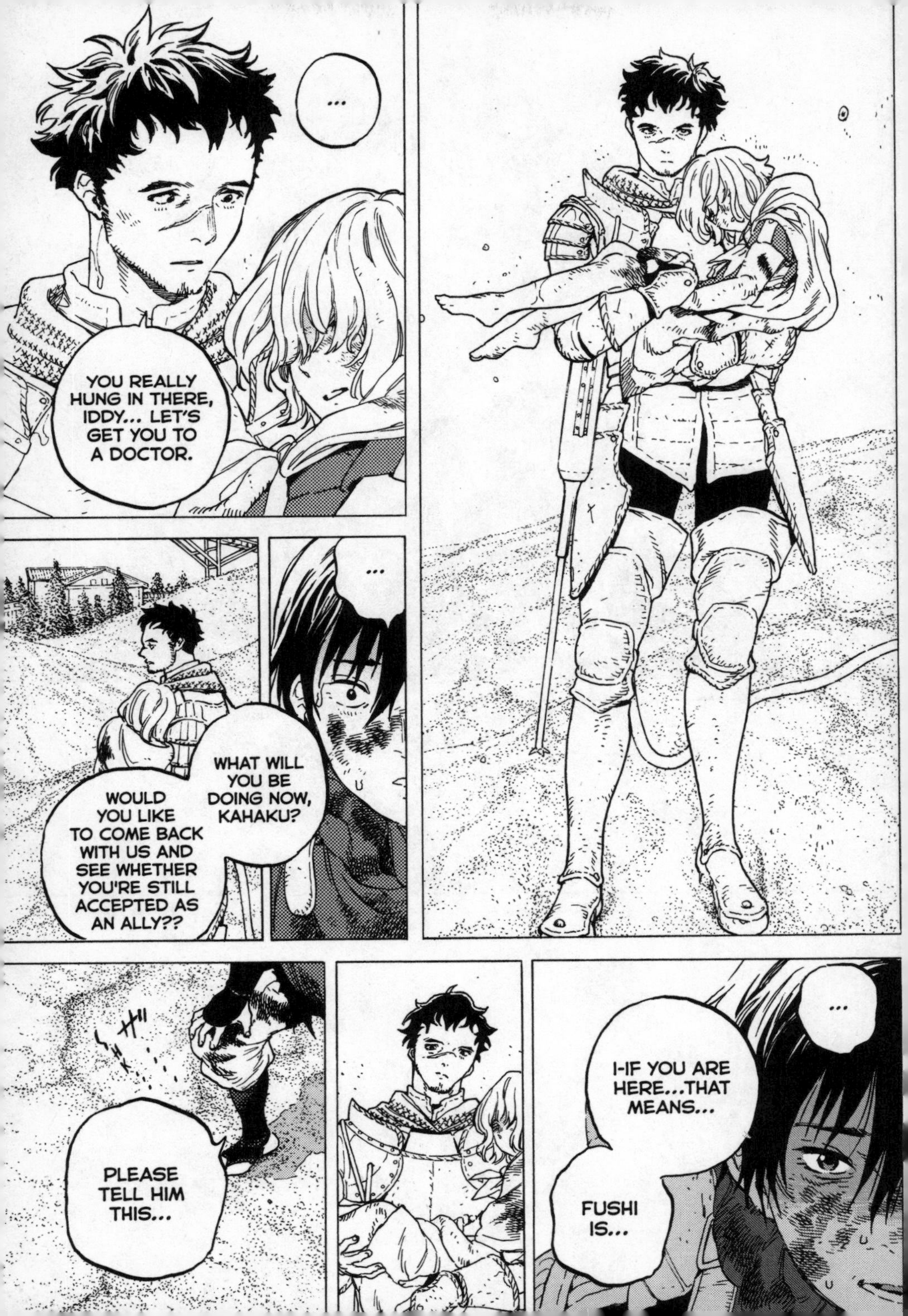
...
YOU REALLY HUNG IN THERE, IDDY... LET'S GET YOU TO A DOCTOR.
...
WHAT WILL YOU BE DOING NOW, KAHAKU?
WOULD YOU LIKE TO COME BACK WITH US AND SEE WHETHER YOU'RE STILL ACCEPTED AS AN ALLY??
...
I-IF YOU ARE HERE...THAT MEANS...
FUSHI IS...
PLEASE TELL HIM THIS...

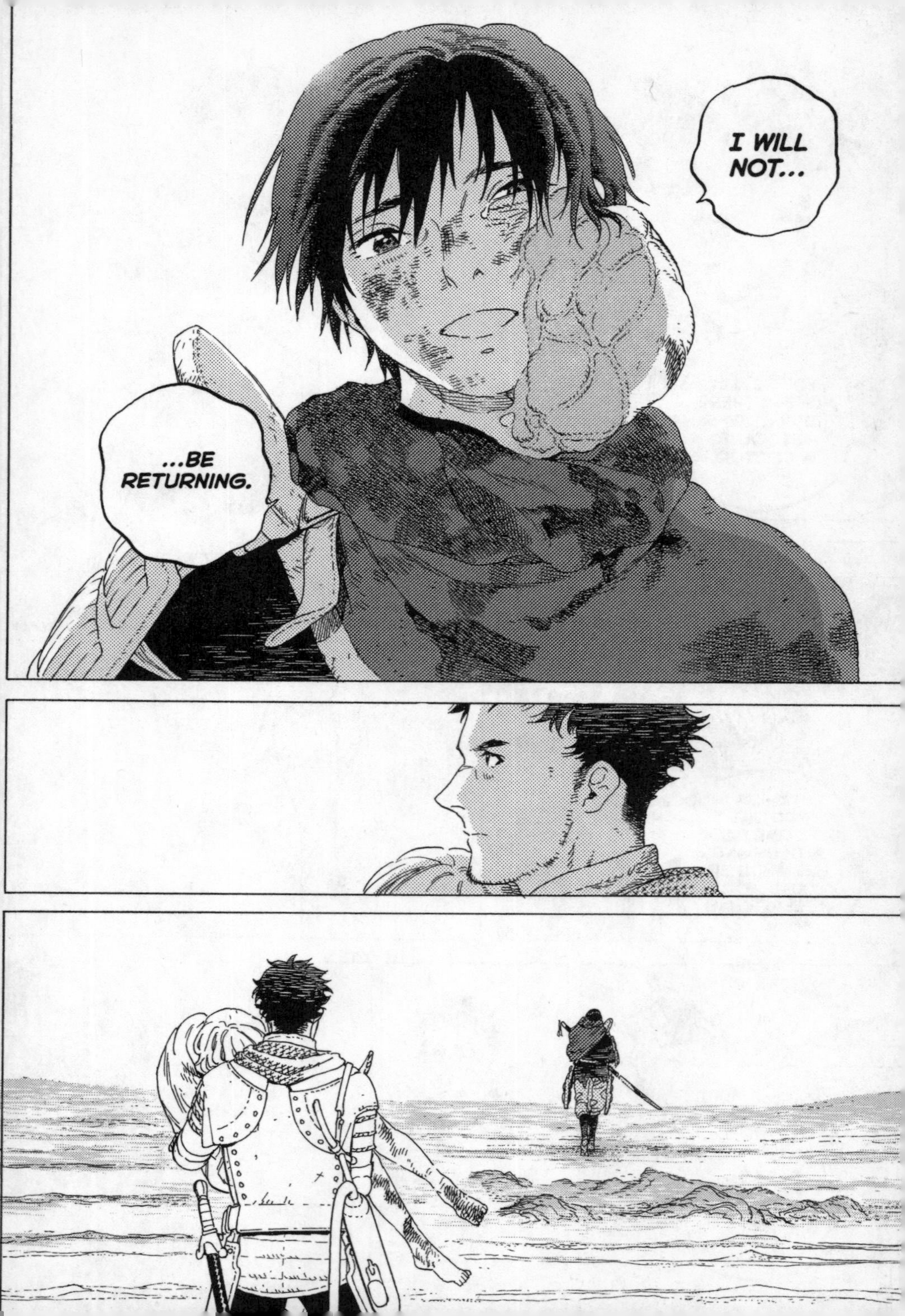
I WILL NOT...
...BE RETURNING.

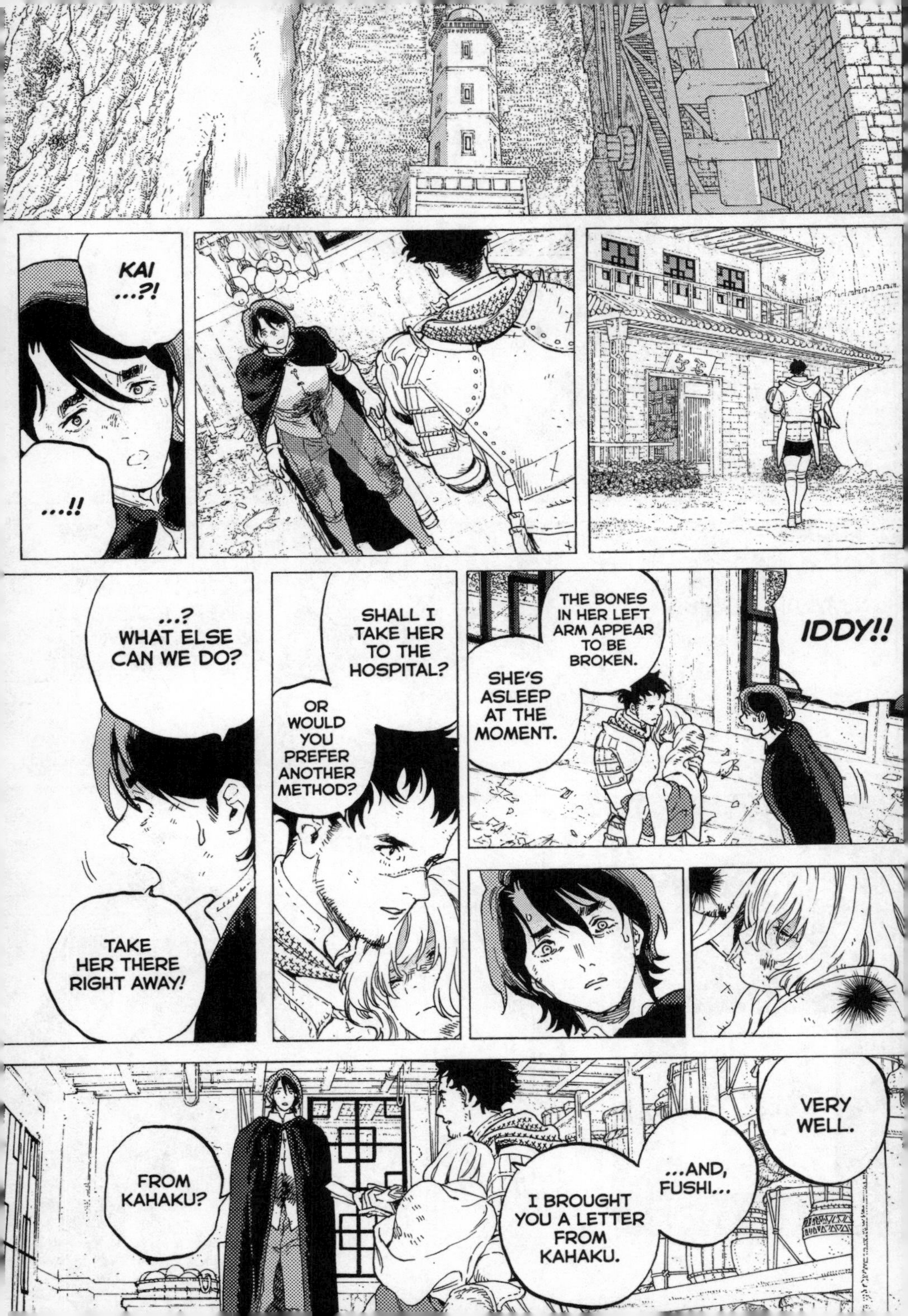
KAI ...?!
...!!
IDDY!!
THE BONES IN HER LEFT ARM APPEAR TO BE BROKEN.
SHE'S ASLEEP AT THE MOMENT.
SHALL I TAKE HER TO THE HOSPITAL?
OR WOULD YOU PREFER ANOTHER METHOD?
...? WHAT ELSE CAN WE DO?
TAKE HER THERE RIGHT AWAY!
VERY WELL.
...AND, FUSHI...
I BROUGHT YOU A LETTER FROM KAHAKU.
FROM KAHAKU?

RUSTLE

THE GUARDIANS SHALL NOW WITHDRAW FROM YOUR LIFE.

BUT SHOULD YOU HAVE NEED AGAIN, MY CLAN IN YANOME WILL HELP YOU AT ANY TIME.

FOR THESE TWO HUNDRED YEARS... WE WERE UNABLE TO DO A SINGLE THING FOR YOU...

MY APOLOGIES.

FAREWELL.

FUSHI...

...COULD HAVE KILLED KAHAKU AT ANY TIME.

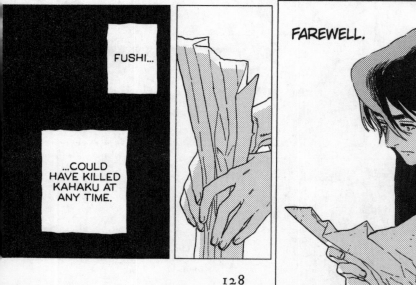

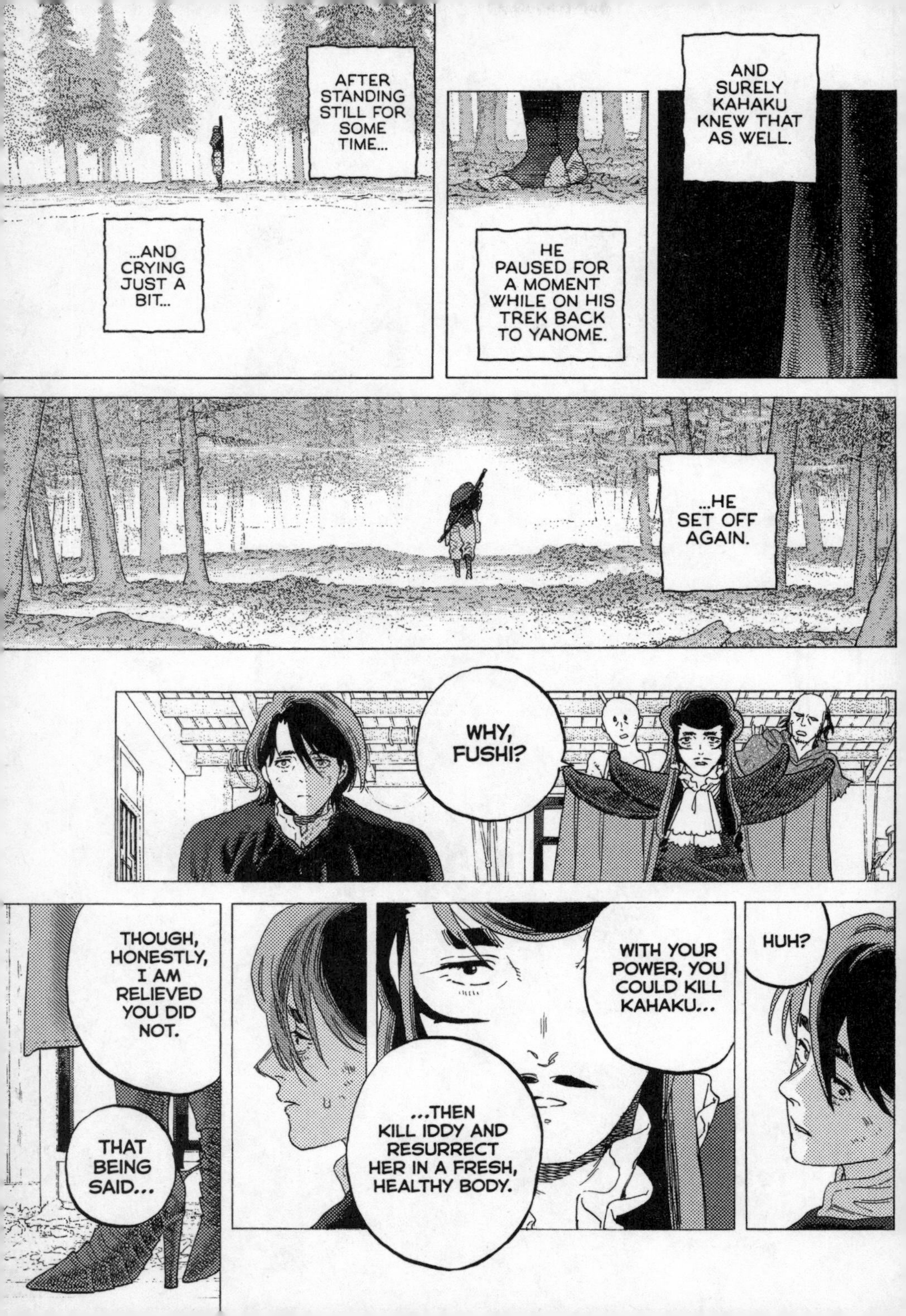
AND SURELY KAHAKU KNEW THAT AS WELL.
HE PAUSED FOR A MOMENT WHILE ON HIS TREK BACK TO YANOME.
AFTER STANDING STILL FOR SOME TIME...
...AND CRYING JUST A BIT...
...HE SET OFF AGAIN.
WHY, FUSHI?
HUH?
WITH YOUR POWER, YOU COULD KILL KAHAKU...
...THEN KILL IDDY AND RESURRECT HER IN A FRESH, HEALTHY BODY.
THOUGH, HONESTLY, I AM RELIEVED YOU DID NOT.
THAT BEING SAID...

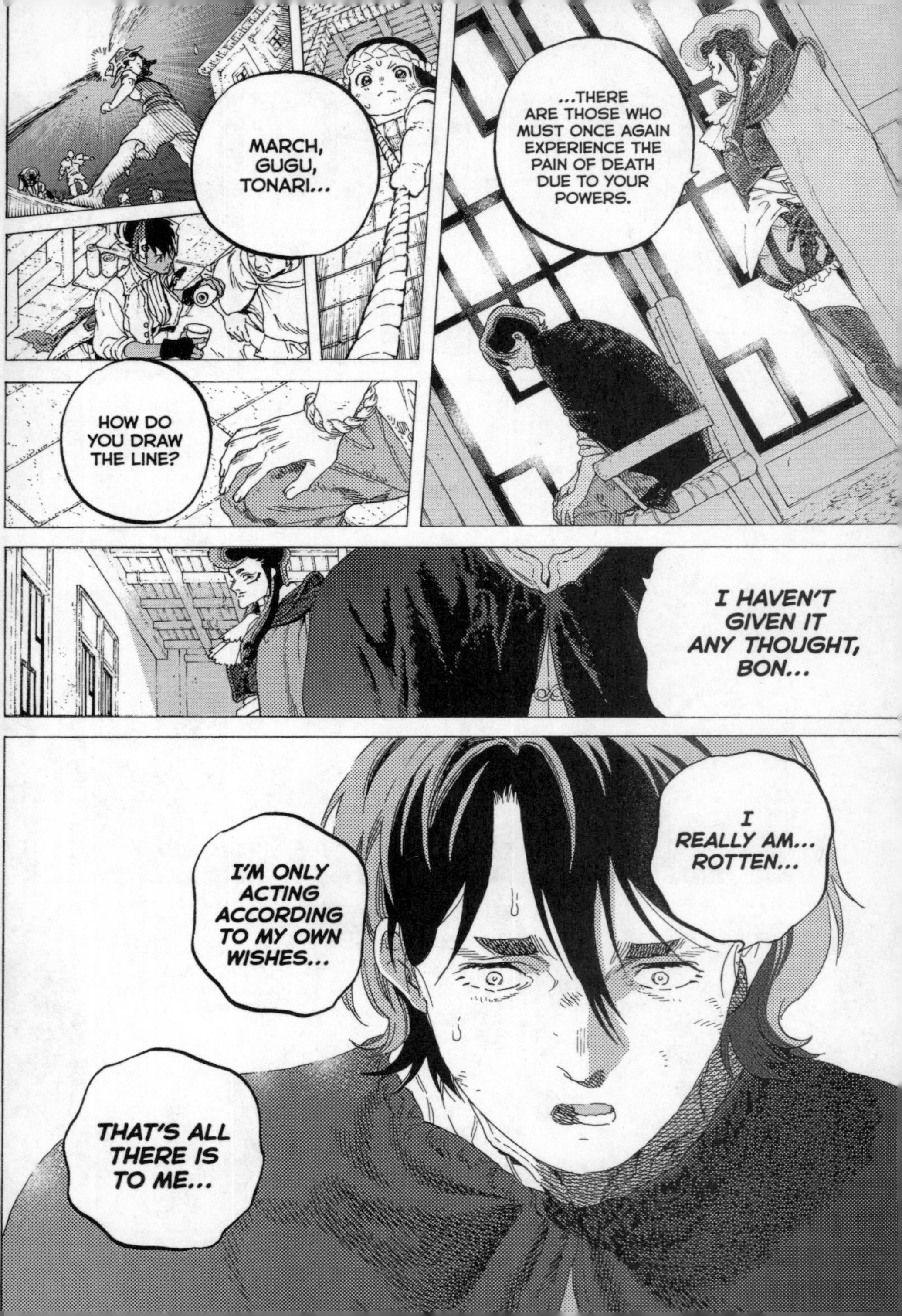
...THERE ARE THOSE WHO MUST ONCE AGAIN EXPERIENCE THE PAIN OF DEATH DUE TO YOUR POWERS.
MARCH, GUGU, TONARI...
HOW DO YOU DRAW THE LINE?
I HAVEN'T GIVEN IT ANY THOUGHT, BON...
I REALLY AM... ROTTEN...
I'M ONLY ACTING ACCORDING TO MY OWN WISHES...
THAT'S ALL THERE IS TO ME...

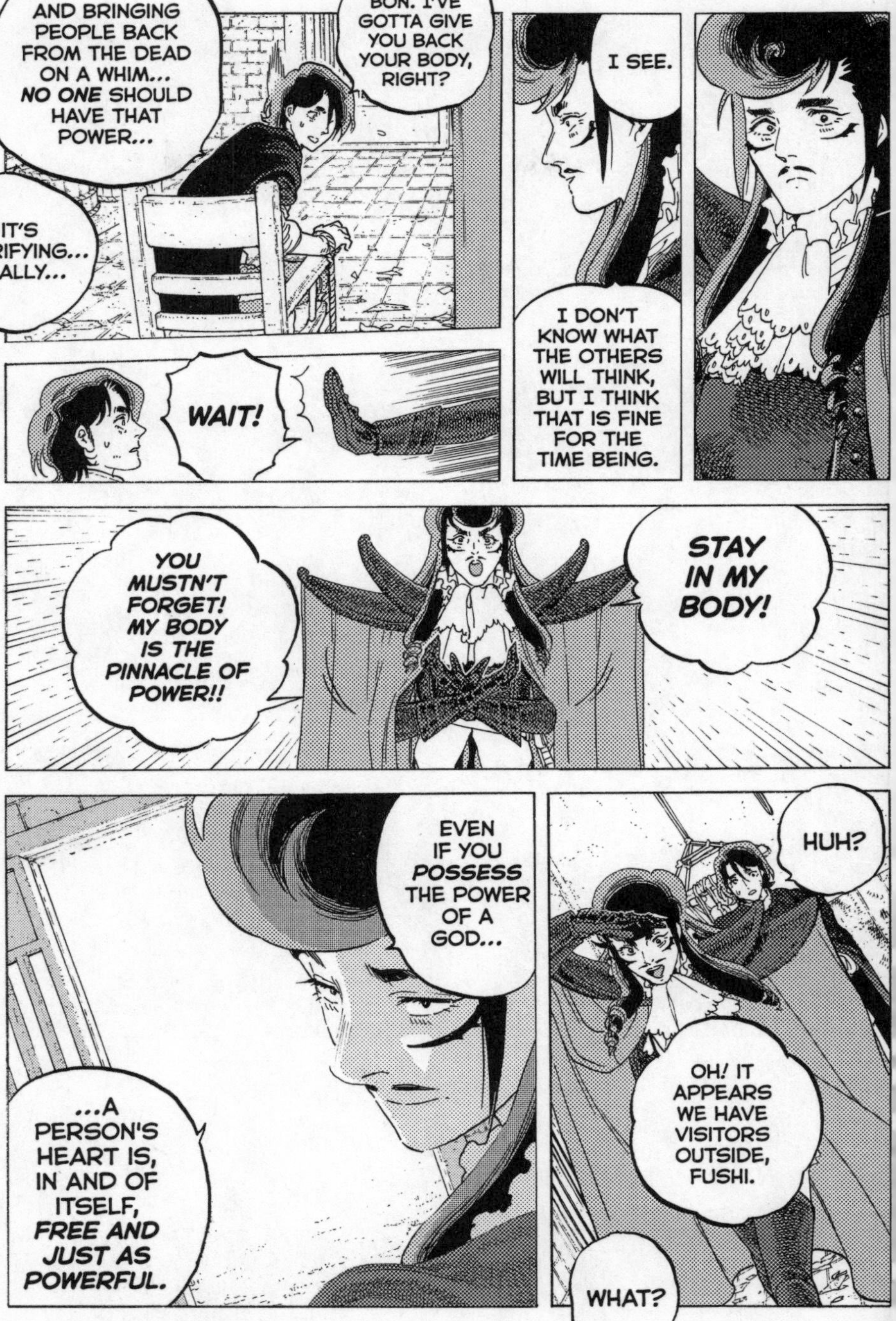
I SEE.
I DON'T KNOW WHAT THE OTHERS WILL THINK, BUT I THINK THAT IS FINE FOR THE TIME BEING.
SORRY, BON. I'VE GOTTA GIVE YOU BACK YOUR BODY, RIGHT?
AND BRINGING PEOPLE BACK FROM THE DEAD ON A WHIM... *NO ONE* SHOULD HAVE THAT POWER...
IT'S TERRIFYING... REALLY...
WAIT!
STAY IN MY BODY!
YOU MUSTN'T FORGET! MY BODY IS THE PINNACLE OF POWER!!
HUH?
OH! IT APPEARS WE HAVE VISITORS OUTSIDE, FUSHI.
WHAT?
EVEN IF YOU *POSSESS* THE POWER OF A GOD...
...A PERSON'S HEART IS, IN AND OF ITSELF, *FREE AND JUST AS POWERFUL.*

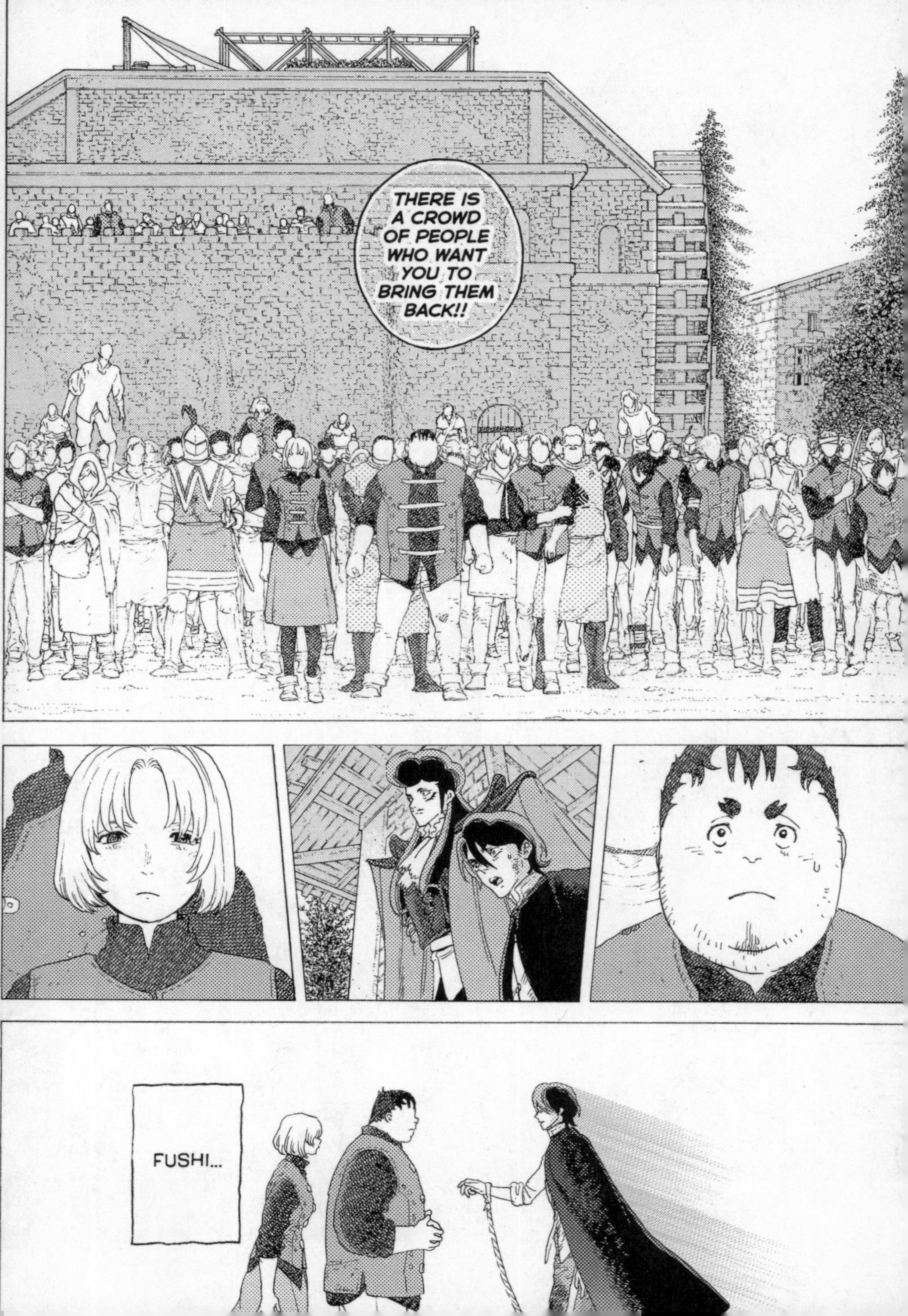
THERE IS A CROWD OF PEOPLE WHO WANT YOU TO BRING THEM BACK!!
FUSHI...

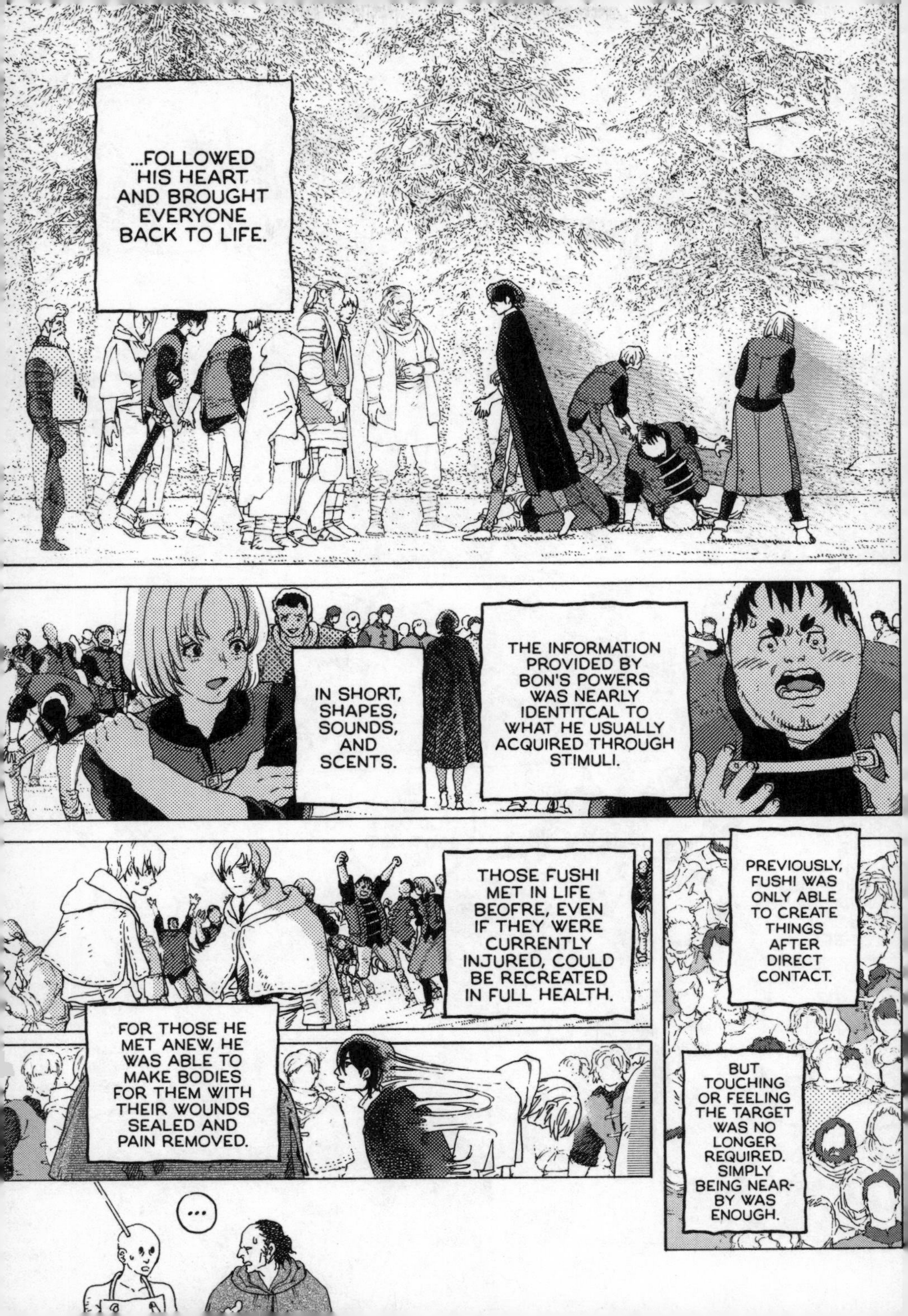
...FOLLOWED HIS HEART AND BROUGHT EVERYONE BACK TO LIFE.
THE INFORMATION PROVIDED BY BON'S POWERS WAS NEARLY IDENTITCAL TO WHAT HE USUALLY ACQUIRED THROUGH STIMULI.
IN SHORT, SHAPES, SOUNDS, AND SCENTS.
PREVIOUSLY, FUSHI WAS ONLY ABLE TO CREATE THINGS AFTER DIRECT CONTACT.
BUT TOUCHING OR FEELING THE TARGET WAS NO LONGER REQUIRED. SIMPLY BEING NEAR-BY WAS ENOUGH.
THOSE FUSHI MET IN LIFE BEOFRE, EVEN IF THEY WERE CURRENTLY INJURED, COULD BE RECREATED IN FULL HEALTH.
FOR THOSE HE MET ANEW, HE WAS ABLE TO MAKE BODIES FOR THEM WITH THEIR WOUNDS SEALED AND PAIN REMOVED.
...

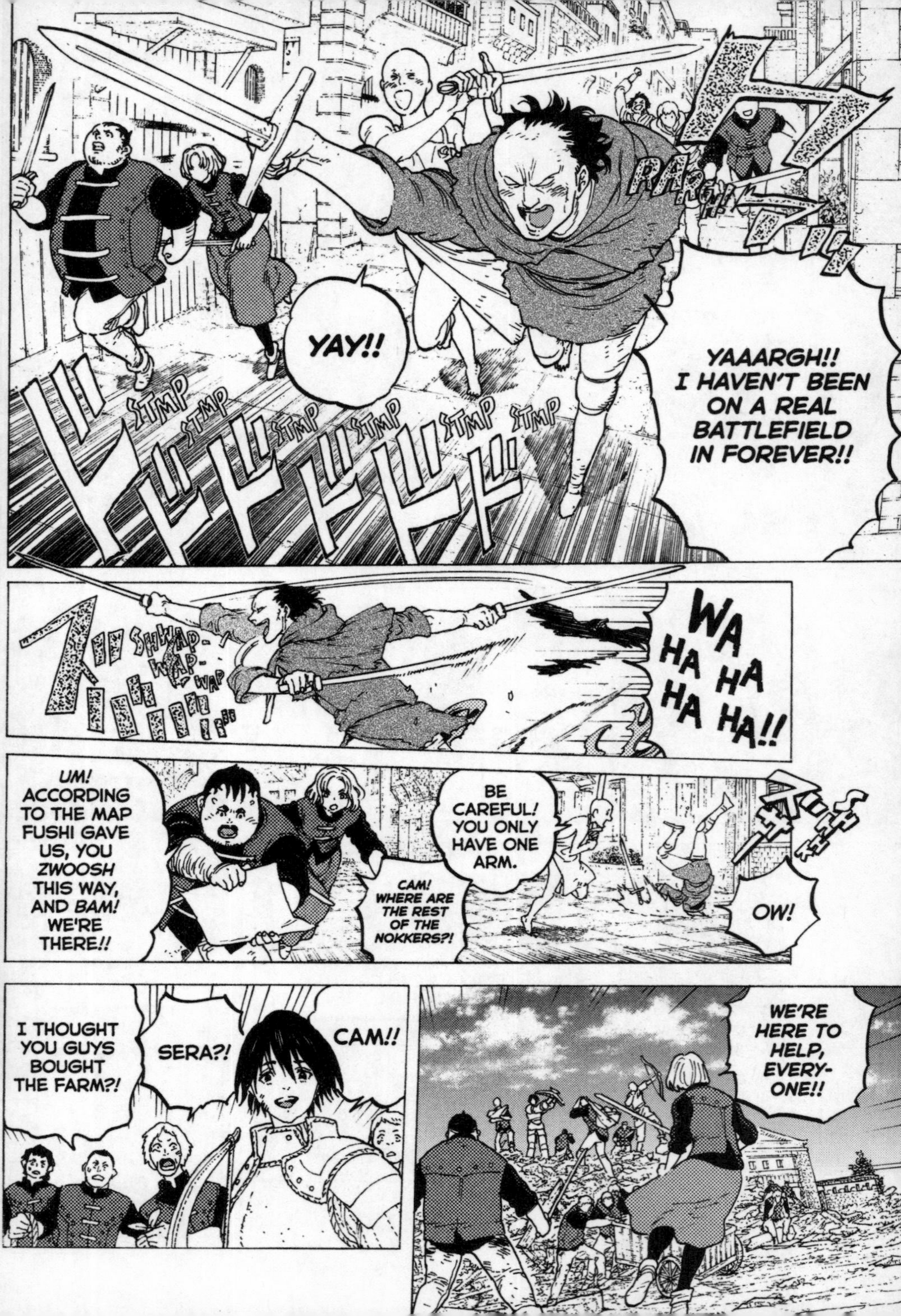
YAAARGH!! I HAVEN'T BEEN ON A REAL BATTLEFIELD IN FOREVER!!
YAY!!
STMP STMP STMP STMP STMP STMP
WA HA HA HA HA HA!!
SHWAP-WAP-WAP
OW!
BE CAREFUL! YOU ONLY HAVE ONE ARM.
CAM! WHERE ARE THE REST OF THE NOKKERS?!
UM! ACCORDING TO THE MAP FUSHI GAVE US, YOU *ZWOOSH* THIS WAY, AND *BAM!* WE'RE THERE!!
WE'RE HERE TO HELP, EVERYONE!!
CAM!!
SERA?!
I THOUGHT YOU GUYS BOUGHT THE FARM?!

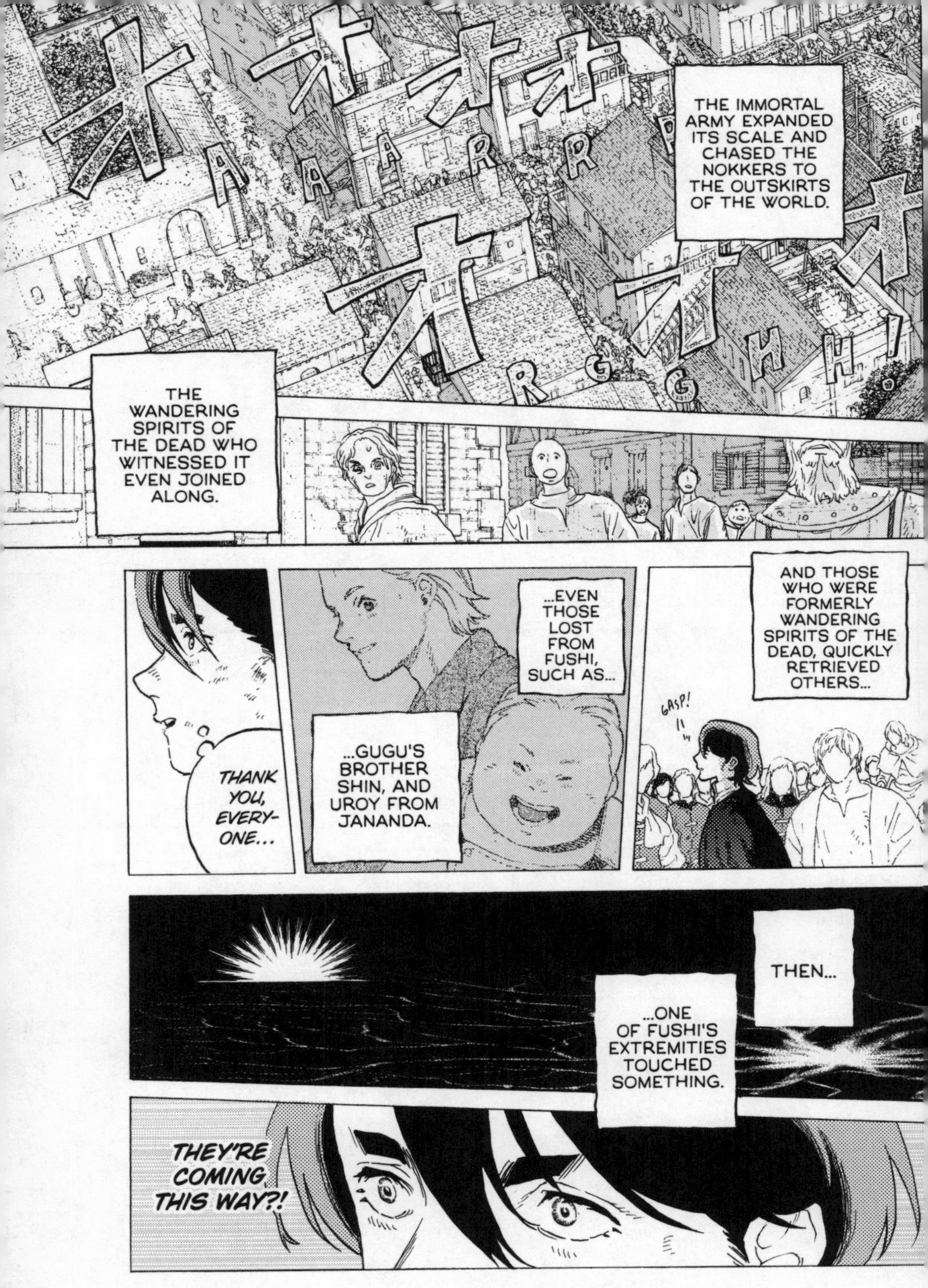
THE IMMORTAL ARMY EXPANDED ITS SCALE AND CHASED THE NOKKERS TO THE OUTSKIRTS OF THE WORLD.
AAARRRRGGHH!
THE WANDERING SPIRITS OF THE DEAD WHO WITNESSED IT EVEN JOINED ALONG.
AND THOSE WHO WERE FORMERLY WANDERING SPIRITS OF THE DEAD, QUICKLY RETRIEVED OTHERS...
GASP!
...EVEN THOSE LOST FROM FUSHI, SUCH AS...
...GUGU'S BROTHER SHIN, AND UROY FROM JANANDA.
THANK YOU, EVERY-ONE...
THEN...
...ONE OF FUSHI'S EXTREMITIES TOUCHED SOMETHING.
THEY'RE COMING THIS WAY?!

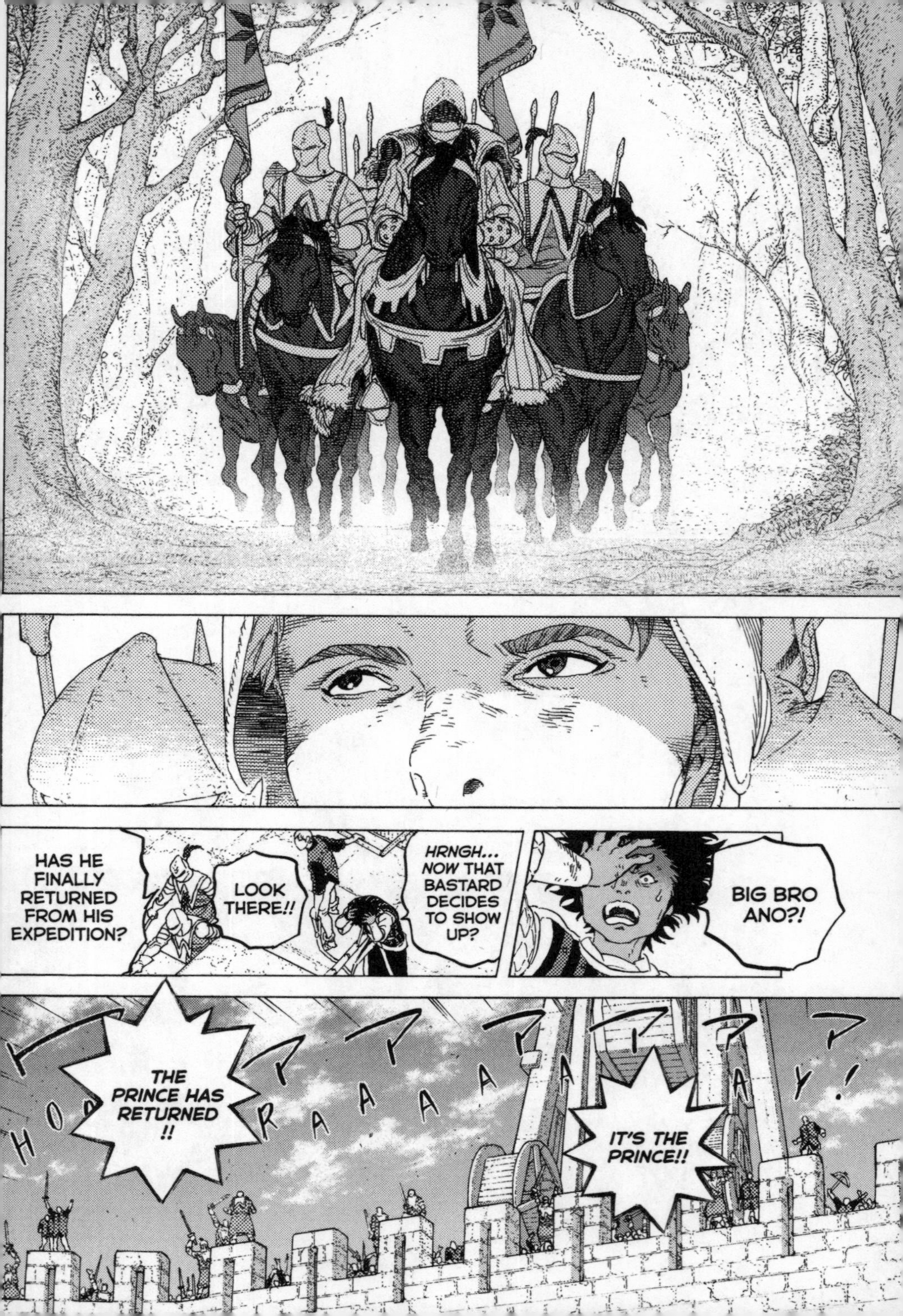
BIG BRO ANO?!
HRNGH... NOW THAT BASTARD DECIDES TO SHOW UP?
LOOK THERE!!
HAS HE FINALLY RETURNED FROM HIS EXPEDITION?
HOORAAAAAY!
IT'S THE PRINCE!!
THE PRINCE HAS RETURNED!!

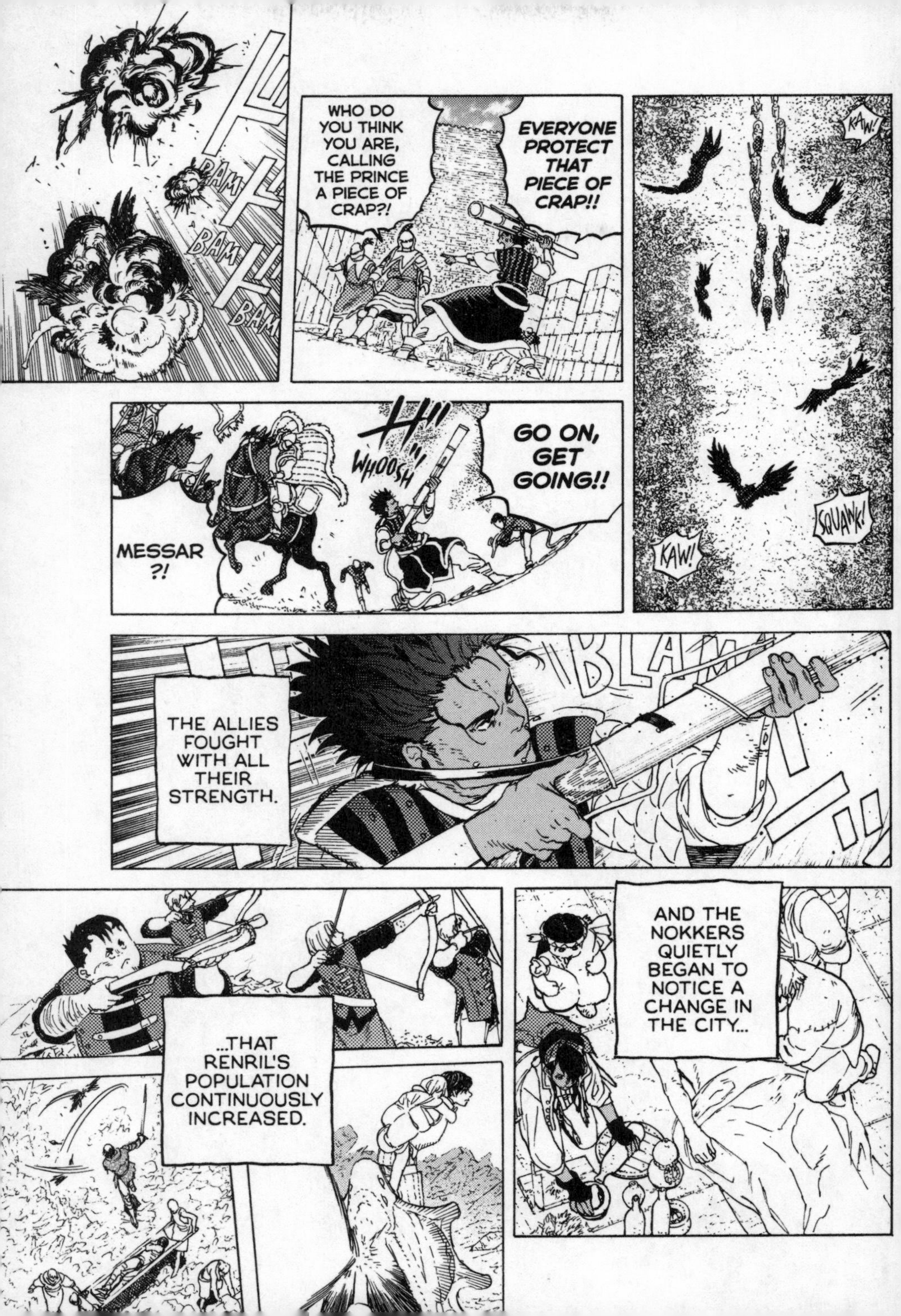
KAW!
SQUAWK!
KAW!
EVERYONE PROTECT THAT PIECE OF CRAP!!
WHO DO YOU THINK YOU ARE, CALLING THE PRINCE A PIECE OF CRAP?!
BAM
BAM
BAM
GO ON, GET GOING!!
WHOOSH
MESSAR ?!
BLAM
THE ALLIES FOUGHT WITH ALL THEIR STRENGTH.
AND THE NOKKERS QUIETLY BEGAN TO NOTICE A CHANGE IN THE CITY...
...THAT RENRIL'S POPULATION CONTINUOUSLY INCREASED.

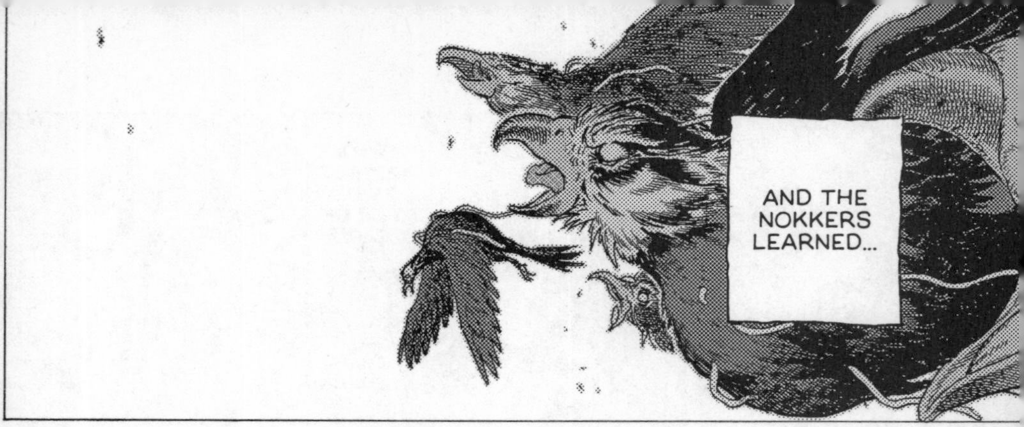
AND THE NOKKERS LEARNED...
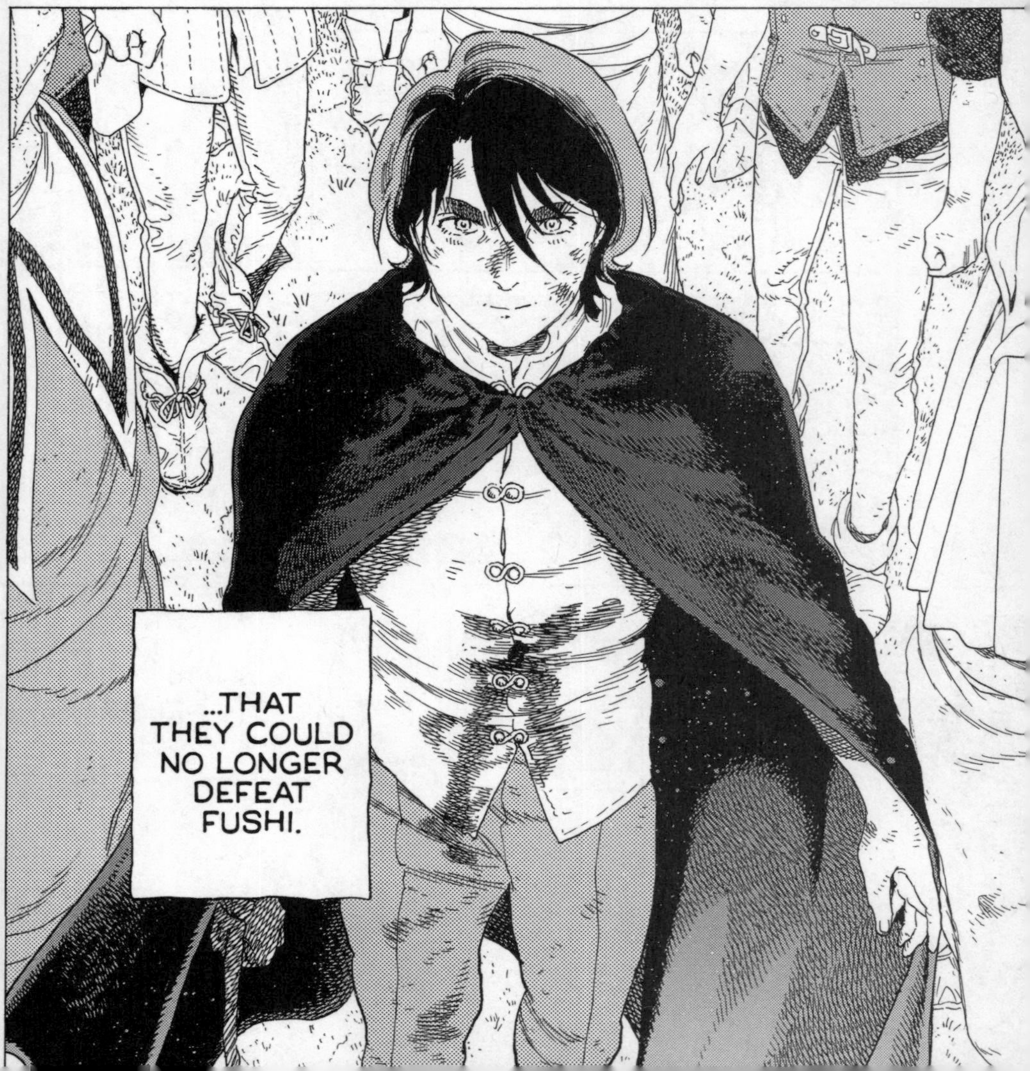
...THAT THEY COULD NO LONGER DEFEAT FUSHI.

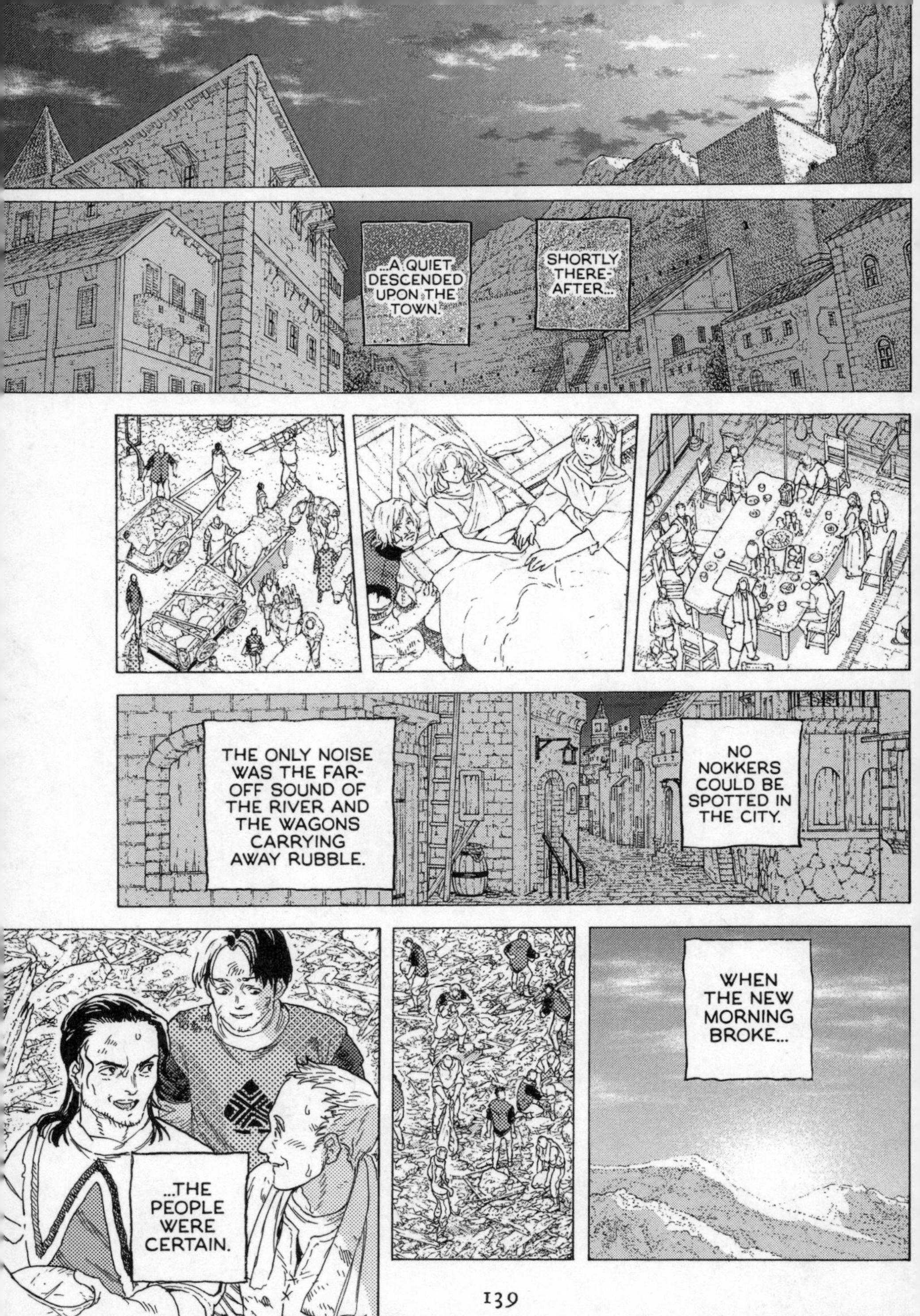

SHORTLY THERE-AFTER...
...A QUIET DESCENDED UPON THE TOWN.
NO NOKKERS COULD BE SPOTTED IN THE CITY.
THE ONLY NOISE WAS THE FAR-OFF SOUND OF THE RIVER AND THE WAGONS CARRYING AWAY RUBBLE.
WHEN THE NEW MORNING BROKE...
...THE PEOPLE WERE CERTAIN.

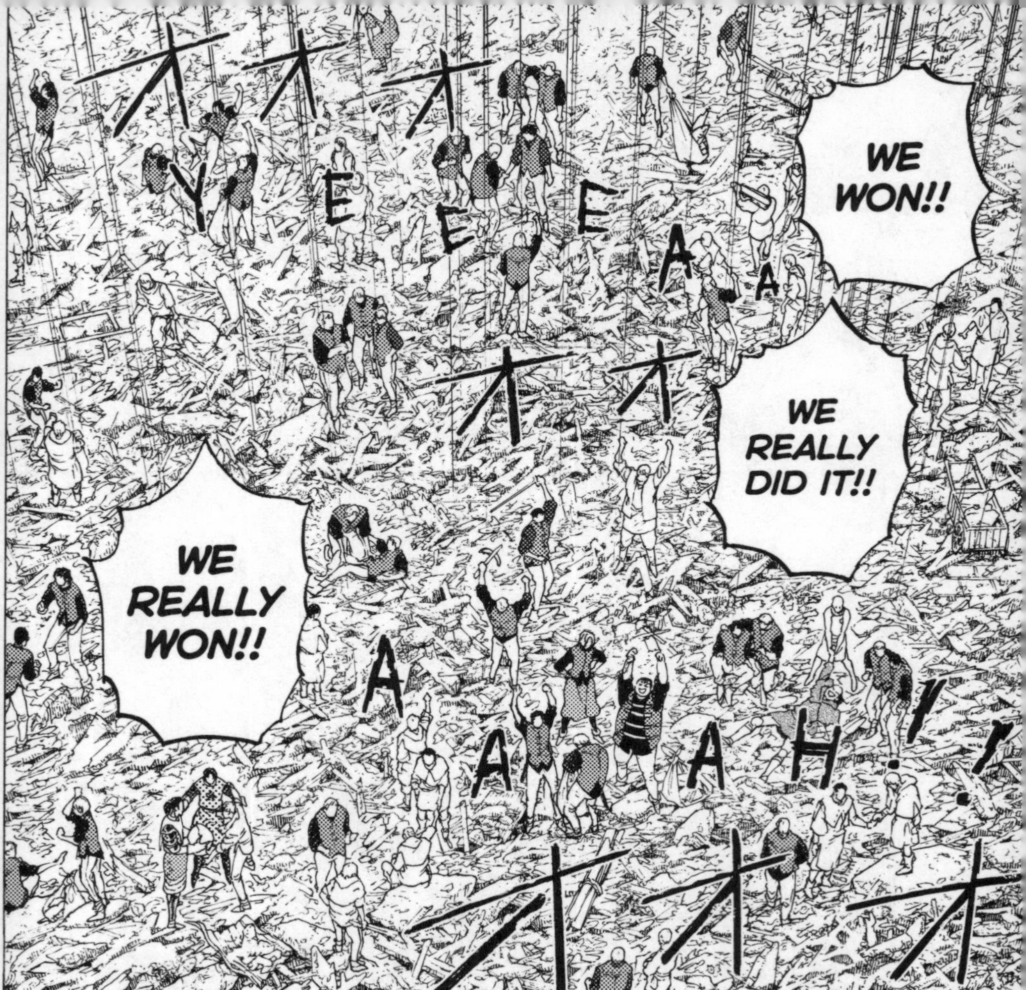
オオオ
YEEEAAAAAH!!
オオ
オオオ
WE WON!!
WE REALLY DID IT!!
WE REALLY WON!!
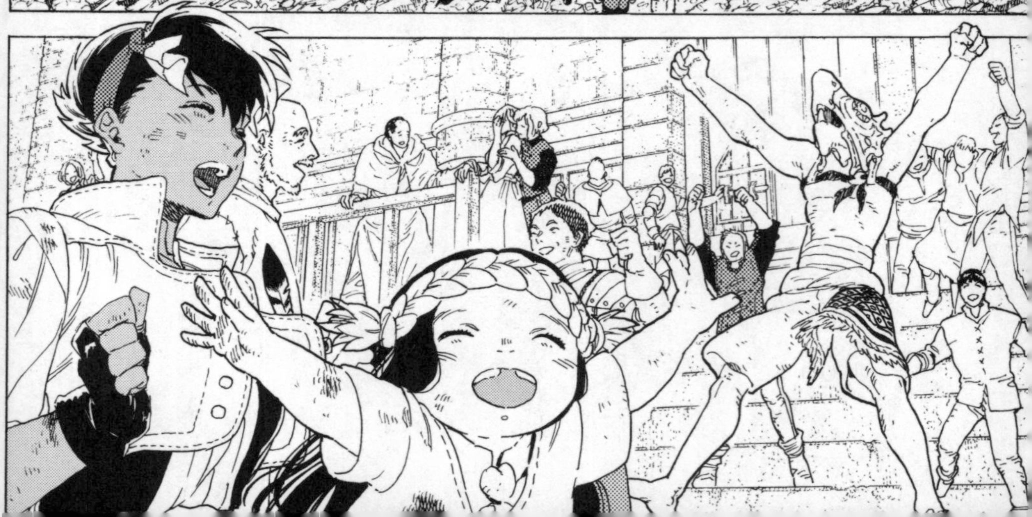

TO YOUR ETERNITY

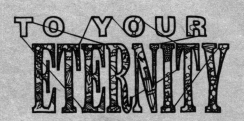

TO YOUR
ETERNITY

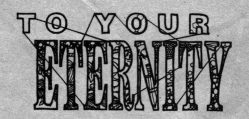

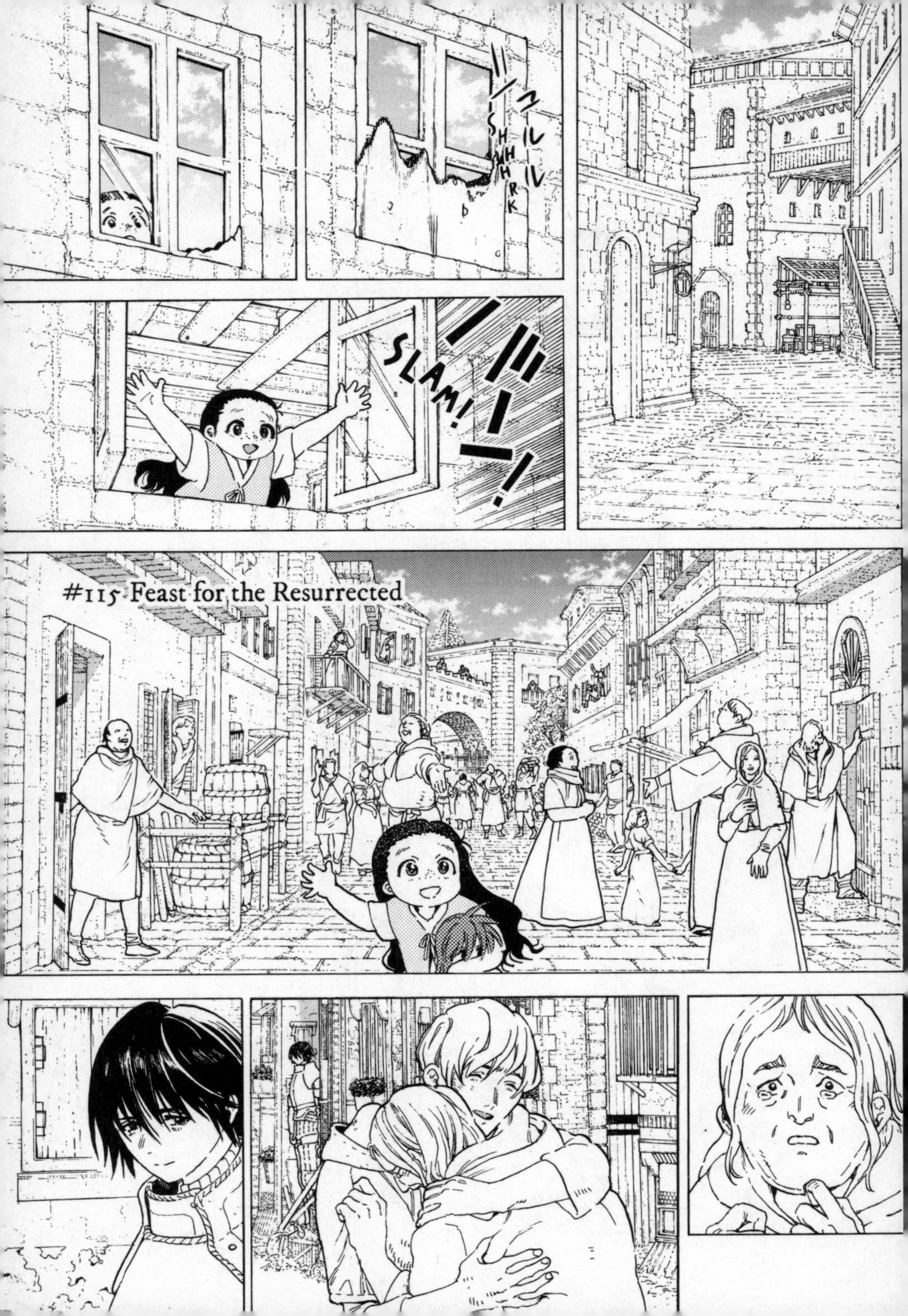
SHHHRK
SLAM!
#115 Feast for the Resurrected

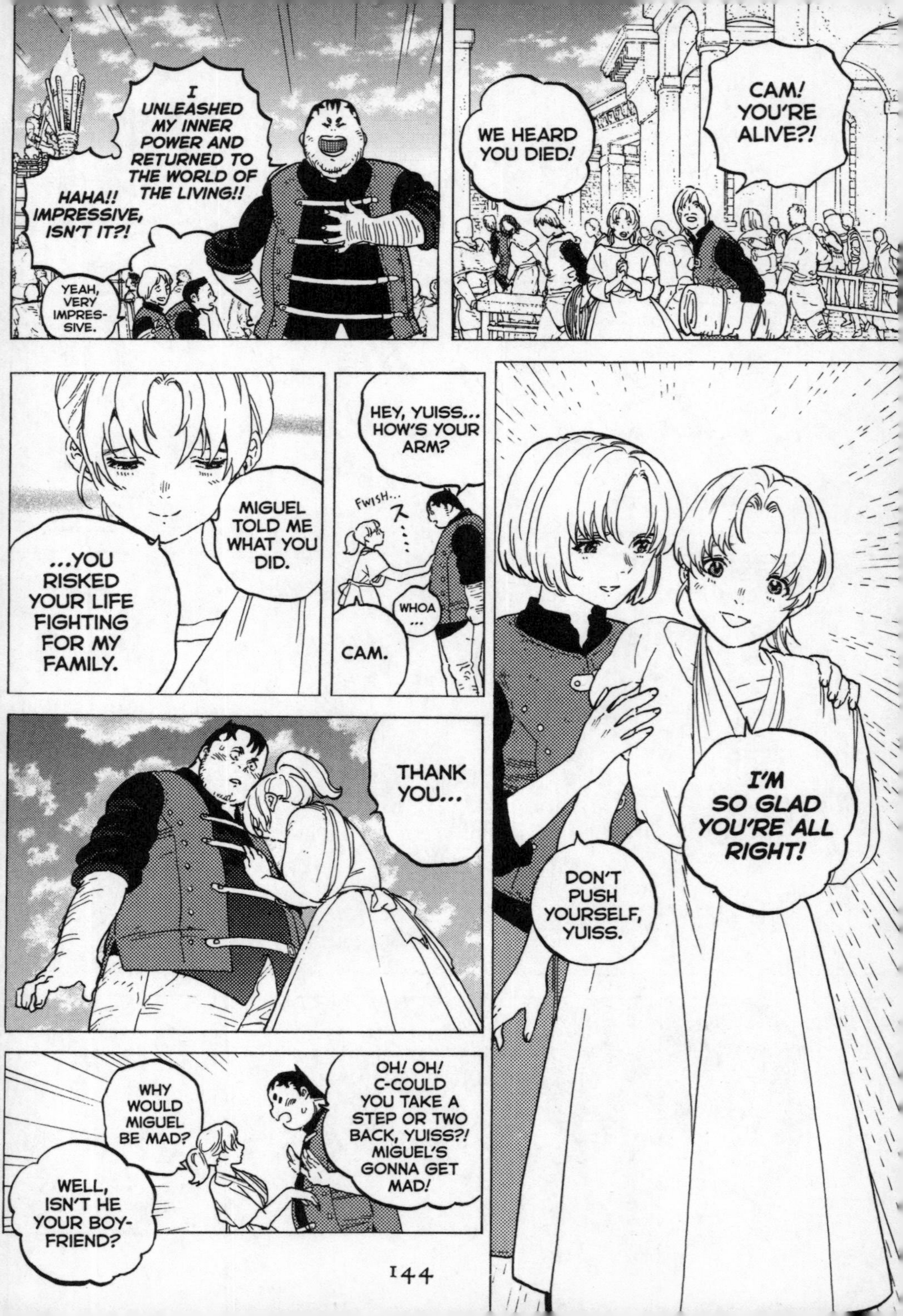
CAM! YOU'RE ALIVE?!
WE HEARD YOU DIED!
I UNLEASHED MY INNER POWER AND RETURNED TO THE WORLD OF THE LIVING!!
HAHA!! IMPRESSIVE, ISN'T IT?!
YEAH, VERY IMPRES- SIVE.
I'M SO GLAD YOU'RE ALL RIGHT!
DON'T PUSH YOURSELF, YUISS.
HEY, YUISS... HOW'S YOUR ARM?
FWISH...
WHOA ...
CAM.
MIGUEL TOLD ME WHAT YOU DID.
...YOU RISKED YOUR LIFE FIGHTING FOR MY FAMILY.
THANK YOU...
OH! OH! C-COULD YOU TAKE A STEP OR TWO BACK, YUISS?! MIGUEL'S GONNA GET MAD!
WHY WOULD MIGUEL BE MAD?
WELL, ISN'T HE YOUR BOY- FRIEND?

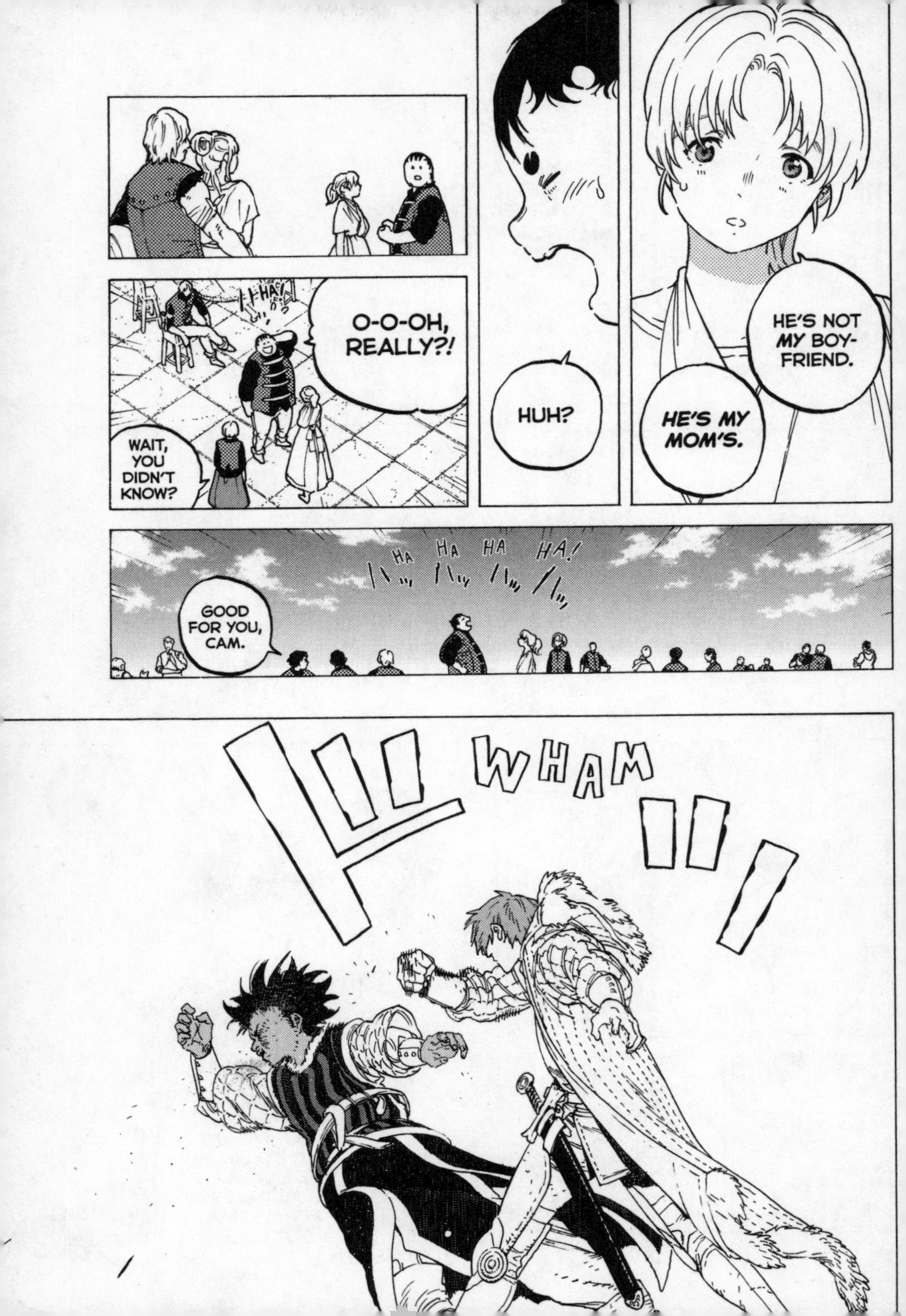
HE'S NOT MY BOY-FRIEND.
HE'S MY MOM'S.
HUH?
O-O-OH, REALLY?!
HA!
WAIT, YOU DIDN'T KNOW?
HA HA HA HA!
GOOD FOR YOU, CAM.
WHAM

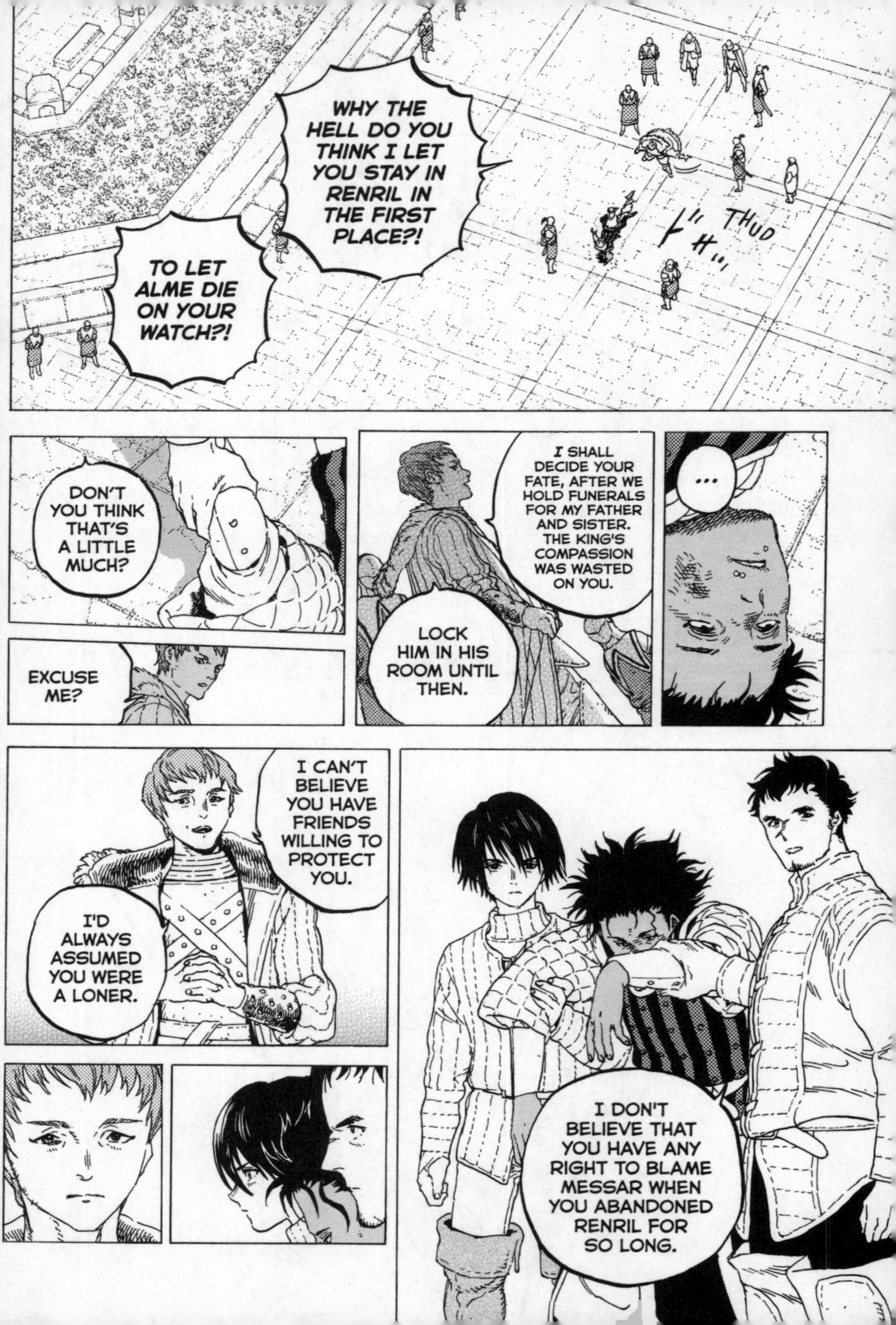
WHY THE HELL DO YOU THINK I LET YOU STAY IN RENRIL IN THE FIRST PLACE?!
TO LET ALME DIE ON YOUR WATCH?!
THUD
...
I SHALL DECIDE YOUR FATE, AFTER WE HOLD FUNERALS FOR MY FATHER AND SISTER. THE KING'S COMPASSION WAS WASTED ON YOU.
LOCK HIM IN HIS ROOM UNTIL THEN.
DON'T YOU THINK THAT'S A LITTLE MUCH?
EXCUSE ME?
I DON'T BELIEVE THAT YOU HAVE ANY RIGHT TO BLAME MESSAR WHEN YOU ABANDONED RENRIL FOR SO LONG.
I CAN'T BELIEVE YOU HAVE FRIENDS WILLING TO PROTECT YOU.
I'D ALWAYS ASSUMED YOU WERE A LONER.

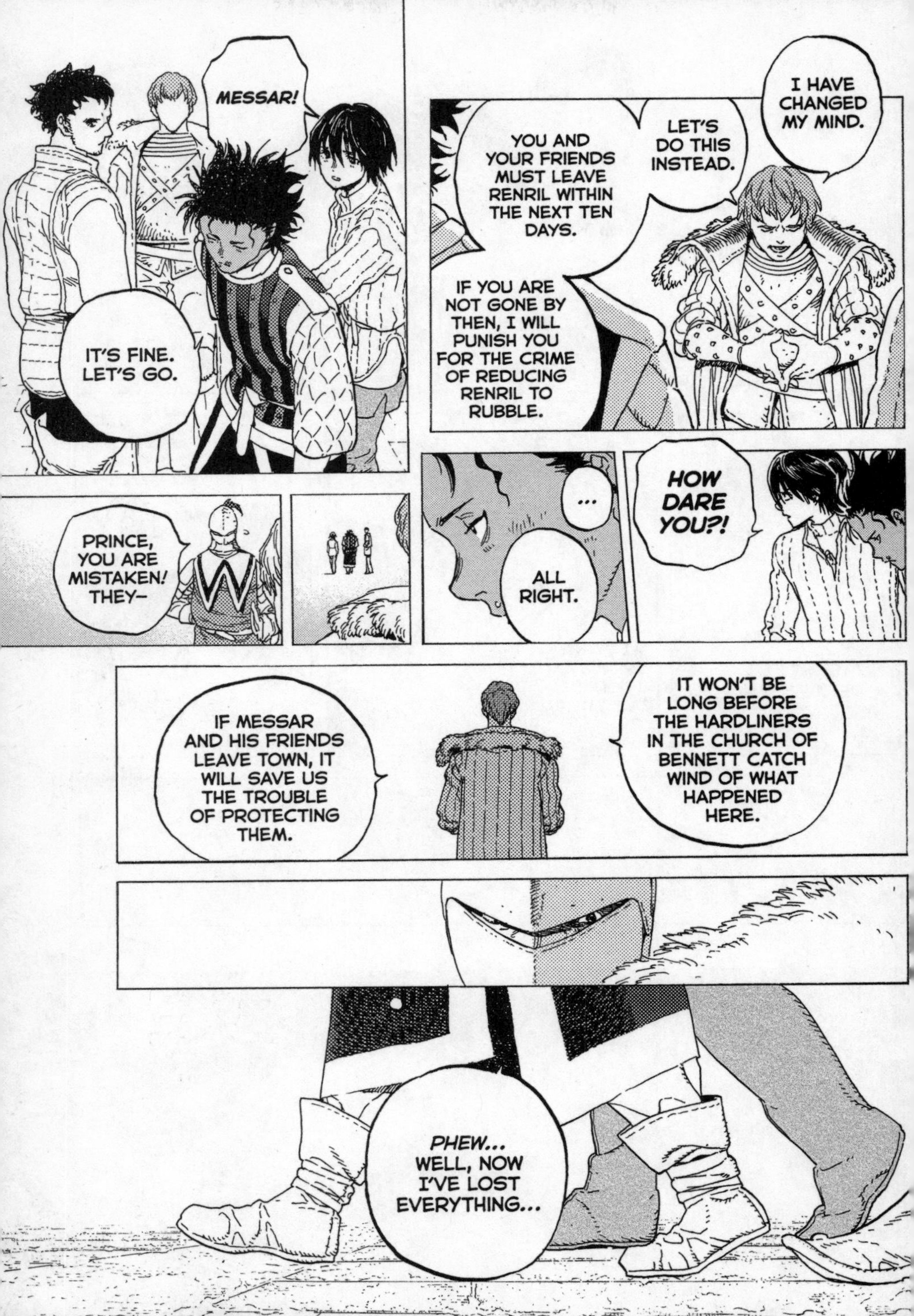
I HAVE CHANGED MY MIND.
LET'S DO THIS INSTEAD.
YOU AND YOUR FRIENDS MUST LEAVE RENRIL WITHIN THE NEXT TEN DAYS.
IF YOU ARE NOT GONE BY THEN, I WILL PUNISH YOU FOR THE CRIME OF REDUCING RENRIL TO RUBBLE.
MESSAR!
IT'S FINE. LET'S GO.
HOW DARE YOU?!
...
ALL RIGHT.
PRINCE, YOU ARE MISTAKEN! THEY–
IT WON'T BE LONG BEFORE THE HARDLINERS IN THE CHURCH OF BENNETT CATCH WIND OF WHAT HAPPENED HERE.
IF MESSAR AND HIS FRIENDS LEAVE TOWN, IT WILL SAVE US THE TROUBLE OF PROTECTING THEM.
PHEW... WELL, NOW I'VE LOST EVERYTHING...

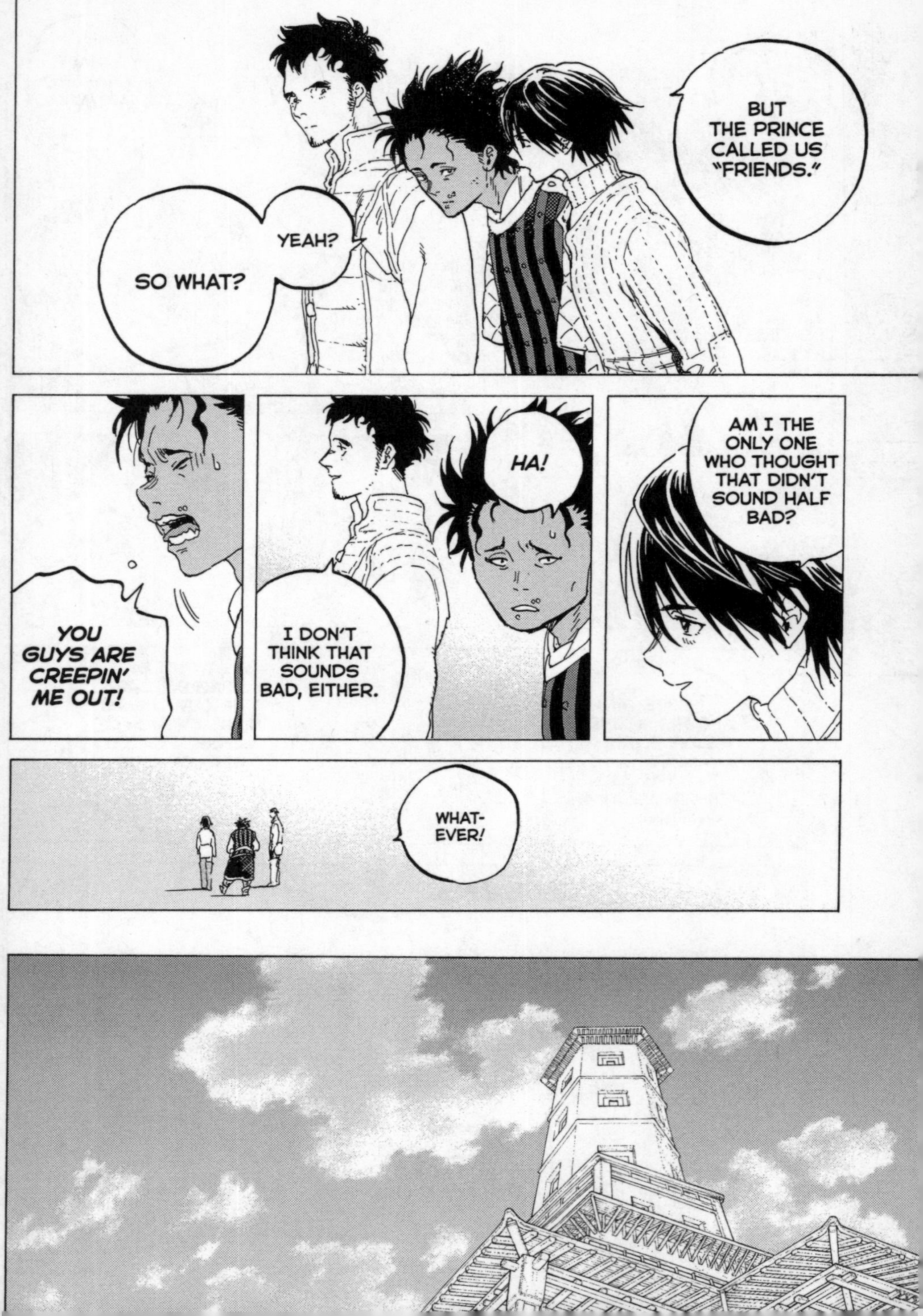
BUT THE PRINCE CALLED US "FRIENDS."
YEAH?
SO WHAT?
AM I THE ONLY ONE WHO THOUGHT THAT DIDN'T SOUND HALF BAD?
HA!
I DON'T THINK THAT SOUNDS BAD, EITHER.
YOU GUYS ARE CREEPIN' ME OUT!
WHAT-EVER!

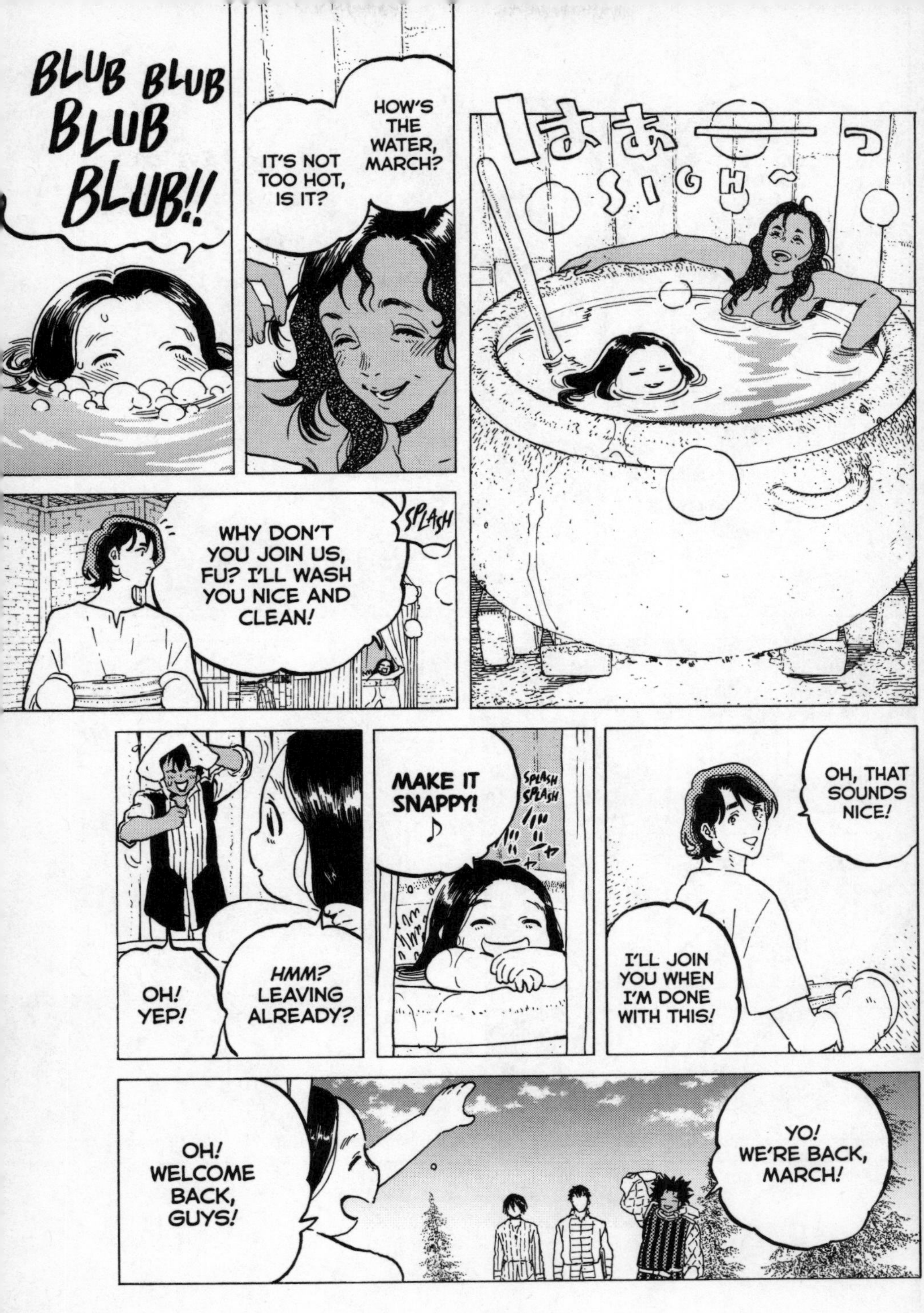
はあーーっ
SIGH~
HOW'S THE WATER, MARCH?
IT'S NOT TOO HOT, IS IT?
BLUB BLUB BLUB BLUB!!
SPLASH
WHY DON'T YOU JOIN US, FU? I'LL WASH YOU NICE AND CLEAN!
OH, THAT SOUNDS NICE!
I'LL JOIN YOU WHEN I'M DONE WITH THIS!
SPLASH SPLASH
MAKE IT SNAPPY! ♪
HMM? LEAVING ALREADY?
OH! YEP!
YO! WE'RE BACK, MARCH!
OH! WELCOME BACK, GUYS!

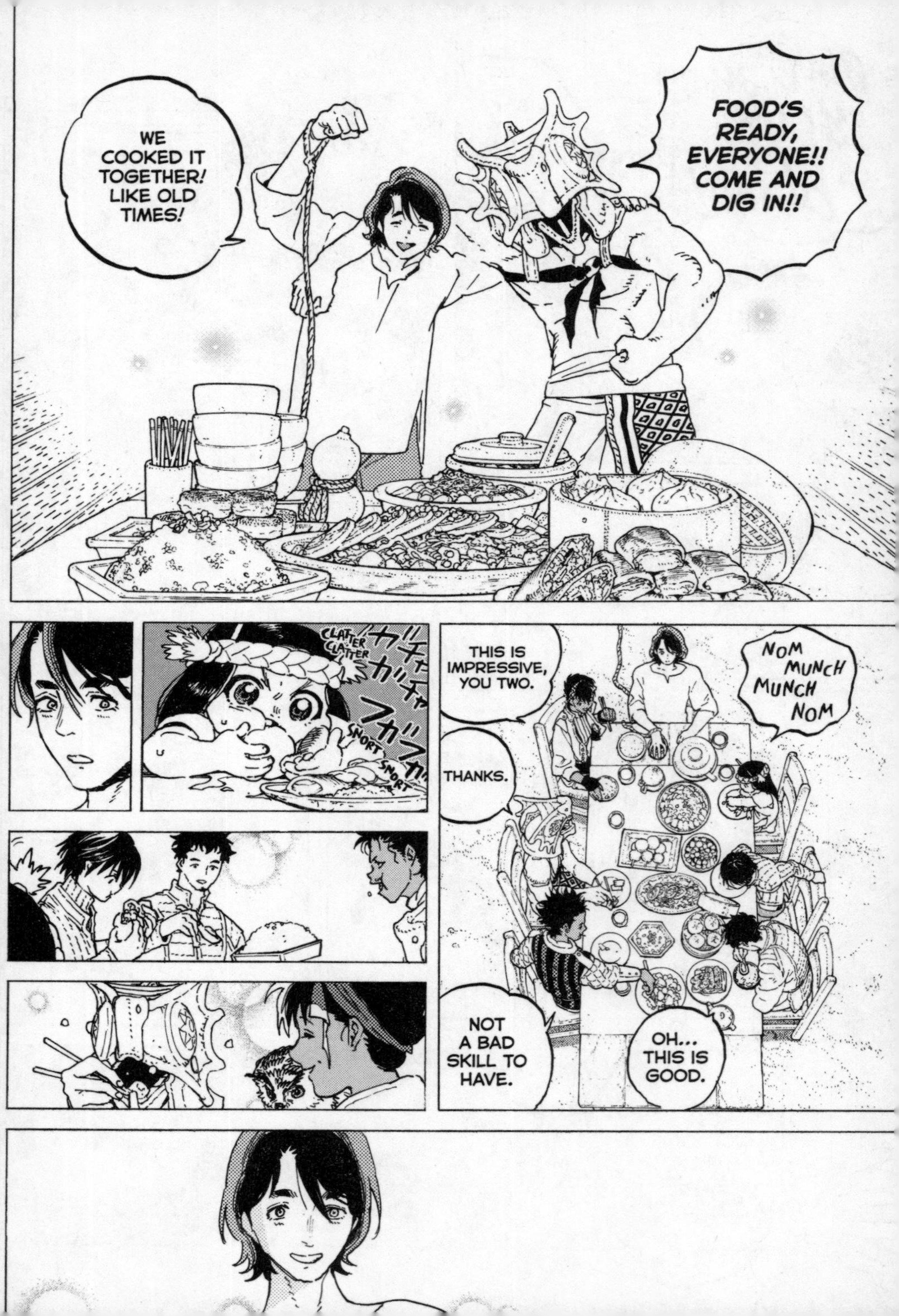
FOOD'S READY, EVERYONE!! COME AND DIG IN!!
WE COOKED IT TOGETHER! LIKE OLD TIMES!
NOM MUNCH MUNCH NOM
THIS IS IMPRESSIVE, YOU TWO.
THANKS.
OH... THIS IS GOOD.
NOT A BAD SKILL TO HAVE.
CLATTER CLATTER
SNORT
SNORT

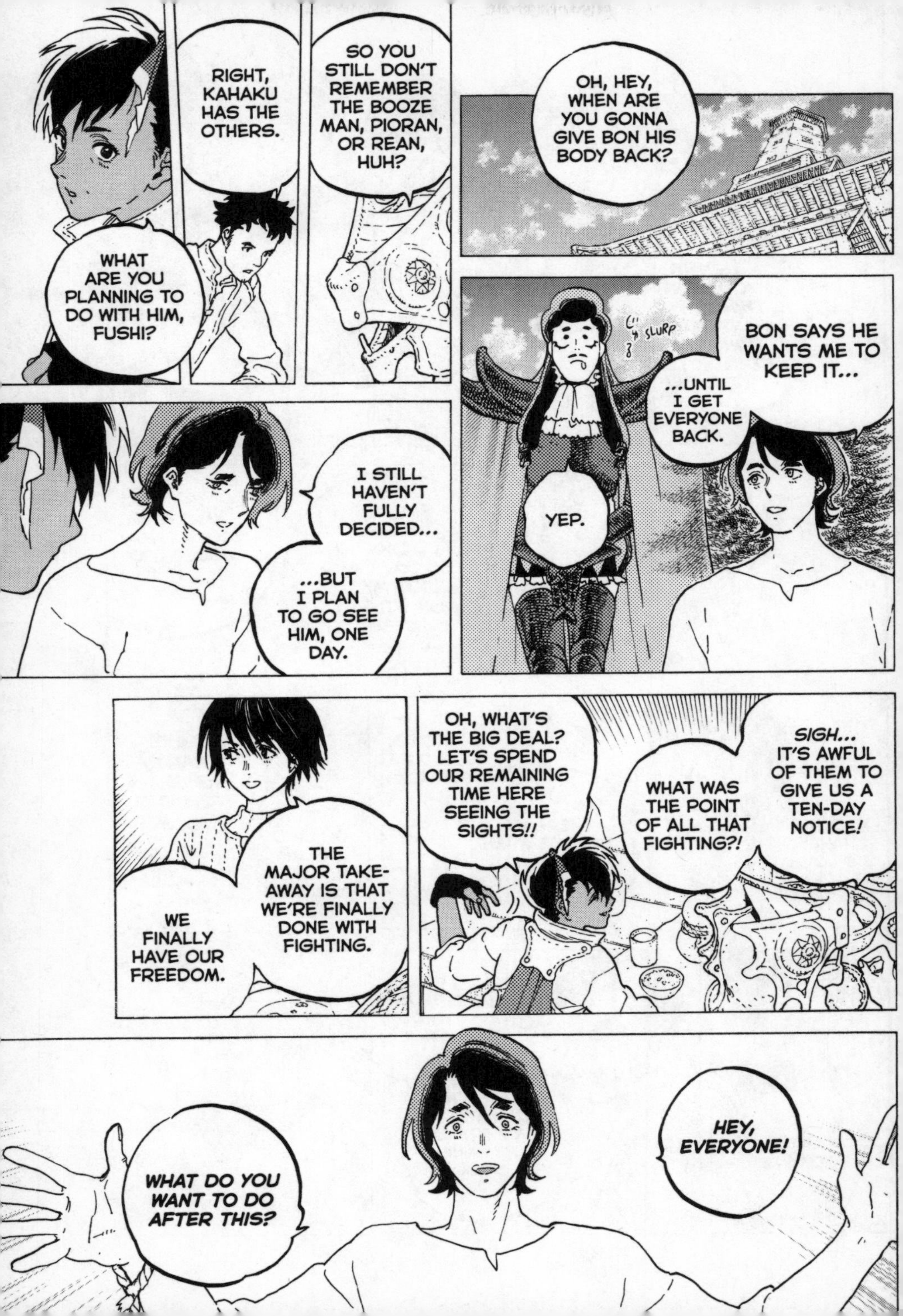
OH, HEY, WHEN ARE YOU GONNA GIVE BON HIS BODY BACK?
BON SAYS HE WANTS ME TO KEEP IT...
...UNTIL I GET EVERYONE BACK.
SLURP
YEP.
SO YOU STILL DON'T REMEMBER THE BOOZE MAN, PIORAN, OR REAN, HUH?
RIGHT, KAHAKU HAS THE OTHERS.
WHAT ARE YOU PLANNING TO DO WITH HIM, FUSHI?
I STILL HAVEN'T FULLY DECIDED...
...BUT I PLAN TO GO SEE HIM, ONE DAY.
SIGH... IT'S AWFUL OF THEM TO GIVE US A TEN-DAY NOTICE!
WHAT WAS THE POINT OF ALL THAT FIGHTING?!
OH, WHAT'S THE BIG DEAL? LET'S SPEND OUR REMAINING TIME HERE SEEING THE SIGHTS!!
THE MAJOR TAKE-AWAY IS THAT WE'RE FINALLY DONE WITH FIGHTING.
WE FINALLY HAVE OUR FREEDOM.
HEY, EVERYONE!
WHAT DO YOU WANT TO DO AFTER THIS?

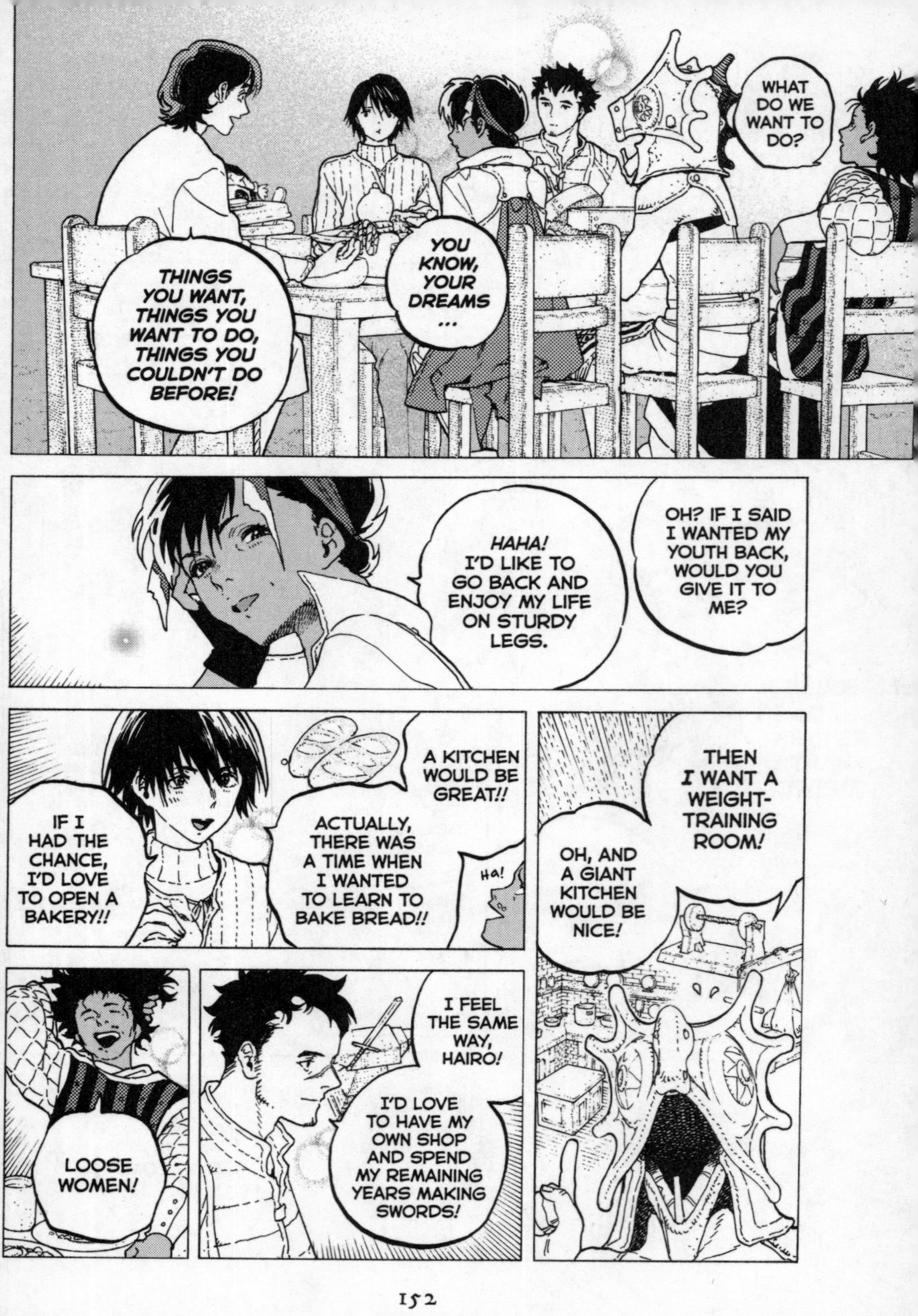
WHAT DO WE WANT TO DO?
YOU KNOW, YOUR DREAMS ...
THINGS YOU WANT, THINGS YOU WANT TO DO, THINGS YOU COULDN'T DO BEFORE!
OH? IF I SAID I WANTED MY YOUTH BACK, WOULD YOU GIVE IT TO ME?
HAHA! I'D LIKE TO GO BACK AND ENJOY MY LIFE ON STURDY LEGS.
THEN *I* WANT A WEIGHT-TRAINING ROOM!
OH, AND A GIANT KITCHEN WOULD BE NICE!
A KITCHEN WOULD BE GREAT!!
ACTUALLY, THERE WAS A TIME WHEN I WANTED TO LEARN TO BAKE BREAD!!
Ha!
IF I HAD THE CHANCE, I'D LOVE TO OPEN A BAKERY!!
I FEEL THE SAME WAY, HAIRO!
I'D LOVE TO HAVE MY OWN SHOP AND SPEND MY REMAINING YEARS MAKING SWORDS!
LOOSE WOMEN!

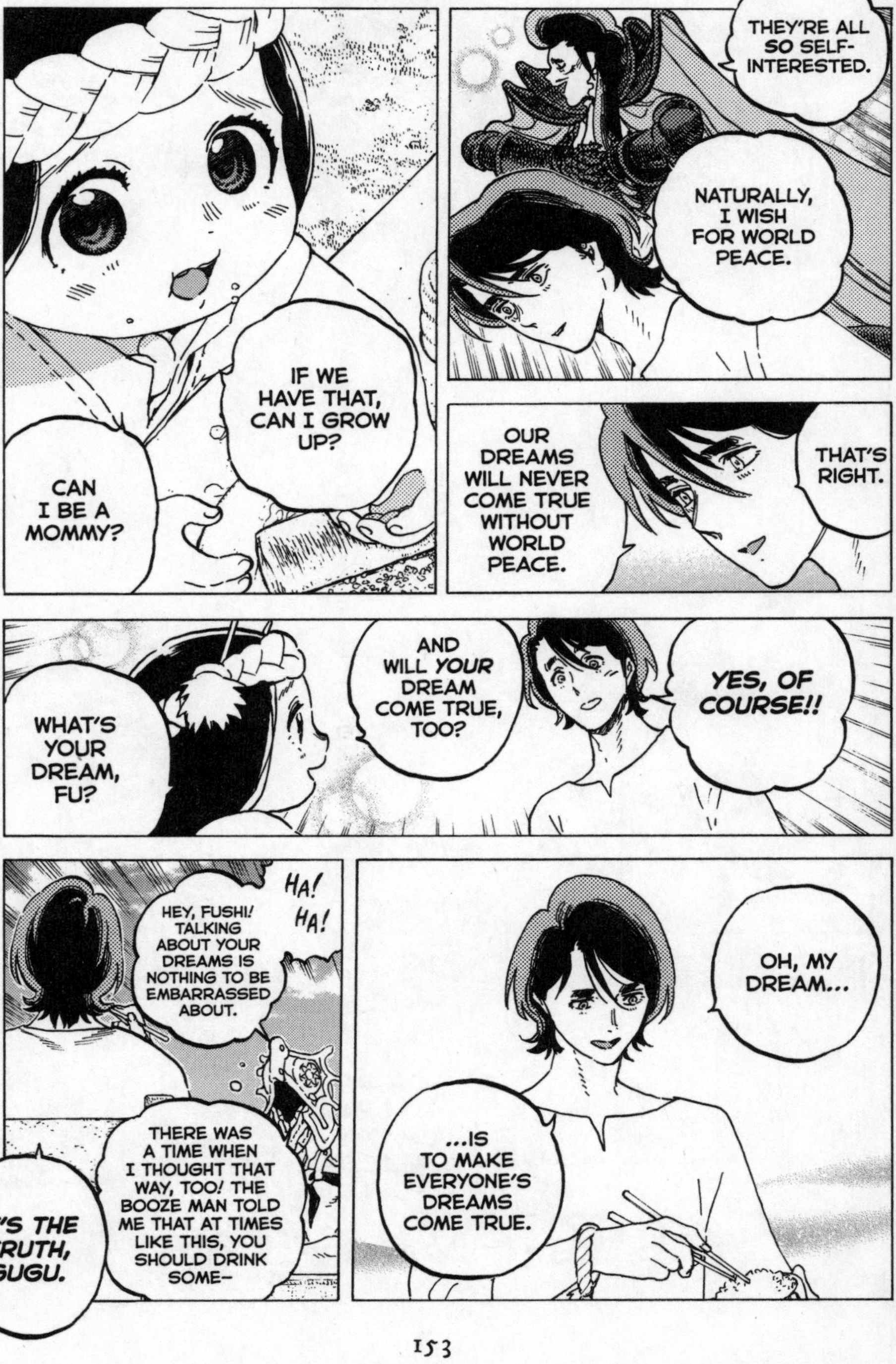
THEY'RE ALL SO SELF-INTERESTED.
NATURALLY, I WISH FOR WORLD PEACE.
THAT'S RIGHT.
OUR DREAMS WILL NEVER COME TRUE WITHOUT WORLD PEACE.
IF WE HAVE THAT, CAN I GROW UP?
CAN I BE A MOMMY?
YES, OF COURSE!!
AND WILL *YOUR* DREAM COME TRUE, TOO?
WHAT'S YOUR DREAM, FU?
OH, MY DREAM...
...IS TO MAKE EVERYONE'S DREAMS COME TRUE.
HA! HA!
HEY, FUSHI! TALKING ABOUT YOUR DREAMS IS NOTHING TO BE EMBARRASSED ABOUT.
THERE WAS A TIME WHEN I THOUGHT THAT WAY, TOO! THE BOOZE MAN TOLD ME THAT AT TIMES LIKE THIS, YOU SHOULD DRINK SOME–
IT'S THE TRUTH, GUGU.

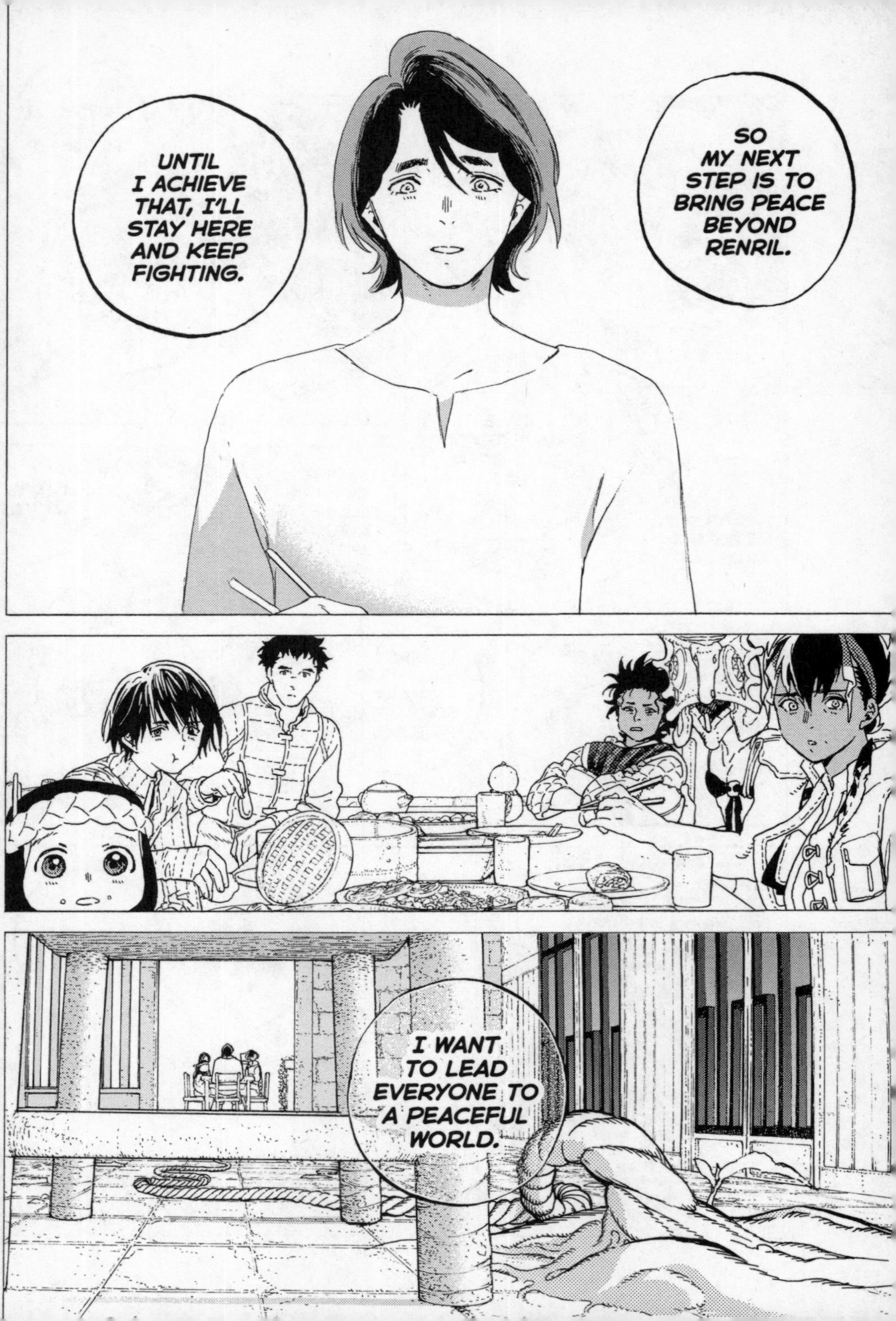
SO MY NEXT STEP IS TO BRING PEACE BEYOND RENRIL.
UNTIL I ACHIEVE THAT, I'LL STAY HERE AND KEEP FIGHTING.
I WANT TO LEAD EVERYONE TO A PEACEFUL WORLD.

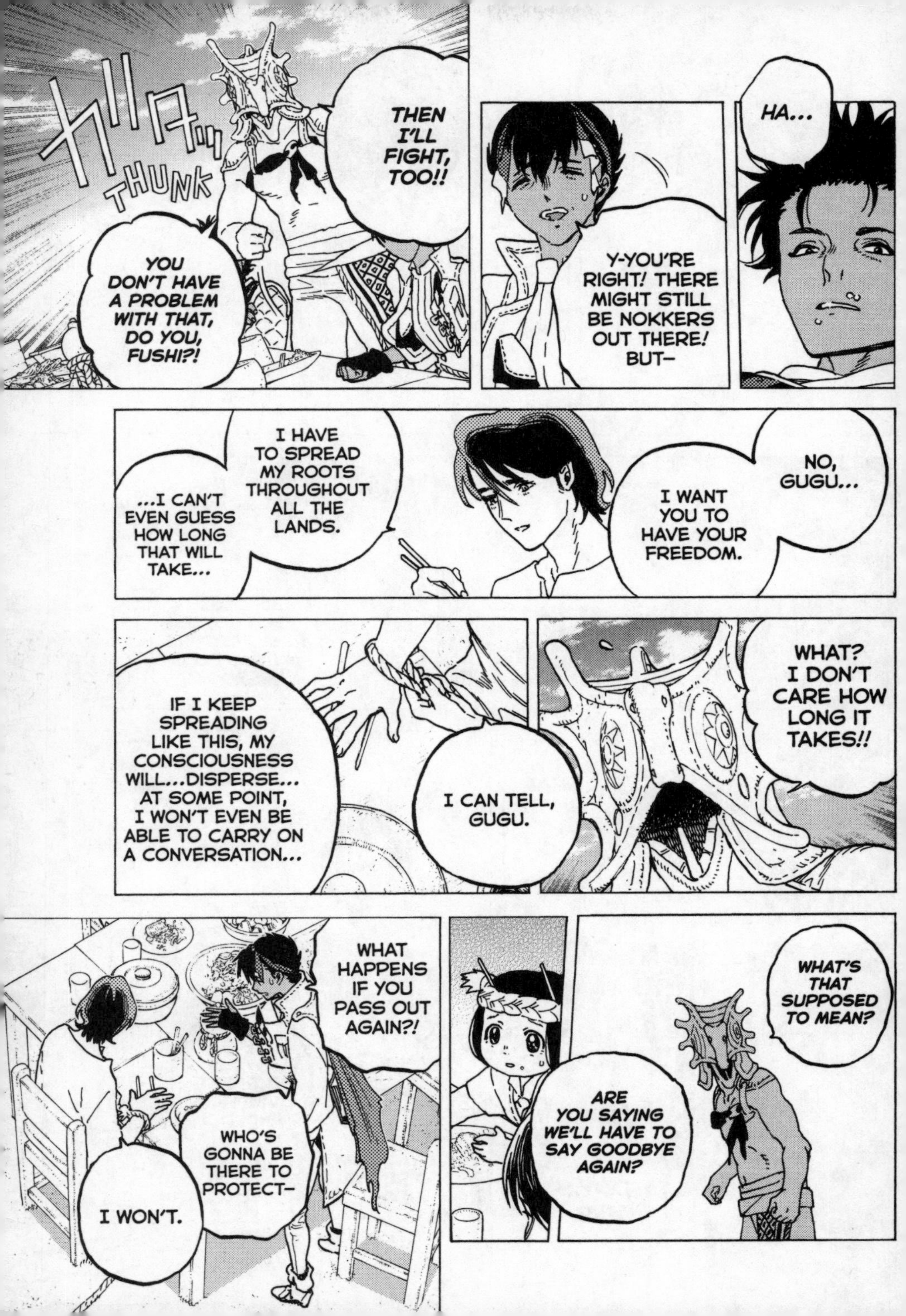
HA...
Y-YOU'RE RIGHT! THERE MIGHT STILL BE NOKKERS OUT THERE! BUT—
THEN I'LL FIGHT, TOO!!
THUNK
YOU DON'T HAVE A PROBLEM WITH THAT, DO YOU, FUSHI?!
NO, GUGU...
I WANT YOU TO HAVE YOUR FREEDOM.
I HAVE TO SPREAD MY ROOTS THROUGHOUT ALL THE LANDS.
...I CAN'T EVEN GUESS HOW LONG THAT WILL TAKE...
WHAT? I DON'T CARE HOW LONG IT TAKES!!
I CAN TELL, GUGU.
IF I KEEP SPREADING LIKE THIS, MY CONSCIOUSNESS WILL...DISPERSE... AT SOME POINT, I WON'T EVEN BE ABLE TO CARRY ON A CONVERSATION...
WHAT'S THAT SUPPOSED TO MEAN?
ARE YOU SAYING WE'LL HAVE TO SAY GOODBYE AGAIN?
WHAT HAPPENS IF YOU PASS OUT AGAIN?!
WHO'S GONNA BE THERE TO PROTECT—
I WON'T.

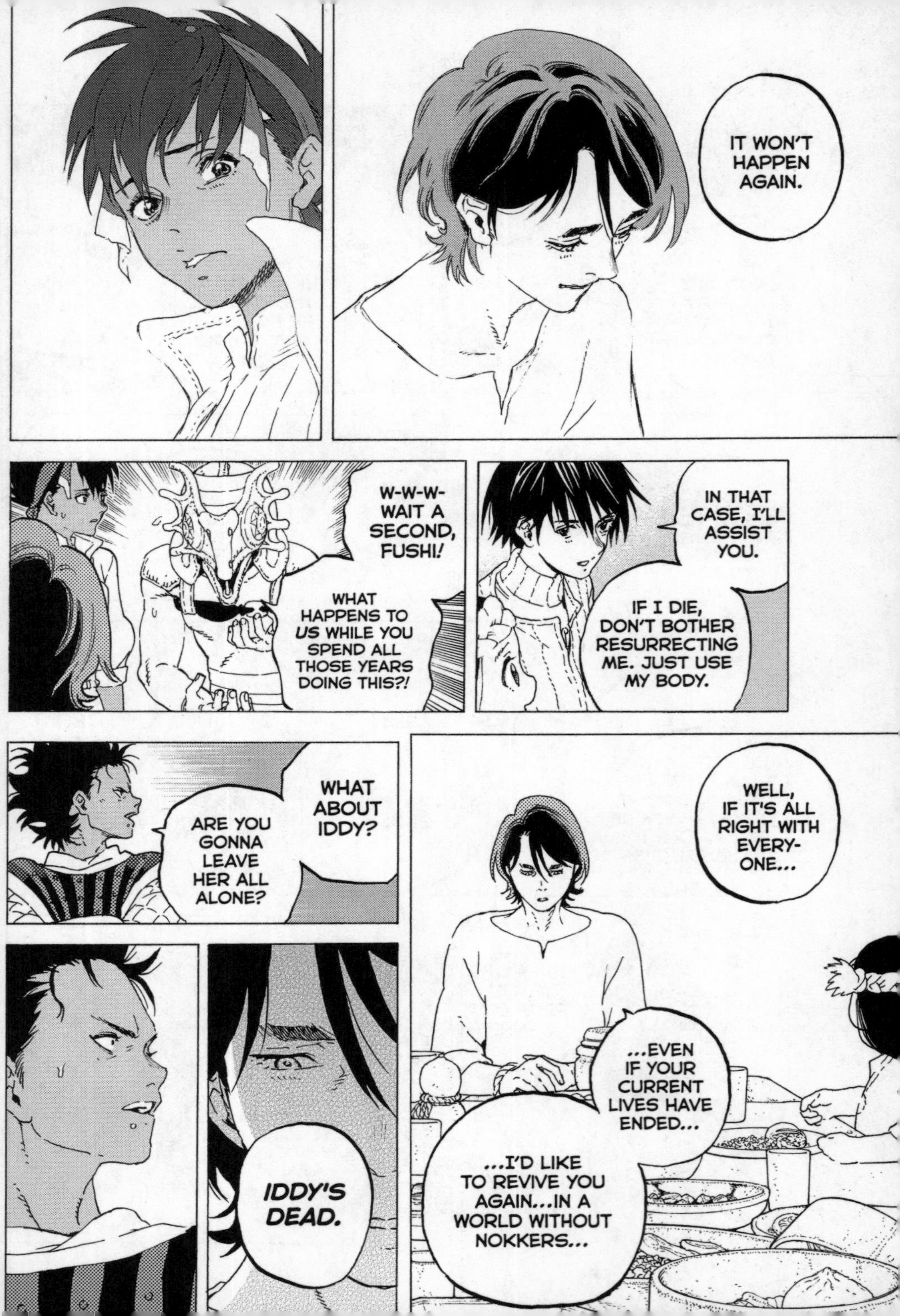
IT WON'T HAPPEN AGAIN.
IN THAT CASE, I'LL ASSIST YOU.
IF I DIE, DON'T BOTHER RESURRECTING ME. JUST USE MY BODY.
W-W-W-WAIT A SECOND, FUSHI!
WHAT HAPPENS TO US WHILE YOU SPEND ALL THOSE YEARS DOING THIS?!
WELL, IF IT'S ALL RIGHT WITH EVERY-ONE...
...EVEN IF YOUR CURRENT LIVES HAVE ENDED...
...I'D LIKE TO REVIVE YOU AGAIN...IN A WORLD WITHOUT NOKKERS...
WHAT ABOUT IDDY?
ARE YOU GONNA LEAVE HER ALL ALONE?
IDDY'S DEAD.

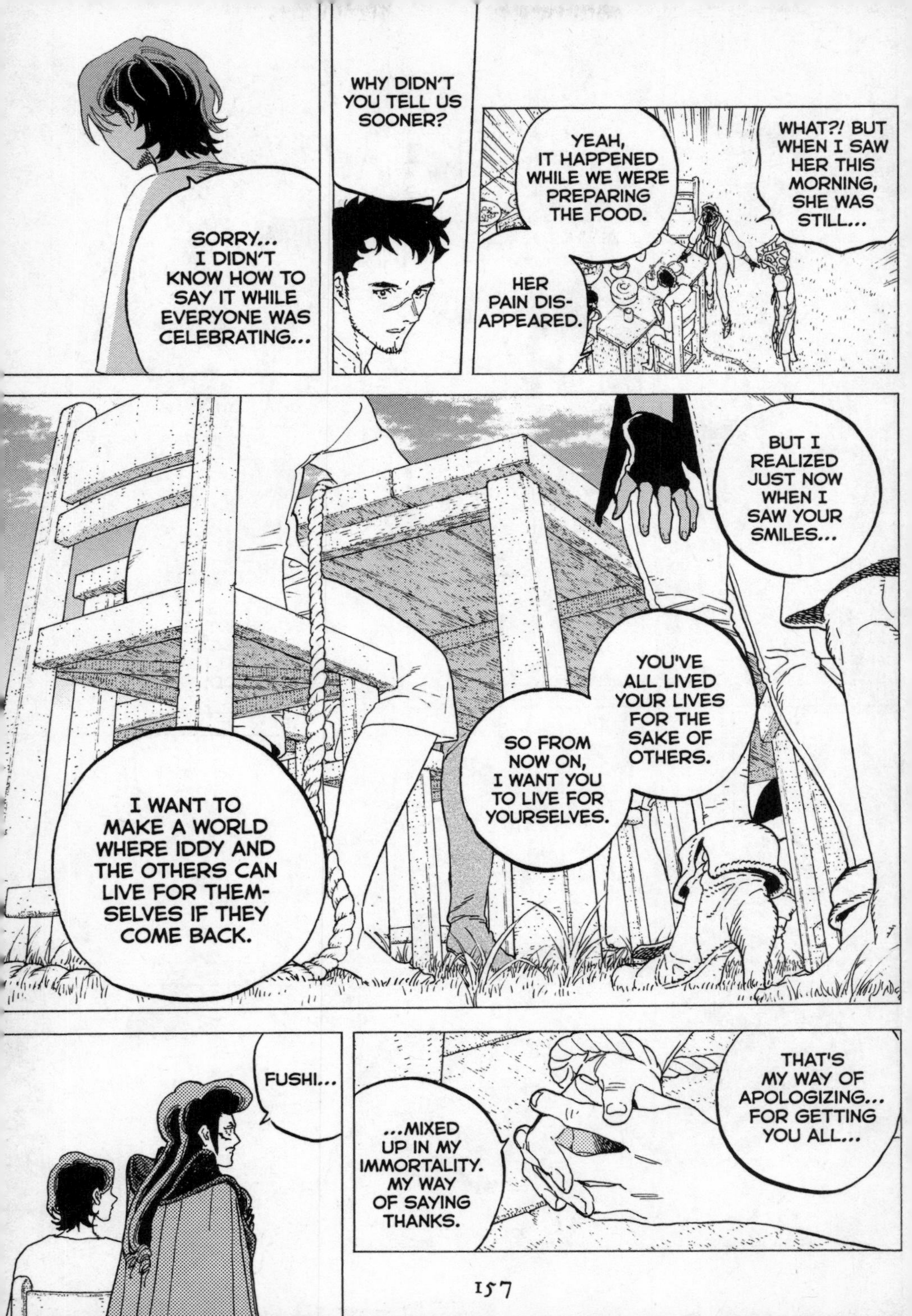
WHAT?! BUT WHEN I SAW HER THIS MORNING, SHE WAS STILL...
YEAH, IT HAPPENED WHILE WE WERE PREPARING THE FOOD.
HER PAIN DIS-APPEARED.
WHY DIDN'T YOU TELL US SOONER?
SORRY... I DIDN'T KNOW HOW TO SAY IT WHILE EVERYONE WAS CELEBRATING...
BUT I REALIZED JUST NOW WHEN I SAW YOUR SMILES...
YOU'VE ALL LIVED YOUR LIVES FOR THE SAKE OF OTHERS.
SO FROM NOW ON, I WANT YOU TO LIVE FOR YOURSELVES.
I WANT TO MAKE A WORLD WHERE IDDY AND THE OTHERS CAN LIVE FOR THEM-SELVES IF THEY COME BACK.
THAT'S MY WAY OF APOLOGIZING... FOR GETTING YOU ALL...
...MIXED UP IN MY IMMORTALITY. MY WAY OF SAYING THANKS.
FUSHI...

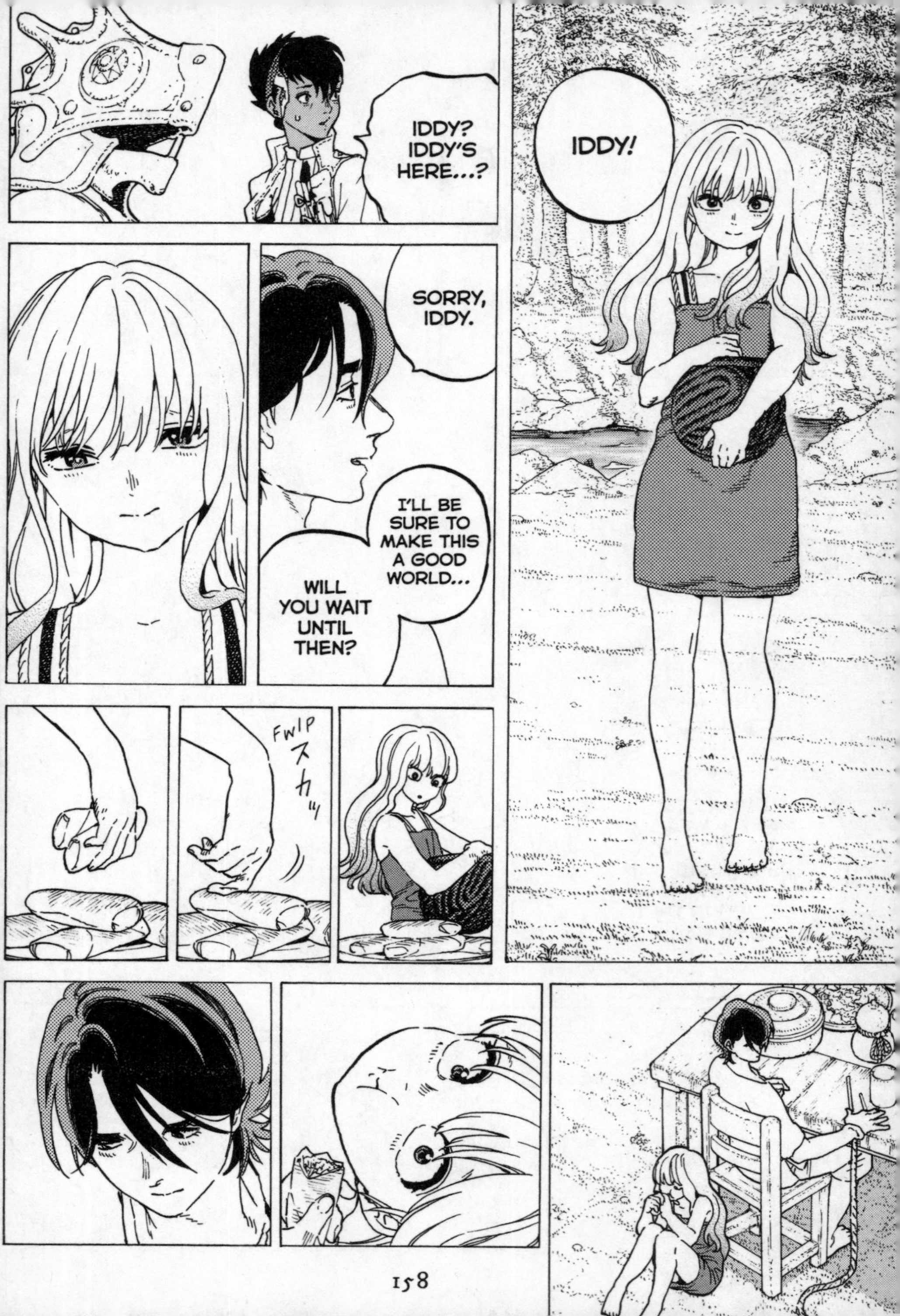
IDDY!
IDDY? IDDY'S HERE...?
SORRY, IDDY.
I'LL BE SURE TO MAKE THIS A GOOD WORLD...
WILL YOU WAIT UNTIL THEN?
FWIP
スカッ

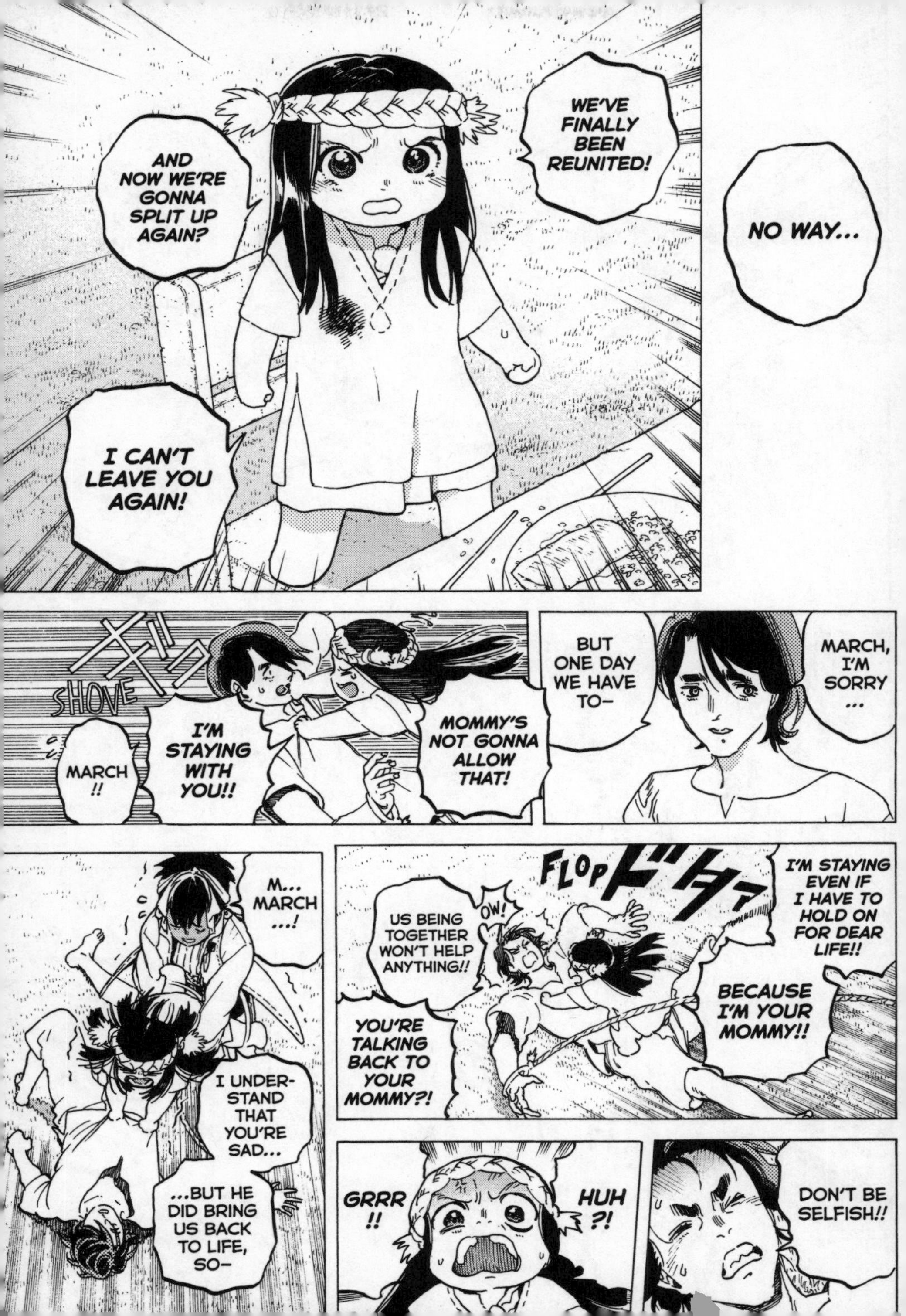
NO WAY...
WE'VE FINALLY BEEN REUNITED!
AND NOW WE'RE GONNA SPLIT UP AGAIN?
I CAN'T LEAVE YOU AGAIN!
MARCH, I'M SORRY ...
BUT ONE DAY WE HAVE TO–
MOMMY'S NOT GONNA ALLOW THAT!
SHOVE
I'M STAYING WITH YOU!!
MARCH !!
FLOP
I'M STAYING EVEN IF I HAVE TO HOLD ON FOR DEAR LIFE!!
BECAUSE I'M YOUR MOMMY!!
OW!
US BEING TOGETHER WON'T HELP ANYTHING!!
YOU'RE TALKING BACK TO YOUR MOMMY?!
DON'T BE SELFISH!!
HUH ?!
GRRR !!
M... MARCH ...!
I UNDER-STAND THAT YOU'RE SAD...
...BUT HE DID BRING US BACK TO LIFE, SO–

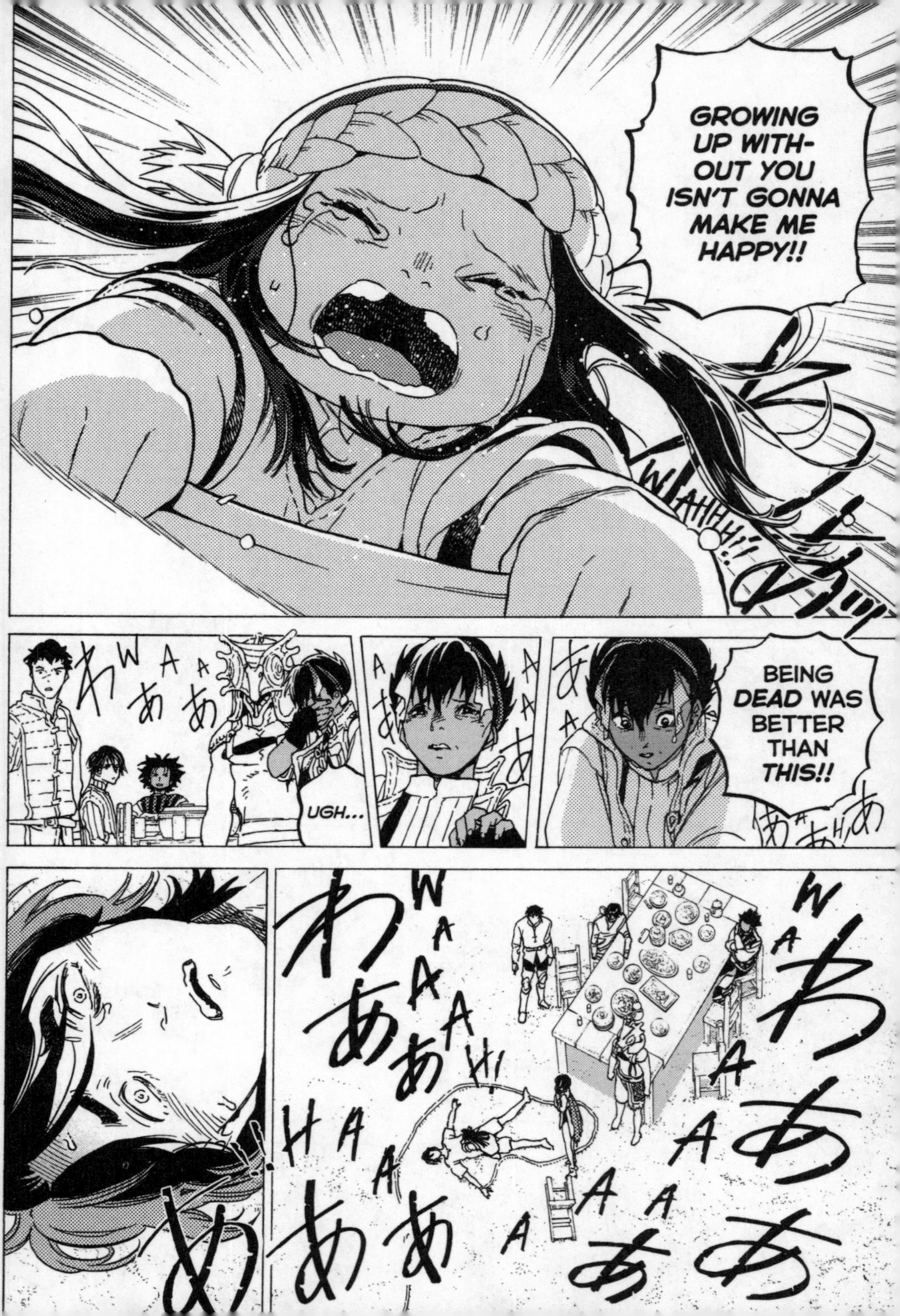
GROWING UP WITH-OUT YOU ISN'T GONNA MAKE ME HAPPY!!
WAHHH!!
BEING DEAD WAS BETTER THAN THIS!!
UGH...
WAAAH!
HAAA

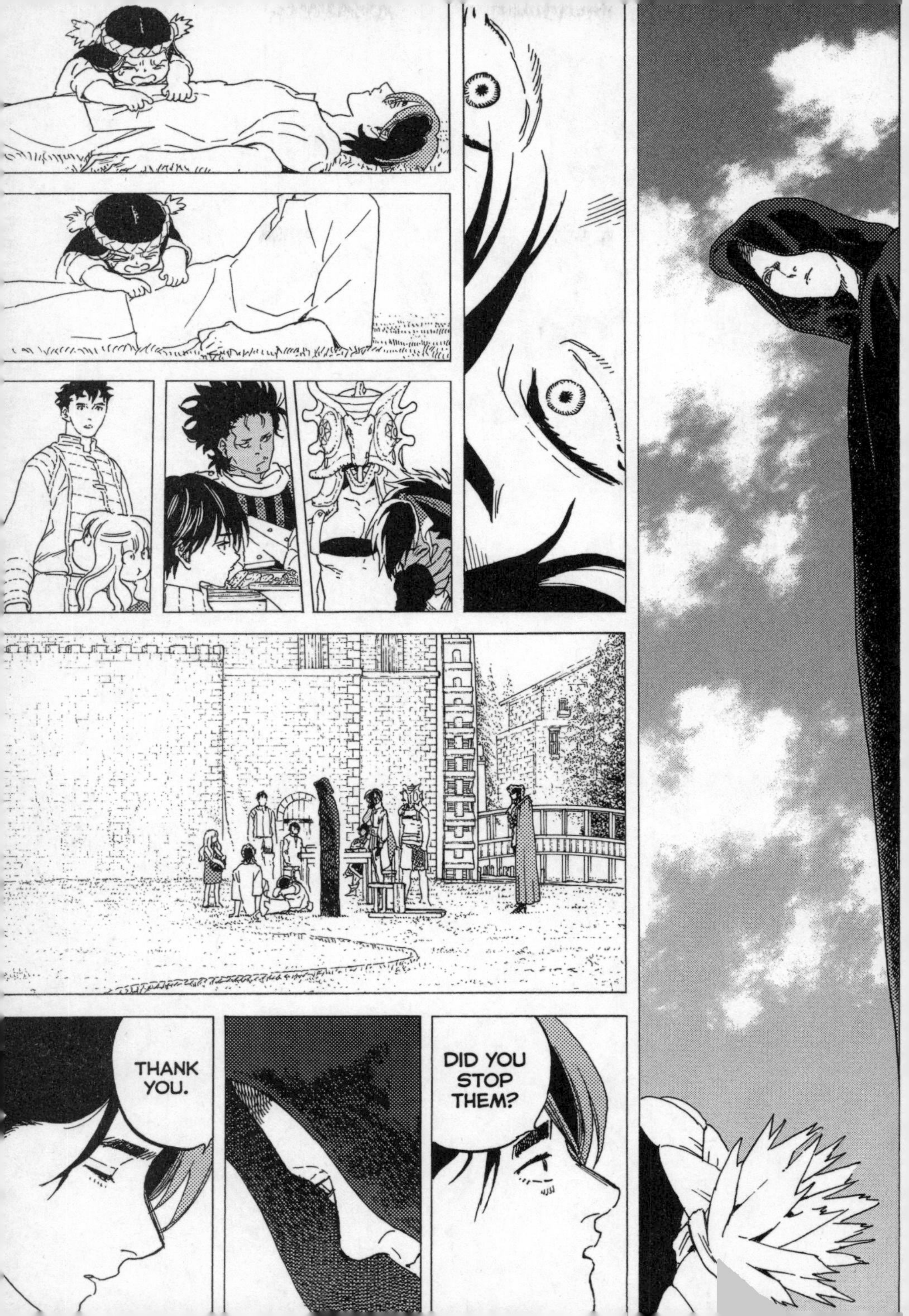
DID YOU STOP THEM?
THANK YOU.

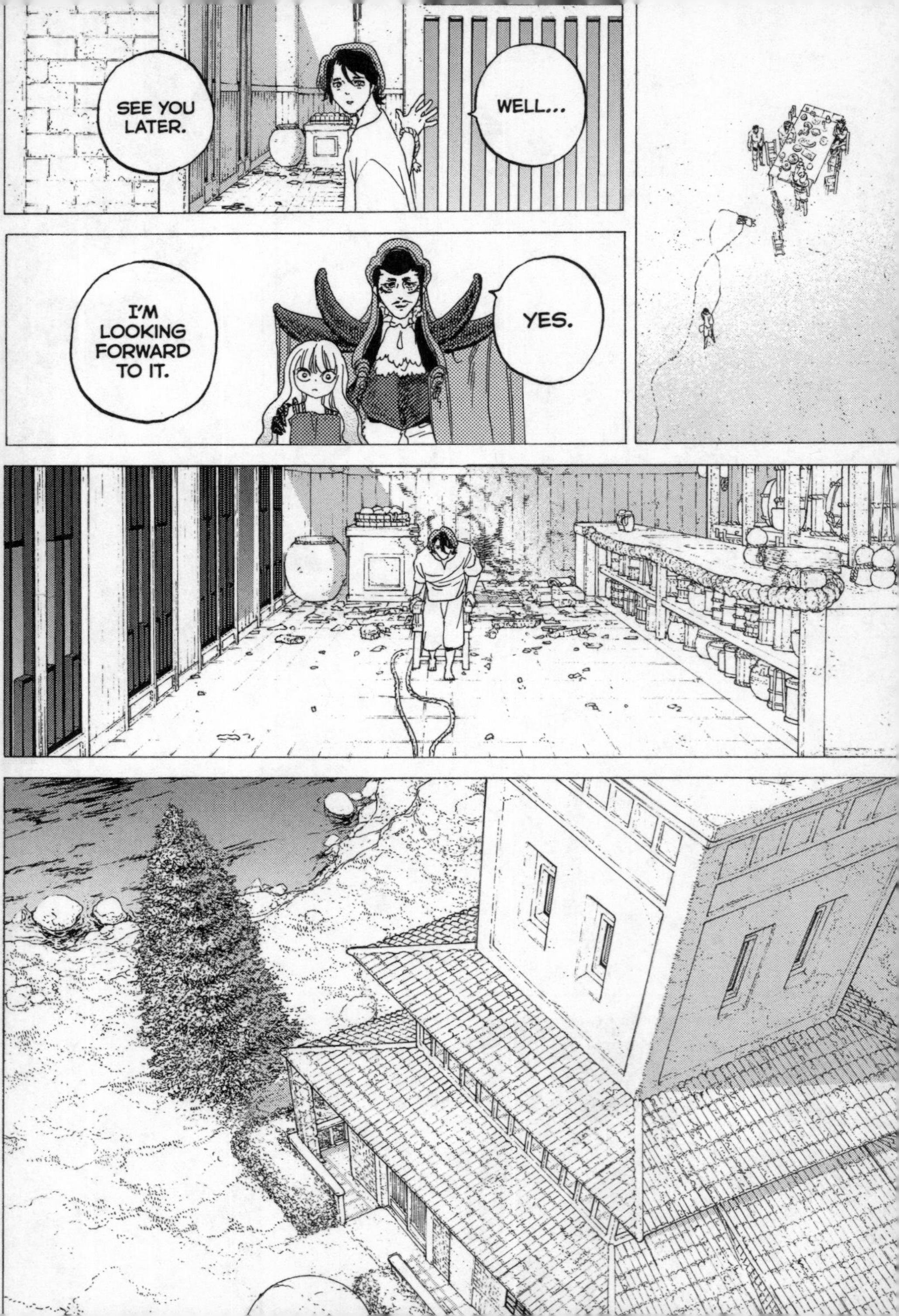
WELL...
SEE YOU LATER.
YES.
I'M LOOKING FORWARD TO IT.

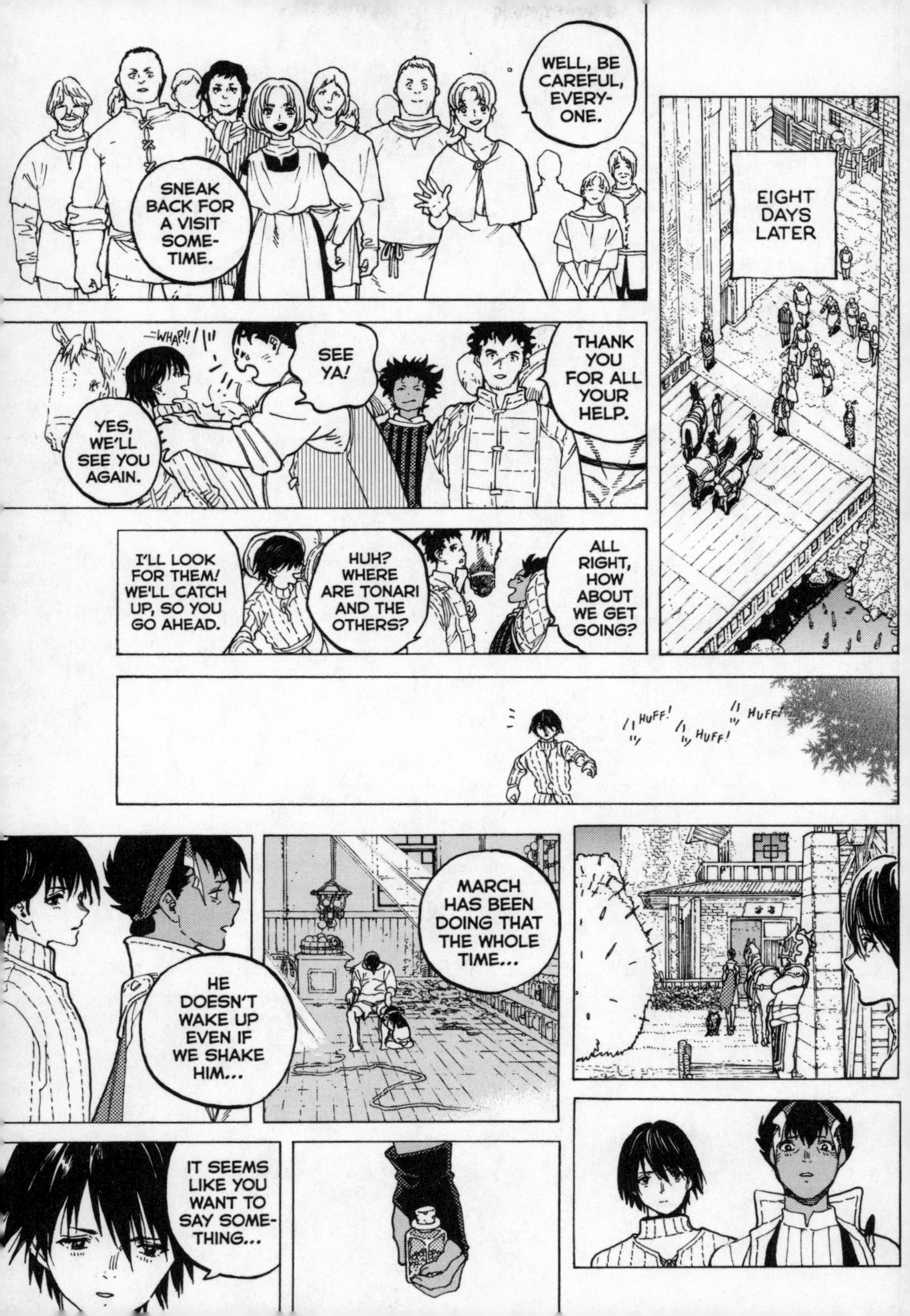
EIGHT DAYS LATER
WELL, BE CAREFUL, EVERY-ONE.
SNEAK BACK FOR A VISIT SOME-TIME.
THANK YOU FOR ALL YOUR HELP.
SEE YA!
WHAP!!
YES, WE'LL SEE YOU AGAIN.
ALL RIGHT, HOW ABOUT WE GET GOING?
HUH? WHERE ARE TONARI AND THE OTHERS?
I'LL LOOK FOR THEM! WE'LL CATCH UP, SO YOU GO AHEAD.
HUFF!
HUFF!
HUFF!
MARCH HAS BEEN DOING THAT THE WHOLE TIME...
HE DOESN'T WAKE UP EVEN IF WE SHAKE HIM...
IT SEEMS LIKE YOU WANT TO SAY SOME-THING...

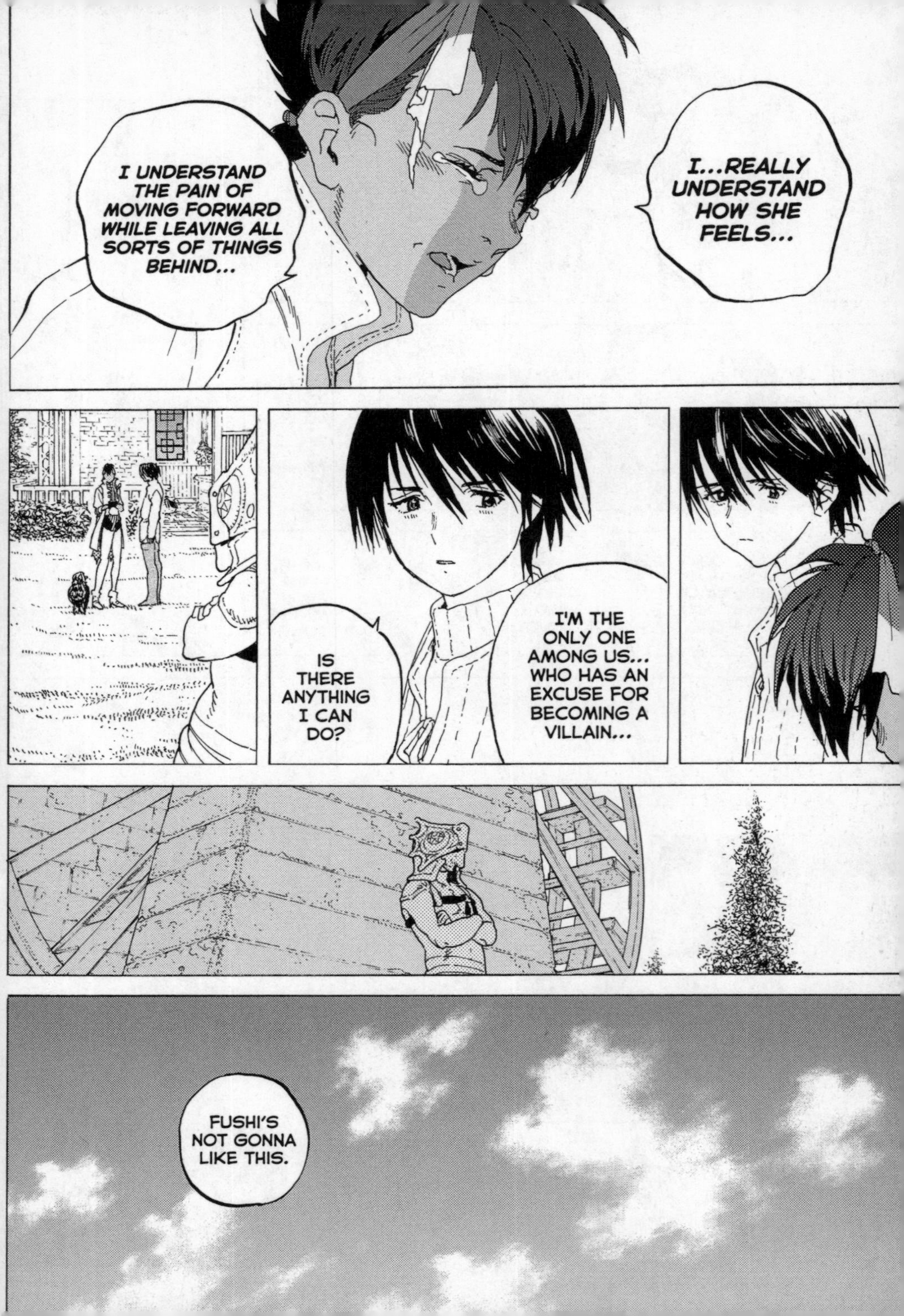
I...REALLY UNDERSTAND HOW SHE FEELS...
I UNDERSTAND THE PAIN OF MOVING FORWARD WHILE LEAVING ALL SORTS OF THINGS BEHIND...
I'M THE ONLY ONE AMONG US... WHO HAS AN EXCUSE FOR BECOMING A VILLAIN...
IS THERE ANYTHING I CAN DO?
FUSHI'S NOT GONNA LIKE THIS.

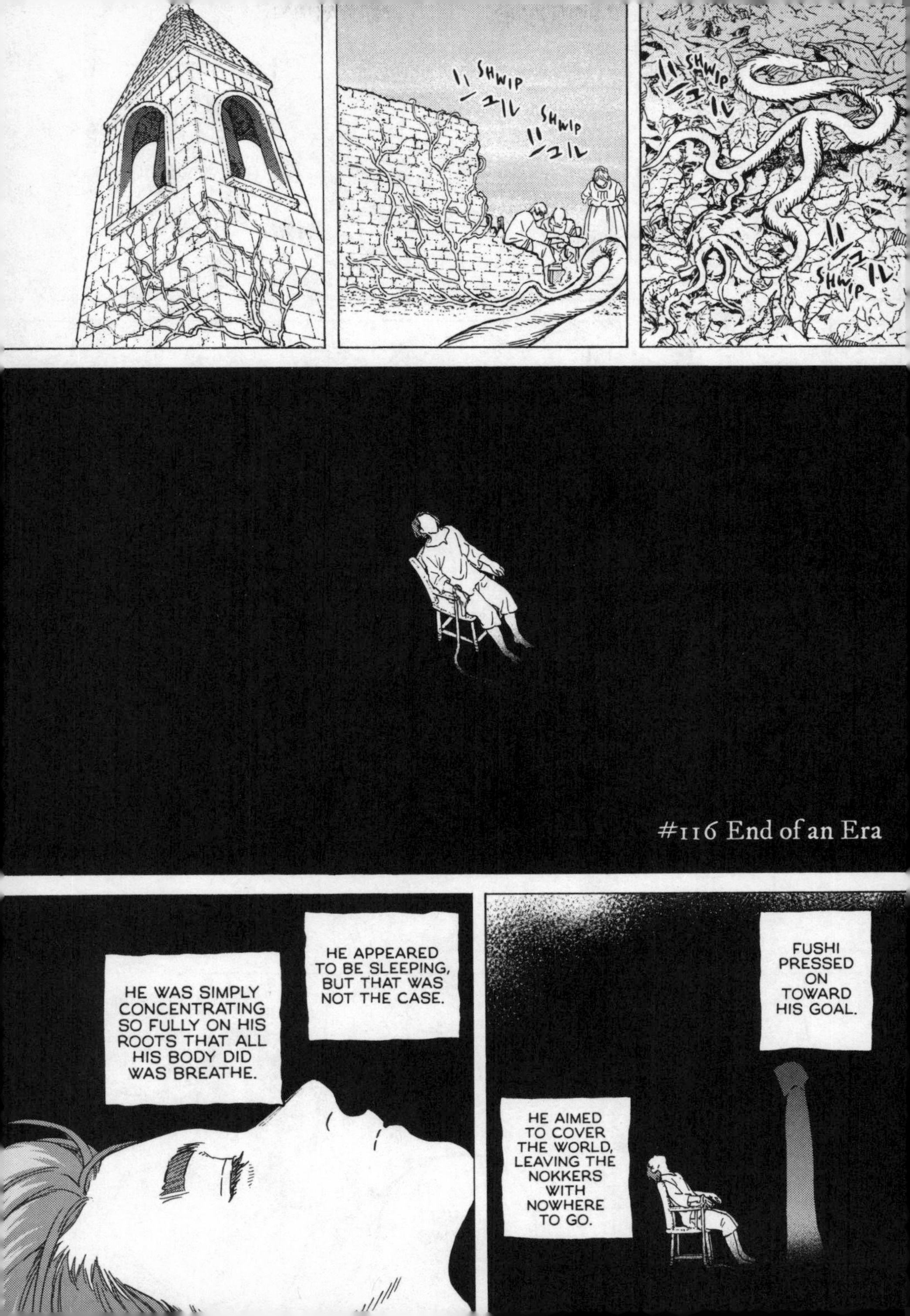
SHWIP
SHWIP
SHWIP
#116 End of an Era
FUSHI PRESSED ON TOWARD HIS GOAL.
HE AIMED TO COVER THE WORLD, LEAVING THE NOKKERS WITH NOWHERE TO GO.
HE APPEARED TO BE SLEEPING, BUT THAT WAS NOT THE CASE.
HE WAS SIMPLY CONCENTRATING SO FULLY ON HIS ROOTS THAT ALL HIS BODY DID WAS BREATHE.

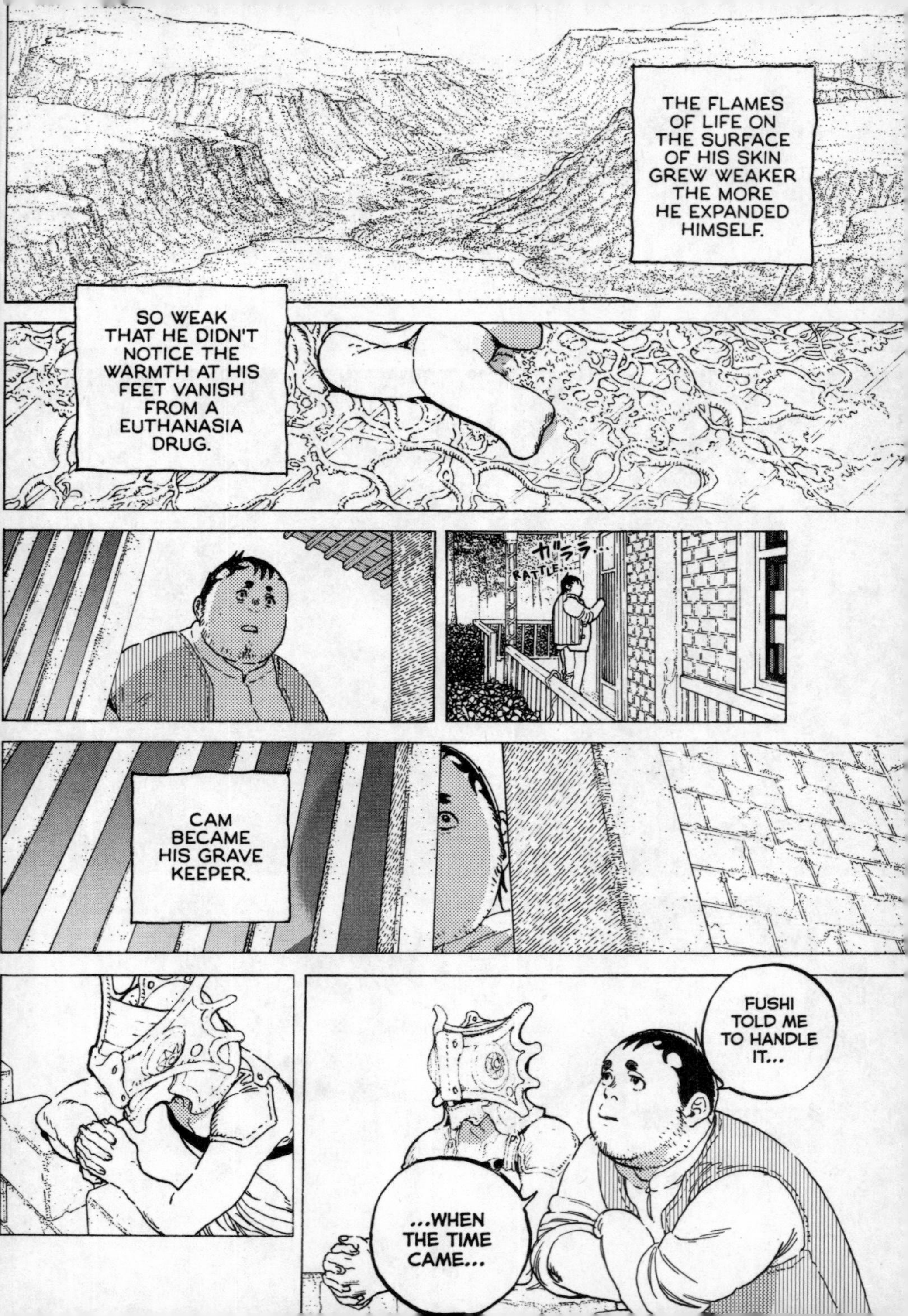
THE FLAMES OF LIFE ON THE SURFACE OF HIS SKIN GREW WEAKER THE MORE HE EXPANDED HIMSELF.
SO WEAK THAT HE DIDN'T NOTICE THE WARMTH AT HIS FEET VANISH FROM A EUTHANASIA DRUG.
ガララ…
RATTLE...
CAM BECAME HIS GRAVE KEEPER.
FUSHI TOLD ME TO HANDLE IT...
...WHEN THE TIME CAME...

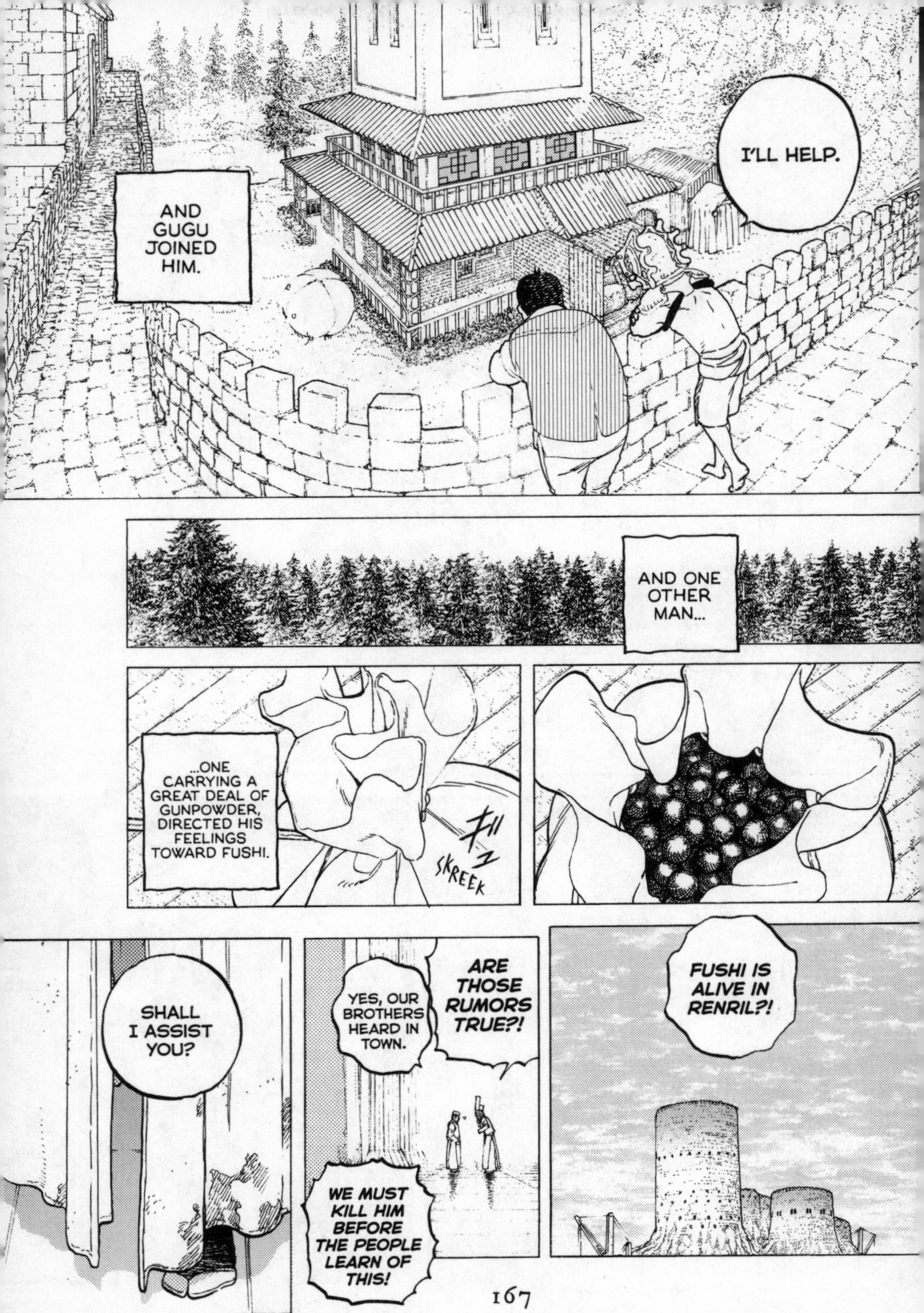
I'LL HELP.
AND GUGU JOINED HIM.
AND ONE OTHER MAN...
...ONE CARRYING A GREAT DEAL OF GUNPOWDER, DIRECTED HIS FEELINGS TOWARD FUSHI.
SKREEK
FUSHI IS ALIVE IN RENRIL?!
ARE THOSE RUMORS TRUE?!
YES, OUR BROTHERS HEARD IN TOWN.
WE MUST KILL HIM BEFORE THE PEOPLE LEARN OF THIS!
SHALL I ASSIST YOU?

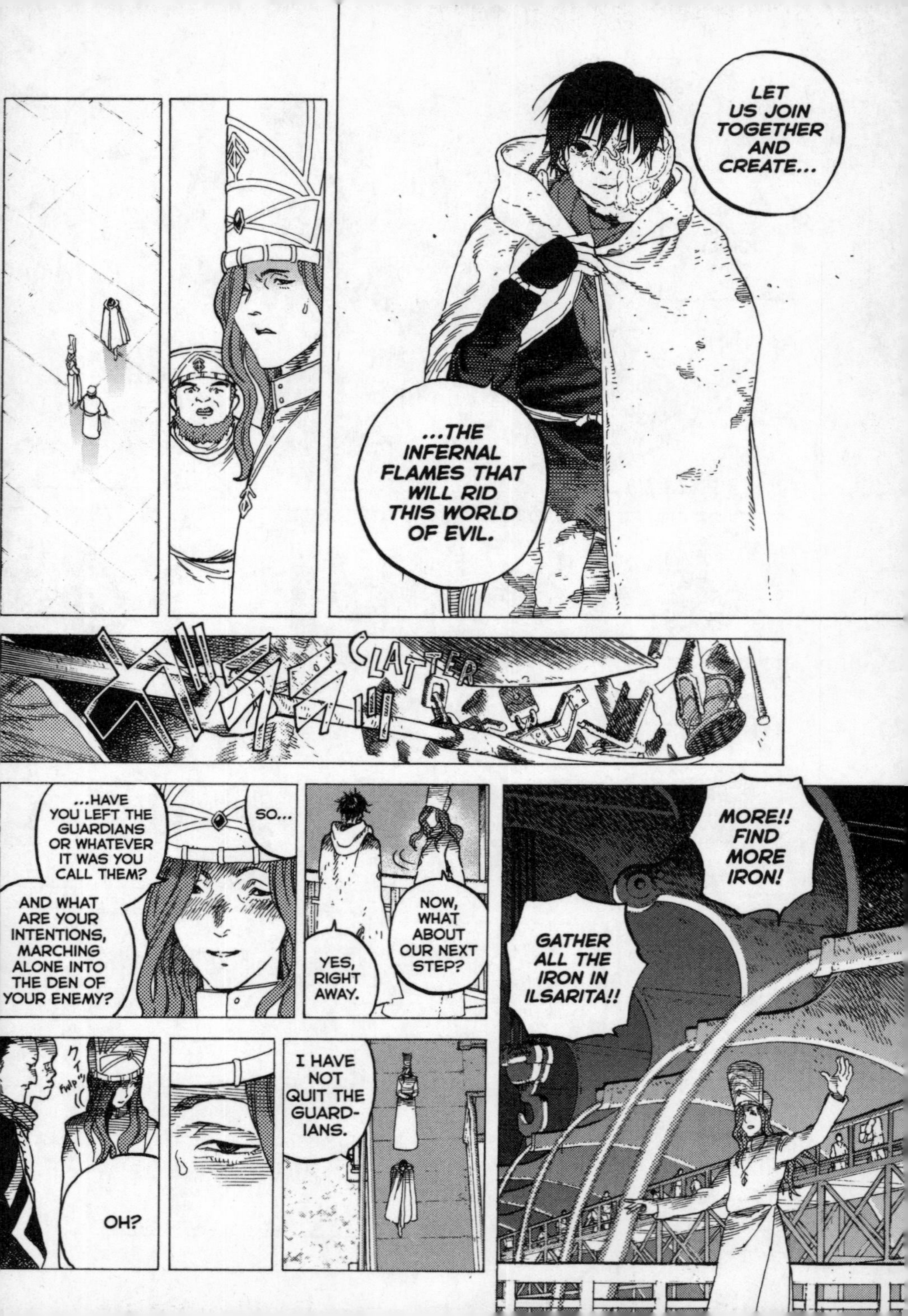
LET US JOIN TOGETHER AND CREATE...
...THE INFERNAL FLAMES THAT WILL RID THIS WORLD OF EVIL.
CLATTER
MORE!! FIND MORE IRON!
GATHER ALL THE IRON IN ILSARITA!!
NOW, WHAT ABOUT OUR NEXT STEP?
YES, RIGHT AWAY.
SO...
...HAVE YOU LEFT THE GUARDIANS OR WHATEVER IT WAS YOU CALL THEM?
AND WHAT ARE YOUR INTENTIONS, MARCHING ALONE INTO THE DEN OF YOUR ENEMY?
I HAVE NOT QUIT THE GUARD-IANS.
OH?

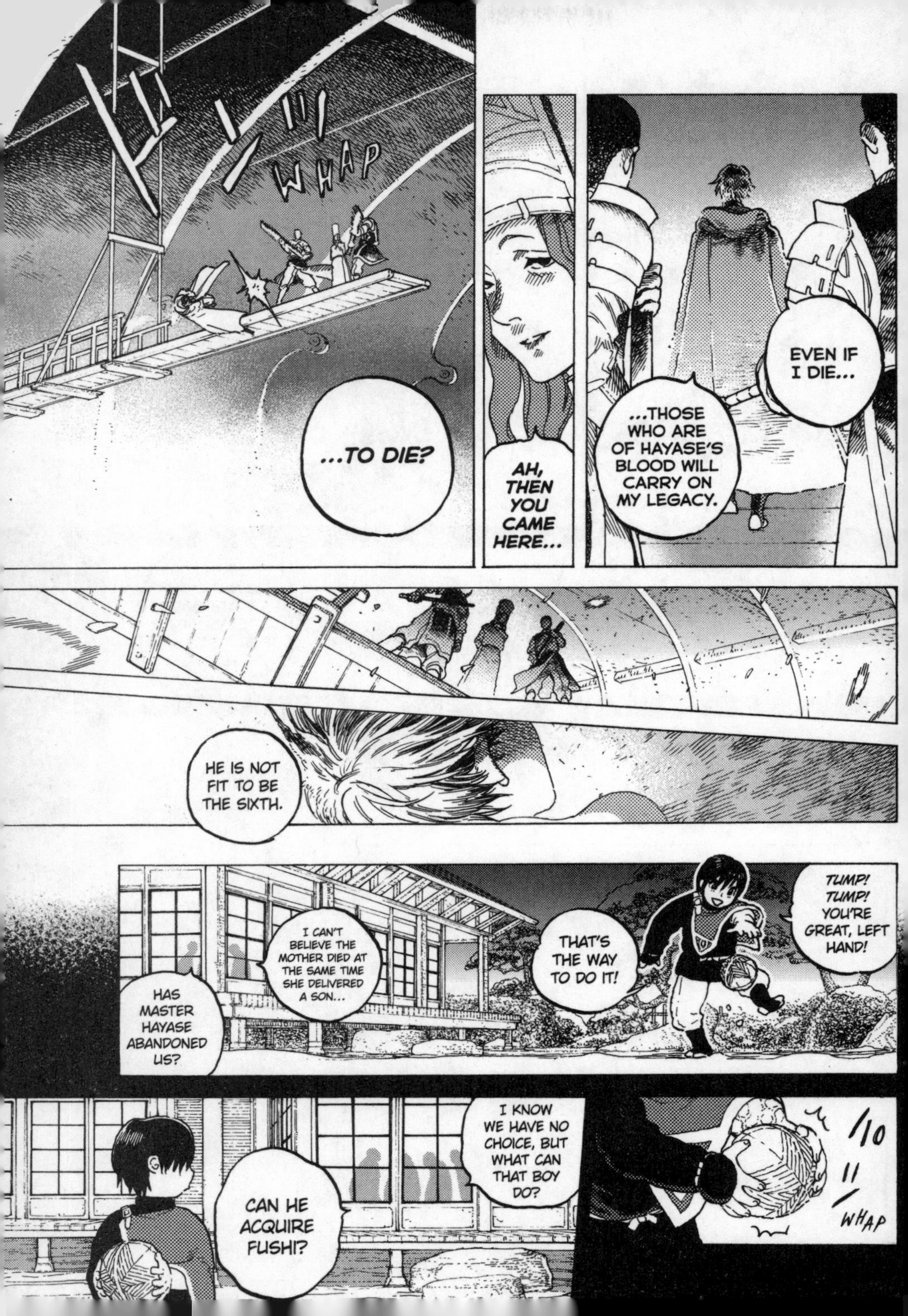
EVEN IF I DIE...
...THOSE WHO ARE OF HAYASE'S BLOOD WILL CARRY ON MY LEGACY.
AH, THEN YOU CAME HERE...
WHAP
...TO DIE?
HE IS NOT FIT TO BE THE SIXTH.
TUMP! TUMP! YOU'RE GREAT, LEFT HAND!
THAT'S THE WAY TO DO IT!
I CAN'T BELIEVE THE MOTHER DIED AT THE SAME TIME SHE DELIVERED A SON...
HAS MASTER HAYASE ABANDONED US?
WHAP
I KNOW WE HAVE NO CHOICE, BUT WHAT CAN THAT BOY DO?
CAN HE ACQUIRE FUSHI?

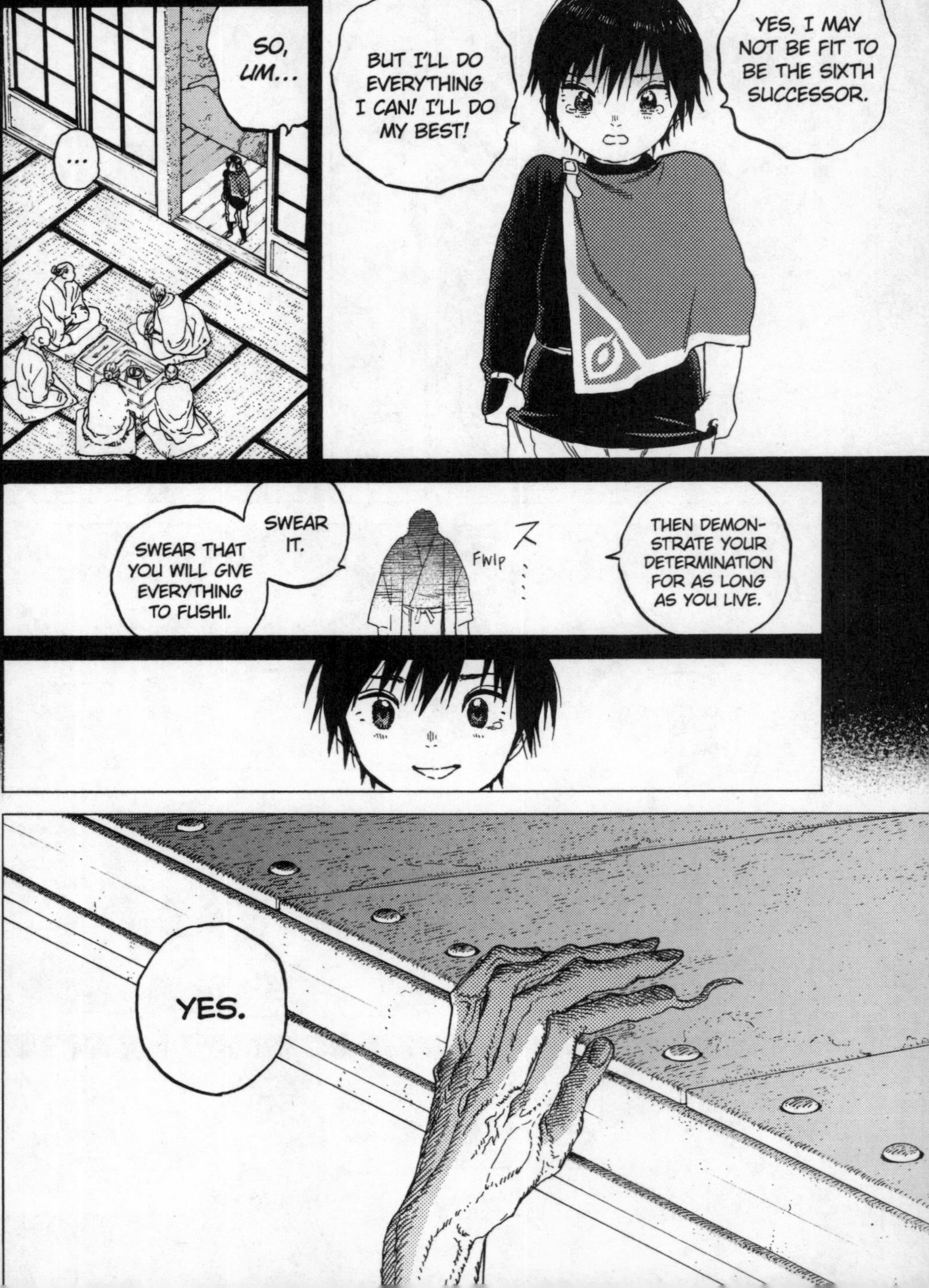
YES, I MAY NOT BE FIT TO BE THE SIXTH SUCCESSOR.
BUT I'LL DO EVERYTHING I CAN! I'LL DO MY BEST!
SO, UM...
...
THEN DEMON-STRATE YOUR DETERMINATION FOR AS LONG AS YOU LIVE.
ス
FWIP
SWEAR IT.
SWEAR THAT YOU WILL GIVE EVERYTHING TO FUSHI.
YES.

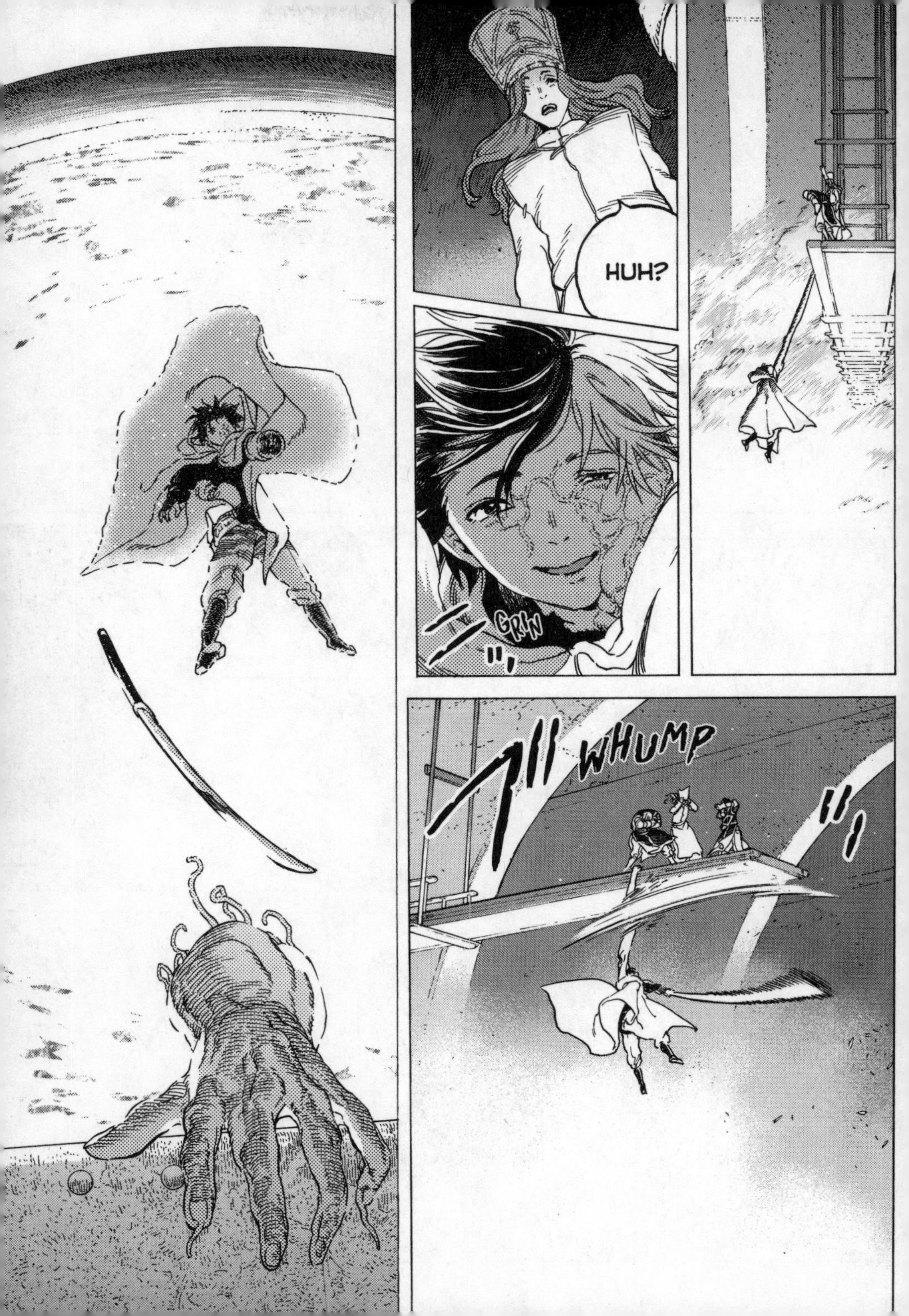
HUH?
GRIN
WHUMP

I LOVE YOU...

...FUSHI.

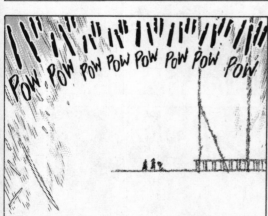

POW POW POW POW POW POW POW POW

SPLOSH

BLUB BLUB

ARGH!

AH!

YAAAAARGH!!

EEK!

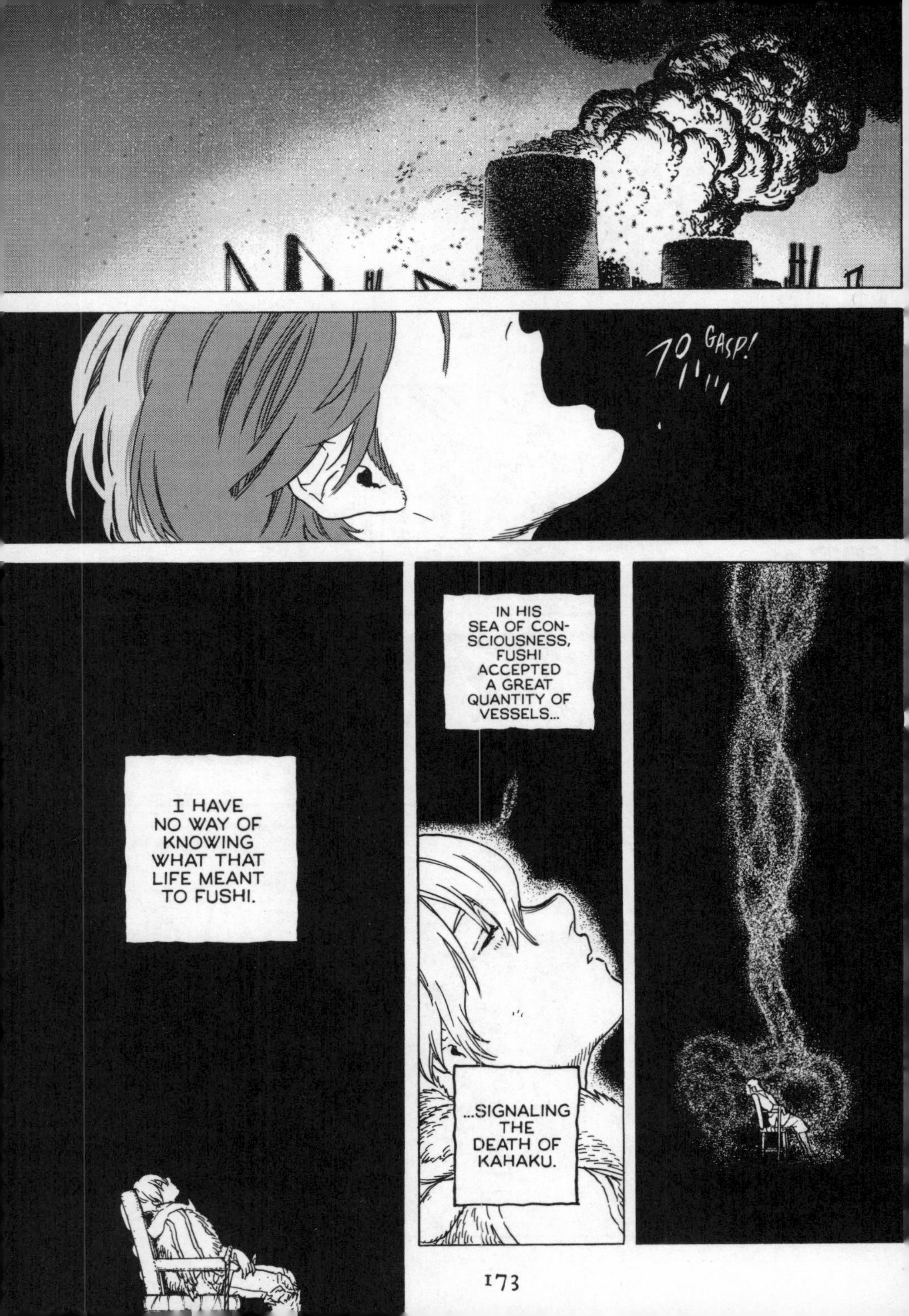
GASP!
IN HIS SEA OF CON-SCIOUSNESS, FUSHI ACCEPTED A GREAT QUANTITY OF VESSELS...
...SIGNALING THE DEATH OF KAHAKU.
I HAVE NO WAY OF KNOWING WHAT THAT LIFE MEANT TO FUSHI.

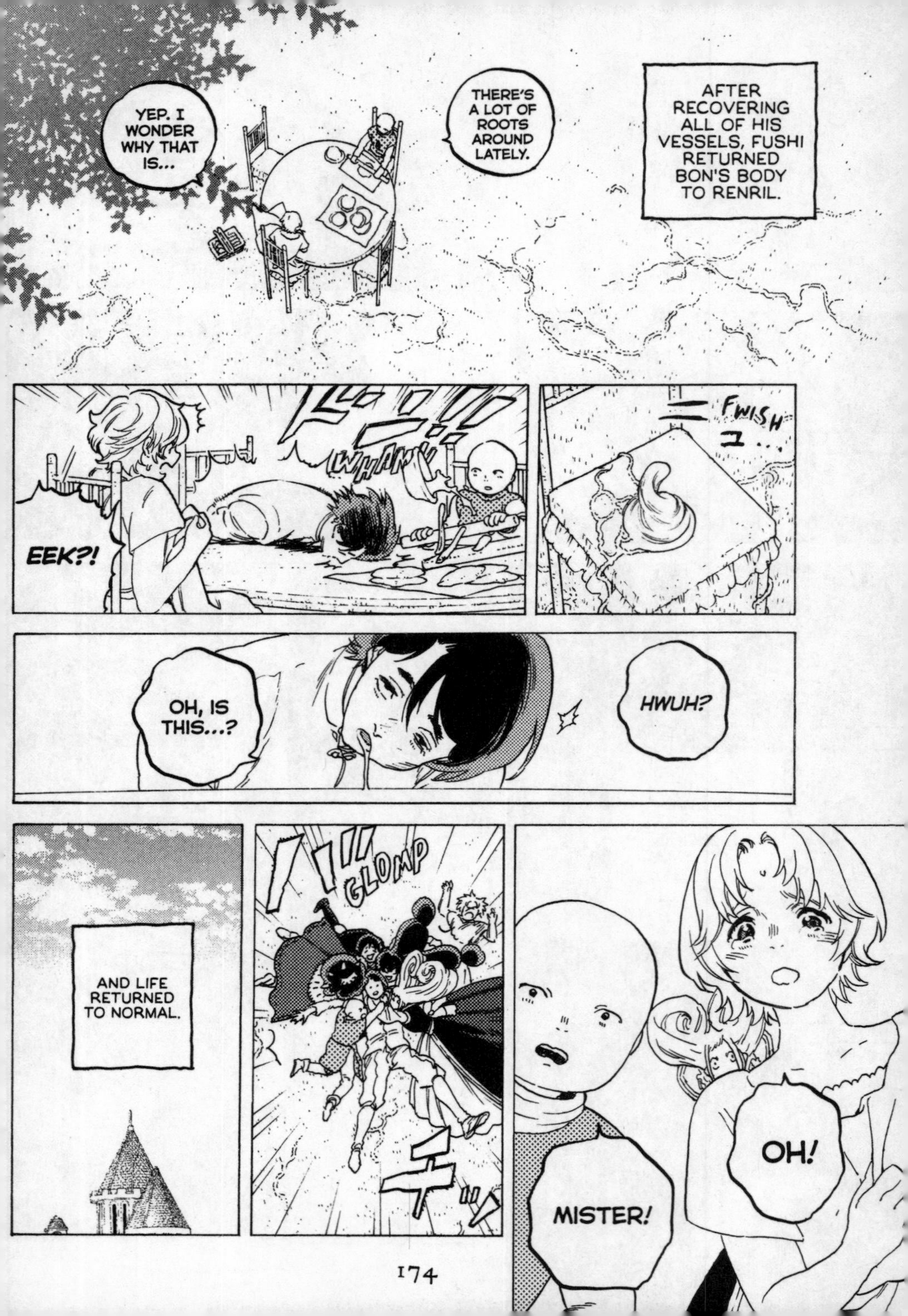
AFTER RECOVERING ALL OF HIS VESSELS, FUSHI RETURNED BON'S BODY TO RENRIL.
THERE'S A LOT OF ROOTS AROUND LATELY.
YEP. I WONDER WHY THAT IS...
FWISH
WHAM
EEK?!
HWUH?
OH, IS THIS...?
OH!
MISTER!
GLOMP
AND LIFE RETURNED TO NORMAL.

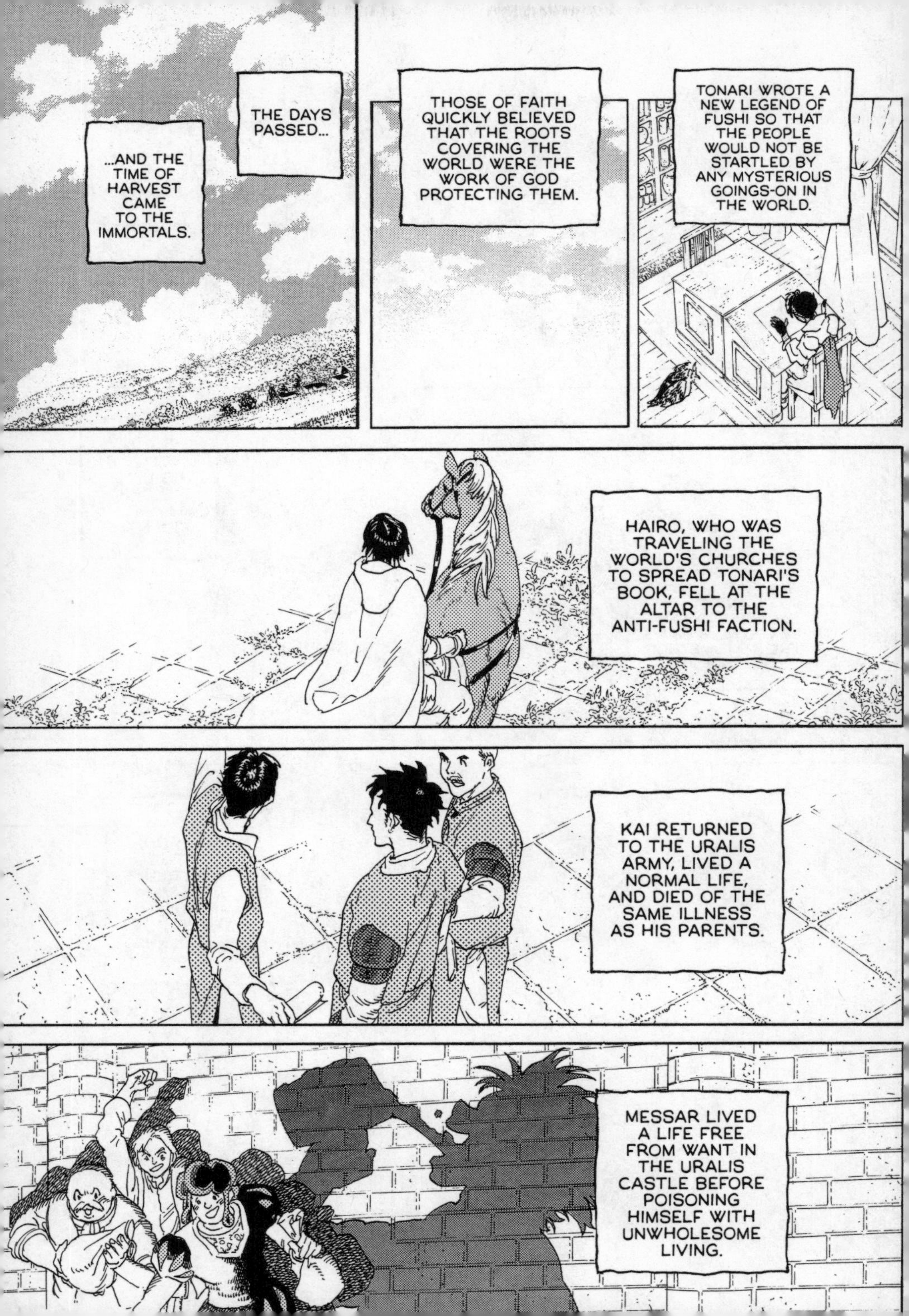
TONARI WROTE A NEW LEGEND OF FUSHI SO THAT THE PEOPLE WOULD NOT BE STARTLED BY ANY MYSTERIOUS GOINGS-ON IN THE WORLD.
THOSE OF FAITH QUICKLY BELIEVED THAT THE ROOTS COVERING THE WORLD WERE THE WORK OF GOD PROTECTING THEM.
THE DAYS PASSED...
...AND THE TIME OF HARVEST CAME TO THE IMMORTALS.
HAIRO, WHO WAS TRAVELING THE WORLD'S CHURCHES TO SPREAD TONARI'S BOOK, FELL AT THE ALTAR TO THE ANTI-FUSHI FACTION.
KAI RETURNED TO THE URALIS ARMY, LIVED A NORMAL LIFE, AND DIED OF THE SAME ILLNESS AS HIS PARENTS.
MESSAR LIVED A LIFE FREE FROM WANT IN THE URALIS CASTLE BEFORE POISONING HIMSELF WITH UNWHOLESOME LIVING.

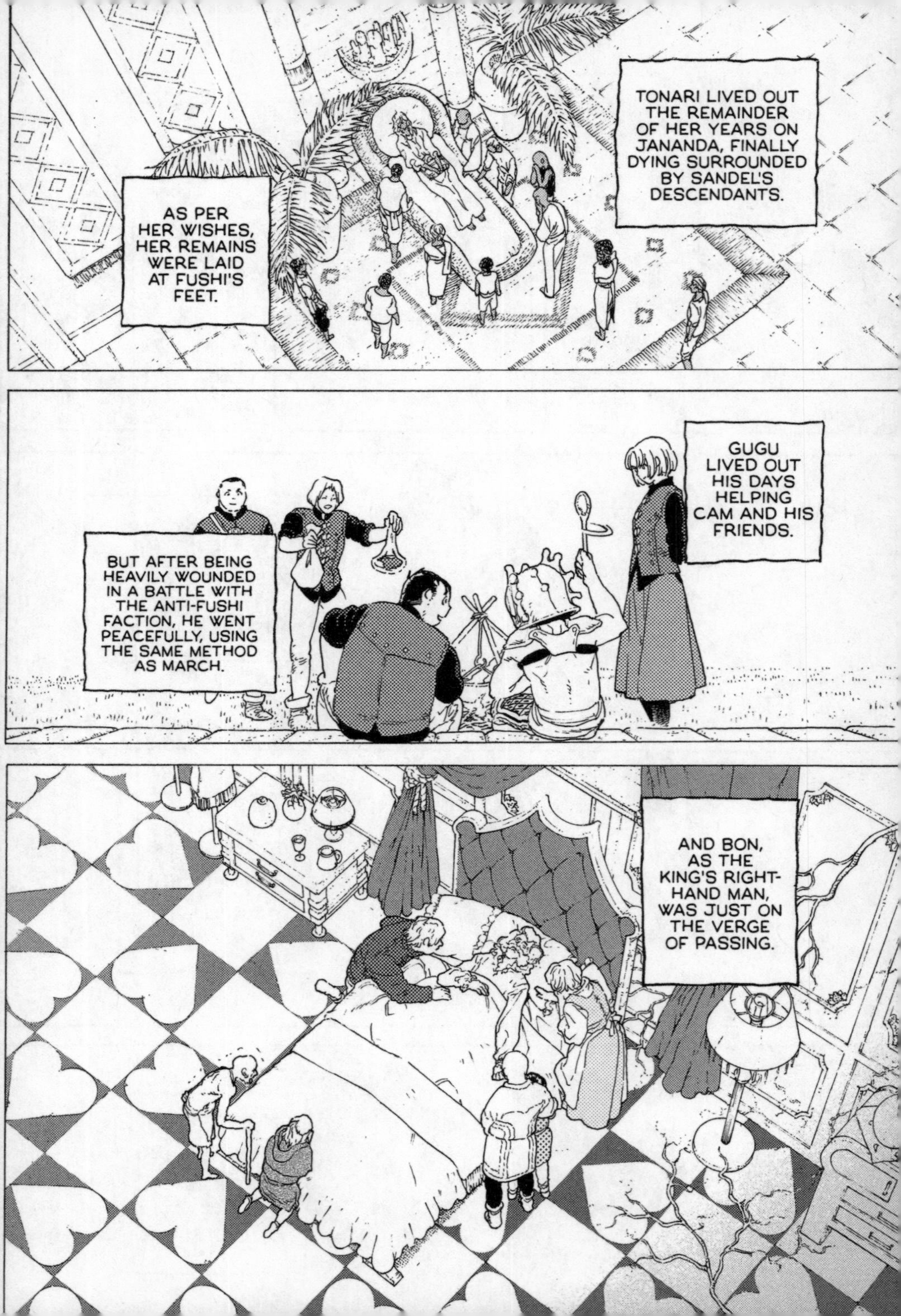
TONARI LIVED OUT THE REMAINDER OF HER YEARS ON JANANDA, FINALLY DYING SURROUNDED BY SANDEL'S DESCENDANTS.
AS PER HER WISHES, HER REMAINS WERE LAID AT FUSHI'S FEET.
GUGU LIVED OUT HIS DAYS HELPING CAM AND HIS FRIENDS.
BUT AFTER BEING HEAVILY WOUNDED IN A BATTLE WITH THE ANTI-FUSHI FACTION, HE WENT PEACEFULLY, USING THE SAME METHOD AS MARCH.
AND BON, AS THE KING'S RIGHT-HAND MAN, WAS JUST ON THE VERGE OF PASSING.

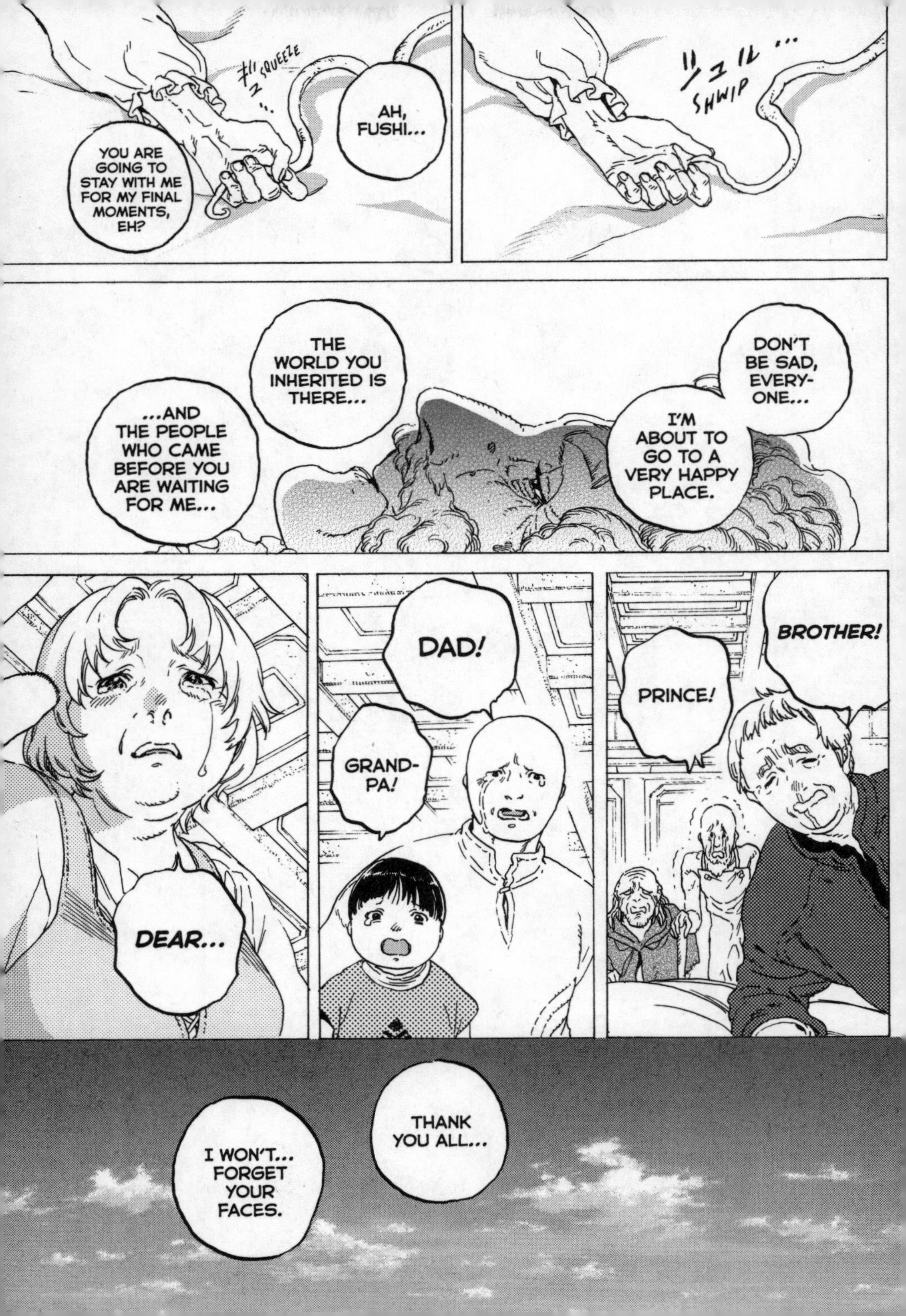
SHWIP
AH, FUSHI...
SQUEEZE
YOU ARE GOING TO STAY WITH ME FOR MY FINAL MOMENTS, EH?
DON'T BE SAD, EVERYONE...
I'M ABOUT TO GO TO A VERY HAPPY PLACE.
THE WORLD YOU INHERITED IS THERE...
...AND THE PEOPLE WHO CAME BEFORE YOU ARE WAITING FOR ME...
BROTHER!
PRINCE!
DAD!
GRAND-PA!
DEAR...
THANK YOU ALL...
I WON'T... FORGET YOUR FACES.

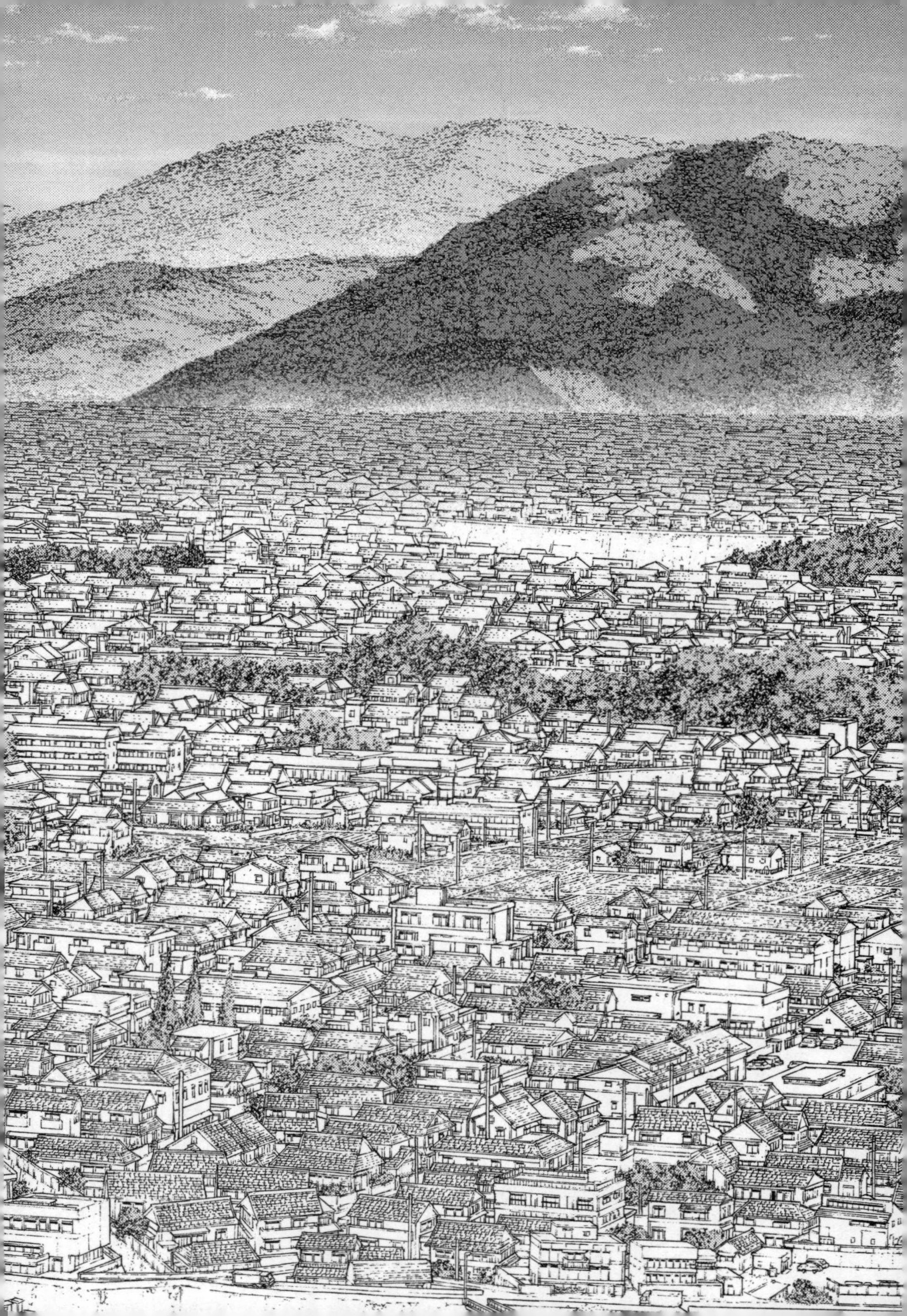

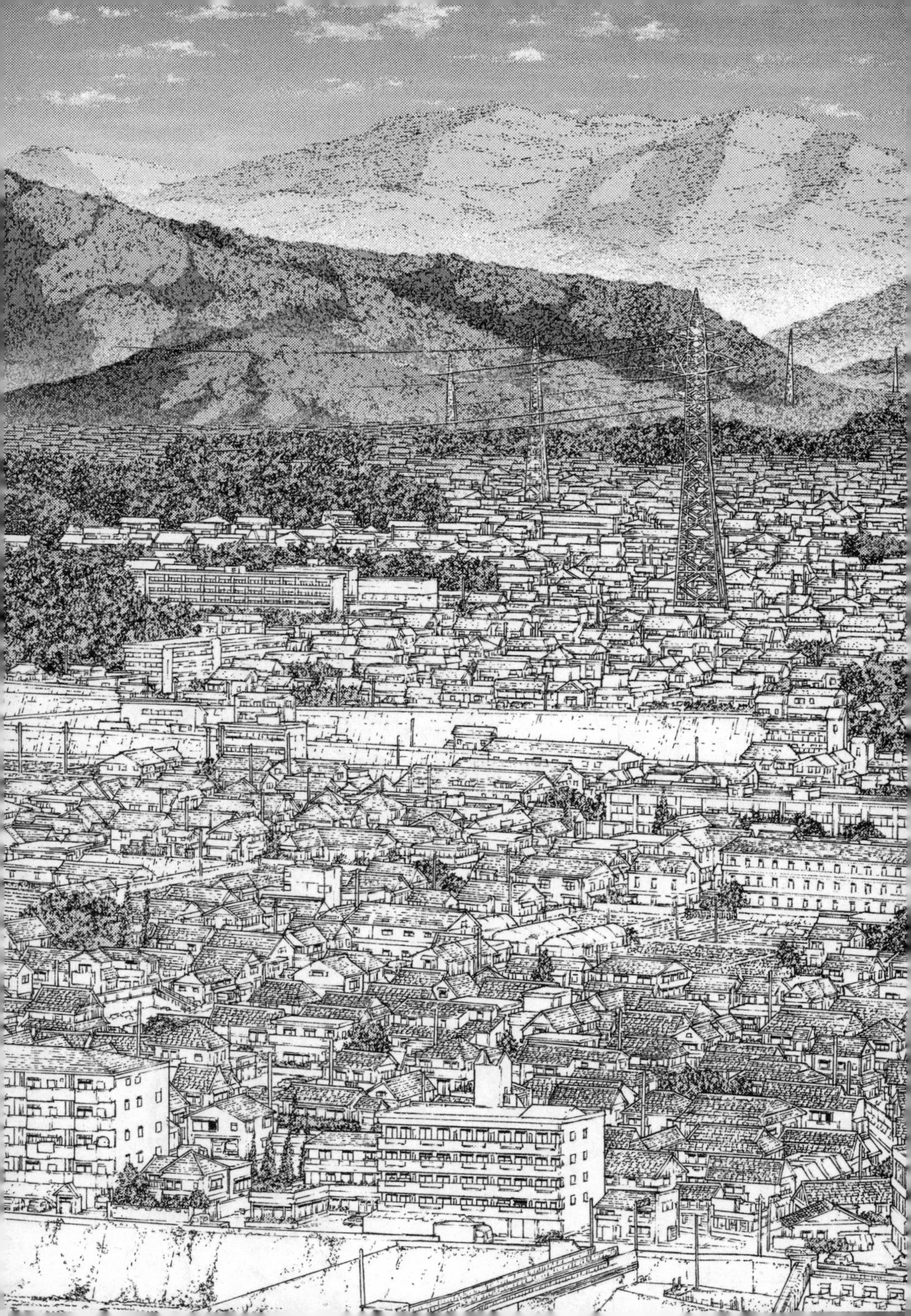

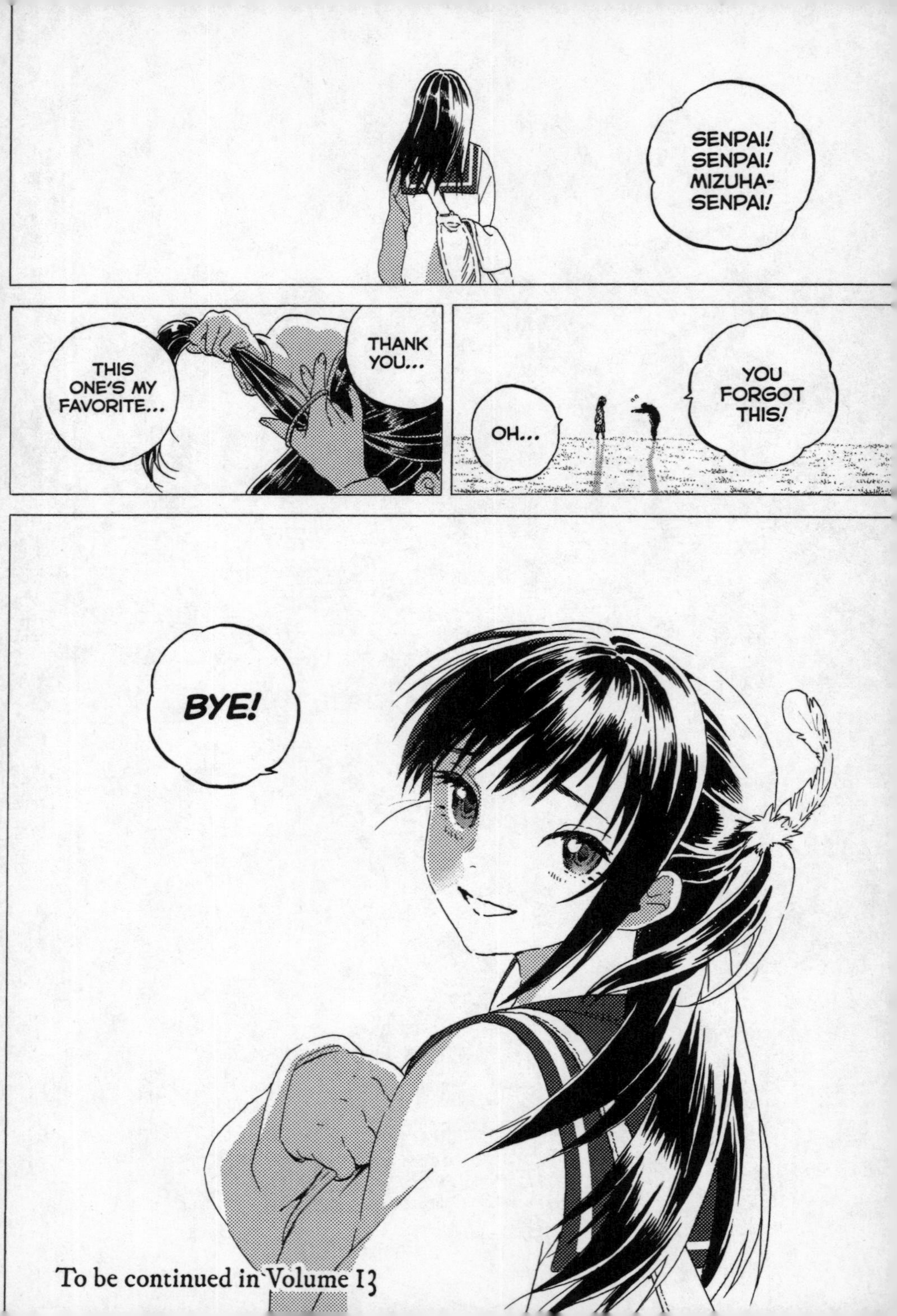
SENPAI! SENPAI! MIZUHA-SENPAI!
YOU FORGOT THIS!
OH...
THANK YOU...
THIS ONE'S MY FAVORITE...
BYE!
To be continued in Volume 13

TO YOUR

ETERNITY

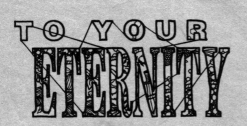

NEXT VOLUME PREVIEW

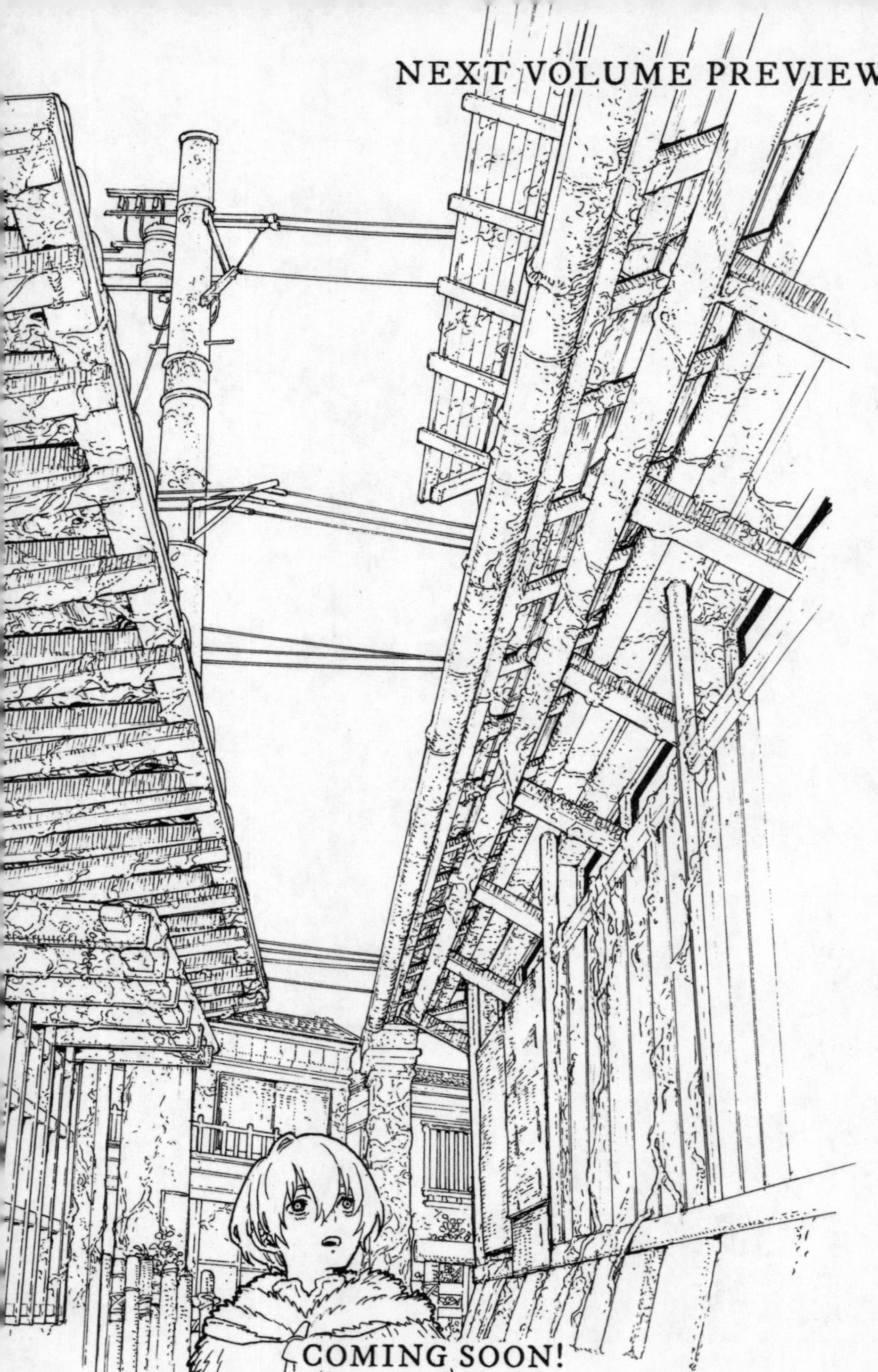

COMING SOON!

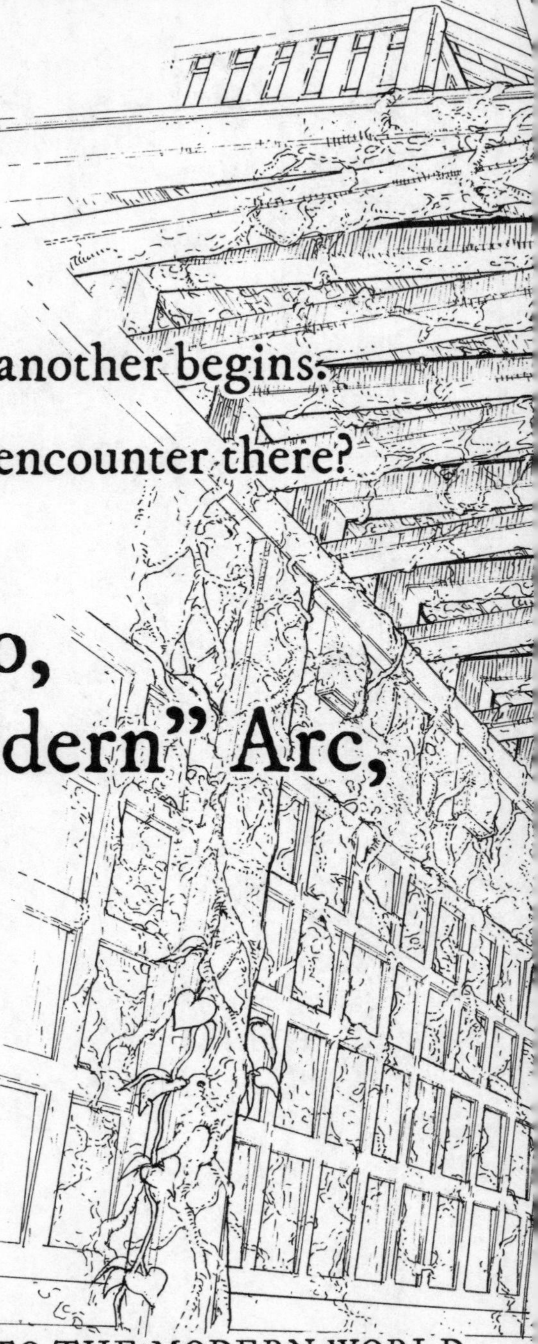

One world ends, another begins.

What will Fushi encounter there?

Part Two, the “Modern” Arc, Begins.

OUR STAGE MOVES TO THE MODERN WORLD— IN VOLUME 13!

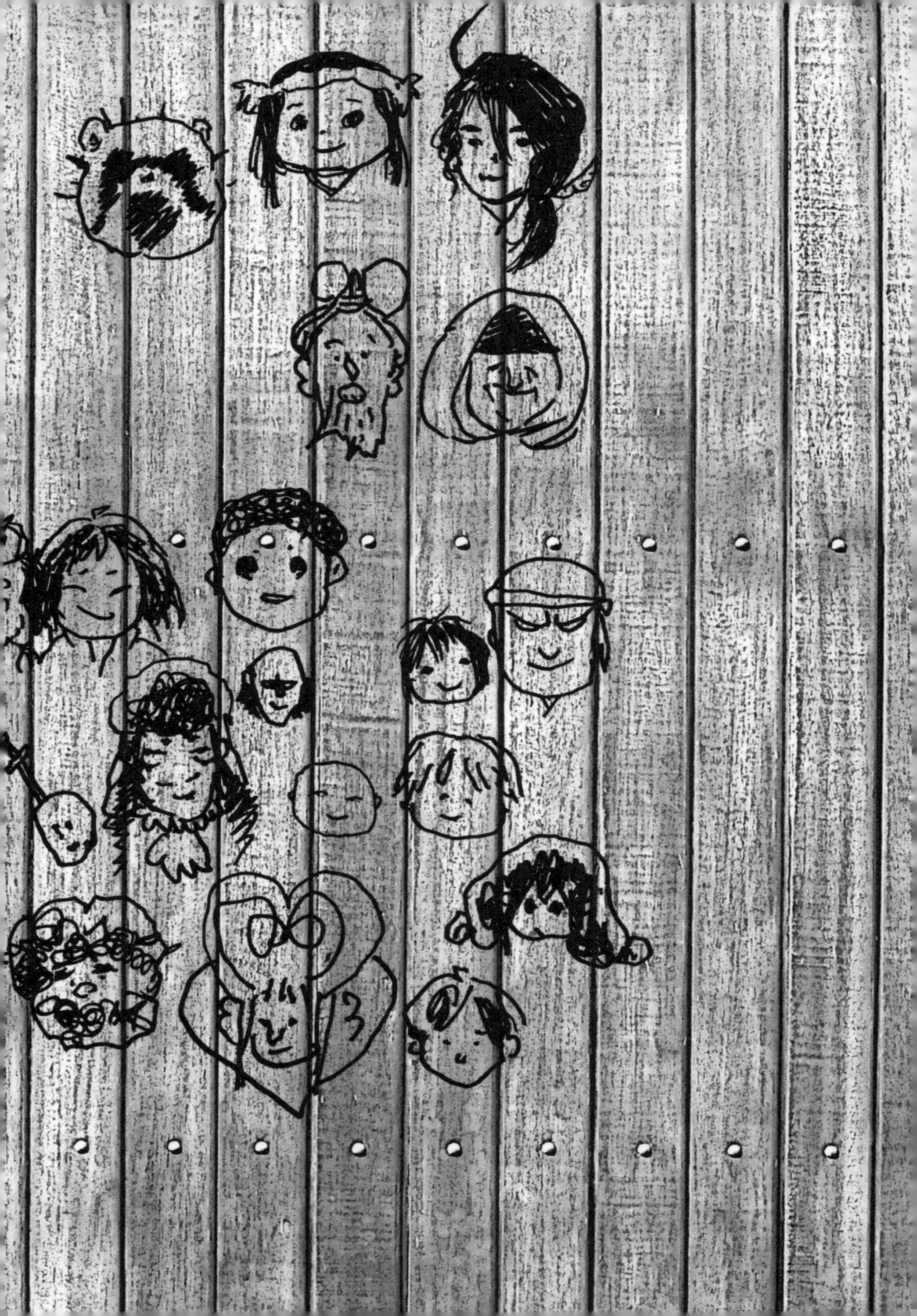

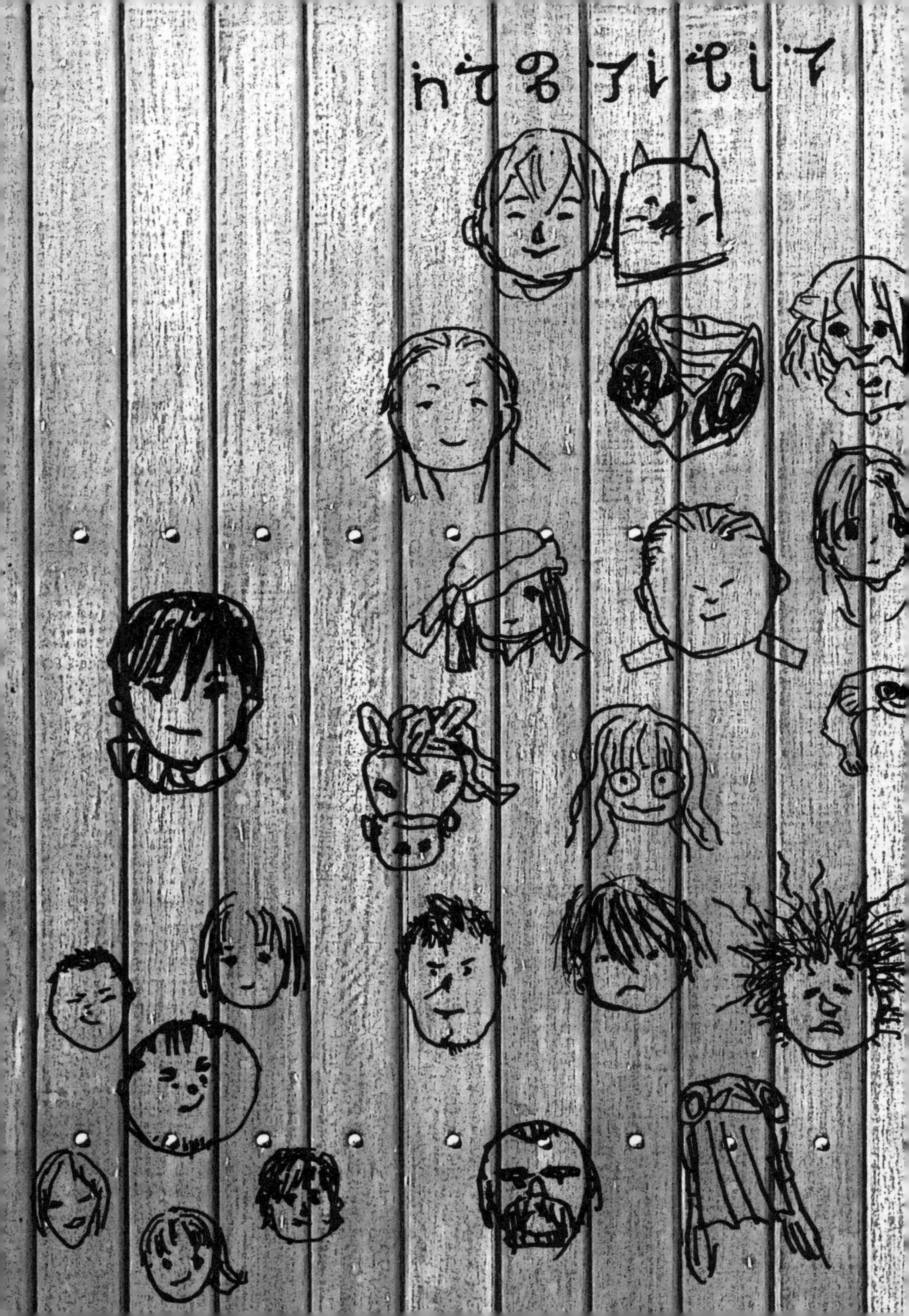

Young characters and steampunk setting, like *Howl's Moving Castle* and *Battle Angel Alita*

Beyond the Clouds © 2018 Nicke / Ki-oon

A boy with a talent for machines and a mysterious girl whose wings he's fixed will take you beyond the clouds! In the tradition of the high-flying, resonant adventure stories of Studio Ghibli comes a gorgeous tale about the longing of young hearts for adventure and friendship!

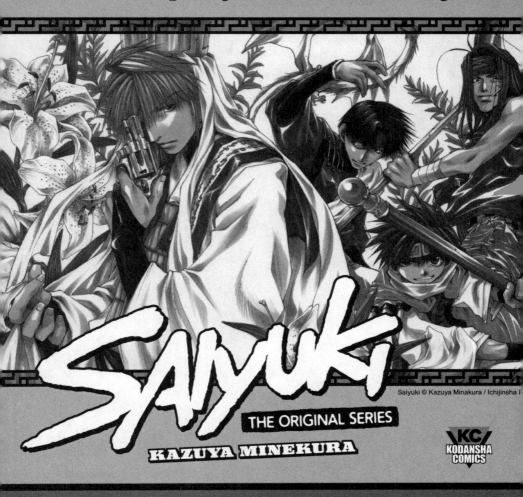

One of CLAMP's biggest hits returns in this definitive, premium, hardcover 20th anniversary collector's edition!

"A wonderfully entertaining story that would be a great installment in anybody's manga collection."
— Anime News Network

"CLAMP is an all-female manga-creating team whose feminine touch shows in this entertaining, sci-fi soap opera."
— Publishers Weekly

Poor college student Hideki is down on his luck. All he wants is a good job, a girlfriend, and his very own "persocom"—the latest and greatest in humanoid computer technology. Hideki's luck changes one night when he finds Chi—a persocom thrown out in a pile of trash. But Hideki soon discovers that there's much more to his cute new persocom than meets the eye.

KC
KODANSHA
COMICS

The art-deco cyberpunk classic from the creators of *xxxHOLiC* and *Cardcaptor Sakura*!

"Starred Review. This experimental sci-fi work from CLAMP reads like a romantic version of *AKIRA*." —Publishers Weekly

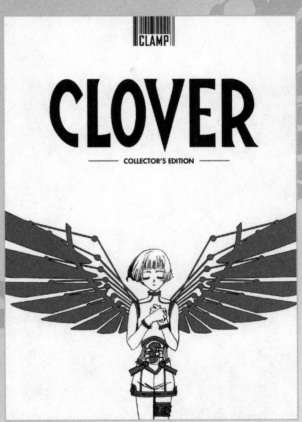

CLOVER © CLAMP·ShigatsuTsuitachi CO.,LTD./Kodansha Ltd.

Su was born into a bleak future, where the government keeps tight control over children with magical powers—codenamed "Clovers." With Su being the only "four-leaf" Clover in the world, she has been kept isolated nearly her whole life. Can ex-military agent Kazuhiko deliver her to the happiness she seeks? Experience the complete series in this hardcover edition, which also includes over twenty pages of ravishing color art!

‹ KAMOME ›
SHIRAHAMA

Witch Hat Atelier

A magical manga
adventure for
fans of Disney
and Studio
Ghibli!

The magical adventure that took Japan by storm is finally here, from acclaimed DC and Marvel cover artist Kamome Shirahama!

In a world where everyone takes wonders like magic spells and dragons for granted, Coco is a girl with a simple dream: She wants to be a witch. But everybody knows magicians are born, not made, and Coco was not born with a gift for magic. Resigned to her un-magical life, Coco is about to give up on her dream to become a witch...until the day she meets Qifrey, a mysterious, traveling magician. After secretly seeing Qifrey perform magic in a way she's never seen before, Coco soon learns what everybody "knows" might not be the truth, and discovers that her magical dream may not be as far away as it may seem...

KC
KODANSHA
COMICS

A Kodansha Comics Trade Paperback Original
To Your Eternity 12 copyright © 2020 Yoshitoki Oima
English translation copyright © 2020 Yoshitoki Oima

Published in the United States by Kodansha Comics, an imprint of Kodansha USA Publishing, LLC, New York.

Publication rights for this English edition arranged through Kodansha Ltd., Tokyo.

First published in Japan in 2020 by Kodansha Ltd., Tokyo as *Fumetsu no Anata e*, volume 12.

ISBN 978-1-63236-799-0

Cover Design: Tadashi Hisamochi (hive&co., Ltd.)
Title Logo Design: Shinobu Ohashi

Printed in the United States of America.

www.kodanshacomics.com

9 8 7 6 5 4 3 2
Translation: Steven LeCroy
Lettering: Darren Smith
Editing: Haruko Hashimoto, Alexandra Swanson
Editorial Assistance: YKS Services LLC/SKY Japan, INC.
Kodansha Comics Edition Cover Design: Phil Balsman

Publisher: Kiichiro Sugawara
Vice president of marketing & publicity: Naho Yamada

Director of publishing services: Ben Applegate
Associate director of operations: Stephen Pakula
Publishing services managing editor: Noelle Webster
Assistant production manager: Emi Lotto, Angela Zurlo